Vulnerable Children and the Law

of related interest

Safeguarding Children from Abroad
Refugee, Asylum Seeking and Trafficked Children in the UK
Edited by Emma Kelly and Farhat Bokhari
ISBN 978 1 84905 157 6
eISBN 978 0 85700 559 5
Best Practice in Working with Children Series

Improving Outcomes for Children and Families
Finding and Using International Evidence
Edited by Anthony N. Maluccio, Cinzia Canali, Tiziano Vecchiato, Anita Lightburn, Jane Aldgate and Wendy Rose
Foreword by James K. Whittaker
ISBN 978 1 84905 819 3
eISBN 978 0 85700 248 8
Child Welfare Outcomes Series

Understanding Costs and Outcomes in Child Welfare Services
A Comprehensive Costing Approach to Managing Your Resources
Lisa Holmes and Samantha McDermid
ISBN 978 1 84905 214 6
eISBN 978 0 85700 448 2
Child Welfare Outcomes Series

Safeguarding Children Across Services
Messages from Research
Carolyn Davies and Harriet Ward
ISBN 978 1 84905 124 8
eISBN 978 0 85700 290 7
Safeguarding Children Across Services Series

Child Protection Systems in the United Kingdom
A Comparative Analysis
Anne Stafford, Nigel Parton, Sharon Vincent and Connie Smith
ISBN 978 1 84905 067 8
eISBN 978 0 85700 254 9

Promoting Children's Rights in Social Work and Social Care
A Guide to Participatory Practice
Margaret Bell
ISBN 978 1 84310 607 4
eISBN 978 0 85700 486 4
Children in Charge Series

Child Well-Being
Understanding Children's Lives
Edited by Colette McAuley and Wendy Rose
Foreword by Dame Gillian Pugh
ISBN 978 1 84310 925 9
eISBN 978 0 85700 393 5

Good Practice in Safeguarding Children
Working Effectively in Child Protection
Edited by Liz Hughes and Hilary Owen
ISBN 978 1 84310 945 7
eISBN 978 1 84642 894 4
Good Practice in Health, Social Care and Criminal Justice Series

Vulnerable Children and the Law

International Evidence for Improving Child Welfare, Child Protection and Children's Rights

Edited by Rosemary Sheehan, Helen Rhoades and Nicky Stanley

Jessica Kingsley *Publishers*
London and Philadelphia

Figure 2.1 on page 45 reproduced from O'Leary and Squire 2009b with permission from Patrick O'Leary and Jason Squire.
Table 2.1 on page 49 reproduced from 2009b with permission from Patrick O'Leary and Jason Squire.
Table 2.2 on page 54 reproduced from O'Leary and Squire 2009b with permission from Patrick O'Leary and Jason Squire.
Figure 9.1 on page 174 reproduced from Connolly and Doolan 2007 with permission from Marie Connolly and Mike Doolan.
Figure 9.2 on page 174 reproduced from Connolly and Doolan 2007 with permission from Marie Connolly and Mike Doolan.

First published in 2012
by Jessica Kingsley Publishers
116 Pentonville Road
London N1 9JB, UK
and
400 Market Street, Suite 400
Philadelphia, PA 19106, USA

www.jkp.com

Library of Congress Cataloging in Publication Data
Vulnerable children and the law : international evidence for improving child welfare, child protection and children's rights / edited by Rosemary Sheehan, Helen Rhoades and Nicky Stanley.
p. cm.
Includes bibliographical references and index.
ISBN 978-1-84905-868-1 (alk. paper)
1. Children--Legal status, laws, etc.--Congresses. 2. Child welfare--Congresses. 3. Child abuse--Congresses. I. Sheehan, Rosemary. II. Rhoades, Helen. III. Stanley, Nicky, 1955-
K639.A6V85 2012
342.08'772--dc23
2011037698

British Library Cataloguing in Publication Data
A CIP catalogue record for this book is available from the British Library

ISBN 978 1 84905 868 1
eISBN 978 0 85700 456 7

Printed and bound in Great Britain

Contents

Part II: Indigenous and Non-national Children and Vulnerability

Part III: Child Welfare and Family Identity

Part IV: Child Welfare and Legal Intervention

Preface and Acknowledgements

Cross-national interest in the rights and best interests of children in the 21st century led to the international conference 'Children and the Law: International approaches to children and their vulnerabilities', hosted by Monash University, Australia, at the Monash Centre in Prato, Italy, 7–10 September 2009. Speakers and delegates addressed emerging social concerns that contribute to the vulnerability of children and young people, ranging from the plight of child refugees and children escaping war and trauma to new forms of child victimisation such as children as soldiers, as well as ongoing concerns about children entering the criminal justice system, the pervasiveness of child sexual abuse, and children harmed by maltreatment and family breakdown. Conference delegates confirmed that the systems responding to such children at risk of harm must be reshaped if they are to better protect children's rights and best interests.

The idea for the book arose out of this conference, convened by Rosemary Sheehan. Research and policy initiatives presented outlined some distinctive needs of children, as noted above. Particular attention was paid to the structural disadvantages and harms experienced by Indigenous children and to the global movement of children and child trafficking. Other key themes were the changing social parameters that are drawing children into and placing increased demands on the youth justice and care and protection systems; and the increasing intersection of mental health problems and legal processes for children. Contributors suggested preventative strategies designed to address the origins and nature of vulnerability for children and outlined plans to offer them more effective protection from changing social and political forces. Though many more children are being identified as in need of care and protection, more needs to be known about their particular needs for support and intervention.

Authors contributing to this book challenge policy-makers and legal and welfare systems to concentrate more on the emerging and ongoing needs children have for care and protection and to resist simply maintaining current approaches, regardless of their efficacy. A range of authors from the UK, USA, Canada, the Netherlands, New Zealand and Australia make a compelling case for further research and reform: if systems are to be successful at addressing the disadvantage and risk associated with these identified child welfare concerns, they must be child-centred and proper attention must be given to the legal, social and political rights and expectations accorded to children by UN and national rights conventions.

This book was made possible by the generous support provided by Stephen Jones and Caroline Walton from Jessica Kingsley Publishers, whose interest in child welfare and social policy matters encourages the kind of research and debate found in this book. Our thanks go also to all those who contributed to the writing of the book, providing a unique cross-national perspective on making a difference for children whose care and protection needs require more targeted advocacy, action and policy from governments and services to better ensure their rights as citizens are upheld.

Rosemary Sheehan, Helen Rhoades and Nicky Stanley

Introduction

Rosemary Sheehan, Helen Rhoades and Nicky Stanley

A critical issue faced by governments and practitioners working in the area of child welfare over the past decade has been the question of what circumstances justify intervention to protect a child. Whilst legal definitions of 'a child in need of protection' have, as their cornerstone, statutory intervention to protect a child from maltreatment, the parameters used to measure this have shifted dramatically in recent years, as political developments and social changes have drawn attention to new situations that place children at risk of harm. Whilst there has been growing awareness of the plight of specific groups of children, such as asylum seekers and unaccompanied minors, other emerging areas of concern – for example, the experiences of children in the justice system, the fracturing of children's relationships and life contexts, the exploitation and trafficking of children and what is needed to work effectively with vulnerable families – have as yet attracted negligible scholarly attention. Most of the existing research on these issues focuses on work with select groups of children, generally in the context of their connections to adults. Moreover, there is a dearth of literature examining the meaning of protective intervention for children whose lives are intersected by the law.

This book offers a comprehensive analysis of issues relating to new and emerging vulnerabilities of children in the 21st century. The rights and best interests of children are confronted by a range of social challenges which draw into question the effectiveness of systems designed to respond to children at risk of harm. Child protection services are dealing with families with increasingly complex issues, often compounded by factors such as family violence, mental illness and substance misuse (Bromfield *et al.* 2010). Child protection services are confronted also by the increased role of legal institutions in children's lives, as well as by national obligations to interventions and policies such as the United Nations Convention on the Rights of the Child

(UNCRC). Child welfare systems in Western nations are increasingly expected to differentiate between the needs of children referred to them and to make distinctions between problems arising from structural and environmental conditions (trafficked children, for example) and problems located within the family. These include parental problems which endanger children – and families who are neglectful or abusive – where the state is required to share parental responsibility (Spratt and Devaney 2009).

The aim of this book is to identify new and emerging child vulnerabilities and to propose what factors promote better recognition and responses from national and community agencies. The contributing authors offer a practical focus on direct work and policy development with vulnerable children. The book is divided into four parts. Common to each part is an examination of children's life contexts and the breadth of issues arising from the intersection of the law with their lives. In the first part of the book, particular attention is given to children as citizens. The second part explores concerns for Indigenous and unaccompanied refugee and immigrant children. In the third part, child welfare and family identity are examined. The fourth and final part deals with statutory protection of children.

Part I

The six chapters in this part of the book identify a range of socio-structural issues which infringe children's rights, with specific attention to the exploitation of children and the consequent social and personal impacts. The authors examine thinking and practices that maintain the structural inequalities children as a social group experience and the political, cultural and ideological changes required to deliver an effective rights agenda for children.

In Chapter 1, Deena Haydon (Northern Ireland) argues that, despite ratification of the UNCRC, there is negligible realisation of the rights of many of the most vulnerable and disadvantaged children and young people in the UK. She locates this disadvantage in the context of persistent poverty and its impact on children's education, health and wellbeing and family relationships: 21 per cent of children in Northern Ireland compared with 9 per cent in Britain live in severe poverty. They are children whose families' capacity to encourage and appropriately care for them is inhibited by poverty and by trauma related to the armed conflict in Northern Ireland. The chapter explores the ways in which complex, often unaddressed, needs and the cumulative effects of economic and social disadvantage are heightened when these young people are in conflict with the law.

Chapter 2 by Patrick O'Leary and Jason Squire (England) presents case studies from Africa and the sub-continent that illustrate the difficulties in establishing a basic system of child rights in the face of humanitarian emergencies, civil unrest and conflict. They outline key principles to set in place an organisational culture of child rights and protection which addresses immediate risks in periods of crisis, and suggest balancing these with essential knowledge of cultural differences and dilemmas. Chief amongst the dilemmas is the understanding that children are citizens in their own right, a construct challenged by the culturally diverse contexts presented in this chapter.

Chapter 3 by Chris Beddoe (England) extends exploration of these dilemmas to include an examination of the recent increase in child trafficking across the UK for purposes of sexual exploitation, forced labour, forced marriage and organised criminal activity. Beddoe outlines UK responses to human trafficking, including legislation to convict traffickers for both sexual exploitation and labour exploitation. The responses are confounded by negligible identification of victims and Beddoe suggests that cultural relativity may inhibit child protection and prevention responses to child victims. The chapter argues that the policy gaps and practice challenges require multi-agency responses if they are to halt child trafficking in the UK.

Chapter 4 by Shelly Whitman (Canada) argues that the use of children as soldiers is the starkest reminder of the exploitation of children and the denial of their rights as citizens. This chapter suggests that it is only by addressing the socio-economic problems in nations which draw children into armed conflict, and providing resources for children's education and employment, that the power of opportunistic leaders is challenged. Whitman outlines the Demobilisation, Disarmament, Reintegration and Rehabilitation approach to the reduction of conflict. This focuses on particular strategies that reduce the use of children as soldiers, improve their life circumstances and seek to ensure that children are recognised as community citizens in their own right.

Chapter 5 by Gladis Molina (United States) turns attention to the plight of unaccompanied children who enter the US each year and enter federal custody in the care of the Office of Refugee Resettlement. The uncertainty surrounding their status places them in a vulnerable position in the legal process, both procedurally and substantively. The author examines the concept of citizenship and argues that best interest considerations must be at the centre of legal process irrespective of their refugee or asylum seeking claims. She presents details of legal representation in federal immigration proceedings and recommends statutory policy and supports that attend to social welfare perspectives as much as to legal interests.

Chapter 6 by Una Convery and Linda Moore (Northern Ireland) extends discussion of children in custody by presenting findings from a study of children in prison in Northern Ireland. The Northern Ireland Human Rights Commission examined the extent to which legislation, policy and practice in reality observed the human rights principle that custody for children should be a last resort. They found negligible attention was given to alternatives to criminalisation and custody, despite consistent research findings that detention is harmful, hugely expensive and relatively ineffective. Those detained were overwhelmingly socially excluded children. The authors argue that greater priority within the youth justice system must be given to meeting these children's best interests rather than concentrating on rights-compliance, and they describe examples of such advocacy approaches.

Part II

The four chapters which comprise Part II of the book address Indigenous and non-national children and vulnerability. Chapter 7 by Suzanne Oliver (Australia) introduces this part with a debate about the effectiveness of changes to welfare provision, law enforcement and land tenure resulting from government initiatives and the impact of these on child protection. In 2007 the *Little Children are Sacred* (*Ampe Akelyernemane Meke Mekarle*) Report was released in Australia, the result of an inquiry by the Northern Territory government into the protection of Aboriginal children from sexual abuse. Widespread violence and sexual abuse of both women and children occurring in Northern Territory communities was combined with poor health, alcohol and drug abuse, unemployment, gambling, pornography, poor education and housing, and a general loss of identity across Aboriginal communities in the Northern Territory. The chapter outlines the gaps that remain in addressing systemic disadvantage and child maltreatment in these communities.

Chapter 8 by Goos Cardol (the Netherlands) turns attention to non-national children termed 'residing aliens', who are increasingly resident in the Netherlands. He describes the Roma as an example of children in need who are outside mainstream Dutch society. These children may have entered Holland as illegal immigrants or as trafficked children and their welfare needs bring them to the attention of child protection agencies. The problems experienced by Roma children challenge accepted standards in Dutch society and create conflict in Dutch law. The author argues that the Child Protection Board must develop child care policy that both guarantees these children's rights as embodied in UNCRO and should also ensure national legislation recognises the distinct and distinctive needs of these children.

Chapter 9 by Rawiri Taonui (New Zealand) discusses how New Zealand has been challenged by major incidences of Maori child abuse and the overrepresentation of Maori in current statistics for child abuse and mortality. Debate has raged around the origins of this ethnoindigenous Maori abuse and also around the best solutions. The author approaches this debate by examining how socio-political and economic and cultural processes have contributed to and exacerbated interpersonal and family violence. This chapter looks both at these origins and at culturally based family programs that challenge child violence and maltreatment. Taonui notes that these programs need to be devolved from centralised non-Maori dominated systems if they are to be successful, as well as being systemically distant from stereotyping and historical racism.

In Chapter 10, Terri Libesman (Australia) debates whether or not international human rights law can offer a framework within which Indigenous children's welfare and wellbeing can be addressed at a local level. Reforms to child welfare legislation in Manitoba, Canada, and Victoria and the Northern Territory in Australia, provide comparative case studies of responses to Indigenous children's welfare which are founded in or derogate from Indigenous children's human rights. Libesman examines how international law can respond in a sensitive manner to culturally and linguistically different communities. She gives attention to how principles of self-determination can be accommodated within universal standards to ensure that both individual human rights and collective values about child welfare and wellbeing are accommodated.

Part III

Chapter 11 by Cathy Humphreys and Meredith Kiraly (Australia) is the first of the four chapters comprising Part III of the book, which gives attention to the theme of child welfare and family identity. The chapter describes research conducted by the authors which examined contact arrangements between infants in 'out of home care' (foster care) and their parents. Recent trends in Children's Court decisions to give high intensity contact to mothers and fathers of infants in foster care has raised questions about how and why such contact arrangements are constructed. The research revealed conflicting understandings about the nature of attachment and differing views about risks and vulnerabilities on the part of welfare and legal decision makers. It found that the level of disruption to infants and their parents, the multiple handling of children and distances travelled did not facilitate reunification. On the basis of their findings, the authors argue that reunification is better supported when attention is given to quality, not quantity, of contact.

Jackie Turton (England) in Chapter 12 identifies ways in which gendering child sexual abuse creates problems for protecting children, and highlights concerns that can arise in terms of children's rights. The author presents findings from research that included adults who have been child victims of female perpetrators, female offenders and practitioners working within child protection. Her research found that perpetrators sought to make the sexualised behaviour appear acceptable, not just to those around them, but to themselves as well. Turton argues that underlying social constructs of motherhood and femininity can offer the opportunity to excuse the sexually abusive behaviour of female perpetrators and silence their child victims.

James Reid (England) in Chapter 13 argues that stereotypes in the UK public discourse on separated families of 'deadbeat dads' and 'obstructive mums' contribute to negative outcomes for children in contested contact proceedings, denying them familial and cultural experiences and contributing to a sense of lost identity. Reid believes these stereotypes are in part encouraged by uncritical approaches to assessment perpetuated by the Framework for the Assessment of Children in Need and their Families (Department of Health 2000). The author suggests that while a framework for intervention is necessary, policy and practice must give equal attention to parental family, culture and community, regardless of with whom the child lives, to ensure children have access to their full identity and to the community that is core to their relational networks.

Chapter 14 by Greg Kelly and Chaitali Das (Northern Ireland) critically examines statutory powers to divest parents of their parental rights and to make adoption orders in relation to their children. In the US and the UK, such statutory orders are justified on the grounds that adoption is better at delivering the 'family for life' that children need. They are also considered to keep children out of state care which is widely perceived as having poor outcomes and being ill equipped to provide the sensitive framework needed for the lifelong care of children. The authors suggest that the tension between the principle that the child's best interests should be the 'paramount consideration' in all decisions in relation to their welfare, and at the same time – as set out in Article 8 of the European Convention of Human Rights – the principle that 'everyone has the right to respect for his family life', has contributed to a divesting of parental rights and familial identity. The authors discuss whether 'modern adoption', now normally including continued contact between child and birth family, provides a more 'proportionate' response to children's needs for permanent placement.

Part IV

Chapter 15 by Lisa Young (Australia) is the first of five chapters which comprise Part IV of the book: child welfare and legal intervention. This chapter examines claims that private family law proceedings in Australia systematically fail to protect children from family violence. Young discusses how recent legislative reforms which emphasise shared parenting arrangements have heightened the risk of children being exposed to violence and abuse. The chapter presents recent findings about violence affecting children in family law matters and proposes specific changes to family law processes to better protect children from violence in parenting disputes.

In Chapter 16, Nicky Stanley, Pam Miller, Helen Richardson-Foster and Gill Thomson (England) argue that police notifications of incidents of domestic violence to statutory children's services constitute an acknowledgement of the harm that domestic violence inflicts on children. This chapter presents findings from the first UK study to examine these notifications in depth. The authors examine the outcomes for children and families and identify practice and policy gaps that must be addressed for real understanding of the impact of family violence on children and the ongoing threat of harm it creates for them.

Chapter 17 by Robert George (England) presents findings from studies undertaken in England and New Zealand in which judges and lawyers were interviewed about deciding relocation disputes – which arise when one parent wishes to move with their child over a geographic distance which substantially affects the child's relationship with the other parent. The author discusses the stark choices which the law makes in its relocation decisions and how seemingly sensible legal positions adopted may prioritise adult preferences and fail to accommodate the long-term psychological welfare of such children.

Chapter 18 by Helen Rhoades (Australia) takes as its starting point policies in numerous jurisdictions, including England, France, Australia and Canada, that are increasingly emphasising the need for non-adversarial dispute resolution processes for managing post-separation disputes over children. The author argues that effective collaboration between parents' legal advisers and dispute resolution professionals who work with separated families is central to these dispute resolution processes. The chapter explores the disciplinary, cultural and policy factors that impede effective collaboration and makes recommendations about strategies for enhancing interprofessional cooperation.

Chapter 19 by Rosemary Sheehan (Australia) turns also to children's best interests but within the child welfare jurisdiction. Sheehan suggests that the framing of child protection as a socio-legal enterprise limits effective collaboration and distracts from a broader child welfare focus. The implications of this for children, and the legal context, are suggested. The chapter presents findings that suggest contemporary child welfare legislation fails to address the practical concerns of child protection. It is argued that approaches which confirm child protection as a shared enterprise across child and community welfare professions offer better attention to a child's needs and family capacity for change to maintain their children in their care.

Chapter 20 concludes this book by discussing the themes which have been identified and developed in the book and outlines some conclusions about what is required to respond effectively to vulnerable children. The Conclusion highlights areas where new research is needed and proposes practice and policy directions that need to be pursued.

Child maltreatment continues to be a significant social problem in many nations (Horsfall, Bromfield and McDonald 2010). Individuals and families presenting to child protection services are increasingly situated within a wider context of exclusion and disadvantage, with problems which are complex and often chronic in nature (Spratt and Devaney 2009). What is clear is that the rapid growth of child protection and the increased role of legal institutions in children's lives challenges policy makers, professionals and governments internationally. We hope that this book encourages ongoing discussion and debate; we hope it contributes to greater understanding of the disadvantage experienced by groups of children from previously unfamiliar contexts. For such groups national strategies are required to reduce their vulnerability to child maltreatment.

References

Bromfield, L., Lamont, A., Parker, R. and Horsfall, B. (2010) *Issues for the Safety and Wellbeing of Children in Families with Multiple and Complex Problems: The Co-Occurrence of Domestic Violence, Parental Substance Misuse and Mental Health Problems* (NCPC Issues 33). Melbourne: National Child Protection Clearinghouse, Australian Institute of Family Studies.

Department of Health (2000) *Framework for the Assessment of Children in Need and their Families.* London: The Stationery Office.

Horsfall, B., Bromfield, L. and McDonald, M. (2010) *Are Social Marketing Campaigns Effective in Preventing Child Abuse and Neglect?* (NCPC Issues 32). Melbourne: National Child Protection Clearinghouse, Australian Institute of Family Studies.

Northern Territory Government Australia (2007) *Ampe Akelyernemane Meke Mekarle: Little Children are Sacred.* Inquiry into the Protection of Children from Sexual Abuse. Available at www.inquirysaac.nt.gov.au/pdf/bipacsa_final_report.pdf, accessed on 28 October 2011.

Spratt, T. and Devaney, J. (2009) 'Identifying families with multiple problems: Perspectives of practitioners and managers in three nations.' *British Journal of Social Work 39*, 418–434.

PART I

Children and Citizenship

Chapter 1

Children's Rights

The Effective Implementation of Rights-based Standards

Deena Haydon

Introduction

This chapter illustrates how children's rights continue to be breached in the UK despite ratification of the *United Nations Convention on the Rights of the Child* (UNCRC) on 16 December 1991. The views and experiences of young people involved with Include Youth – a non-government organisation (NGO) working to promote and protect the rights of children in conflict with the law in Northern Ireland – provide evidence of the impacts of structural inequalities and how these limit realisation of their rights for some of the most 'vulnerable' and 'disadvantaged' children and young people in this UK jurisdiction. The chapter concludes with an outline of the legal, ideological and political changes required for more effective implementation of rights-based standards.

UNCRC general principles

In 1989 the UNCRC established children (under-18s) as 'rights-holders' in every aspect of their lives. According to the UNCRC Preamble, signatories to the Convention affirm the principles agreed by the United Nations in various Charters, Declarations, Covenants and Rules. These include: recognising the 'equal and inalienable rights of all members of the human family' without distinction of any kind, as well as 'the dignity and worth of the human person'; acknowledging children's entitlement to 'special care and assistance' and that every child 'should be fully prepared to live an individual life in society... brought up in the spirit...of peace, dignity, tolerance, freedom, equality and solidarity'; recognising that, 'in all countries in the world, there are children living in exceptionally difficult conditions, and that such children need special consideration'; and affording the family 'the necessary protection and assistance' to 'fully assume its responsibilities within the community' (UN General Assembly 1989, p.1).

The UNCRC is 'the most comprehensive, legally binding document on the treatment of children' (Kilkelly 2008, p.188). An 'easily understood advocacy tool', it 'promotes children's welfare as an issue of justice rather than one of charity' (Veerman 1992, p.184). UNCRC Articles provide 'a directional framework' for institutionally based policies and practices, 'recognising the role of the state in supporting families and carers in the development, socialisation and welfare of children' (Scraton and Haydon 2002, p.313). The UNCRC outlines general principles that should underpin policy and practice: guaranteeing rights to each child 'without discrimination of any kind' (Article 2); ensuring 'the best interests of the child' are a primary consideration in all actions concerning children (Article 3); recognising every child has the 'inherent right to life', ensuring 'to the maximum extent possible the survival and development of the child' (Article 6); and assuring the child's 'right to express...views freely in all matters', her/his views being given due weight in accordance with the child's age and maturity (Article 12). The UN Committee on the Rights of the Child (2001) recognises the importance of a holistic approach to human rights, which is lived as well as learned.

Assessing realisation of children's rights in the UK

The UN Committee notes that, through ratification, a State takes on obligations under international law to implement the UNCRC including action 'to ensure the realisation of all rights in the Convention for all children in their jurisdiction' (UN Committee on the Rights of the Child 2003, paragraph 1). In July 2007, the UK Government submitted its third and fourth consolidated periodic reports to the UN Committee. The devolved administrations of Northern Ireland, Scotland and Wales produced information for inclusion in the UK Government report. The Children and Young People's Unit in Northern Ireland's Office of the First Minister and Deputy First Minister (OFMDFM) commissioned consultations with children and young people to inform the Northern Ireland report (Haydon 2007) and reports were submitted by youth-led organisations in Scotland (Article 12), Wales (Funky Dragon) and England (Children's Rights Alliance for England; see Child Rights International Network 2008). Other submissions included a combined report by the four UK Children's Commissioners, a report from the Northern Ireland Human Rights Commission and briefings by specific lobbying groups. Alliances of NGOs also submitted reports from each of the four UK jurisdictions (Children's Rights Alliance for England 2008; Croke and Crowley 2007; Haydon 2008a; Scottish Alliance for Children's Rights 2008).

Alongside significant issues within individual jurisdictions, the NGO alliances raised serious common concerns. Regarding UNCRC general principles, the 'welfare' of the child rather than 'best interests' is prioritised in UK legislation. This reinforces paternalism, in which children are perceived as vulnerable and dependent on adults. The principle of non-discrimination is undermined by the persistence of high levels of child poverty throughout the UK. Inequalities between the richest and poorest children are evident in the limited opportunities and negative outcomes experienced by children living in poverty. In addition, those who are under 18 years of age (including young parents) receive lower wages for paid work and less welfare benefits than adults. Jurisdiction-specific legislation does not protect effectively against discrimination or promote equal opportunities for all children, especially those who have consistently experienced unequal treatment and provision of services (such as children with disabilities; children from minority ethnic communities; asylum seekers and refugees; lesbian, gay, bisexual, trans-gendered (LGBT) young people; 'looked after' children and care leavers). Nor is Article 12 effectively realised in legislation, policy and practice impacting on children's lives, as their views are not routinely sought or acted on. Regarding juvenile justice, the current low age of criminal responsibility – ten years in England, Wales and Northern Ireland, and eight years in Scotland, although the minimum age of prosecution was raised to 12 years in August 2010 – is not compliant with the UNCRC or *General Comment No. 10* (UN Committee on the Rights of the Child 2007) and custody is not a measure of last resort.

Children's rights violations in Northern Ireland

In June 2009, the Northern Ireland population was 1,788,896, of whom 24.2 per cent (432,814) were aged under 18 (NISRA undated). A significant proportion of these children live in poverty – more than

122,000 (29%) in income poverty (DSD 2007); approximately 170,000 (38%) go without basic necessities (Save the Children 2007); and an estimated 44,000 (10%) live in severe poverty (Magadi and Middleton 2007). Between 2001 and 2004, persistent poverty affected 21 per cent of children in Northern Ireland compared with 9 per cent in Britain (Monteith, Lloyd and McKee 2008). Entitlement to free school meals is an indicator of economic deprivation, and in Northern Ireland 22 per cent of primary school pupils, 26 per cent of non-selective secondary school pupils and 7 per cent of those attending selective grammar schools are entitled to free school meals (DENI 2011).

Poverty negatively impacts on children's education, health and wellbeing, family relationships and social activities (Horgan 2009; Horgan and Monteith 2009; McLaughlin and Monteith 2004; Save the Children 2007). For example, the 'hidden' costs of education (uniforms, books and equipment, school trips, extra-curricular activities) disproportionately affect families living in poverty (Horgan 2007). Differences in educational attainment reflect socio-economic inequalities at every level – those entitled to free school meals leave school with fewer qualifications, are less likely to enter Further or Higher Education and are more likely to be unemployed than those who are not entitled to free school meals (DENI 2010). Infant mortality rates for children born to parents living in more deprived areas are a third higher than for Northern Ireland as a whole, and children living in these areas are almost twice as likely to have experienced dental decay (Chief Medical Officer 2007). Young people from poorer families are more likely to smoke, drink alcohol and abuse solvents or drugs than young people from wealthier backgrounds (Save the Children 2007). The rate of teenage pregnancy is highest in the areas of Northern Ireland with greatest social and economic deprivation (Kenway *et al.* 2006) and between 1999 and 2003 the suicide rate was 17.0 per 100,000 in economically deprived areas as opposed to 8.2 per 100,000 in wealthier communities (DHSSPS 2006).

The experiences of young people in conflict with the law illustrate their complex, often unaddressed, needs and the cumulative impacts of economic and social disadvantage. Many live in families where their parents' capacity to encourage and appropriately care for them is inhibited by poverty, trauma related to the armed conflict in Northern Ireland (which affected thousands of individuals, families and communities between 1969 and the beginning of the 'peace process' in 1998), and their personal experiences of compromised parenting.

When asked what support families need, these young people emphasise parental support:

> Parenting classes...so they can give kids more self-confidence and self-esteem. But some parents can't give it to their kids if they never had it themselves – they wouldn't know how to. (Haydon 2009, p.38)

Lack of support can lead to breakdown in family relationships, neglect and abuse, resulting in children being placed in care. As one young person describes, experiences of childhood trauma and separation from parents are often exacerbated by negative perceptions about 'looked after' children and their family situation:

> I pretended to them [other kids] that my foster parents and family were my real family. It made me feel bad. I would have liked to have told them: 'I am in the care system.' I didn't because I was worried they would tease me and treat me badly or differently. (Haydon 2009, p.40)

Another young person's comment reflects how many 'looked after' children experience emotional instability and feelings of rejection by their parents: 'People don't think their family care about them, so they don't care about themselves' (Haydon 2009, p.42). Further, they feel that residential staff have minimal emotional attachment to the young people in their care, leading to less empathy and understanding of individuals' needs:

> Your family would forgive you for things that care staff wouldn't.
>
> If you do one thing wrong [when in residential care], they phone the peelers [police]. It's supposed to be a home, where you live. If you were living with your Mum and Dad, they wouldn't phone the police when you broke a cup!... [Care] staff call the police too quickly – for smashing cups, I was done for criminal damage. They could have just made me pay it back. (Haydon 2009, p.42)

The Criminal Justice Inspectorate (CJINI 2008, p.vii) notes that the over-representation of children from residential care placements is a 'longstanding feature of juvenile custody in Northern Ireland'. This over-representation extends throughout the criminal justice system. In 2006, 11 per cent of 'looked after' children aged ten and over were cautioned or convicted, compared with 1 per cent of 10–17-year-olds found guilty of offences in Northern Ireland that year (NSPCC 2009). During 2006–2007, 30 per cent of all admissions to the Juvenile Justice Centre (where 10–17-year-olds are held in custody) came from 'looked after' care backgrounds. The percentage of 'looked after' children in the Centre fluctuated between 22 per cent and 58 per cent of all residents on any given day, and 'looked after' children had on average twice as many admissions as non-looked after children (CJINI 2008).

Most children in conflict with the law have had poor educational experiences. One young person explains how under-achievement often leads to disruptive behaviour in school:

> If you feel you're not very smart in school. That makes you mess about, to take the notice off you not being smart. It takes the focus off it – you can say it's 'cos you've been messing about, that's why you're not doing well. (Haydon 2009, p.18)

Others highlight the significance of undiagnosed special educational needs: 'I was told I was stupid, thick an' all. I never found out I was dyslexic 'til I came here [to a voluntary project]'; and how unidentified needs or lack of appropriate support can prompt truanting: 'Left school at 14. They never gave me any support so I just left' (Haydon 2009, p.29). Contrasting their experience of mainstream education with provision in the Juvenile Justice Centre, young people emphasise the smaller classes and individualised approach: 'Outside teachers just write on a board and make you write it down. Here, they talk to you more, see what help you need' (Haydon 2009, p.29).

Limited access to age-appropriate, affordable play facilities and safe social space are priorities for children (Haydon 2007; Kilkelly *et al.* 2004; NICCY 2008). Young people in conflict with the law are clear that lack of provision increases the likelihood of involvement in risk-taking or 'anti-social' behaviour: 'Most people get into crime at the start because they're bored and have nothing to do' (Haydon 2009, p.32). But when spending time in their neighbourhood with friends, young people feel targeted by the police:

> You're prevented from standing on the streets. If the cops come by, they know young people and start going at them… If you're in large groups, you're told to separate.
>
> [Police] tell you to move on but there is nowhere to go. And then when you move on, they tell you to move on from there. You can't win. (Haydon 2009, p.60)

Young people define 'police harassment' as being continuously stopped, questioned, moved on and threatened with Anti-Social Behaviour Orders (McAlister, Scraton and Haydon 2009; Nelson *et al.* 2010). They consider that name-calling and ridicule by police officers exacerbates violent confrontations, maintaining that fighting the police is an expression of their resistance to age discrimination.

In some communities, young people are moved on and threatened with severe punishment or exiling by paramilitaries (former Republican or Loyalist combatants involved in the armed conflict) who resist the involvement of the police in their communities and informally regulate perceived 'anti-social' behaviour: 'There's not enough to do, so young people steal cars… But they shouldn't get knee-capped for doing that, or put out of the country [by paramilitaries]' (Haydon 2009, p.23). In 2007, 29 per cent of young people who completed the Northern Ireland *Young Persons Behaviour and Attitudes Survey* worried about threats by paramilitaries and 2.8 per cent had been threatened by paramilitaries in the previous 12 months (OFMDFM 2011). For many young people, there is a correspondence between the State's use of punitive measures and the punishments administered by members of their local community (Haydon and Scraton 2008; Lloyd 2009):

> What we need is a bit of support and understanding – what we get told is we're bad and end up on the receiving end of police and paramilitaries. (Young person in Haydon 2009, p.8)

Young people acknowledge that alcohol and drug use can affect their behaviour – reducing inhibitions and providing the impetus for involvement in offending:

> People start stealing, mugging people and doing robberies, to get money to pay for drugs.
>
> It's normal to do drugs, everybody does – that makes you more likely to do stuff, you have no inhibitions. (Haydon 2009, pp.18–19)

There is, however, a lack of awareness about available health services: 'Loads don't know who their doctor is'…'I haven't got a clue!'; and poor mental health is a common experience: 'There are not enough mental health services – self-harm and suicide are problems in Northern Ireland' (young people cited by Haydon 2009, p.34). Significant issues include: anxiety about family circumstances, domestic violence, bereavement, depression, bullying in school, and inter-generational trauma which is a legacy of the conflict in Northern Ireland. The impacts of the circumstances described are evidenced in the recorded issues faced by those held in custody – of the 30 children in the Juvenile Justice Centre on 30 November 2007, eight were on the child protection register, 14 had a statement of educational needs, 20 had a diagnosed mental health disorder, 17 had a history of self-harm and eight had attempted suicide (CJINI 2008).

How could international rights-based standards be more effectively implemented?

International standards articulate the principles that should underpin legislation, policy and practice. However, these are not implemented effectively in the UK, undermining realisation of their rights for many children in Northern Ireland and Britain. Following its examination of the UK Government, the *Concluding Observations* of the UN Committee on the Rights of the Child (2008) raised numerous concerns. In response, the UK Government produced a joint commitment to take action and each jurisdiction produced an action plan. But more fundamental changes are required.

Recognising the structural inequalities experienced by children

As stated by Scraton and Chadwick (1991, p.180):

> In order to understand the dynamics of life in advanced capitalist societies and the institutionalisation of ideological relations within the state and other key agencies it is important to take account of the historical, political and economic contexts of classism, sexism, heterosexism and racism. These categories do not form hierarchies of oppression, they are neither absolute nor are they totally determining, but they do carry with them the weight and legitimacy of official discourse.

As individuals and as a social group, children also experience structural inequalities derived in the determining context of 'age'. Within this, there is a distinction between 'ageism' and 'adultism'. While ageism may apply to both children and older people, adultism 'as an oppressive material and intellectual force' is specific only to children and young people:

> ...adultism becomes institutionalised and mediated through social structures and their processes and policies...material

> power is complemented by persistent ideologies of subservience and subjugation to silence the voices and nullify the actions of young people… No other group of people could have been so systematically ignored… (Scraton 1997, p.xiii)

In research and consultation with children and young people, lack of participation is the most frequently raised concern. They resent that they are not encouraged to express their views, their opinions are not taken into account, and they are not involved in making decisions (Haydon 2007; Kilkelly *et al.* 2004; McAlister *et al.* 2009). This is particularly so for children deemed 'troublesome'. As one young person states: 'People think ones like us are just hoods. Nobody ever asks us what we think, or what we want' (Haydon 2009, p.13).

Power differentials between adults and children are manifested interpersonally (in relationships between children and parents, community members or adults working with them) and institutionally (through the reproduction of social and material inequalities in schools, colleges, health services, accommodation, welfare and employment). Consequently, children experience discrimination and marginalisation in personal, social and community interactions and have limited involvement in private or public decision-making processes. When asked how they are perceived, young people's responses reflect their experience of exclusion:

> No adults treat young people with respect – I wear a hood, I am a hood.
>
> Young people are not valued in our society. We are all labelled as bad news, as trouble, nagged at. (Haydon 2009, p.14)

Children and young people express frustration about the negative assumptions of adults (Haydon 2007; McAlister *et al.* 2009). A typical comment is that people 'Automatically think you're up to no good because of your appearance – clothes and age' (young person in Haydon 2009, p.14). Adults' power and control over children's space, bodies and time – expressed as a demand for obedience – is defined as 'age-patriarchy' by Hendrick (2005, p.398). More contentiously, Haydon and Scraton (2000, pp.447–448) use the term 'child hate' to reflect 'the systemic and interpersonal prevalence of harm, abuse, degradation, exploitation, fear, rejection and exclusion endured by children in their daily encounters with adult worlds'.

Using international standards as a framework

Criticisms of the UNCRC tend to focus on its conceptualisation of 'rights' and the limitations imposed by language that circumscribes State responsibilities. Fortin (2003) acknowledges the contested relationship between moral/legal rights and social ideas about how children should be treated or the level of autonomy they should be granted, noting there is no 'test' providing guidance about what rights children have or should have. Alderson (2008, p.18) contends that UNCRC rights are aspirational as they are realisable only 'to the maximum extent of available resources' and conditional rather than absolute because they are affected by the 'evolving capacities of the child', the 'responsibilities, rights and duties of parents' and 'national law'.

Despite these limitations, Kilkelly (2008, pp.188–191) outlines the benefits of international standards. They are a useful 'auditing tool', representing 'a common reference point against which progress can be usefully measured'. They provide the 'potential for legal argument based on standards that are international rather than national in character'. They are a framework for 'rights-based analysis that allows states' failings to be highlighted, but also comprise indicators of best practice as to how such shortcomings can be addressed'. While 'establishing minimum standards, on which states should build, they also have a wide universal application to states emerging from conflict and those apparently on the irreversible road to punitiveness'. Importantly, they are 'a constant reference point or benchmark, not susceptible to the vagaries of public opinion', which 'gives them both credibility and a sense of timeless value'.

Challenging resistance to 'rights'

Fortin (2003, p.18) argues that the language of rights 'is a politically useful tool to ensure achievement of certain goals for children'. Rights take on particular significance in protecting the weak, the vulnerable, the oppressed or the minority interest (Scraton and Haydon 2002). For Freeman (2007, p.7), children's rights are 'no more or less important than rights generally'. Regardless of age, rights 'recognise the respect their bearers are entitled to. To accord rights is to respect dignity: to deny rights is to cast doubt on humanity and on integrity.' As Freeman (2007, p.8) states:

> Without rights the excluded can make requests, they can beg or implore, they can be troublesome; they can rely on, what has been called, *noblesse oblige*, or on others being charitable,

> generous, kind, cooperative or even intelligently foresighted. But they cannot demand, for there is no entitlement.

Freeden (1991, p.11) proposes that a 'satisfactory theory of basic rights' has to meet three criteria: 'rational and logical standards' (philosophical); 'translatable into codes of enforceable action' (legal); and 'terms that are emotionally and culturally attractive' (ideological). UK Government ratification of international human rights standards implies acceptance of their principles and provisions as rational and logical, but the second and third criteria remain contested in terms of children's rights in the UK. Although the UNCRC is legally binding through ratification, it has not been incorporated into domestic law. The only statutorily available human rights instrument that can be utilised in cases of alleged rights violations is the *European Convention on Human Rights* (ECHR), as the *1998 Human Rights Act* made the ECHR domestically justiciable. The UNCRC has been cited in judgments in the High Court in Northern Ireland, although there has not been a consistent approach regarding its standing or applicability and Judges have ruled that the Northern Ireland Executive or UK Government are under no obligation to enforce international provisions or treaties not introduced into domestic law (Haydon 2008b).

In terms of ideology, Franklin (2002, p.3) argues:

> ...discussion of children's rights has achieved a degree of respectability. Instead of being dismissed as 'utopian nonsense' or mere 'political correctness' the idea that children possess rights which adults should respect and help to promote now informs aspects of government policy and legislation, the policy of voluntary sector and charitable organisations as well as the practice of welfare professionals.

Despite this shift, significant emotional and cultural resistance to children's rights continues. For example, in Northern Ireland the promotion of human rights has been a central element within 'peace' agreements. However, the long and disputed process of developing recommendations for a *Bill of Rights for Northern Ireland* highlighted major disparities in interpretation of 'rights' amongst political parties, disagreements over the role of the State in articulating and implementing rights, and lack of consensus about defining children's rights (Bill of Rights Forum 2008; NIHRC 2008).

Prioritising children's participation

There is a key ideological tension between a child's right to 'protection' (promoting their welfare and protecting them from harm, abuse and exploitation) and their right to 'autonomy' (recognising their evolving capacity for decision-making, self-determination, independence and responsible action). Protection is generally prioritised, albeit on the basis of questionable assumptions. Children are presumed vulnerable, dependent and not competent to take on responsibilities. They are dependent on adults to meet their basic needs, and their relative lack of knowledge or experience contributes to both physical and emotional vulnerabilities, but focusing on their need for care and protection as a result of 'incompetence' reinforces a deficit-based perception of children and young people as well as doubtful assumptions about adult competence.

Like any other 'stage' of life, childhood and youth are periods of dynamic change and adaptation as individuals gain experience and understanding, develop additional skills and negotiate relationships and events. Although children may resist responsibilities associated with adulthood, they do want to be involved in decision-making processes and to have access to age-appropriate information or support in making informed choices and establishing independence. Children are structurally vulnerable because they are socially and politically excluded and considered subordinate to adults. This structural vulnerability increases their physical and emotional vulnerability. Because children are not listened to, they are disempowered and vulnerable to exclusion, abuse or exploitation by adults.

A further assumption is that their evolving intellectual capacity defines children as 'less than adult'. In fact, children are often more competent than adults assume *if* issues are explained in language, or using examples, that they understand. Having less knowledge and experience does not invalidate children's views. They require opportunities to develop skills to express their views, listen, engage in reciprocal relationships with adults and make informed decisions. The final assumption is that adults, assumed to be competent, act in children's best interests. This is difficult to assess if the child's views and wishes are not taken into account in decision-making. Consequently, children consider participation central:

> Adults think 'Kids should be seen and not heard' – in politics, the community, everywhere... They should be seen, and heard. But you have to be seen first to be heard. (Young person in Haydon 2009, p.8)

Developing a positive rights-based agenda for children

Developing a positive rights-based agenda requires recognition that children are unique individuals and legitimate rights-holders, not dependent on acceptance of responsibility or attainment of adult status. International standards do not link children's rights to responsibilities. There is not a social contract between the child and the State, nor is there an expectation that the child should accept responsibilities to ensure realisation of their rights. For every child under 18 years of age, rights are universal entitlements, not rewards or privileges. The UN Committee on the Rights of the Child (2005, paragraph 1) 'wishes to encourage recognition that young children are holders of all rights enshrined in the Convention and that early childhood is a critical period for realisation of these rights'.

As duty-bearers, the State and its agencies are responsible for ensuring that every child has access to appropriate health care, education, play and leisure opportunities, an adequate standard of living, a supportive family or alternative care and protection from abuse or exploitation. In prioritising the child's wellbeing and personal development, responsibility for those deemed 'at risk of offending' should be located in children's services (education, health, social care), with provision of support through locally available community-based services which identify and address the needs articulated by children and their families (see: The Riyadh Guidelines, OHCHR 1990a). For those who have committed offences, the priority should be diversion from the criminal justice system and decriminalisation, with disposals focusing on rehabilitation rather than punishment and retribution. One young person with experience of custody suggests that 'Harsh punishment doesn't work. It makes you harder, it makes you feel like a bigger man. It's like, "I can take that, what do I care?"' (Haydon 2009, p.68).

Any reaction should be in proportion to the personal circumstances of the offender and the gravity of the offence (see: The Beijing Rules, OHCHR 1985). Community-based alternatives to custody (for example, supported accommodation, bail support schemes and remand fostering) should ensure that custody is used as a last resort, for the shortest possible period, and only for those presenting serious immediate risk to themselves or others (see: The Tokyo Rules, OHCHR 1990b; The Havana Rules, OHCHR 1990c). According to these international standards, the rights of those held in secure facilities should be protected and young people should receive care, protection, education and vocational training, programs and activities to help them assume socially constructive and productive roles on release. As young people articulate, loss of liberty is the punishment for those in custody:

> Prison shouldn't be about punishing – you shouldn't get punished by the people in prison. The staff aren't there to punish you, they're there just to look after you… They're there to correct you, help you change your ways.
>
> You're not sent to prison for it to be hard – it's about taking your freedom. The punishment is not being able to go out in your community, being free. (Haydon 2009, p.67)

To conclude, the State should play a key role in bridging the gap between rhetoric and reality concerning children's rights. Achievement of this objective is dependent on recognition of the impacts of structural inequalities and development of child-focused, time-bound measures to address these. This requires provision of appropriate resources and articulation of political commitment to the promotion, protection and realisation of their rights for *all* children, including the most disadvantaged and marginalised:

> Young people like us already get the blame for near enough everything. I suppose it's easy to do that – blame it on the teenagers. But people just don't know the lives we lead, the problems a lot of us have. (Young person in Haydon 2009, p.17)

References

Alderson, P. (2008) *Young Children's Rights: Exploring Beliefs, Principles and Practice.* London: Jessica Kingsley Publishers.

Bill of Rights Forum (2008) *Bill of Rights Forum: Final Report. Recommendations to the Northern Ireland Human Rights Commission on a Bill of Rights for Northern Ireland.* 31 March 2008.

Chief Medical Officer (2007) *Your Health Matters. The Annual Report of the Chief Medical Officer for Northern Ireland 2006.* June 2007. Belfast: DHSSPS.

Child Rights International Network (2008) *CRC Session 49, September–October 2008.* Available at www.crin.org/Alternative-Reports/session.asp?CRCID=53, accessed on 3 February 2012.

Children's Rights Alliance for England (2008) *Implementation of the Convention on the Rights of the Child. NGO Alternative Report to the Committee on the Rights of the Child – England.* London: CRAE.

CJINI (Criminal Justice Inspection Northern Ireland) (2008) *Inspection of Woodlands Juvenile Justice Centre.* May 2008. Belfast: CJINI.

Croke, R. and Crowley, A. (eds) (2007) *Stop, Look, Listen: The Road to Realizing Children's Rights in Wales. Wales NGO Alternative Report.* Cardiff: Wales Programme of Save the Children.

DENI (Department of Education Northern Ireland) (2010) *Qualifications and Destinations of Northern Ireland School Leavers 2008/09.* Statistical Press Release. Bangor: DENI.

DENI (2011) *Enrolments at Schools and in Funded Pre-School Education in Northern Ireland 2010/11 (Revised).* Statistical Release, 25 March 2011. Bangor: DENI.

DHSSPS (Department of Health, Social Services and Public Safety) (2006) *Protect Life. A Shared Vision: The Northern Ireland Suicide Prevention Strategy and Action Plan 2006–2011.* Belfast: DHSSPS.

DSD (Department of Social Development) (2007) *Households Below Average Income, Northern Ireland 2005–2006.* Belfast: DSD.

Fortin, J. (2003) *Children's Rights and the Developing Law* (2nd edition). London: LexisNexis.

Franklin, B. (2002) 'Children's Rights: An Introduction.' In B. Franklin (ed.) *The New Handbook of Children's Rights: Comparative Policy and Practice.* London and New York: Routledge.

Freeden, M. (1991) *Rights.* Buckingham: Open University Press.

Freeman, M. (2007) 'Why it remains important to take children's rights seriously.' *International Journal of Children's Rights 15,* 1, 5–23.

Haydon, D. (2007) *United Nations Convention on the Rights of the Child. Consultation with Children and Young People.* Belfast: Office of the First Minister and Deputy First Minister. Available at Available at www.ofmdfmni.gov.uk/report-on-consultations-5.pdf, accessed on 26 January 2012.

Haydon, D. (2008a) *Northern Ireland NGO Alternative Report. Submission to the United Nations Committee on the Rights of the Child for Consideration during the Committee's Scrutiny of the UK Government Report.* Belfast: Save the Children and Children's Law Centre.

Haydon, D. (2008b) *Additional Information from Northern Ireland in Response to the List of Issues Relating to Implementation of the Convention on the Rights of the Child in the UK: Summary of Additional Information, Suggested Questions, Executive Summary and Actions Required.* Belfast: Save the Children NI and Children's Law Centre.

Haydon, D. (2009) *Developing a Manifesto for Youth Justice in Northern Ireland. Background Paper.* Belfast: Include Youth.

Haydon, D. and Scraton, P. (2000) '"Condemn a little more, understand a little less": The political context and rights implications of the domestic and European rulings in the Venables–Thompson case.' *Journal of Law and Society 27,* 3, 416–448.

Haydon, D. and Scraton, P. (2008) 'Conflict, regulation and marginalisation in the North of Ireland: The experiences of children and young people.' *Current Issues in Criminal Justice 20,* 1, 59–78.

Hendrick, H. (ed.) (2005) *Child Welfare and Social Policy: An Essential Reader.* Bristol: Policy Press.

Horgan, G. (2007) *The Impact of Poverty on Young Children's Experience of School.* York: Joseph Rowntree Foundation/Save the Children.

Horgan, G. (2009) *Speaking Out Against Poverty. Voices of Children Living in Disadvantaged Areas.* Belfast: Save the Children Northern Ireland.

Horgan, G. and Monteith, M. (2009) *What Can We Do to Tackle Child Poverty in Northern Ireland?* York: Joseph Rowntree Foundation.

Kenway, P., Macinnes, T., Kelly, A. and Palmer, G. (2006) *Monitoring Poverty and Social Exclusion in Northern Ireland.* York: Joseph Rowntree Foundation.
Kilkelly, U. (2008) 'Youth Justice and Children's Rights: Measuring Compliance with International Standards.' *Youth Justice 8*, 3, 187–192.
Kilkelly, U., Kilpatrick, R., Lundy, L., Moore, L. *et al.* (2004) *Children's Rights in Northern Ireland.* Belfast: NICCY.
Lloyd, T. (2009) *Stuck in the Middle (Some Young Men's Attitudes and Experiences of Violence, Conflict and Safety).* Jordanstown: Centre for Young Men's Studies, University of Ulster/YouthAction NI.
Magadi, M. and Middleton, S. (2007) *Measuring Child Poverty in the UK.* London: Save the Children.
McAlister, S., Scraton, P. and Haydon, D. (2009) *Childhood in Transition: Experiencing Marginalisation and Conflict in Northern Ireland.* Belfast: Queen's University Belfast/ Save the Children/Princes Trust.
McLaughlin, E. and Monteith, M. (2004) *The Bottom Line.* Belfast: Save the Children.
Monteith, M., Lloyd, K. and McKee, P. (2008) *Persistent Child Poverty in Northern Ireland.* Belfast: Save the Children.
Nelson, E., McBride, R-S., O'Riordan, O. and Smyth, P. (2010) *Beyond the Margins: Building Trust in Policing with Young People.* Belfast: Achieve Enterprises and Institute for Conflict Research.
NICCY (Northern Ireland Commissioner for Children and Young People) (2008) *Children's Rights: Rhetoric or Reality. A Review of Children's Rights in Northern Ireland 2007/08.* Belfast: NICCY.
NIHRC (Northern Ireland Human Rights Commission) (2008) *A Bill of Rights for Northern Ireland: Advice to the Secretary of State for Northern Ireland.* Belfast: NIHRC.
NISRA (Northern Ireland Statistics and Research Agency) (undated) *Estimated Population by Sex and Age, 30 June 2009.* Available at www.nisra.gov.uk/archive/demography/ publications/annual_reports/Table2.1_2009.xls, accessed on 18 February 2011.
NSPCC (National Society for the Prevention of Cruelty to Children) (2009) *Key Child Protection Statistics in Northern Ireland,* June 2009. Available at www.nspcc.org.uk/ inform/research/statistics/key_child_protection_statistics_in_northern_ireland_pdf_ wdf48712.pdf, accessed on 24 March 2011.
OFMDFM (2011) *Good Relations Indicators, 2010 Update.* Available at www.ofmdfmni. gov.uk/good_relations_indicators_-_2010_update-4.xls, accessed on 26 January 2012.
OHCHR (Office of the High Commissioner for Human Rights) (1985) *United Nations Standard Minimum Rules for the Administration of Juvenile Justice.* The Beijing Rules. Adopted by General Assembly resolution 40/33 of 29 November 1985.
OHCHR (1990a) *United Nations Guidelines for the Prevention of Juvenile Delinquency.* The Riyadh Guidelines. Adopted by General Assembly resolution 45/112 of 14 December 1990.
OHCHR (1990b) *United Nations Standard Minimum Rules for Non-custodial Measures.* The Tokyo Rules. Adopted by General Assembly resolution 45/110 of 14 December 1990.
OHCHR (1990c) *United Nations Rules for the Protection of Juveniles Deprived of their Liberty.* The Havana Rules. Adopted by General Assembly resolution 45/113 of 14 December 1990.
Save the Children (2007) *A 2020 Vision: Ending Child Poverty in Northern Ireland. Annual Child Poverty Report 2007.* Belfast: Save the Children.

Scottish Alliance for Children's Rights (2008) *The NGO Report (Scotland) 2008 to the United Nations Committee on the Rights of the Child.* Edinburgh: SACR.

Scraton, P. (ed.) (1997) *'Childhood' in 'Crisis'?* London: UCL Press.

Scraton, P. and Chadwick, K. (1991) 'The Theoretical and Political Priorities of Critical Criminology.' In K. Stenson and D. Cowell (eds) *The Politics of Crime Control.* London: Sage.

Scraton, P. and Haydon, D. (2002) 'Challenging the Criminalisation of Children and Young People: Securing a Rights-based Agenda.' In J. Muncie, G. Hughes and E. McLaughlin (eds) *Youth Justice: Critical Readings.* London: Sage.

UK Government (2007) *The Consolidated Third and Fourth Periodic Reports of the United Kingdom of Great Britain and Northern Ireland.* 16 July 2007. CRC/C/GBR/4.

UN Committee on the Rights of the Child (2001) *General Comment No. 1. The aims of education. Article 29 (1) (2001).* 17 April 2001. CRC/GC/2001/1.

UN Committee on the Rights of the Child (2003) *General Comment No. 5. General measures of implementation of the Convention on the Rights of the Child (arts. 4, 42 and 44, para. 6).* 27 November 2003. CRC/GC/2003/5.

UN Committee on the Rights of the Child (2005) *General Comment No. 7. Implementing child rights in early childhood.* 1 November 2005. CRC/C/GC/7.

UN Committee on the Rights of the Child (2007) *General Comment No. 10. Children's rights in juvenile justice.* 25 April 2007. CRC/C/GC/10.

UN Committee on the Rights of the Child (2008) *Concluding Observations. United Kingdom of Great Britain and Northern Ireland.* 20 October 2008. CRC/C/GBR/CO/4.

UN General Assembly (1989) *Convention on the Rights of the Child,* Resolution 44/25. 20 November 1989.

Veerman, P.E. (1992) *The Rights of the Child and the Changing Image of Childhood.* Dordrecht: Martinus Nijhoff Publishers.

Chapter 2

Child Protection in Humanitarian Emergencies

Patrick O'Leary and Jason Squire

Introduction

Visually the picture of children suffering in disasters or conflict is emotionally compelling and prompts the international community towards action. Few people will forget the image of a vulture standing ready to pounce on a starving child in Southern Sudan in 1993 (Kleinman and Kleinman 1996), or the footage of children in the Occupied Palestinian Territories having lost limbs after unknowingly playing with an unexploded military ordnance (Watts 2009). Globally there is in excess of 200 million children affected by humanitarian crises (Save the Children 2007). In the 2004 tsunami in South East Asia one-third of all victims were children (UNICEF 2009) and in the 2009 Haiti earthquake young children had very high mortality rates in the months immediately following the disaster (Kolbe *et al.* 2010). The Darfur conflict in Sudan has seen more than 1.4 million children displaced; of these over 700,000 children have only known a life mitigated by conflict (UNICEF 2008).

In the decade up to the year 2000, 66.5 million children were affected by natural disasters and in excess of 10 million were affected by conflict (IFRCRCS 2001, cited in Penrose and Takaki 2006). The nature of conflict has dramatically transformed over the years, with more than 90 per cent of casualties in modern-day conflicts being civilians and more than half being children; worldwide 17 million children have been either internally or externally displaced by war

(IPCCPE 2006). Humanitarian emergencies are often more severe and sustained in the developing world where infrastructure and services are poorly resourced and prepared. Child mortality and injury following disasters are significantly heightened (Linnan *et al.* 2007), and infant mortality increases dramatically during and after disasters (Rajaratnam *et al.* 2010). As a result the developing world has a substantial reliance on international aid and assistance from non-government organisations (NGOs). Therefore it is imperative for organisations delivering child protection programming in emergencies to be professionally equipped to carry out accountable and punctual interventions.

In this chapter we present an approach to child protection in humanitarian emergencies. This approach draws on experiences and evaluative research gained from the child protection programming of Terre des hommes Foundation Lausanne (Tdh) in a number of countries (Nepal, Pakistan, Sri Lanka and Sudan) where humanitarian crises have occurred and Tdh has provided an emergency child protection focused response (see O'Leary and Squire 2009a, b). A number of challenges are identified for child protection programming and the corresponding ways these issues can be addressed through a systematic process of policy, planning and practice.

Child protection risks in emergencies

In the aftermath of a humanitarian emergency there are many risks, not only arising directly from the crisis but also from people's increased vulnerability. Children are the most vulnerable in this environment. In the chaos during and after a crisis, children can be separated from their families, who may have been killed, maimed, or forced to flee. These conditions are often further complicated by volatile and complex socio-political conflict, especially evident in countries such as Lebanon, Pakistan, Sri Lanka and Sudan. Many risks arise from increases in the fragility of natural protection systems within families and communities. It is frequently acknowledged that disasters lead to an increased exposure for children to exploitation and violence, along with risks associated with the immediate impact of the disaster such as access to clean drinking water, sanitation and unsafe play areas. Even in these seemingly hopeless conditions children and families can be incredibly resilient. Indeed it is the aim of emergency aid programs to harness this resiliency with the goal being a return to normalcy as quickly as possible, which differs significantly from developmental aid programs which promote changes in knowledge, attitudes and practices, often over an extended period, even years. Emergency aid programs range from weeks to months with specific, often quite narrow, objectives. Within this concise framework, the most resilient, and often the most visible, are more likely to be able to access assistance and engage with humanitarian intervention programs. Distribution of emergency aid often encounters the stronger survivors, but reaching the most vulnerable children can be a significant challenge. This requires high quality assessments and intervention strategies, coupled to systematic and accountable monitoring within a professional framework.

Many child protection risks identified in an emergency are often pre-existing and are generally exacerbated by the conditions and effects of the disaster. These pre-existing risks may already constitute a serious breach of child rights and in some cases these violations can be more life threatening than some of the risks attributable to the disaster that first prompted intervention. This can create dilemmas about priorities and intervention planning, especially where mandates and funding for interventions are solely focused on the impact of the disaster, not on structural reforms or long-term change. Borrowing from the 2009 protection funding guidelines of the European Commission for Humanitarian Aid (ECHO), a primary donor in humanitarian crisis, they clearly state their focus is on 'non-structural' activities which 'contributes to human rights but does not address them as such' (2009, p.5). ECHO seeks to fund punctual projects which have a clear focus on 'responsive' and short-term 'remedial' interventions to the human rights needs of affected individuals or groups, rather than 'environment building' actions. In this context we assert that emergency interventions require clear child protection objectives.

In the immediate aftermath of a disaster the focus of intervention is on the human survival needs of food, water, shelter and life-preserving medical care. Within a rights framework the priority is to ensure this distribution reaches children. Often the failure of these resources to reach children is related to child protection problems arising from the disaster. Family separation is a common problem in emergencies, and reunification with primary caregivers is a priority when first identifying unaccompanied or separated children. Emergencies disrupt social order and result in dysfunctional support and protective structures, leaving children and adolescents vulnerable to exploitation in many forms. Armed conflict can make boys and girls targets to be recruited into armed forces, exposing them to extreme risks and later psychological harm. The high numbers of children who are separated from families are at risk to trafficking, child labour and opportunistic crime such as sexual assault and/or robbery. Tremendous stress can leave children exposed to disproportionate punishment and other physical harm from things such as gender-based violence and civil unrest. Emergencies have often caused damage to the physical environment, leaving few safe areas for children to play or exposing them to risks such as landmines or stagnant water. The experience of surviving an emergency can cause psychological distress, adversely affecting children's social and emotional development. Of course community and children's survival in these situations give important indications of strength and resilience. These are important factors to utilise and support when considering any intervention.

Emergency contexts

Humanitarian emergencies can be slow in onset, such as drought, famine or increasing political tensions, or they can be rapid in onset, such as tsunamis, earthquakes or landslides (Delaney 2006). Complex emergency situations pose particular difficulties and are characterised by complex and interacting economic and socio-political factors that are often compounded by natural events (Delaney 2006). In emergency and conflict situations children face a heightened risk of displacement and human rights abuses. The breakdown of law and order disrupts critical economic systems, including material and social infrastructure, which in turn increases children's risk of exposure to violence, exploitation, abuse, separation from families, and recruitment into armed forces or sexual slavery (IPCCPE 2006).

Whilst child protection in emergency contexts is increasingly becoming a priority throughout the world, a coherent approach to protecting children in conflict and emergencies is often absent, particularly in terms of a lack of agreement in the definition of what constitutes child protection in emergency contexts (IPCCPE 2006). This confusion resides in four main areas: a limited understanding of child rights as a conceptual framework; a lack of situational analysis; insufficient understanding of the social aspects of child protection; and insufficient integration with community services and community networks (IPCCPE 2006). Organisations have also called for systemic and accountable interventions that emphasise both quality and sustainability (Save the Children 2007; UNICEF 2006).

Historically, humanitarian interventions in emergency and conflict-affected contexts have focused on prioritising physical and medical issues over social, psychological or psychosocial issues (Williamson and Robinson 2006). This implies that medical and physical issues can be effectively addressed in isolation from the psychosocial dimensions of the situation. Williamson and Robinson (2006) argue that it is more beneficial to consider the interrelatedness of the biological, material, social and psychological dimensions of human functioning. Inadequate attention to psychosocial responses in emergency contexts has been found to be a significant contributor to the failure of programs (Williamson and Robinson 2006). In emergency contexts it is therefore necessary to consider responses to psychosocial issues holistically as part of a comprehensive set of responses to enable populations to achieve an adequate level of wellbeing. For Tdh and their response to vulnerable children in emergencies, the connection and interplay between a child's material, social and psychological needs cannot be separated when the intention is to create a consciousness of normalcy (Terre des hommes 2008). The internal and external factors that facilitate a child's sense of wellbeing, primarily achieved through feelings of being safe, greatly impacts on their return to a normalcy of psychosocial functioning.

Cycle of response in humanitarian disasters

A range of models exist amongst humanitarian agencies in regard to emergency responses; generally these follow a number of phases, as illustrated in Figure 2.1.

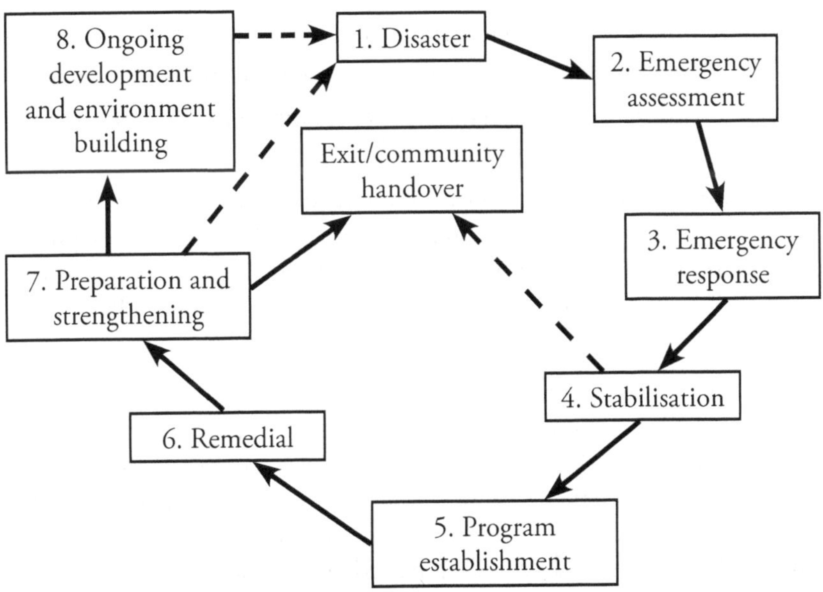

FIGURE 2.1 Emergency cycle
Source: O'Leary and Squire 2009b

Phases can vary in length from a few months to two years. Within this cycle there are important complementary stages to manage each of the phases within the cycle:

1. *Prerequisites.* Emergency assessments follow an exploratory mission or receipt of rapid assessment documentation from major donors or government actors; several components are identified, including field and modalities (framework) of intervention, local and national context, resource mapping, and existing study documentation.
2. *Strategic planning.* After an in-depth analysis of the prerequisites and objectives a consensus is reached on a strategic plan. This stage is essential but time consuming, and the working conditions in emergency contexts often do not allow the planning team to fully assess the situation due to the critical nature of the response needed.
3. *Operational programming.* This involves the conversion of the strategic plan to activities with timeframes and will result in the development of a monthly or annual operation and implementation plan.
4. *Implementation/execution.* Execution of the activities as set out in the operational plan.
5. *Monitoring/evaluation.* Indicators are established to ensure adequate monitoring of all stages of a project.
6. *Capitalisation.* This stage aims to maintain the best practices as models and learn from possible mistakes.
7. *Readjustment/withdrawal.* Some readjustment may be required as a result of the evaluation process of the previous phase. Withdrawal of NGO will result in the project being handed over to a local NGO or government partner, or the project comes to an end.

During the primary phase of a humanitarian aid crisis there is an understandable tendency to apply a 'blanket response' approach, namely little discrimination on who receives aid. Once the initial trauma and other effects of the emergency have receded and some control is achieved, there will be a shift toward focusing on the most vulnerable children and providing remedial activities.

Understanding child protection issues in humanitarian emergencies

In many developing world child populations, morbidity and mortality from preventable causes such as poor hygiene, unsafe water, inadequate sanitation, low rates of immunisation and malnutrition are substantial, and in emergencies these issues can be seriously exacerbated. These are often pre-existing issues of child survival and development. There are numerous problems of protection arising directly as a result of the disaster; however, often the intersection of these issues at a time of an emergency can make it difficult to precisely attribute the cause of the problem. For example, as a direct result of the 2005 earthquake in the North West Frontier region of Pakistan, children were separated from parents and consequently deprived of the basic survival needs of food and shelter; this is an emergency-induced problem. As a result children under five years of age had the highest mortality rate (Sullivan and Hossain 2009). In the same location there was a significant pre-existing protection problem of child labour in sand mines. This problem was made worse because of labour shortages immediately following the earthquake. Similarly, in the El Geneina Region of Darfur in Sudan, internally displaced people who were housed in camps had poor access to clean water for drinking and washing, making hygiene a major problem for infections in young children. This is an emergency-induced problem because it is a direct result of their displacement and compounded by the often rapid increase of arrivals and the abilities of humanitarian actors and the Sudanese government to respond in an insecure environment. In the same camps a pre-existing problem of sexual abuse of children was reported by the community. This violation of children exists in most communities around the world, but its prevalence can increase in camps because of the social environment (for example, families sharing confined temporary accommodation) and weakened community protection structures (O'Leary and Squire 2009b).

Often emergencies occur in the context of an ongoing chronic crisis such as civil war which adds to the complexity for program implementation and determining aetiology. A good example of this was in Eastern Sri Lanka where Tdh intervened following the acute crisis caused by the tsunami in 2004. Prior to this, the region had been affected by internal conflict, primarily between the ruling Sinhalese (Buddhist) government and sections of the Tamil (Hindu) minority. Many children had not been registered or had lost their birth certificates due to the ongoing military conflict. Instability within the country due to civil war led to the inconsistent delivery of government services in contested districts. The absence of birth certificates present a child protection risk because this can prevent a child from being eligible for education, health care and citizenship rights. These risks were compounded by the tsunami, as well as creating further risks such as displacement and a lack of shelter and clean drinking water. This can make it difficult to accurately classify problems as 'emergency induced' or 'pre-existing'. Regardless, these issues harm children and in themselves can require an emergency response. This can make the humanitarian response complex, requiring careful planning to determine priority risks and needs matched to a flexible intervention model to facilitate adaptation and change. During the life of an emergency project program initiatives can spark additional risks. For example, in Sri Lanka as part of Tdh's psychosocial recovery project, a number of safe play centres were established to assist children and their community to regain a sense of normalcy. These also provided clear locations where children would gather and thereby became ideal sites for child soldier abductions. Tdh had to manage both of these child protection risks concurrently and could not avoid or disregard one over the other due to the objectives of their project. Table 2.1 provides examples of various problems children experience in countries we examined.

Humanitarian-aid-induced problems should not be underestimated. Most pertinent is to guard against any risks that staff (international and national) may pose as they gain access to vulnerable children and their communities. An organisational Child Protection Policy and Code of Conduct which establishes clear guidelines and standards of practice provides an excellent starting point for training, monitoring and responding. A crucial dilemma, particularly in emergency contexts, is the time-limited nature of the intervention and subsequent impact these interventions can have on communities once humanitarian work is scaled down and/or terminated. Additionally, new expectations can be created and new 'needs' can emerge as a result of service provision that prior to the emergency did not exist.

Ethical challenges and cultural sensitivities

A rights-based philosophy has dominated many of the recent macro responses to child protection. This has largely been led by Western governments and organisations. In humanitarian emergencies there can be serious challenges to implementing a rights-based approach, because an interventionist approach is often needed to ensure that lives can be saved and the immediate suffering alleviated. The dilemma here is balancing

TABLE 2.1 Emergency-induced risks/problems; child survival and development issues; pre-existing problems; and humanitarian-aid-induced problems in each of the countries selected for this research[1]

<table>
<tr><th>PROBLEM</th><th>PAKISTAN</th><th>SRI LANKA</th><th>SUDAN</th><th>NEPAL</th></tr>
<tr><td rowspan="9">Emergency induced</td><td>Few safe play areas</td><td>Child registration</td><td>Few safe play areas</td><td>Child trafficking</td></tr>
<tr><td>Child labour</td><td>Legal ownership rights</td><td colspan="2">Child recruitment and abduction</td></tr>
<tr><td colspan="3">Acute medical problems</td><td>Family conflict</td></tr>
<tr><td>Child trafficking</td><td colspan="3">Attacks from militias and military</td></tr>
<tr><td colspan="4">Orphaned or abandoned</td></tr>
<tr><td colspan="4">Psychosocial distress and mental disorders</td></tr>
<tr><td colspan="4">Displaced and unaccompanied children/separation from family</td></tr>
<tr><td colspan="4">School attendance</td></tr>
<tr><td colspan="4"></td></tr>
<tr><td rowspan="7">Pre-existing</td><td>Juvenile justice</td><td>Child registration
Children involved in armed groups</td><td>Disabled children</td><td>Play areas</td></tr>
<tr><td colspan="3">Educational resources</td><td></td></tr>
<tr><td colspan="3">Early marriage</td><td></td></tr>
<tr><td>Child labour</td><td colspan="2">Child trafficking</td><td></td></tr>
<tr><td colspan="4">Corporal punishment</td></tr>
<tr><td colspan="4">Physical and sexual abuse/violence and neglect</td></tr>
<tr><td colspan="4">Gender-based violence and discrimination</td></tr>
</table>

PROBLEM	PAKISTAN	SRI LANKA	SUDAN	NEPAL
Child survival and development	Poor personal and household hygiene practices			
	Malnutrition and unsafe water/sanitation			
	Child registration		Child registration	
	Lack of educational and vocational training facilities			
	Lack of health care services to respond to chronic medical/disability problems			
Humanitarian aid induced	Dependency for referral to medical care	Dependency on referral to resources	Dependency for food and shelter	Reliance on agency resources rather than self-sustained resources
	Suspicion of NGO	Risk of institutional abuse	Reliant community leadership	Unsustainable funding and fears of termination
	Effect of terminating of project (local staff and communities)	Threats/violence from militias or other political religious groups for accepting support from NGO		Community tensions with local staff and volunteers
	Potential to undermine indigenous support structures and resilience			

Source: O'Leary and Squire 2009b

the needs of children within the immediate crisis while balancing the need for communities to have the power to decide and participate in the intervention process and planning. There are essentially two polarised positions that have emerged in regard to child protection in developing nations. First, the need to be culturally sensitive and demonstrate cultural competency, and second, the contrasting need to challenge norms within cultures that sanction the harsh or neglectful treatment of children (Maiter, Alaggio and Trocmé 2004). Whilst it is often argued that when working in culturally diverse contexts it is necessary to take a culturally relative stance, this approach is not necessarily appropriate for child protection work, which requires the use of rapidly executed risk assessment tools within short periods of time (Maiter *et al.* 2004). That is not to deny however the need for workers to be culturally sensitive, but rather highlights the need to promote children's wellbeing and welfare as a fundamental priority.

Modern conceptions of childhood are both socially and historically specific. There is increasing recognition that much of the literature and legislation has been drawn from the Western, middle-class, male construction of childhood as being the 'essential' childhood and has been prescribed as a universal application (Alanen 1994; Burman 1995). In contemporary times under the United Nations, the international convention on children's rights has been defined by the West and exported to developing countries (Boyden 1997), who have ratified and agreed to much of its contents.

It is therefore important that child protection intervention from humanitarian agencies does not impose a system which assumes that developed countries know how to best protect children, while at the same time failing to protect children from violations of rights because these are said to be 'cultural' or 'traditional'. Some protection risks might be explained or even dismissed under these loaded terms (for example, child labour, early marriage and physical punishment). However, often these cultural, religious and traditional teachings do not promote or condone these protection risks or in other cases there are strict guidelines on how such practices are carried out (UNICEF and Al-Azhar University 2005). Invariably this creates tensions and dilemmas but can also lead to conflict, and in extreme cases to life-threatening situations for international and national humanitarian aid staff. It is therefore critical for international humanitarian aid organisations to engage and identify all power structures within communities, such as women, who can often be less visible and not heard as readily in communities who are dominated by patriarchy. If this is not done it can leave the impression that violations of child rights are unanimously supported by communities (for example, gender discrimination in education). This can be misleading as there are often contrary views amongst a substantial proportion of the population. However, even within this considered approach, care needs to be taken not to disrupt established systems of governance which might put sectors of the community in a precarious position after the emergency intervention stops. The fundamental questions that need to be reflected on during the assessment and planning of emergency aid programs are: How long are we going to be here for and what change can really be effected? Are we creating needs and doing harm? Who is acknowledging this as a problem? What are the security risks for all parties?

Intervention on controversial or sensitive child protection issues require organisations to commit to processes that facilitate community participation and ownership to bring about change or support individual children in the long term, which can be problematic in emergency projects. In the short term, it could be the case that there is a need to manage them within the culturally specific conditions, which can often challenge the principles of child rights organisations and the protection of children, when laid across international standards.

Sensitive protection issues require critical analysis to determine what, if any, action is necessary. Central here is the ethical principle of 'do no harm'; other principles are the inherent tensions between 'duty of care' and 'self-determination'. Embedded in these issues are considerations of consent at individual, family and community levels. Consent is complex and in regard to children requires awareness of the child's capacity to comprehend and rationally process information in an environment free from coercion. It is often the case that humanitarian aid organisations receive a perception of consent, but this can be based on misunderstandings from both parties on what they are consenting to and what it actually means for individual children, families and communities. For example, in Pakistan, children involved in labour consented to receive assistance to attend school but incorrectly assumed that their family would be compensated for lost wages. This example from Pakistan highlights the importance of ensuring children and their families understand exactly what is being agreed by encouraging dialogue that elicits understanding. For staff who do not speak the local language or dialects, quality translation is critical. A smile or nod of the head should not be assumed as an indication of consent and understanding.

It is a frequent part of an humanitarian aid organisation's daily life to be managing community relations, often based on avoiding conflict to ensure access to communities, regardless of signed agreements and/or promises of full cooperation. Informed consent is not always easy to obtain in situations of emergencies and therefore requires professional ethical practice guidelines. If consent is not prioritised we may inadvertently infer that they (child, family or community) do not have the capacity to know what is best for themselves. This can lead to assumptions that people wilfully make the 'wrong choice'. As a result, not seeking consent takes power away from already disempowered people and gives the message that their choices will be overridden (Leighton 2007). This can add to people's sense of helplessness and erode trust in organisations. Nevertheless consent is not a simple binary of yes or no, as other issues of responsibility, within both legal and duty of care frameworks, cannot be ignored. Where dilemmas arise it is always important to gain organisational support which involves local national staff as much as possible. National staff are a crucial element in navigating and securing community relationships and cannot be disregarded or overlooked.

Confidentiality is an important ethical consideration to maintain the integrity of any child protection initiative. This requires staff to be mindful of their professional responsibility to protect information on individuals, families and communities, through being careful regarding who they discuss cases with and ensuring secure storage of personal information. Storage of information should be carefully considered in relation to the purpose of this information and potential risks if it were obtained by an outside party. This can be particularly critical in insecure locations where militias and/or governments would be interested in obtaining the personal details of families or particular individuals of interest to them.

Guidelines and standards of practice

An important outcome of prior research in this area (see O'Leary and Squire 2009a, b) is a continuum of practice (Table 2.2) for establishing child protection programs that are consistent with the ethos and conceptual frameworks of Tdh. This type of conceptual framework was first developed for domestic violence practice and policy guidelines (O'Leary, Chung and Zannettino 2004). Similarly a 'dos and don'ts' framework has been used and is promoted in the Inter-Agency Standing Committee's Guidelines on Mental Health and Psychosocial Support in

TABLE 2.2 The continuum matrix of practice: policy and practice in child protection programs in emergencies

UNACCEPTABLE FORM	MINIMUM FORM	OPTIMUM FORM
Project commencement and organisational structure		
• Implementation without needs assessment or community consultation • Program design relying purely on a crisis response without consideration to the impact of the intervention on the community in the long term • No community consultation processes to facilitate participation • No basic staff or volunteer induction in child protection policy, ethics and methods • No clear lines of authority, decision-making responsibilities or reporting structures	• Clear documentation of community consultation and needs assessment • Basic organisational chart and tools for reporting processes within this structure • Strategies and process for community and child participation • Process for decision making, e.g. case conferences • Planning within the use of other Tdh resources and guides, e.g. project management cycle and log frames • Strategies for future handover or closure of project	• Established recruitment criteria for local staff • Continuing Professional Development and Training Program with links to local and/or international institutions • Organisational chart regularly reviewed and updated • Organisational culture of child protection at all levels of operations • Established agreements with local partner organisations for handover or development after emergency project conclusion
Methods, system and accountability		
• No specific assessment tools to target the most vulnerable children • No utilisation of child protection tools and methods gained from Tdh organisational capitalisations and resources • No adaptation of these resources for local cultural and environmental context • Little or no formal process for recording information • No systemic process of recording actions in child protection or numbers of beneficiaries • No assessment of risk or prioritising	• Basic start up using existing Tdh tools and methods with appropriate training, that target the most vulnerable children • Gradual adaptation of these tools and methods to suit local needs and context • Where child-friendly spaces are used, a basic registration of children attending operates in all centres • Use of standard tools for recording information, e.g. assessment, case planning and evaluation	• Progression towards greater group sophistication in child protection operations • Intervention on chronic and sensitive issues of child rights violations that existed prior to emergency with application of the principles of do no harm • Assessment of protection needs of child beneficiaries attending Tdh services • Increased sophistication of child protection tools and greater involvement of non-specific protection staff

Community participation and leadership		
• No links to community leaders, local stakeholder organisations and national authorities in child protection • No representation from senior Tdh country management including expatriates in key child protection decisions • No succession planning for local staff to take up key leadership positions • No structure for grievances to be raised with Tdh	• Expatriate and local staff share key roles in day-to-day operations • Induction and training is provided to all protection staff • Community leaders and other stakeholders play key part in regular consultation meetings • Intervention is community based or progressing towards this • Natural and appropriate community child protection strategies are nurtured	• Selection of appropriate child protection issues are community driven • Most protection staff are local or nationally based staff • Protection activities are led and owned by community leaders and volunteers, which include less visible groups such as women and children • Prevention activities are the prime focus
Development, exit and capitalisation		
• No evidence of program improvement or growth in line with changing in context and needs • No formal evaluations or capitalisations (negative or positive) • No advance warning of changes or withdrawal of services • Resources are not adequately identified for the continuation of specific sustainable program initiatives	• Early planning or program change towards exit and/or community handover • Documentation of capitalisation on basic strengths and weaknesses • Strategies that encourage community ownership and sustainability with child protection initiatives • Support of local staff with expertise to carry on child protection activities within local organisations or other initiatives	• Potential for progression into sustainable social development initiative either through direct Tdh involvement or through other sources (e.g. local partner organisations) • Emergency readiness at program completion, i.e. clear community initiatives to intervene in child rights violations • Detailed review and evaluation to maximise capitalisations

Source: O'Leary and Squire 2009b

Emergency Settings (2007). The application and examination of child protection interventions along a continuum of practice provides a more realistic and dynamic frame for program development that acknowledges the evolving and visionary aims of an intervention. At the same time this continuum not only provides a standard of practice to aspire to, it also sets out some guidelines that detail what is not acceptable in the design and operation of child protection systems and methods.

In an environment where the language of 'best practice' is commonplace, few guides for organisations actually identify what is unacceptable in the implementation of child protection projects in humanitarian aid. Best practice often diminishes the complex and challenging process of establishing a child protection initiative in emergency contexts. To deal with this reality the continuum of practice provides a set of minimum standards which flow through to a set of optimum characteristics for projects to aspire to in their evolution. This fluid approach is promoted to respond to unpredicted challenges and to manage them as they evolve with a holistic vision of the child protection response. It is often part of a humanitarian aid organisation's methodologies and funding requirements to apply the principles of 'project cycle management' (see Terre des hommes 2001). There is an ongoing responsibility to identify strengths and weaknesses within programs in order to develop strategies to navigate the various challenges present both for the responding organisation and the recipients of humanitarian aid.

Conclusion

Responding to children in humanitarian emergencies is no longer a matter of delivering food, water, medicine and shelter. Albeit a good place to start, it requires a professional conceptualisation of protection and identification of risks. Understanding the ethical principles and cultural sensitivities of the local context is critical. It has been noted for some time that relief work in emergencies requires strong coordination and planning with field staff having professional qualifications (Salama *et al.* 2004), and this is especially true for child protection staff. Professions such as social work have important contributions to make in improving protection responses in emergencies. Funding from public and private donors increasingly demands accountability structures to deliver quality services to show the impact of emergency relief. These structures also offer the opportunity for the international community to enhance the quality of child protection programming in emergency contexts.

Recognition of child rights and the duty to act decisively to protect children at serious risk must be balanced with a critical knowledge of cultural differences and dilemmas. Moving beyond the initial crisis phase towards intervention with chronic risks that arise or are exacerbated in an emergency requires careful strategic planning. This is not always easy in emergency contexts as a climate of urgency can quickly supersede attempts to preserve the targeted intervention. Guidelines and professional frames offer some important structures for this while also providing a line of accountability to donors and beneficiaries alike.

Endnote

1. These are not exhaustive lists of problems but rather broad issues that were faced in the selected countries.

References

Alanen, L. (1994) 'Gender and Generation: Feminism and the "Child Question".' In J. Qvortrup, M. Bardy, G. Sgritta and H. Wintersberger (eds) *Childhood Matters: Social Theory, Practice and Politics.* Aldershot: Ashgate.

Boyden, J. (1997) 'Childhood and the Policy Makers: A Comparative Perspective on the Globalisation of Childhood.' In A. James and A. Prout (eds) *Constructing and Reconstructing Childhood* (2nd edition). London: Routledge Falmer.

Burman, E. (1995) 'The abnormal distribution of development: Policies for southern women and children.' *Gender, Place and Culture: A Journal of Feminist Geography 2,* 1, 21–36.

Delaney, S. (2006) *Protecting Children from Sexual Exploitation and Sexual Violence in Disaster and Emergency Situations.* Bangkok: ECPAT International.

ECHO (2009) *Humanitarian Protection: DG ECHO's Funding Guidelines.* European Commission: Director General for Humanitarian Aid Office. Brussels: ECHO.

Inter-agency Planning Consultation on Child Protection in Emergencies (IPCCPE) (2006) *Identifying Gaps – Child Protection in Emergencies.* A discussion paper for the Inter-agency Planning Consultation on Child Protection in Emergencies, 13–14 December 2006. Geneva: IPCC.

Inter-Agency Standing Committee Guidelines (2007) *IASC Mental Health and Psychosocial Support in Emergency Settings.* Geneva: IASC.

Kleinman, A. and Kleinman, J. (1996) 'The appeal of experience; the dismay of images: Cultural appropriations of suffering in our times.' *Daedalus 125,* 1, 1–23.

Kolbe, A.R., Hutson, R.A., Shannon, H., Trzeinski, E. *et al.* (2010) 'Mortality, crime and access to basic needs before and after the Haiti earthquake: A random survey of Port-au-Prince households.' *Medicine, Conflict, and Survival 2,* 4, 281–297.

Leighton, S. (2007) 'Ethical Issues in Working Therapeutically with Vulnerable Children.' In P. Vostanis (ed.) *Mental Health Intervention and Services for Vulnerable Children and Young People.* London: Jessica Kingsley Publishers.

Linnan, M., Giersing, M., Linnan, H., Cox, R. *et al.* (2007) 'Child mortality and injury in Asia: Policy and programme implications.' *Special Series on Child Injury 4*, IWP 2007–08. Italy: UNICEF, Innocenti Research Centre.
Maiter, S., Alaggio, R. and Trocmé, N. (2004) 'Perceptions of child maltreatment by parents from the Indian subcontinent: Challenging myths about culturally based parenting practices.' *Child Maltreatment 9*, 3, 309–324.
O'Leary, P.J. and Squire, J. (2009a) 'Case management: Systems and accountability.' *Social Work in Child Protection Projects*. Lausanne: Terres des hommes Foundation.
O'Leary, P.J. and Squire, J. (2009b) 'Field and research capitalisations in child protection.' *Social Work in Child Protection Projects*. Lausanne: Terres des hommes Foundation.
O'Leary, P.J., Chung, D. and Zannettino, L. (2004) *Comparative Assessment of Good Practice in Programs for Perpetrators of Domestic Violence*. Canberra: Partnerships Against Domestic Violence, Office of Status of Women, Prime Minister and Cabinet, Commonwealth of Australia.
Penrose, A. and Takaki, M. (2006) 'Children's rights in emergencies and disasters.' *Lancet 367*, 698–699.
Rajaratnam, J.K., Marcus, J.R., Flaxman, A.D., Wang, H. *et al.* (2010) 'Neonatal, postneonatal, childhood, and under-5 mortality for 187 countries, 1970–2008: A systematic analysis of progress towards Millennium Goal 4.' *Lancet 375*, 1988–2008.
Salama, P., Spiegel, P., Tolley, L. and Waldman, R. (2004) 'Lessons learned from complex emergencies over past decade.' *Lancet 364*, 1801–1813.
Save the Children (2007) *Child Protection in Emergencies: Priorities, Principles and Practices*. Stockholm: The International Save the Children Alliance and Save the Children.
Sullivan, K.M. and Hossain, S.M. (2009) 'Earthquake mortality in Pakistan.' *Disasters 34*, 1, 176–183.
Terre des hommes (2001) *Project Cycle Handbook*. Lausanne: Terres des hommes Foundation.
Terre des hommes (2008) *Child Protection Manual for Intervention in Humanitarian Crisis* (2nd edition). Lausanne: Terres des hommes Foundation.
UNICEF (2006) *The State of the World's Children: Excluded and Invisible*. New York: UNICEF.
UNICEF (2008) *Sudan: Darfur – Overview*. Available at www.unicef.org/sudan/overview.html, accessed on 1 February 2012.
UNICEF (2009) *Helping Children Recover from the Asian Tsunami*. London: UNICEF UK.
UNICEF and Al-Azhar University (2005) *Children in Islam: Their Care, Upbringing and Protection*. Cairo: Al-Azhar University.
Watts, H.G. (2009) 'The consequences for children of explosive remnants of war: Land mines, unexploded devices, and cluster bombs.' *Journal of Pediatric Rehabilitation Medicine 2*, 3, 217–227.
Williamson, J. and Robinson, M. (2006) 'Psychosocial interventions, or integrated programming for well-being?' *Intervention: The International Journal of Mental Health, Psychosocial Work and Counselling in Areas of Armed Conflict 4*, 1, 4–25.

Chapter 3

Children in the Shadows

Child Trafficking in the UK

Christine Beddoe

Introduction

Child trafficking can be described as the movement of children for the purpose of exploitation. In order to identify child victims it is essential that professionals understand and react to all manifestations of exploitation, not just sexual exploitation. Over a number of years the UK has developed a comprehensive response to human trafficking including a National Action Plan, the UK Human Trafficking Centre, a formal identification mechanism and legislation to convict traffickers for both sexual exploitation and labour exploitation. However, formal identification of victims by government agencies is well below what non-government organisations (NGOs) believe to be the real picture. Overall conviction rates for child trafficking are low and convictions for labour exploitation are in single digits despite child trafficking for labour exploitation being consistently recorded as the most significant in terms of numbers of suspected victims found. Child trafficking is unquestionably a form of child abuse, but is cultural relativity inhibiting child protection and prevention responses?

Definition of human trafficking

The standard definition of human trafficking is contained within Article 3 of the Protocol to Prevent, Suppress and Punish Trafficking in Persons, Especially Women and Children (hereafter known as 'the Palermo Protocol'), which supplements the United Nations

Convention against Transnational Organized Crime (UNODC 2004). The Palermo Protocol was adopted by resolution on 15 November 2000 and entered into force on 25 December 2003. It was signed by the UK government on 14 December 2000 and ratified on 9 February 2006 (United Nations 2000).

Article 3 states:

> For the purposes of this Protocol:
>
> (a) 'Trafficking in persons' shall mean the recruitment, transportation, transfer, harbouring or receipt of persons, by means of the threat or use of force or other forms of coercion, of abduction, of fraud, of deception, of the abuse of power or of a position of vulnerability or of the giving or receiving of payments or benefits to achieve the consent of a person having control over another person, for the purpose of exploitation. Exploitation shall include, at a minimum, the exploitation of the prostitution of others or other forms of sexual exploitation, forced labour or services, slavery or practices similar to slavery, servitude or the removal of organs.
>
> (b) The consent of a victim of trafficking in persons to the intended exploitation set forth in subparagraph (a) of this article shall be irrelevant where any of the means set forth in subparagraph (a) have been used.
>
> (c) The recruitment, transportation, transfer, harbouring or receipt of a child for the purpose of exploitation shall be considered 'trafficking in persons' even if this does not involve any of the means set forth in subparagraph (a) of this article.
>
> (d) Child' shall mean any person under 18 years of age.

This definition clarifies that the scope of trafficking in relation to children is much broader than with adults. It is not necessary for there to have been threats, the use of force or any other coercion used. The rationale behind this is that a child is not able to consent to his or her own exploitation, and that extends to anyone under the age of 18. A working definition of child trafficking can be readily explained as the movement of children for the purpose of exploitation.

The Palermo Protocol was followed by a regional treaty, the Council of Europe Convention on Action against Trafficking in Human Beings (hereafter the European Convention) (Council of Europe 2005). The definition of trafficking contained within this directly mirrors that used by the United Nations. The Convention was adopted by Ministers of the Council of Europe in 2005 and entered into force on 1 February 2008. It sets out minimum standards for the protection of victims of trafficking, and for the investigation and prosecution of traffickers.

The UK government signed the European Convention in March 2007, and ratified it in December 2008. However, it did not come into force within the UK until 1 April 2009, the date at which the current UK trafficking framework became active.

Between 2007 and 2010 the UK government made some important progress in combating child trafficking, strengthening legislation to prosecute traffickers, including a separate section on children within the National Action Plan on Trafficking, and introducing a formal victim identification structure called the National Referral Mechanism or NRM. In 2006 the government launched the UK Human Trafficking Centre in Sheffield under the auspices of South Yorkshire police. The UK Human Trafficking Centre (UKHTC), now based in Birmingham and part of the Serious Organised Crime Agency, is a multi-agency unit that provides a point of coordination for the development of expertise and cooperation to combat the trafficking of human beings. The multi-agency nature of UKHTC tends more towards government and law enforcement agencies, although it is host to a number of initiatives where NGOs participate.

However, despite these measures, the actual number of child victims being supported by Local Authority Social Services is still unknown and the number of convictions for child trafficking, although not centrally recorded, is thought to be in single digits.

In 2009 a group of 11 UK NGOs formed an alliance called the Anti-Trafficking Monitoring Group to act as watchdog over the government's implementation of the European Convention. The group published its first report in 2010 with significant criticism, particularly of the NRM:

> The principal response of the Government to their obligations as party to the Convention was the establishment of an identification system called the National Referral Mechanism (NRM). The OSCE suggest that NRMs should be a multi-agency coordination system and their every stage an opportunity to help trafficked persons. The system appears to be relying excessively on the discretion of officials who receive minimal training to staff a mechanism supported by flawed legal guidance relating to who should be identified as victims of trafficking, and without a formal appeals process. This fails to

> consistently identify and assist people who have been trafficked. Furthermore, the system appears to be putting more emphasis on the immigration status of the presumed trafficked persons, rather than the alleged crime committed against them. (Anti-Trafficking Monitoring Group 2010, p.9)

A recurring theme in the Anti-Trafficking Monitoring Group report is the problem caused when government agencies fail to identify victims because of the conflation of people smuggling and human trafficking. In other words, when victims of exploitation fall through the gaps it is most likely because they are thought of as immigration offenders or people coming to the UK to work illegally.

The National Referral Mechanism

The UK government introduced a formal system of identification for victims of trafficking on 1 April 2009. This is known as the National Referral Mechanism (NRM), and a positive final decision unlocks particular benefits and entitlements for victims enshrined in the Council of Europe Convention on Action Against Trafficking in Human Beings, which the UK ratified in 2008. Within the NRM system, a referral is made to the Competent Authority, comprising of either the UK Border Agency (UKBA) or the UK Human Trafficking Centre (UKHTC). Referrals can only be made by authorities designated as first responders. In the case of children this means police, local authorities and UKBA; no NGO can refer and referral is not mandatory. The procedures immediately following a referral can lead to a positive 'reasonable grounds' decision with a low burden of proof which opens a gateway for a 'conclusive grounds' decision where further information can be gathered and tested and a decision given within 45 days. The NRM, particularly for children, has proved to be controversial and problematic. A report by 12 local authorities published in February 2011 came to the conclusion that, whilst there were some benefits to the NRM, 'there are concerns about the actual benefits to the child of the NRM process itself, especially where asylum issues are also involved, and that the NRM is often not in the best interests of the child' (London Local Safeguarding Children Board 2011, p.30).

The NRM process fails to acknowledge the time-intensive and complex procedures involved in obtaining a child's full disclosure of abuse, particularly when the child is still controlled by fear, threat or other means. As such it relies heavily on other material evidence such as police investigations and prosecutions in formalising decisions about who is a victim of trafficking for the purpose of accessing support under the European Convention.

The available data from the NRM and published by the UK Human Trafficking Centre (UK Human Trafficking Centre 2011) suggests the numbers of children receiving a positive 'conclusive grounds' decision are well below the estimates of what the Anti-Trafficking Monitoring Group and other NGOs believe there should be. The latest statistics released from the UK Human Trafficking Centre show that:

- between 1 April 2009 and 30 June 2010, 215 (26%) of the 843 cases of all potential victims of human trafficking referred under the National Referral Mechanism relate to children. By 31 December 2010, the number of children referred had increased to 322 (26%) of the total 1254 referrals of human trafficking. There was an increase of 107 child referrals in 6 months and a consistent pattern of 1 in 4 referrals being a child
- between 1 April 2009 and 31 December 2010, the highest recorded exploitation type for child referrals was labour exploitation, including domestic servitude (142 children), whilst sexual exploitation related to 99 child cases. A further 81 cases involved abuse where the primary exploitation type was unknown
- 21 children were under 10 years of age at the time of referral
- between 1 April 2009 and 31 December 2010, 106 of the 322 referrals of children were given a positive 'conclusive grounds' decision formalising their status as a trafficked person. Just over half of these decisions relate to trafficking for sexual exploitation (51%).

Caution should be used when interpreting these figures as they do not represent all suspected cases of trafficking because this is not a mandatory reporting system and so vulnerable children who are believed to be trafficked can be looked after by local authority children's social services without going through this formal procedure. What is of particular interest within these published statistics is that the number of final or 'conclusive grounds' decisions (121) related to children equals just over five victims per month since the NRM became active in April 2009. No other documentation is published that records the fate of the remaining child cases.

Identification

The 'numbers game' is not new for any sector fighting for resources, but the human catastrophe of not formally identifying victims of abuse and exploitation has tragic consequences. Additionally, when statutory authorities prevent a more robust national analysis by not systematising data gathering and data sharing, there is also a significant risk that victim support agencies lose funds, refocus or simply disappear, creating a downward spiral where abused and exploited people remain in the shadows.

Beyond the NRM there is no systematic process of data collection, analysis and reporting on child trafficking across the United Kingdom of Great Britain and Northern Ireland. The UK Human Trafficking Centre has not published any reports on child trafficking since it was established in 2006. The centre does not lead trafficking operations as that is the responsibility of individual police forces; it does, however, support police with tactical advice and intelligence-sharing capabilities and acts as a UK focal point for international investigations.

The devolved governments and administrations in Scotland, Wales and Northern Ireland are responsible for their own local authorities, including children's social services, and there are 43 individual police forces across the UK. However, information about trafficked children is not only held by local authorities and by the police; the UK Border Agency (including border control, immigration and asylum services) and the Crown Prosecution Service also obtain data on cases of children who have been trafficked as part of other responsibilities, but this information is not collated or analysed centrally. NGOs routinely use Freedom of Information requests and parliamentary questions to obtain non-published government statistics on human trafficking, but this is piecemeal and information sources and dates do not often correspond.

A raft of significant but small-scale primary research projects on child trafficking have been undertaken by organisations such as ECPAT UK (ECPAT UK 2004, 2007, 2009) primarily using interviews with social workers, support agencies and police in specific geographic locations to gather case studies and to identify trends and responses. The first government report on child trafficking was published by the London-based Child Exploitation and Online Protection centre (CEOP), a government agency tasked with gathering and sharing information on child exploitation, mostly but not exclusively on the sexual abuse of children in an on-line setting.

The 2007 Scoping Project on Child Trafficking in the UK report published by CEOP (CEOP 2007) surveyed police forces and other statutory agencies, supplementing information with cases from NGOs. This resulted in 330 children from 44 countries documented as known or suspected to be trafficked in an 18-month period to December 2006. A second report (CEOP 2009) by CEOP published in 2009 identified a further 325 children from 52 countries over a 12-month period to 29 February 2008, but not all police forces responded to their survey. In fact only 21 (of 43) UK police forces responded, and of those only 17 provided any intelligence (CEOP 2009). The third and most recent CEOP report (CEOP 2010) published in December 2010 identified 287 children from 47 countries in a 12-month period to February 2010. Again only 21 UK police forces responded to the CEOP survey but with only 10 providing intelligence (CEOP 2010).

Investigations and convictions

Despite it being four years since the opening of the UK Human Trafficking Centre, the number of successful convictions of traffickers seems remarkably low against even the most conservative NRM estimate of victims. The UKHTC records information received from police forces across the UK on human trafficking convictions, but data is not specifically disaggregated by age or gender of victim, and therefore there is no straightforward way of obtaining data related to the conviction of criminals who have trafficked children:

> Statistics held by the UKHTC show that there were 33 convictions for trafficking for sexual exploitation in 2009 and 17 convictions in 2010 (adult and child victims). There are 65 cases still pending from arrests in 2009 and 2010. (House of Commons Debate, 26 April 2011, c356W)
>
> There were three convictions for trafficking for labour exploitation in 2009 and comparable figures are not yet known for 2010. (House of Commons Debate, 3 November 2010, c861W)

Apart from an incongruously low number of overall trafficking convictions for both adult and child victims, the most notable conclusion from this comparison is that convictions for labour exploitation are extremely low.

What's going wrong?

Without a comprehensive and systematic approach to data collection vulnerable children are left even more at risk as the government has to make policy and allocate resources on partial and incomplete information and professionals are not aware of national or regional trends. If the trafficking of children is about the movement of children for the purpose of exploitation then it is vital that all professionals understand the fundamental concept of exploitation in all its manifestations. Notwithstanding that sexual exploitation is often under-reported, professionals – including police – are more likely to understand sexual abuse and prostitution of children as a crime. What is becoming evident is that police investigations of trafficking for labour exploitation do not result in prosecutions, or even worse that investigations are not happening at all. In 2009 ECPAT UK published a report on child trafficking in Wales (Kelly 2009) based on research and interviews with child welfare professionals and police. The research identified 32 cases of children suspected as being trafficked in four locations: Cardiff, Newport, Swansea and Wrexham. ECPAT UK was the first UK organisation to claim publically that cultural relativism was preventing children, especially victims of labour exploitation, from being identified. ECPAT UK states that 'certain practices or behaviours were described to us as cultural in origin so services did not intervene despite concerns of exploitation. Thus it was not unusual for Roma children to wash cars…or for Bangladeshi boys to live with strangers in a take-away' (Kelly 2009, p.46). The conclusion to this report was that to dismantle a culture of disbelief and embed a successful child protection response it requires a combination of the right level of knowledge, attitude and effective practice of all the professionals working on the case.

Child trafficking and labour exploitation

The trafficking in children for labour exploitation is likely to be under-reported in the UK on account of the difficulties children face disclosing their experiences and general attitudes towards child labour, particularly migrant children who are often seen as illegal workers or children helping the family with illegal work. It is not unusual for traffickers to intensively groom children by telling them exactly what to say, or what not to say, to the authorities, and this can be seen by government agencies, particularly immigration and police authorities, as a direct challenge to the child's credibility if a child changes their story during an investigation. In trafficking for labour exploitation the initial accounts from children most often refer to the adult as a member of the family, and as such the distinction between a child helping the family and exploitative child labour is blurred.

The government's statutory guidance on safeguarding children who may be victims of trafficking states:

> Children who have been trafficked may be reluctant to disclose the circumstances of their exploitation or arrival into the UK for fear of reprisals by the trafficker, owner or pimp or out of misplaced loyalty to them. (HM Government 2007, paragraph 5.15)

The same guidance also notes that children may initially give a false account to the authorities, having been coached to do so by their traffickers:

> It is likely that the child will have been coached with a story to tell the authorities in the UK and warned not to disclose any detail beyond the story, as this would lead them to being deported. (HM Government 2007, paragraph 7.2)

This is supported by CEOP research:

> It is often argued that vague background stories containing insufficient corroborative detail are an indication that a story is false. Authorities may subsequently conclude that the individual is an economic migrant who will seek to claim asylum and obscure the truth to avoid identification and prevent deportation, therefore discounting the possibility that the individual is a victim of trafficking. It should be noted, however, that coaching victims to provide a vague story is a measure of control, as the agent wants to ensure that the victim is not immediately deported. The victim will comply by recounting a fabricated story believing they are in the process of being facilitated, whilst the trafficker hopes to stall authorities long enough to get the victim out of their control and into exploitation. Traumatic events and age of the child may also have an impact on the clarity of the story. (CEOP 2010, p.19)

Domestic servitude

ECPAT UK's first study on child trafficking in 2004, *Cause for Concern*, identified 15 cases in London of child trafficking for domestic servitude including one case that additionally involved exploitation through prostitution (ECPAT UK 2004). Subsequent research studies undertaken by ECPAT UK into trafficking in Wales (Kelly 2009) and England's North-West, North-East and West Midlands (ECPAT UK 2007) similarly identified concerns in relation to trafficking for domestic servitude. The research in all of these regions found a lack of practitioner confidence in identifying victims of child trafficking for domestic servitude.

The trafficking in children for the purpose of domestic servitude was identified by CEOP as the second most commonly identified form of labour exploitation in the UK during the period 1 March 2009 to 28 February 2010. Eleven per cent (25) of the potential child victims of trafficking identified by CEOP's research were believed to have been trafficked for domestic servitude (CEOP 2010). This figure relates to 18 girls and seven boys, with the youngest child identified as eight years of age (CEOP 2010).

Case-based evidence from ECPAT UK and CEOP show that trafficking for labour exploitation in domestic household settings is hidden and exploited children are regularly passed off as family members from adults within the same ethnic community. Although domestic servitude is most reported from the West African community, it is not exclusively an African issue. Children are brought to the UK by people known to their family, but once landed they have their documents removed, are denied education and made to work over 12 hours a day doing domestic chores and looking after younger children. They are physically beaten, emotionally abused and threatened. Sexual abuse of girls is also a feature of trafficking for domestic exploitation, to the extent that it may be unclear whether the purpose of trafficking is in fact for sexual exploitation rather than for domestic exploitation or a combination of both.

Forced labour

Much less is known about the trafficking of children in the UK for other types of forced labour. Evidence of the exploitation of children for forced labour emerged in ECPAT UK's research into trafficking in England's North-West, North-East and West Midlands (ECPAT UK 2007). Police and local authorities reported suspicions of trafficking for labour and debt bondage in the West Midlands in relation to regular arrivals into the area of large numbers of Afghan boys aged 14–16 years who, though in education, regularly went missing and showed physical signs of manual work and fatigue. The trafficking of three Bangladeshi boys in restaurant work and two Chinese girls in the catering industry through organised networks was also identified (ECPAT UK 2007). ECPAT UK's research in Wales identified concerns in relation to a number of boys living with unrelated adults and exploited in takeaways and kebab shops.

In October 2010, news agencies reported the identification by the Gangmasters Licensing Authority (GLA) of seven children in forced labour picking onions on a farm near Worcester (BBC 2010). The children were among 50 Romanian workers who also appeared to have been exploited as the report indicated intelligence suggesting that a household of 40 people would be paid less than £100 a week for the work. Serious child protection concerns were identified in relation to the children discovered at the farm as well as the possibility that more children had been trafficked and exploited:

> The seven children, aged between nine and 15, were being made to work from 7.30 in the morning until dusk, dressed in thin summer clothes, as temperatures dropped close to zero.
>
> Wellington boots that looked suitable for a five-year-old were also found in the field, suggesting even younger children had worked there. Investigators for the GLA say it is the first time they have come across such young children working in fields in the UK.
>
> They were brought to the field in the back of a box van, with no food or water for the day. Six of the children have been taken into local authority care. Some were working alongside parents, but others appeared to have been brought to the farm on their own.

Forced criminality

Children are also trafficked to the UK for a range of criminal activities including the cultivation of cannabis, street crime (such as fake DVD selling, bag snatching, pick-pocketing and begging) and benefit fraud.

There is increasing evidence that children from South East Asia, particularly Vietnam, are being trafficked to the UK and forced to work cultivating cannabis. Traditionally, cannabis has been imported into the UK by drug traffickers, but the extent of home cultivation in the

UK has grown rapidly and now accounts for a significant amount of cannabis consumed in the UK. While there are many sole-use growers cultivating cannabis, there has also been an explosion of large-scale, commercial production of cannabis over the last decade, organised by criminal networks.

The number of cannabis factories identified in the UK has also risen dramatically in the last two years, from 3032 factories identified by police forces in 2007/2008 to 6866 factories identified in the year 2009/2010 (ACPO 2010). Over 1.3 million cannabis plants have been seized in this two-year period, equating to a street value of £150 million (ACPO 2010).

Private suburban homes still account for the vast majority of all commercial cannabis factories identified since April 2008, though factories have also been identified in industrial/commercial premises, agricultural premises, non-dwellings (sheds, outhouses, garages) and public/open areas (ACPO 2010). It is estimated that criminal gangs can make up to several hundred thousand pounds of profit a year from a three-bedroom house converted into a cannabis factory. However, the police are noticing a steady increase in the number of factories discovered in agricultural and industrial commercial premises as the latter offer the opportunity of greater profits from the larger yields possible in larger premises (ACPO 2010). Properties boarded up as a result of the recession have also been attractive to criminals and a growing number of disused industrial commercial properties have been used for commercial cannabis cultivation (ACPO 2010).

Child trafficking for exploitation in cannabis farms

In its most recent strategic threat assessment, the Centre for Child Exploitation and Online Protection (CEOP) identified that the cultivation of cannabis was the second most common form of exploitation of children (after sexual exploitation) and 18 per cent (39 children) of the total number of children identified as potential victims of trafficking in the UK were believed to have been exploited in cannabis farms. Ninety per cent (34) of the victims were boys and the general age range of victims was 13 to 17 years.

Once transferred to the cannabis factories, trafficked children are forced to sleep on floors and in cupboards. They endure extremely hazardous conditions in the factories. These include constant heat and light, noxious fumes and the risk of fire and electrocution due to the illegal rewiring of the electricity supply. Children hold the lowest position in the criminal enterprise and are forced to work as 'gardeners', tending and watering cannabis plants (CEOP 2010), and in other roles including the illegal and dangerous diversion of electricity to the farms, and breaking and entering the premises of rival cannabis producers (ACPO 2010).

Criminal gangs may use violence to ensure compliance of those working the factories (ACPO 2010). Children are also subjected to emotional abuse and sometimes physical abuse (CEOP 2010), the long-term consequences of which are discussed below. Debt bonds may be high. The report of the Association of Chief Police Officers cites an example of a girl told she had a debt of £17,000 to be paid off through two years' work in a cannabis factory (CEOP 2010).

Street crime

CEOP report that 9 per cent (20) of the children identified as potential victims of trafficking in the period 2009/2010 were exploited through their forced involvement in street crime (CEOP 2010). This involves activities such as selling illegal copies of DVDs, bag snatching, pick-pocketing and begging. In other words, it is the criminal exploitation of their labour.

Between 2007 and 2010 Operation Golf, a specialist Joint Investigation Team (JIT) between the Metropolitan Police Service and the Romanian National Police, investigated organised crime networks involved in the trafficking of children from the Romanian Roma community into London for forced criminality.

According to Operation Golf, over 1000 children from one Romanian town were found to have been trafficked into Western Europe for labour and sexual exploitation over a four-year period. This trafficking network is thought to be responsible for trafficking over 168 children to the UK for forced criminality (Anti-Slavery International 2010). In October 2010, a further 28 children were recovered in a major policing operation in East London conducted as part of Operation Golf (Metropolitan Police 2010).

Police estimate that the profits generated for traffickers are significant, with each 'trained' child able to generate up to £100,000 a year through begging and the theft of credit cards, cash and mobile phones (Anti-Slavery International 2010). Children recovered from these sorts of trafficking situations in the UK have been identified as suffering severe abuse and neglect in situations involving both family members and third parties.

In July 2010, Romanian nationals G. and S. Mihai were convicted in a British court of neglect, physical abuse and the exploitation of seven children aged between two and 15 years for forced begging, theft and benefit fraud:

> When the police arrived, most of the children were found sleeping on the floor of the sparsely furnished house in the Berkshire town with little food.
>
> Four required dental treatment and three suffered from infestations of head lice. One of the youngest children was later found to have scarring consistent with cigarette burns and another with a lesion. The injuries happened while the children were in their parents' care, the court was told. (*The Guardian* 2010)

Conclusion

Children who have been trafficked have faced dreadful experiences of abuse, neglect and physical and emotional control. More than anything these children need to be treated as children and provided with the care and support that is the right of every child in the UK regardless of their nationality or immigration status. The Council of Europe Convention on Action Against Trafficking in Human Beings contains various provisions which are specific to children regarding their protection and assistance. The European Convention confirms that procedures concerning children must be different from those concerning adults. However, although children thought to be trafficked can be looked after by the UK welfare system until they turn 18, the greatest barrier to accessing specialist long-term support is the failure to be formally identified as a victim of trafficking combined with the lack of police investigation or prosecution. Even though there is a growing body of case-based research on child trafficking in the UK, both by government agencies and NGOs, the actual number of *formally* identified child victims by the government national referral mechanism is much smaller. The picture of child trafficking to the UK is fragmented because there is no mandatory data collection and analysis. Child labour across the UK is acknowledged in published research reports, but the conviction rate for trafficking for labour exploitation, whether adult or child, is significantly lower than trafficking for sexual exploitation. Whether this is related to a wider culture of disbelief or evidential challenges, it is clearly a significant barrier to a successful positive identification in the NRM process.

References

Anti-Slavery International (2010) *London's Met Police Help Bust Child Trafficking Gang in Romania.* Available at www.antislavery.org/english/press_and_news/news_and_press_releases_2009/200410_londons_met_police_help_bust_child_trafficking_gang_in_romania.aspx, accessed on 19 December 2011.

Anti-Trafficking Monitoring Group (2010) *Wrong Kind of Victim: One Year On, an Analysis of UK Measures to Protect Trafficked Persons.* London: The Anti-Trafficking Monitoring Group.

Association of Chief Police Officers (ACPO) (2010) *'Three Years On...' Findings from the UK National Problem Profile: Commercial Cultivation of Cannabis.* Available at www.acpo.police.uk/documents/crime/2010/201008CRICCC01.pdf, accessed on 12 March 2011.

BBC (2010) 'Child onion pickers highlights exploitation problem.' Available at www.bbc.co.uk/news/uk-11617664, accessed on 22 December 2011.

Child Exploitation and Online Protection Centre (CEOP) (2007) *A Scoping Project on Child Trafficking in the UK.* Available at http://ceop.police.uk/Documents/child_trafficking_report0607.pdf, accessed on 22 December 2011.

Child Exploitation and Online Protection Centre (CEOP) (2009) *Strategic Threat Assessment – Child Trafficking in the UK.* London: CEOP.

Child Exploitation and Online Protection Centre (CEOP) (2010) *Strategic Threat Assessment – Child Trafficking in the UK.* London: CEOP.

Council of Europe (2005) *Council of Europe Convention on Action against Trafficking in Human Beings: CETS 197.* Available at www.coe.int/t/dghl/monitoring/trafficking/Docs/Convntn/CETS197_en.asp#TopOfPage, accessed on 12 March 2011.

End Child Prostitution, Pornography and Trafficking of Children for Sexual Purposes (ECPAT UK) (2004) *Cause for Concern? London Social Services and Child Trafficking.* London: ECPAT UK.

End Child Prostitution, Pornography and Trafficking of Children for Sexual Purposes (ECPAT UK) (2007) *Missing Out – A Study of Child Trafficking in the North-West, North-East and West Midlands.* London: ECPAT UK.

End Child Prostitution, Pornography and Trafficking of Children for Sexual Purposes (ECPAT UK) (2009) *Bordering on Concern: Child Trafficking in Wales. London: ECPAT UK.* Available at www.ecpat.org.uk/sites/default/files/bordering_on__concern_english.pdf, accessed on 22 December 2011.

Her Majesty's (HM) Government (2007) *Working Together to Safeguard Children – Safeguarding Children Who May Have Been Trafficked.* Nottingham: DCSF Publications.

Kelly, E. (2009) *Bordering on Concern – Child Trafficking in Wales.* Cardiff: ECPAT UK and the Office of the Children's Commissioner for Wales.

London Local Safeguarding Children Board (2011) *Final Monitoring Report: Local Authority Pilots of the London Safeguarding Children Guidance and Toolkit.* London: London Safeguarding Children Board.

Metropolitan Police (2010) *Children Safeguarded in Major Operation.* Available at http://content.met.police.uk/News/Children-safeguarded-in-major-operation/1260267437629/1257246745756, accessed on 19 December 2011.

The Guardian (2010) 'Romanians jailed for making their children beg and steal.' Available at www.guardian.co.uk/uk/2010/jul/30/romanians-jailed-children-beg-steal, accessed on 19 December 2011.

UK Human Trafficking Centre (2011) *UK Human Trafficking Centre Statistical Data.* Available at www.ukhtc.org, accessed on 6 February 2012.

United Nations (2000) *Status of UN Treaties, Chapter XVIII, 12.a.* Available at http://treaties.un.org/Pages/ViewDetails.aspx?src=TREATY&mtdsg_no=XVIII-12-a&chapter=18&lang=en, accessed on 12 March 2011.

United Nations Office on Drugs and Crime (UNODC) (2004) *United Nations Convention against Transnational Organized Crime and the Protocols Thereto.* Available at www.unodc.org/documents/treaties/UNTOC/Publications/TOC%20Convention/TOCebook-e.pdf, accessed on 12 March 2011.

Chapter 4

Child Combatants and Peace Processes

Challenges of Inclusion and Exclusion

Shelly L. Whitman

Introduction

> There can be no keener revelation of a society's soul than the way in which it treats its children. (Nelson Mandela)

In many areas of the world we must recognise that the great majority of the population is below the age of 18 years. There are an estimated 2.2 billion people in the world below the age of 18 years and two billion of these children live in the developing world (World Population Awareness 2010). Yet, despite such demographics, we often fail to hear the voices of young people and, even worse, we fail to address their needs. If children are the future, then surely they should also be our priority. Unfortunately, the use of children as soldiers is the starkest reminder to the entire world that we have failed miserably to uphold the rights of children. This failure is indicative of the current balance of power that defines our world in which greed, exploitation of the innocent and inaction far too often prevail. As Graça Machel stated: 'our collective failure to protect children must be transformed into an opportunity to confront the problems that cause their suffering' (Machel 2001, p.xi).

The phenomenon of child soldiers is not new, but has gained increasing attention from the international community over the last 10–15 years. However, there is little evidence to prove that such attention has resulted in fewer children being utilised in armed conflict. In fact, there is much evidence to suggest that efforts to demobilise children are often thwarted by re-recruitment processes. Current estimates suggest that 250,000 children are used as combatants worldwide (Office of the United Nations Special Representative of the Secretary-General on Children and Armed Conflict 2009). This estimate may be conservative, as gaining accurate data on the use of children is extremely difficult to obtain. Armed groups rarely give accounts of how many children are in their ranks, and understanding who is a child is also difficult in countries where documentation is absent or doctored and family structures have been destroyed. In addition, many developing nations often rely on children as a human resource due to the demographics of their societies. In Sierra Leone, during the armed conflict, children under the age of 18 comprised 70 per cent of the fighters (Singer 2006).

It is the intention of this chapter to address the need to include child soldiers within peace processes as key stakeholders in the attainment of peace. The conditions that create the space for children to be utilised as combatants are created by opportunistic leaders, socio-economic problems, and a lack of opportunities for education and employment. It is therefore imperative that we begin to discuss how to include child soldiers in this debate and how to address Disarmament, Demobilization and Reintegration (DDR) effectively so as not to exclude a key segment of society. Children have the ability to contribute to peace through positive engagement and peace building efforts that will hopefully assist in ensuring future hostilities will not occur. By placing children at the top of the agenda, we then are forced to try to find resolution to the very roots of conflict. Currently, we place children's rights at the bottom of the agenda or as an add-on item.

Child soldiering problem

Under the UN Convention on the Rights of the Child (CRC), a child is defined as any individual under the age of 18 years. The CRC is one of the most universally accepted international conventions, with 139 signatories and 192 parties to the Convention (United Nations Treaty Collection 2011). Graça Machel asserted that child soldiering is a global problem that occurs more systematically than most analysts have previously suspected (Machel 2001). The Paris Principles define a child soldier as: 'any person under the age of 18 years who is or has been recruited or used by an armed force or group in any capacity, including, but not limited to, children used as fighters, cooks, porters, messengers, spies or for sexual purposes' (United Nations 2007, p.7). This definition includes girls recruited for sexual purposes and for forced marriage. It does not, therefore, only refer to a child who is carrying or has carried arms. Children who are vulnerable to recruitment into armed groups are often those who come from the poorest sections of society, who do not have families, and who are located in conflict zones (Brett and McCallin 1998). Some children are forcibly taken and others are considered 'volunteers'. For those children who are forcibly taken or recruited, they often are faced with the choice of joining or death. In addition, many must watch their families be murdered by the armed groups and others must commit the murders themselves. Graça Machel points out that joining an armed group is often a response to a variety of pressures – economic, social and cultural (2001). There is much evidence to point to the need for survival as the primary reason for joining an armed group. If survival is a key reason for joining, then it is paramount we address the socio-economic voids within many developing nations. How is it possible that children can obtain food, security, medical attention, clothing and education more readily from an armed group than through their communities, families and governments?

Children are often utilised as soldiers for a variety of reasons. Their comparative agility, small size and the ease with which they can be psychologically controlled are all advantageous to armed groups. Small arms and light weapons have made it easy for children to manipulate and carry such weapons. Children are also used as spies, messengers, porters and cooks, and for standing guard, clearing landmines, stealing and foraging for food as well as participating in combat roles. Armed groups see children as a cheap and easily obtained human resource in many parts of the world (Singer 2006). Child soldiers are often plied with alcohol and drugs prior to going into battle. This assists with creating a sense of fearlessness and distance from the brutality of their duties. It also creates an additional burden of ridding children of such addictions in addition to the physical and psychological consequences of child soldiering. Many children are maimed or killed in battle and the physical consequences are lifelong reminders for these children. There are many psychological consequences of children's participation in armed conflict that range from aggression and revenge to anxiety to fear, grief and depression. It can also result in low self-esteem, guilt and violent behaviour, shame, and a lack of trust in others (Machel 2001).

Many children are not welcomed back into their families and communities after they have served as combatants. It is not easy for the communities to forget the terror that may have been imposed by the child soldiers. It must also be borne in mind that creating a fear of children by communities is often a deliberate tactic used by armed groups. The use of children in war carries a high risk also for children in a war zone who may not be involved with armed groups – identifying who is a threat and who is not is difficult and makes all children potential targets (Singer 2006). In addition, the families now have the burden of caring for physically or psychologically affected children and this often stretches the limited resources beyond the capacity of the families. There is also a significant proportion of children who find it difficult to accept their roles as children and submit to the authority of a family and school setting and not as commanders in an armed group; this has been particularly true of girl soldiers (Lee 2009).

Girl soldiers are also used in combat roles. However, there are additional burdens they undertake, such as becoming 'wives' or being used as sexual slaves. It is estimated that 40 per cent of the child soldiers used globally are girl soldiers (McKay and Mazurana 2004). The consequences of such abuse are: the contraction of HIV/AIDS and sexually transmitted diseases, psychological trauma, unwanted pregnancies, and humiliation and shame that are often associated with such survivors from the reactions from their families and communities. Once a girl becomes associated with an armed group and is used sexually, she becomes identified socially as a 'military wife' and is most often considered to no longer have any value in society (Verhey 2004).

Failure to protect

The Convention on the Rights of the Child and the Optional Protocol on the Involvement of Children in Armed Conflict outline the need to protect children. The Optional Protocol specifically addresses the illegality of recruiting children under the age of 15 years and using children under the age of 18 years to participate in direct hostilities. Article 3(3) states that:

> States Parties that permit voluntary recruitment into their national armed forces under the age of 18 years shall maintain safeguards to ensure, as a minimum, that: (a) Such recruitment is genuinely voluntary; (b) Such recruitment is carried out with the informed consent of the person's parents or legal guardians; (c) Such persons are fully informed of the duties involved in such military service; and (d) Such persons provide reliable proof of age prior to acceptance into national military service.

United Nations Resolution 1612 is a key instrument in the fight against the use of child soldiers and supplements the Optional Protocol. It is the first United Nations Security Council resolution to call for a monitoring and reporting mechanism that would result in sanctions if non-compliance occurs. UN SC Resolution 1612 focuses on six grave violations related to children in armed conflict: the killing or maiming of children; the recruitment and use of children as soldiers; attacks on hospitals or schools; denial of humanitarian assistance for children; abduction of children; and rape and other grave sexual abuse of children (Office of the UN Special Representative of the Secretary-General on Children and Armed Conflict 2009). In July 2009, UN SC Resolution 1882 was also passed and makes specific links between the use of children as soldiers and the crimes of sexual violence that so often characterise current war situations.

In addition, the International Criminal Court has also made the issue of the criminality in the use of child soldiers one of their initial test cases. International attention has been brought to the issue, but the major problem has been translating this attention and international legal standards into action that assists with the reduction of the number of children recruited and used in armed conflicts.

Democratic Republic of the Congo and Sierra Leone: Case studies

It is estimated that approximately 120,000 of the 250,000 children used as child combatants are within Africa (Twum-Danso 2003). It is therefore important to discuss the African continent with respect to child soldiers and peace processes, while also recognising that child soldiers are a global phenomenon and not one that is specific to Africa. Two cases in particular that raise some very important questions in this regard are the Democratic Republic of the Congo (DRC) and Sierra Leone.

Democratic Republic of the Congo

Out of the total population of 62 million people in the DRC, over 50 per cent are estimated to be under 18 years of age (Watchlist on Children and Armed Conflict 2003). It has been reported by UNICEF that as many as one-third of the DRC's children have been forced to take up arms (UNICEF 2003). According to the United Nations, each and every armed group participating in the conflict in the DRC has used children as soldiers. Fighting in the Eastern section of the DRC has been particularly violent and the abuse of civilians rife. Aid workers in Ituri have estimated that more than half of the estimated 15,000 fighters who make up the Union of Congolese Patriots (UPC) are under the age of 18 years, and some as young as eight years (BBC News 2003). The UPC defends its use of children as soldiers by arguing that they are providing orphans with the much needed social services they otherwise could not afford.

Kadogos is the Swahili name given by the Congolese to the child soldiers; it means little ones who fight. Many of the armed groups in the DRC do not hide the fact that they use children. Former President Laurent Kabila had used child soldiers to support his military since 1996. Laurent Kabila had repeatedly promised the international community that his government would demobilize and reintegrate the child soldiers. However, on 7 August 1998, an official communiqué was aired on national radio calling for the children and youth between the ages of 12 and 20 years to enlist in the Congolese Armed Forces in response to the Congolese Rally for Democracy's (RCD) insurgency from the East (Human Rights Watch 2003). Laurent Kabila was assassinated in 2001, at which point his son Joseph Kabila assumed the Presidency. The National Armed Forces of the DRC (FARDC) had however continued to use child soldiers but are now in a formal demobilisation and reintegration process to attempt to ensure children are no longer a part of this army.

In March 2003, the Pretoria Agreements were signed by all of the Congolese Parties to the conflict to install a transitional government in the DRC. Since this agreement, a democratic election has taken place for the first time in the DRC's history in 2006. At the same time, in 2009, the International Criminal Court has taken up the case against Thomas Lubanga, a former rebel leader in the Northeast of the country, as the first test case for the Court. One of the charges against Mr Lubanga relates to his use of children as soldiers in the DRC. It was discouraging to many when, on 15 July 2010, ICC Trial Chamber I ordered the release of Thomas Lubanga:

> ICC judges argued that an accused cannot be held in preventative custody on a speculative basis, namely that at some stage in the future the proceedings may be resurrected. However, the order was not implemented with immediate effect. The Prosecution appealed the decision. On 8 October 2010, the ICC Appeals Chamber reversed Trial Chamber I's July 2010 decision to stay proceedings and to release the accused. Appeals judges

> stated that although the prosecutor did not comply with the Trial Chamber's orders relating to protection issues, judges should first have tried applying sanctions before imposing the drastic measure of a stay of proceedings. The defendant remains in custody and the trial has resumed. (Coalition for the International Criminal Court 2011)

It is hoped that the case against Mr Lubanga will result in a successful prosecution for his crimes against children in the DRC. A successful prosecution will be an important rallying point for child rights activists globally and will send a clear signal to those who use and recruit child soldiers that they may will be held responsible by international courts. Such attention to this matter is key in ending the use of children in armed conflict.

The inclusion of children in the peace process in the DRC was minimal at best. At no point within the process were children ever represented as an entity that had significant contributions for peace in the DRC. Youth groups did participate in some of the civil society delegations to the process, but were not elected to represent the youth in the Inter-Congolese dialogue process.

Resolutions and final agreements that were reached during the peace process did have provisions related to children and youth in the DRC. Resolution DIC/CDC/03 specifically mentions the demobilisation and reintegration of child soldiers. Both the Humanitarian and Economic and Social Committees of the Inter-Congolese dialogue recognised the problems that plagued the youth in the DRC that often lead to their use as child soldiers. However, the issues related to children and youth appeared as 'add-ons' and not priorities for the peace process in the DRC.

While the DRC has successfully undergone its first democratic elections and has put in place a new government of national unity, the East is still ravaged with many problems, ranging from human rights violations to underdevelopment. The UN and children's rights groups have been working to extract children from armed groups. Children as young as five years are still recruited and used in the conflict. Many also argue that the policies of 'release and reintegration' have not been met with real solutions or development opportunities. This is evidenced by the fact that one in five children will die before they reach their fifth birthday in the DRC (Watchlist on Children and Armed Conflict 2003). However, one bright ray of light was the creation of a Children's Parliament in 2002 by the United Nations. The parliament advocates for justice on behalf of children in the DRC and hears cases of abuse and neglect as well as lobbying for the release of child prisoners (McCrummen 2007). The creation of other children's parliaments across Africa has taken root and may be an important means of getting children's rights on the political agenda.

Sierra Leone

Eleven years of civil war in Sierra Leone has devastated the population in a wide variety of ways. The use of children as soldiers in Sierra Leone has been fairly well documented and has received world-wide attention. It is estimated that during the conflict in Sierra Leone, 50 per cent of the population was under the age of 18 years and more than 10,000 children served as soldiers for the various fighting factions (Amnesty International 2000).

In 1998, the National Committee for Disarmament, Demobilization and Reintegration (NCDDR) was formed. This particular office was also required to deal with child soldiers. The NCDDR stated that they were not able to disarm all the children and many may have simply melted into their communities. Abdullah and Muana argue that:

> central to an understanding of the war in Sierra Leone is the role of alienated youth, especially lumpen youth in the urban and rural areas, for whom combat appears to be a viable survival alternative in a country with high levels of urban employment, where the economy is dominated by a precious mineral sector in long-term decline. (Twum-Danso 2003, p.39)

The mobilisation of youth in Sierra Leone has its roots in the political past of the country as a strategy that targeted a group most affected by decades of economic decline and social degradation (MacIntyre and Thusi 2003). In 1999, the Lomé Agreement was signed to address the need for peace in Sierra Leone. The agreement was historic as it made provisions for dealing with issues related to children and youth and established the Office for Children's Protection. It also recognised the need to have a UN Officer for the Protection of Children as part of the peacekeeping mission. This was an important recognition to the special needs of children in Sierra Leone and war generally.

Once it was clear that the end of the conflict had arrived in Sierra Leone, donor programs to address the impact of war were initiated (MacIntyre and Thusi 2003). However, one of the biggest problems that occurred was the lack of funding for youth rehabilitation programs. The main focus was on the rehabilitation of the child soldiers and not the wider problems that had caused the youth to become disenfranchised. UN money for Sierra Leone totalled US$34 million in the mid 1990s, yet only $965,000 was earmarked for child soldiers.

If lack of political articulation can lead to the use of violence to express your frustrations, then it is key to involve children and child soldiers in dialogue and peace-building. Most youth in places such as Makeni were of the opinion that before the war they were hardly involved in decision-making, and the positive outcome of the war was that it made people in positions of authority realise the need to include children in such processes (MacIntyre and Thusi 2003). The Ministry of Youth and Sport created a youth radio program for youth to express their views. It has allowed the expression of ideas on the future of Sierra Leone and the promotion of talent.

Resources and exploitation of children

In both the DRC and Sierra Leone, resource exploitation has fuelled the conflicts. Children have been used to guard mine-rich areas, physically mine for the minerals and used as slaves. In addition, the resources have been used to maintain the conflict and have caused greater numbers of children to be forcibly recruited by armed groups. The exploitation of such resources depends upon the 'Western' need and greed for such goods at low cost. Using children to maintain a war or to mine the areas in which minerals are located must be borne in mind when dealing with conflict and peace agreements. It is often viewed as not in the best interests of the West to ensure long-term peace and stability due to the short-term gains received by governments and multinational companies. Albert Hirschman, Robert Baldwin and others have argued that resource industries were unlikely to stimulate growth in the rest of the economy, particularly if foreign multinationals dominated resource extraction and were allowed to repatriate their profits instead of investing them locally (Baldwin 1966; Hirschman 1958; Ross 1999). This needs to change, and if it is recognised by the consumer that our products originate from such sources, it may help in getting children included in the peace process.

Peace processes and child soldiers

UN Security Council Resolution 1612 is an important step forward with respect to the welfare of child combatants. Paragraph 8.a states: 'Make recommendations to the Council on possible measures to promote the protection of children affected by armed conflict, including through recommendations on appropriate mandates for peacekeeping missions and recommendations with respect to the parties to the conflict.' The Convention on the Rights of the Child provides some guidance on child-focused reconstruction in a post-conflict environment. However, many states do not undertake the obligations set out under the CRC.

The traditional discourse on international security has most often characterised children as victims of conflict, occasionally as perpetrators and even less so as both victims and perpetrators. Children are often lumped with women and viewed as members of larger groups of 'vulnerable populations' that are not traditionally viewed as key actors to the conflict. Scholars have relegated children to the margins, or, even more commonly, entirely excluded children as political actors (Hellman, Holmberg and Wagnsson 2010).

As a result, children are, however, not represented at the peace table. Quite often the very people who recruit and exploit children are the people who are negotiating peace agreements. While it is true that they must be dealt with in order for the conflict to be halted, it is also remarkable that children as combatants have not even been 'thought about' as participants at the peace table given the large numbers of children who may be used in conflict. The exclusion of child soldiers is therefore in part due to the practicalities of doing so and in part due to the sociological underpinnings. Policy makers often do not realise the extent of the conflict's impact upon children. Partly too, it stems from the fact that the parties to treaties seldom consider the knowledge and advice of those who advocate on behalf of children, such as non-governmental organisations. Rather, NGOs are expected to support already-agreed-to post-conflict strategies (Watson 2008).

The problems associated with the inclusion of children in peace processes are often related to the wider societal norms that exist. In many African nations children are taught to be respectful of their elders and not to challenge their authority. Elders do not consult children on matters such as peace and conflict resolution. It should however also be pointed out that Western societies do not fare much better, as quite often children and youth are marginalised as well, especially when in many the right to vote is not available until at the age of 18 years.

Many would also argue that the traditional settings for peace negotiation do not provide adequate space for children to participate. In fact, those at the negotiation table are often a very elitist group of representatives who have access to power and wealth. Getting these actors to understand the need to hear children's concerns must become a precondition for participation at the peace table.

In addition, organising the children who were combatants is often difficult. Children may be fearful of being recognised as a child soldier for fear of the repercussions that could occur from their communities and any new government that may be installed. This requires funding and commitment from the United Nations to create offices that deal specifically with such issues. This is where groups such as Ishmael Beah's Network of Young People Affected by War (NYPAW) may be a very valuable tool that could be mobilised to support youth in such processes. NYPAW is an organisation of young men and women who have survived war, some former child soldiers and others not, working towards efforts of greater accountability for the protection of children's rights.

Following on from UN Security Council Resolution 1325, groups such as UNIFEM have lobbied and organised women's groups to push for their inclusion within the peace processes of countries such as the DRC, Sierra Leone and Burundi. The Secretary-General's Special Representative on Children and Armed Conflict, as well as UNICEF, need to take a lead role in ensuring this process occurs for children. Young people must not be seen as problems or victims, but rather as key contributors in planning and implementing long-term solutions (Machel 2001).

In 1996, approximately 5000 children in Colombia created a grand exhibit of pictures, poems and letters on the theme of peace. The Student Council drew up a declaration asking the warring factions for 'peace in our homes, for them not to make orphans of children, to allow us to play freely in the streets and for no harm to come to our small brothers and sisters'. This led to a national campaign called the Children's Movement for Peace. A national children's referendum had been organised and nearly three million children voted. The children's vote helped inspire a peace mandate that was later supported by more than 10 million citizens and made peace the focus of the subsequent presidential campaign (Machel 2001).

The above case demonstrates the immense potential that children have to influence the overall peace efforts of a particular country. Such efforts can not only affect the rights of children, but may positively impact the rights of all citizens.

The UNSRSG's report of March 2009 states that the Department of Political Affairs has recently revised its Operational Guidance on DDR in order to integrate the consideration of children and armed conflict issues that facilitate or impede peace processes (Office of the

United Nations Special Representative of the Secretary-General on Children and Armed Conflict 2009). It further states that DPA's UN mediation focal point system seeks to ensure that children and armed conflict issues are taken into account early on in the strategic thinking and planning phase of a peace process. It is critical that this guidance becomes entrenched in all peace processes. The Department of Political Affairs and the UN SRSG for Children in Armed Conflict recommend the following key issues be implemented as a Peace Agreement Checklist:

1. Child soldiers' issues should be addressed when appropriate throughout the agreement rather than in a particular article.
2. The word child soldiers should be defined to avoid the exclusions of vulnerable children within the armed forces and this should include the Paris Principles definition.
3. Recruitment and use of child soldiers should be considered as a violation of any ceasefire.
4. The section regulating the role and composition of armed forces should provide that the minimum age for recruiting and enlisting persons to armed forces is 18 years of age.
5. Conversion of child soldiers into the regular armed forces as part of conversions programs for militias and other combatants should be prohibited.
6. Provisions regarding the return and release of detainees or POWs should expressly refer to the release of children, giving them priority over the adults.
7. The government should have the obligation in the agreement to design and implement a program for the tracing and reunification of such children with their family.
8. The parties should request the assistance and international funds from the international community in the design and implementation of such programs.
9. The agreement should create a commission to locate children disappeared during the armed conflict.

(United Nations Peacemaker 2009)

Children are sources of knowledge, and child combatants have knowledge that can further help to understand the root causes of conflict. Their experiences have forced them to mature and obtain skills which should be harnessed. It is imperative that we do not forget the agency and resilience of child combatants. They have developed coping mechanisms and negotiation skills inside their armed groups and within a conflict setting that many adults do not comprehend. In addition, they have knowledge about recruitment techniques, desires for peace, and hopes for the future (Johnson *et al.* 2012). It must be borne in mind that exclusion of child combatants can result in a group of further disaffected young people that now have combat skills as well as feelings of revenge and anger that can so easily disrupt peace efforts. In Sri Lanka and Sierra Leone, the repeated breakdown of peace settlements was often complicated by the fact that child soldiers help conflict groups rapidly return to the theatre of war; in short children make wars easier to start and harder to end (Singer 2006).

> Child recruitment into armed forces and groups is illegal in international law. Therefore, child demobilisation and reintegration is a human rights issue and is not contingent on any other political negotiation. The mechanisms and structures for the release and reintegration of children should be set up before a formal peace agreement is signed, a peacekeeping mission deployed and an adult DDR structure established. Progress should be made by armed forces and groups on child release before more complex and national processes begin, such as SSR or power sharing negotiations, and apparent legitimacy should not be given to child recruitment through the integration of children into adult DDR processes, even though, for the purposes of planning the budget and the DDR programme itself, children should be included in the count of persons qualifying for demobilisation/release and reintegration. (United Nations Disarmament, Demobilization and Reintegration Resource Centre 2006, p.1)

DDR is an essential element to the success of any peaceful settlement of a conflict. If children are not included adequately within the DDR processes then peace will be extremely difficult to achieve in cases where large groups of children have been used as combatants. It is imperative to ensure that peace agreements contain provisions specifically related to the release and demobilisation processes for child soldiers. Mediators and guarantors of such peace agreement processes must be briefed on the implications such provisions will have on the long-term peace process and immediate cessation of hostilities. The inclusion of child soldier clauses has the potential to create an important starting point of agreement amongst conflicting parties. Additionally, peace missions, DDR and long-term development goals cannot be effectively designed without the initial inclusion of provisions related to child soldiers.

Peace agreements

Strategies to ensure inclusion of child soldier provisions in a peace agreement may include the following:

1. Invite child protection specialists to the negotiation table. Such specialists should routinely create briefing material related to the need to include provisions related to child soldiers.
2. Provide briefing sessions on child protection to the armed groups and negotiation participants.
3. Child protection advisers should seek input from former child soldiers or youth with respect to the negotiation table.
4. Ensure the UN SRSG for Children and Armed Conflict is included in high-level peace negotiations.
5. Provide incentives to the negotiation participants for inclusion of child protection measures. Such incentives may include an amnesty for those who abide by the new provisions or a seat within the new governing structures.
6. Ensure all armed actors and political participants have input into the provisions related to child soldiers and long-term recovery processes.
7. Invite local community leaders such as educators, medical doctors, religious leaders and youth groups to participate in the negotiation processes.
8. Provide specific provisions that could be included in the peace agreements. Reference should be made to the United Nations Department of Political Affairs Guidelines on Child Issues in Peace Agreement Checklist.
9. Ensure media attention that positively highlights the willingness to agree on such provisions. This must include a campaign to relay such information back to the local communities.

Out of more than 135 international peace agreements created in the past 15 years, only eight have specific provisions related to child soldiers. The impact on DDR is profound when it comes to the inclusion of specific provisions related to the use of children in armed conflict. Sierra Leone's peace accord was a landmark document as it provided just such a provision. This resulted in direct programs for children by UNICEF, Save the Children and CARITAS that stressed the need to abide by the peace accord. Resources can be requested from the international community as the peace accord will determine the need to fulfil specific agreements.

Peacekeeping missions receive their mandates from peace agreements. It is therefore imperative that peace agreements are as specific as possible with respect to child soldiers. If these issues are flagged prior to the UN peacekeeping missions being created then it forces those who create the mandates to make specific provisions for release and reintegration of former child soldiers.

Including child soldiers in peace agreements can allow for positive contributions to peace by these youth that would otherwise be shunned from society. If communities recognise their positive contributions, this can change perceptions of former child soldiers. In addition, this may allow child soldiers to change their own self-perceptions. Policy makers need to understand that inclusion of youth groups, former child soldiers and specific provisions related to child soldiers in a peace process can assist with the attainment of long-term peace. There is a need to conduct studies on long-term cost-benefit analysis along these lines to provide evidence of the importance to include.

There is a danger of merely adding children into the peace process for the sake of appearing to include children. It is important that peace negotiators are educated about the language of the provisions that need to be included. Adult negotiators must not manipulate the processes but commit to real change. Peer-led programs should be created in which support and education is provided to former child soldiers to assist with the need to affect and participate in peace processes.

Conclusion

> Why don't we put world leaders in a room alone and unarmed and it's up to them to finish the conflict by themselves and they're not let out until they finish it? Even though it's mean, they have to live side by side to know each other better. Isn't it better than having other people's lives taken away from them? I have no idea, even children are better at making friends than they are. (Young Sri Lankan girl, age not specified, cited by United Nations Children's Fund 2009)

Children need to be an entity that has specific and meaningful representation in peace-building efforts. We must not view them as an add-on in a peace process but as integral to the resolution of conflict. From the earliest stages of the peace-building efforts, the needs and roles that children play in the conflict must be a key issue to be addressed and understood. Children can provide opportunities for compromise and conflict resolution and therefore must be part of the negotiation process. Few associated with parties to a conflict would want to risk the international condemnation associated with deliberately ignoring the needs of children, but this requires awareness on behalf of the world to call to attention those that ignore children at their peril. If we move away from the notions of including only those who are 'powerful' and instead move towards including those who are 'knowledgeable', we may find that children, particularly in conflict zones, would be most well suited at the peace table (Watson 2008).

Children may provide key answers to conflict resolution. Children are not the sources of conflict, but should be viewed as the resource for resolution.

References

Amnesty International (2000) *Sierra Leone: Childhood – A Casualty of Conflict.* London: Amnesty International. Available at www.amnesty.org/en/library/asset/AFR51/069/2000/en/363960d1-de07-11dd-a3e1-93acb0aa12d8/afr510692000en.pdf, accessed on 28 October 2011.

Baldwin, R.E. (1966) *Economic Development and Export Growth: A Study of Northern Rhodesia 1920–1960.* Berkeley, CA: University of California Press.

BBC News (2003) 'DR Congo "awash" with child soldiers.' Available at http://news.bbc.co.uk/1/hi/world/africa/2772575.stm, accessed on 28 October 2011.

Brett, R. and McCallin, M. (1998) *Children: The Invisible Soldiers.* Stockholm: Radda Barnen.

CIA World Factbook (2010) Available at www.ciafactbook.com, accessed on 12 March 2010.

Coalition for the International Criminal Court (2011) *The Lubanga Case.* Available at www.iccnow.org/?mod=drctimelinelubanga, accessed on 28 October 2011.

Coalition to Stop the Use of Child Soldiers (2004) *Child Soldiers: Global Report 2004.* Available at www.child-soldiers.org/document/get?id=966, accessed on 28 October 2011.

Hellman, M., Holmberg, A. and Wagnsson, C. (2010) 'The centrality of non-traditional groups for security in the globalized era: The case of children.' *International Political Sociology 4*, 1–14.

Hirschman, A.O. (1958) *The Strategy of Economic Development.* New Haven, CT: Yale University Press.

Human Rights Watch (2003) *The Use of Child Soldiers in the Democratic Republic of the Congo.* Was available at www.hrw.org, accessed on 30 July 2003.

Johnson, K., Morantz, G., Seignior, H., Whitman, S. and Zayed, T. (2012) 'From youth affected by war to advocates of peace: Roundtable discussion with former child combatants.' *International Journal of Peacekeeping 16*, 1–2.
Lee, A.J. (2009) *Understanding and Addressing the Phenomenon of 'Child Soldiers': The Gap Between the Global Humanitarian Discourse and the Local Understandings and Experiences of Young People's Military Recruitment.* Master of Science thesis, University of Oxford.
Machel, G. (2001) *The Impact of War on Children.* Vancouver: UBC Press.
MacIntyre, A. and Thusi, T. (2003) 'Children and youth in Sierra Leone's peace-building process.' *African Security Review 12*, 2. Available at www.iss.co.za/pubs/asr/12No2/Content.html, accessed on 10 May 2010.
McCrummen, S. (2007) *The Washington Post.* 'Children's Parliament Sets High Bar in Congo.' 11 August 2007. Available at www.washingtonpost.com/wp-dyn/content/article/2007/08/10/AR2007081002154.html, accessed on 1 April 2011.
McKay, S. and Mazurana, D. (2004) *Where are the Girls? Girls in Fighting Forces in Northern Uganda, Sierra Leone and Mozambique: Their Lives During and After War.* Montreal: Rights and Democracy.
Office of the United Nations Special Representative of the Secretary-General on Children and Armed Conflict (2009) *Children Affected by Armed Conflict.* Available at www.un.org/children/conflict/english/index.html, accessed on 14 March 2010.
Ross, M.L. (1999) 'The political economy of the resource curse.' *World Politics 51*, 2.
Singer, P.W. (2006) *Children at War.* Berkeley, CA: University of California Press.
Twum-Danso, A. (2003) *Africa's Young Soldiers: The Co-option of Childhood.* Pretoria: Institute for Security Studies.
UNICEF (2003) *Information by Country – DRC.* UNICEF. Available at www.unicef.org/infobycountry/drcongo.html, accessed on 30 July 2003.
United Nations (2007) *The Paris Principles on Children Associated with Armed Groups or Armed Forces.* Available at www.un.org/children/conflict/_documents/parisprinciples/ParisPrinciples_EN.pdf, accessed on 30 April 2010.
United Nations Children's Fund (2009) *Machel 10 Year Strategic Review: Children and Conflict in a Changing World.* Available at www.childrenandwar.org/wp-content/uploads/2009/12/msr2_en.pdf, accessed on 23 November 2010.
United Nations Disarmament, Demobilization and Reintegration Resource Centre (2006) *5.30 Children and DDR.* New York: United Nations Disarmament, Demobilization and Reintegration Resource Centre. Available at www.unddr.org/iddrs/05/30.php?search_phrase=children, accessed on 28 October 2011.
United Nations Peacemaker (2009) *Children and Peace Agreements Checklist.* New York: United Nations Department of Political Affairs. Available at http://peacemaker.unlb.org/index1.php, accessed on 1 July 2010.
United Nations Treaty Collection (2011) Available at http://treaties.un.org, accessed on 1 March 2011.
Verhey, B. (2004) *Reaching the Girls: Study on Girls Associated with Armed Forces and Groups in the Democratic Republic of the Congo.* London: Save the Children UK.
Watchlist on Children and Armed Conflict (2003) *The Impact of Armed Conflict on Children in the Democratic Republic of the Congo.* Available at http://watchlist.org/reports/pdf/dr_congo.report.pdf, accessed on 12 March 2011.
Watson, A. (2008) 'Can there be a kindered peace?' *Ethics and International Affairs 22*, 35–42.
World Population Awareness (2010) *Children.* New York: International Herald Tribune. Available at www.overpopulation.org/children.html, accessed on 10 April 2010.

Chapter 5

Unaccompanied Children as Illegal Immigrants in the United States

Gladis E. Molina

Introduction

This chapter is divided into three parts. To begin, I will provide an overview of unaccompanied children in the United States (US). The second part of the chapter will discuss the legal process, including issues of custody and legal representation, which the children must face in the US as immigrants without status. The final part will focus on some of the social welfare issues, such as trauma, that must be dealt with once the children are in the US.

I have been working with immigrant children who enter the US without status and unaccompanied by a parent or legal guardian since 2006. These children come from a range of countries, including Argentina, Brazil, China, Colombia, Cuba, the Dominican Republic, Ecuador, India, Peru, and Somalia. However, the overwhelming majority of the unaccompanied children with whom I have worked come from Mexico and three Central American countries, namely El Salvador, Guatemala, and Honduras. When addressing the issue of what factors force and motivate the journey of unaccompanied children to the US, the chapter will mainly draw on the circumstances of children in these four countries.

Part 1: The children

US federal law, namely section 462 of the *Homeland Security Act 2002* (HSA), defines an 'Unaccompanied Alien Child' (UAC) (referred to as an 'unaccompanied child or children' in this chapter) as a child who 'has no lawful immigration status in the US; has not attained 18 years of age; and with respect to whom there is no parent or legal guardian in the US; or no parent or legal guardian in the US is available to provide care and physical custody.' Children come to the US from around the world, but children from Mexico and Central America account for the overwhelming majority of unaccompanied children in the US (Bhabha and Schmidt 2011; Haddal 2007). Bhabha and Schmidt report that 'the number of unaccompanied and separated children in federal custody has remained steady (7509 unaccompanied children in fiscal year 2010), despite a marked decline in overall immigration enforcement apprehensions' (2011, p.1).

Lucia Rodriguez, an unaccompanied child who made the journey to the US, states, 'the most important thing for everyone to understand is why a child comes to this country... We do not all come for the same reason, but we come here with the best hopes and ideas for our future. For many of us, we face dangerous situations in our country' (Somers, Herrera and Rodriguez 2010, p.322). During the 1980s, Central American countries, such as El Salvador and Guatemala, experienced civil conflict. Though the Central American civil wars of the 1980s have ended, violence continues to threaten children's safety and welfare in Central America. Rather than official civil wars, today the violence and terror stem from the government's inability to control street gangs that beat, rape, and kill people (*Los Angeles Times* 2009). Unaccompanied children from Central America tell how street gangs recruit young people to join their ranks through violent means or the threat of violence; how gang members target victims for extortion and beat and/or kill those who refuse to give in to their demands; and how girls who refuse advances from gang members are sexually assaulted. Similarly, in Mexico the security of children has been threatened by the violence ensuing from drug wars between cartels (*Los Angeles Times* 2010). Children who are orphaned, abandoned, or left behind by their parents, or who live in extreme poverty, are particularly vulnerable because they have little protection against this violence and a sense of personal and communal security constantly evades them. Thus, this lack of security often leads to unaccompanied children making the dangerous journey to the US.

In addition to the lack of security, unaccompanied children also flee their homelands because of their vulnerability as children. In his personal account, Pedro Herrera, who also made the journey to the US as an unaccompanied child, explains: 'I became used to assaults by adults – they took advantage of me, mistreated me, robbed me and abused me. Who could I go to complain to and seek help?' (Somers *et al.* 2010, p.318). Pedro adds: 'In my country, of course there are rights of the child, but in the halls of the government representatives and for the persons of a higher economic class. I was basically one more number amongst all of the children who work on the streets, sleeping in cartons, without a life, without a future' (Somers *et al.* 2010, p.318).

Lucia notes: 'Childhood in the United States is very different because it is respected more… In my country, children also have rights. But in my country, you belong to your family and no one will explain to you the rights you have as a child… A child is treated however adults want to treat them. The child is not valued in her thoughts and what could happen to her' (Somers *et al.* 2010, p.320).

Some family members exploit and abuse children in their care. In *Enrique's Journey*, the bestselling book in the US about unaccompanied children, Sonia Nazario (2007) writes about children who are left behind by their parents, who leave the children in search of security in their own lives, with the goal of reunifying with the children under better circumstances. The children are often left in the care of extended family members, such as grandparents, aunt/uncles, and, in some instances, older siblings, some barely adults themselves. Some of the children left behind are physically and emotionally abused, and the girls may even become victims of sexual abuse. Others are abused at the hands of their own parents, or live with parents who fail to protect them from abuse by the parent's partner, or are sent away to the US because the parents can no longer provide for the children at home. For these children, seeking refuge from child abuse and exploitation is a motivation for embarking on a journey to reach the US.

A child's poverty is linked to their lack of protection and overall vulnerability. Lucia adds, 'In my country, if you are poor you cannot go to school. Instead, the focus is to learn something [so that] you can work to defend yourself' (Somers *et al.* 2010, p.320). Because of their poverty, some children cannot expect to receive the basic tools in order to secure a future for themselves. Lucia is not alone in her thinking. Amnesty International's Secretary General, Irene Khan (2009), asserts this point as a central theme in her book, *The Unheard Truth: Poverty and Human Rights*. Khan notes that, 'Poor people live in perpetual insecurity, and their insecurity reinforces their poverty... They have no rights in relation to those who exercise power over them... Without rights they are insecure, and insecurity means they are less able to fight their deprivation. The state constantly fails poor people... Whether through deliberate repression or through indifference, those in power do not hear the voices of poor people' (pp.9–11).

Given the context of their lives in the home country, these children look to the US with a spirit of hope. However, few fully realize the suffering they may endure to reach the US. In a 2010 report titled *Invisible Victims: Migrants on the Move in Mexico*, Amnesty International documents the stories of Central American migrants who are victims of kidnappings, assaults, and rapes in Mexico. In its report, Amnesty International notes that the dangerous journey places all migrants at risk of abuse, 'but women and children – particularly unaccompanied children – are especially vulnerable' (2010, p.5). Amnesty International calls on the government of Mexico to promote the recognition of migrants' rights, provide them with aid when they are victims of violent crimes, and to protect them equally under the law. In 2011, the *El Paso Times* featured a special report on the journey of a little girl from El Salvador through Mexico, where she suffered sexual abuse.

Part 2: The legal process

Apprehension and detention

When unaccompanied children come to the US, they will have contact with several government agencies upon apprehension by the immigration authorities. Their first encounter is typically with the US Department of Homeland Security (DHS), which is the government agency charged with the protection of American borders and enforcement of the immigration laws. DHS carries out the majority of these tasks through two of its agencies: (1) Customs and Border Protection (CBP), and (2) Immigration and Customs Enforcement (ICE). CBP is the agency that patrols the borders and will take into custody immigrants without status who are apprehended near land borders. ICE is the agency that enforces immigration laws in the interior parts of the US. When DHS encounters non-citizens in the US, it can take them into custody to determine whether they have lawful immigration status in the US. When DHS takes custody of non-citizens, it questions them about their country of origin and their reasons for being in the US. In South Texas, on a weekly basis, I interviewed children within a few days after being interrogated by DHS and they reported feeling scared, uninformed, and at times intimidated by the tone of voice and questioning by DHS officials.

After questioning a non-citizen, DHS must determine whether to keep custody of the non-citizen by placing them in a federal immigration detention center or releasing them from DHS custody. When DHS apprehends a non-citizen who appears or claims to be a child, it must ascertain whether the child is one who comes under the federal definition of an Unaccompanied Alien Child (UAC); this classification triggers provisions under the HSA with respect to the care of these children while they are held in federal detention. In practice, DHS makes the determination about whether a child is a UAC based on information obtained from the child and the circumstances of the child's apprehension at the time that DHS takes custody of the child. For example, if a child was apprehended by DHS without a legal guardian or parent, a child can be classified as a UAC. DHS also classifies a child as a UAC if the child is apprehended with non-parent relatives. In addition, DHS can classify a child as a UAC where the child has one or both parents present in the US, but the parents are not willing to take care and custody of the child. Where a child has one or both parents in the US, DHS has the discretion to contact the parent(s) and inquire about the parent(s)' availability to take custody of the child. In cases where DHS contacts a parent and learns that the parent is not willing to take custody of the child from DHS (often because the parents(s) are afraid that DHS will take custody of them as well because they are undocumented), then DHS will classify the child as a UAC. In these cases, DHS's classification is consistent with federal law because the law takes into account the availability of parents in the US to take care and custody of the child.

Care while in federal custody

Under section 462 of the HSA, DHS is required to transfer care and custody of all UACs to the Office of Refugee Resettlement (ORR), a federal agency housed within the US Department of Health and Human Services (HHS). Pursuant to the HSA, ORR has the responsibility for 'coordinating and implementing the care and placement of unaccompanied alien children who are in Federal custody by reason of their immigration status.' The HSA defines 'placement' as 'the placement of an unaccompanied alien child in either a detention facility or an alternative to such a facility.' ORR carries out its statutory responsibility by subcontracting with facilities across the US to provide food, housing, care, and social services to the children entrusted in ORR's care while the children are in federal custody. The social services provided by ORR facilities include counseling and reunification services. Initially, ORR places all children transferred to their care in detention facilities, such as foster care programs, youth shelters, and therapeutic and secure centers. As a way of placing children in non-detention facility alternatives, social workers at the detention facilities will work with potential sponsors who wish to file a request with ORR that the child be released into their care. During this process, ORR facilities staff will work to reunite the children with relatives, including parents, as well as non-relatives who can demonstrate a history of involvement with the child and who have a clear background criminal check. In practice, ORR must communicate with DHS before it can issue the final approval on the reunification process. While section 462 of the HSA has transferred the care of unaccompanied children to ORR, DHS continues to exercise control over the custody of children while in ORR care. This is supported by the practice that ORR facilities must physically produce the children to DHS whenever DHS officials request to meet with a child transferred to ORR care from DHS. Thus, unaccompanied children are technically under the federal custody of DHS, but just in the care of ORR.

Immigration court

The US Department of Justice (DOJ) houses the Executive Office of Immigration Review (EOIR), which is the agency that oversees the immigration courts across the US. Federal judges presiding over the immigration courts hear and adjudicate cases filed by DHS for prosecution. During the interrogation process, DHS produces a document known as the 'Record of Deportable Alien' (Immigration Form I-213), which serves as the basis for the factual allegations that are lodged in a federal complaint, the 'Notice to Appear' (Immigration Form I-862). When DHS files the Notice to Appear with the immigration court, the filing of such a document officially places a non-citizen in removal proceedings, which is the legal process where a non-citizen must present legal defenses in order to avoid being ordered to be removed from the US. Immigration judges hear cases for both adults and children, whether they are detained or non-detained. When children are detained in federal custody in the care of ORR, ORR facilities ensure that the unaccompanied children are present in the immigration court for their removal proceedings. Where children have been released from federal custody through ORR's reunification process, the sponsor is responsible for bringing the child to court.

Prosecution by DHS

As a matter of law, DHS has the prosecutorial discretion whether to file a Notice to Appear with an immigration court. The current general practice of DHS, however, is to file a Notice to Appear for unaccompanied children whom it places in federal custody in the care of ORR. When DHS files a Notice to Appear with the immigration court against an unaccompanied child, DHS's prosecutorial interests are represented by government attorneys working for the legal division within ICE.

Legal representation for unaccompanied children

In the US, there is no law which requires that children facing removal proceedings be appointed counsel at the federal government's expense, even for children who are detained in federal custody in ORR care. The American immigration court process was not conceived with the participation of children in mind. In practice, children must conform to the space and legal procedures in court as if they were small adults. But children are not small adults. Children lack the intellectual capacity to understand the legal interests that are at stake in these removal proceedings, how to protect their substantive rights, and, more importantly, to recognize and discuss their own vulnerabilities. This is perhaps a reflection of the underlying principle that children are not expected to migrate to other countries without their parents. DHS's response is to proceed before the immigration court so that government attorneys may advance the prosecutorial interests of the US government. Meanwhile children in the immigration court are left to their own devices. The result is that children may not be able to present defense claims adequately to prevent an immigration judge from issuing a removal order. In the end, the vulnerability of unaccompanied children is only increased with the absence of legal representation in the legal process. Without legal counsel, a child may not identify the most viable claim to present in her defense; will not understand the procedural steps to follow in order to preserve rights to a claim; and, because of a lack of information and understanding of the workings of a workroom, will likely delay the operations of a courtroom. In a 2010 report on immigration in the US, the Inter-American Commission on Human Rights (IACHR) expressed concerns that such a vulnerable group does not have access to government-appointed counsel. As part of its recommendations, the IACHR report calls on the US to provide government-appointed counsel to unaccompanied children facing immigration proceedings (IACHR 2010). Similarly, the Immigration Commission of the American Bar Association published a report in which it recommends that legal representation should be provided to unaccompanied minors at government expense (American Bar Association 2010).

Programs for unaccompanied children facing the legal process

The HSA charged ORR with the responsibility of developing a plan to be submitted to Congress on how to ensure that qualified and independent legal counsel is timely appointed to represent the interests of unaccompanied alien children who are in federal custody by reason of their immigration status. A subsequent federal law, the William Wilberforce Trafficking Victims Protection Reauthorization Act of 2008 (TVPRA), mandates that the 'Secretary of Health and Human Services shall ensure...that all unaccompanied alien children who are or have been in the custody of the Secretary [of Health and Human Services] or the Secretary of Homeland Security...have counsel to represent them in legal proceedings or matters.' In addition, the language of the TVPRA states that 'to the greatest extent practicable, the Secretary of Health and Human Services shall make every effort to utilize the services of pro bono counsel who agree to provide representation to such children without charge.' To help address the needs of unaccompanied children through the legal process, ORR is funding two projects: (1) the Legal Orientation Program, and (2) Pro Bono Representation.

The Legal Orientation Program (LOP) project serves children in federal custody in ORR care by providing general information about the legal process through Know Your Rights presentations at ORR facilities. Generally, a Know Your Rights presentation explains to children why they are in federal custody, the ORR reunification process, and the immigration court process. The Pro Bono Representation project provides funding to non-governmental organizations to recruit, train, and match attorneys with children in need of legal representation. Under the Pro Bono Representation project, ORR does not cover any legal costs for representation of the children's immigration case, and instead these costs are borne by the private attorneys volunteering their services. Because the language of the TVPRA mandates the Secretary of Health and Human Services to serve unaccompanied children who have been in the custody of ORR or DHS by ensuring that they have counsel to represent them in legal proceedings, the Pro Bono Representation project now serves children who have been released from federal custody and reunified with family or a trusted adult caregiver.

Organizations that receive ORR funding cannot provide legal representation of the children during removal proceedings. Thus, unaccompanied children can only look to the LOP project as a means to understand the legal process and, if they cannot afford a lawyer, the children look to the Pro Bono Representation project as a means to secure legal representation without charge, or face the daunting task of representing themselves opposite an attorney for DHS in immigration court.

The law: Defending against removal

In the US, there is no law supporting the proposition that an unaccompanied child is exempt from being placed in removal proceedings or that immigration protection or benefits must be afforded to unaccompanied children. Additionally, immigration courts do not employ a best interest of the child framework when deciding whether to grant a claim for defense or to justify withholding removal for a child. Thus, in order for a child to successfully defend against removal proceedings in immigration court by presenting a defense claim, such as asylum, the child must meet the requirements that are generally applicable under the law. As mentioned earlier, children from Central America and Mexico flee due to violence in their home countries stemming from drug cartels and street gang persecution and fear returning. These children can certainly present an asylum claim to the US government, but access to presenting a claim does not necessarily provide unaccompanied children the due protection under their circumstances.

As Somers notes, 'the lack of substantive framework for children's asylum claims and the application of adult standards to children have impeded progress for unaccompanied children in obtaining... protection' (Somers *et al.* 2010, p.376). In practice, the immigration courts, and its reviewing body, the Board of Immigration Appeals (BIA), still have not made it clear whether children fleeing gang violence and persecution in Central America or violence from the drug cartel violence in Mexico will be protected under US asylum laws. Meanwhile, children presenting asylum claims do so with the uncertainty of whether the substantive law will protect them or not. The current legal uncertainty of these claims is in part explained by the

US apprehension of opening the floodgates to requests for protection by unaccompanied children. As Bhabha and Schmidt point out, 'these are precisely the types of claims which elicit concerted opposition, skepticism and controversy from US decision makers. The critical arguments...often have less to do with doubts about a child's actual fear of persecution and need for protection, and more to do with government concerns about the potential impact of positive precedents on the number of future claimants' (2011, p.12). Though the asylum law has a discretionary element, which could arguably take into account a best interest analysis, immigration judges cannot grant asylum solely based on a child's best interest line of reasoning, because asylum claims must still be rooted in some protected ground under the current laws.

In 1990 a unique immigration benefit, known as Special Immigrant Juvenile Status (SIJS), was added to section 101 of the federal immigration code. SIJS allows for a look at the best interest of the child and is the only defense claim crafted for children. SIJS affords protection for children who are present in the US, for whom it has been determined that reunification with one or both parents is not viable due to abuse, abandonment, neglect, or similar circumstances, and for whom it would not be in their best interest to be returned to their home country. Section 101 of the code requires that the determination about the best interest of the child be made by a state juvenile court or in administrative proceedings, rather than by a federal immigration judge or DHS officials. SIJS provides much-needed protection for vulnerable immigrant children in the US.

The current law still does not provide clear protection for children who are victims of abuse and other violent crimes during their journey to the US, such as a child from Central America who suffers a rape in Mexico. In such a case, the child has to present the legal argument of how her past rape in Mexico will be linked to a well-founded fear of future persecution in her home country. Additionally, the child's claim must still be rooted in claiming protection from persecution on the account of one of the protected grounds, such as religion, political opinion, or membership in a particular social group. Similarly, in trafficking cases, where the child is being brought to the US to engage in commercial sex acts or for forced labor, it is uncertain whether there is a defense claim under the trafficking laws if the child was destined for trafficking but was able to escape from the traffickers before reaching the US, and nevertheless made it to the US on her own.

Currently, section 101 of the immigration code requires that a child be present in the US 'on account of' being trafficked. Upon raising a claim for defense under the anti-trafficking laws, a child who escapes from their traffickers before reaching the US will be questioned as to whether her ultimate arrival in the US is a voluntary act as opposed to being due to her trafficking circumstances. As an alternative defense, such a child may have to resort to applying for asylum for fear of being harmed by the traffickers in the home country.

Lastly, the current law does not provide protection for unaccompanied children who reunify with a parent in the US, where the parent is legally able to live and work in the US under the Temporary Protective Status (TPS) program. The TPS program affords immigration protection from removal to individuals from countries designated by the US government due to exceptional circumstances, such as natural disasters. Some of the unaccompanied children from Central America who reunify with their parents in the US have parents who currently have immigration protection under the TPS program. However, the TPS program does not allow such a parent proactively to bring the child to the US in a lawful manner. Thus, while parents in the TPS program can live lawfully in the US, their children cannot be reunified with their parents through a lawful means, and avoid entering the US without status.

Part 3: The social welfare issues

Once a child secures legal representation, the child's legal needs are the issues that become of primary importance to a lawyer, but the child's underlying social services needs are equally, if not more, important to the child's overall social welfare. Attorneys representing an unaccompanied child experience that working on the child's legal case is not an independent operation from the social needs of the child. These social needs include ensuring that a child's basic necessities, such as housing, school, and stability, are met, coordinating appropriate counseling services to deal with past trauma, and presenting a child's best interests. In the course of a legal case, lawyers can expect to be called upon to help the child address some of these social needs as they come up in the course of legal representation. A lawyer representing unaccompanied children is more likely to be called upon to help the children meet social needs because these children are newcomers and they have not built a support system. Additionally, they are unaware of their surroundings and systems (such as schools) in a new place. Lastly, the children may have been placed in the care of an adult, such as a distant relative, where the placement turns out to be less than ideal because the child is unable to build a comfortable relationship of trust with such a caregiver, or because the caregiver ends up neglecting or abusing the child. In many cases, the caregiver has not seen the child in many years. This may be true even in cases where ORR has reunified the child with parents who feel like strangers to the child because of the years of family separation. A lawyer's ability to address the social needs raised in the course of a legal case, however, is limited, and thus a child's overall social welfare cannot be adequately addressed without having systems in place to address the social needs of unaccompanied children.

Coordination of social services

To best serve unaccompanied children, attorneys would greatly benefit from working with social workers on the children's cases. A social worker can assist the attorney to coordinate a client's case and ensure that a child's social welfare needs, including emotional support and stability, are being met. Meeting the child's needs enhances the child's ability to cooperate with the attorney on the legal case, tell her story, and can help the experience be less traumatic for the child. If a child's needs are not being met, the child may feel overwhelmed by having to juggle, all on their own, the changing situations, and cope by withdrawing altogether from the legal case. When there is no person in a role to coordinate social services for a child, the attorney may have to play the role of a social worker, but the attorneys are not equipped with the resources, training, or the information necessary to best help the child meet these needs.

As discussed earlier, while the children are in the care of ORR, they receive social work services through an assigned case manager at the ORR facility. The case workers coordinate the paperwork for the children, make appointments for professional services, arrange transportation to such appointments, and address concerns the child may have which affect their overall welfare. Attorneys who work with unaccompanied children in ORR facilities routinely communicate and work with the caseworkers. For children out of ORR care, ORR funds follow-up social services to children which are provided by non-governmental organizations. These services include home visits to ensure that the child's release from ORR continues to be safe, help in enrolling the child in school, if needed, and access to other services the child may need, including legal services, by referring the child to programs such as the Pro Bono Representation project, discussed earlier. The follow-up services, however, are not provided to all children, only those who ORR determines present issues of concern such as trafficking and special risks, including a history of past sexual abuse. Theoretically, children formerly in ORR care who do not receive follow-up social services can look to their state of residence for help. In reality, however, unaccompanied children may lack access to social services due to state budget constraints and state laws that prevent immigrants without status from accessing social services.

Dealing with trauma

Unaccompanied children arrive in the US with several layers of trauma due to life in the home country and events along the journey. Some of them have suffered emotional, physical, and sexual abuse, including rape, or have been witnesses to horrifying acts of violence. Others carry deep resentment towards a parent who left them behind. As an attorney prepares a child's legal case, past trauma resurfaces and the child must process the emotions and memories produced by past trauma. Not addressing the child's need to process and cope with past trauma only adds to the child's anxiety caused by the legal process. While an attorney can read a child's expressions, finding a professional to work with the child's needs is optimal. Children in ORR care receive counseling services, but those released from ORR are not guaranteed such services. Helping these children obtain services to cope with past trauma in their lives is important in ensuring their emotional stability and overall long-term welfare.

Best interest considerations

As discussed earlier, immigration judges cannot make best interest determinations for children. In addition, a lawyer representing an unaccompanied child in immigration proceedings is not charged with advancing the child's best interests from a social welfare perspective, but is rather charged with advancing her legal interests. Nevertheless, when a child faces a legal system, the issue of her best interest enters into the equation, and to address this issue in the immigration context, in 2004, ORR funded a pilot project aimed at presenting the best interest of unaccompanied children in ORR care. Using these funds, the Immigrant Child Advocacy Project (ICAP) was launched at the University of Chicago. Currently, ICAP trains volunteers to serve as child advocates in two cities where ORR has facilities, Chicago, Illinois, and Harlingen, Texas, and ICAP and ORR are working to expand the program nationally (Bhabha and Schmidt 2011). The role of the child advocate is to formulate the best interests of the child by gathering information about the child from all sources, such as ORR records, the child's attorney, and family members, including family outside the US. The child advocates play a role similar to a guardian *ad litem* attorney, but the advocates are not attorneys for the child. After the passage of the TVPRA in 2008, ORR now has the official authority to enage in the appointment of child advocates for certain children in ORR care. The TVPRA states that 'the Secretary of Health and Human Services is authorized to appoint independent child advocates for child trafficking victims and other vulnerable unaccompanied alien children.' To this end, the TVPRA mandates that 'a child advocate shall be provided access to materials necessary to effectively advocate for the best interest of the child.' The formal inclusion of the role and appointment of child advocates in unaccompanied children's cases is an important step because there is no federal law which grants immigration judges the authority to appoint child advocates or guardians *ad litem* for a child. Bhabha and Schmidt note that 'this lack of legal support is partly a reflection of the more general, adult-centric focus of immigration (unlike juvenile or family) law, where children's issues have largely been an afterthought' (2011, p.10).

Now that there is a federal law that provides for the appointment of child advocates, the challenge will be to figure out what immigration judges are to do with a child's best interest determination, because there is no federal authority that enables an immigration judge to take into account the best interest of the child when deciding whether or not to grant protection. Thus, the federal law leaves children with a legal framework, as expressly stated in the TVPRA, which understands that a best interest determination should be made within the context of certain children, and yet it provides the adjudicators, namely the immigration judges, no framework within which to give weight to such a determination. In other words, as one tries to match the aim of the TVPRA with the current immigration laws, the principle of a child's best interests may not have a compatible fit within the immigration framework. This emphasizes the notion that in the US the legal process engages unaccompanied children in a framework where they are viewed as immigrants without status rather than as children for whom best interest considerations must become part of the legal analysis. Federal lawmakers could provide more certainty in the protection rights for unaccompanied children. The uncertainty places unaccompanied children in a continued vulnerable position in the legal process, both procedurally and substantively.

> As one of only two countries not having ratified the [Convention on the Rights of the Child], the US has no binding international obligation (unlike its Canadian and European counterparts) to ensure that the child protection obligation trumps the immigration control pressure. Instead, its conflicting mandate continues to result in a bifurcated set of policies which straddle and oscillate between two views of migrant children: innocent victims of harsh circumstances in need of protective care on the one hand, and delinquent and potentially dangerous outsiders requiring detention, punishment and expulsion on the other. (Bhabha and Schmidt 2011, p.2)

Conclusion

The US policies toward unaccompanied children are still a work in progress.

As a concluding point, I turn again to Lucia Rodriguez, whose parents are both in the US under the TPS program. In Lucia's words:

> I sometimes feel that no one is listening to me and will not value what I have to say. I talk to my attorneys, but they do not have the power to make decisions. It is very hard for me to see my future now after I came here with certain hopes. My greatest dream is to continue studying. Without any documentation, I do not think I will be able to go to a university. It just feels like I am in an impossible situation. (Somers *et al.* 2010, p.322)

References

American Bar Association (2010) *Reforming the Immigration System: Proposals to Promote Independence, Fairness, Efficiency, and Professionalism in the Adjudication of Removal Cases.* Washington, DC: American Bar Association.

Amnesty International (2010) *Invisible Victims: Migrants on the Move in Mexico.* London: Amnesty International Publications.

Bhabha, J. and Schmidt, S. (2011) 'From Kafka to Wilberforce: Is the U.S. government's approach to child migrants improving?' *11–02 Immigration Briefings 1.* New York: Thomson Reuters.

El Paso Times (2011) 'Special report: Salvadoran girl survives abuse, bureaucracy on journey north.' Available at www.elpasotimes.com/news/ci_18066369, accessed on 28 October 2011.

Haddal, C. (2007) *Unaccompanied Alien Children Policies and Issues.* Congressional Research Service (CRS) Report for Congress LR33896. Washington, DC: US Congress.

Inter-American Commission on Human Rights (IACHR) (2010) *Report on Immigration in the United States: Detention and Due Process*. Washington, DC: Organization of American States.

Khan, I. (2009) *The Unheard Truth: Poverty and Human Rights*. London: W.W. Norton and Company.

Los Angeles Times, The (2009) 'El Salvador Battles on Epidemic of Violence.' May 13, p.A1, p.A19.

Los Angeles Times, The (2010) 'Mexico Under Siege.' November 7, p.A1, pp.A18–19.

Nazario, S. (2007) *Enrique's Journey*. New York: Random House Trade Paperbacks. (Original work published 2006.)

Somers, M., Herrera, P. and Rodriguez, L. (2010) 'Constructions of childhood and unaccompanied children in the immigration system in the United States.' *U.C. Davis Journal of Juvenile Law and Policy 14*, 2, 311–380.

Chapter 6

Children, Vulnerability and Rights

Protecting the Rights of Children in Custody in Northern Ireland

Una Convery and Linda Moore

Introduction

This chapter draws upon primary research conducted by the authors and reported in *Still in Our Care: Protecting Children's Rights in Custody in Northern Ireland* (Convery and Moore 2006). This primary research was conducted for the Northern Ireland Human Rights Commission using its statutory powers of investigation under the Northern Ireland Act 1998 and focused on the Juvenile Justice Centre for Northern Ireland (JJC) used for the detention of remanded and sentenced boys and girls aged 10 to 17. Thirteen of the 25 children detained at the time of fieldwork were interviewed along with custodial care staff, managers and other professionals. The regime was observed over a two-week period; formal interviews were supplemented by informal discussions, for example during mealtimes. The research findings and recommendations are discussed here, and subsequent developments regarding children's incarceration analysed. There is also discussion of conditions for children in Hydebank Wood Young Offenders Centre, a penal institution for children and young people (aged 15 to 23) which acts as a default placement for boys deemed too persistent in their offending, or considered too difficult to manage within the JJC.

Northern Ireland is in transition from over 40 years of violent conflict; however, although the level of fatalities is much reduced, violence persists and many children do not feel safe (McAlister, Scraton and Haydon 2009). Since *Still in Our Care* was published, there have been significant developments within the criminal justice system, most notably the devolution of justice and policing to the locally elected government. However, as evidenced by subsequent research and inspections, significant breaches of rights persist regarding the use of custody for children.

Vulnerabilities and rights

The UNCRC has consistently criticised the United Kingdom (UK) criminal justice system for its low age of criminal responsibility (10 years in England, Wales (E&W) and Northern Ireland), recommending 12 years as a minimum, and preferably an age of 14–16 (UNCRC 2007). The criminalisation of children is exacerbated within the UK context (and elsewhere) by societal and political intolerance, fuelled by negative media coverage, leading to increasingly punitive responses (Scraton 2004). Children in conflict with the law are viewed as 'other', 'undeserving' of care or rights (Goldson 2009) and are 'responsibilised', held to be accountable for their (offending) behaviour and for its consequences (Muncie 2008). There has been a significant rise in the use of custody for children in E&W and, although this trend is not paralleled in Northern Ireland, the demonisation of children and young people is also a problem here (McAlister *et al.* 2009), with many 'increasingly alienated from, and hostile to, both the police and adult members of their own communities' (Byrne and Jarman 2011, p.436).

The UN Convention on the Rights of the Child (CRC) Article 37b forbids the detention of children except as a last resort and for the shortest appropriate time, and also requires the provision of effective alternatives. The UN Standard Minimum Rules for the Administration of Juvenile Justice (Beijing Rules 1985) Article 17.1 states children should not be deprived of their liberty unless 'adjudicated of a serious act involving violence against another person or of persistence in committing other serious offences'. Yet at least one million children are incarcerated worldwide and, as Paulo Sérgio Pinheiro (2006, p.195), UN independent expert on violence against children, states, custodial detention is often used as 'a substitute to adequate care and protection systems'. Noting that the 'threshold' for depriving children of their liberty should be higher than for adults, the UN Special Rapporteur on Torture, Manfred Nowak (UNGA 2009, p.2), notes that 'too many children are still deprived of their liberty, in spite of the existence of clear norms at the international level'. Globally the majority of incarcerated children are in pre-trial detention, not convicted of any crime (Volz 2010), and the UN Committee on the Rights of the Child (UNCRC 2007, paragraph 80) observes that 'in many countries, children languish in pre-trial detention for months or even years, which constitutes a grave violation of Article 37b of CRC'. Article 37c of the CRC also expressly forbids the detention of children in adult institutions, yet this continues to happen in many jurisdictions including Northern Ireland.

Goldson (2009, p.92) observes that 'child prisoners are both inherently and structurally vulnerable', carrying with them existing vulnerabilities and then rendered more vulnerable through experiences of custody. Farrant (2001) reports (on E&W) that 90 per cent of incarcerated young people under the age of 21 have mental health problems, and the experience of prison, including overcrowding and lack of constructive activities, has a negative impact on their mental health. Ng *et al.* (2011) observe the negative impact of detention in adult prisons on children's mental health, and, on the whole, depriving children of their liberty has 'very negative consequences for the child's harmonious development and seriously hampers his/her reintegration in society' (UNCRC 2007, paragraph 11). As Hollingsworth (2008, p.241) notes, 'many children leaving custody are more vulnerable than before they were incarcerated'.

Scraton and McCulloch (2009) expose the processes of incarceration as operating on a continuum of violence. From the stigmatisation of being labelled an 'offender'; through degrading processes of reception; loss of autonomy over every-day decision-making; strip searching; routine lock-downs and use of isolation cells; physical restraint and use of force; subjection to institutional discipline and staff discretion; separation from friends, family and community – all of these contribute to damage and loss of sense of 'self'. Goldson (2009, p.94) highlights that practices such as searching and restraint 'frequently assume violent and harmful forms', and Lord Carlile (2006) recommends that handcuffs should not be used on children; physical interventions should be severely restricted and force never used to secure compliance. Lyon, Dennison and Wilson (2000) state that young people in custody are often keen to use the time constructively, but find themselves frustrated by petty discipline and lack of positive opportunities. Overall, prison is a 'dislocating experience, unconnected to their lives outside' (p.xi). Too often custodial staff are inadequately trained, coupled with a lack of appropriate supervision and accountability, and the small number of girls in custody are poorly provided for (Pinheiro 2006). For some children, the release sought from the pains of imprisonment culminates in death, and the UNCRC (2008) remains 'very concerned' about deaths and the prevalence of self-injury among children in custody. However, the stock response of the authorities to this situation is 'denial' and 'impunity' (Goldson 2009).

Children and the particular circumstances of Northern Ireland

In the context of Northern Ireland as a society in transition from violent conflict, children's vulnerabilities are increased. Over 3700 people have died and more than 40,000 have been injured during the conflict (Edwards and McGrattan 2010), a sizeable proportion of whom were children and young people (Smyth *et al.* 2004). Horgan and Kilkelly (2005, p.6) cite evidence that the conflict has had a 'traumatising effect on far larger numbers of children and young people than was formerly acknowledged'. The particular circumstances facing children in Northern Ireland include: 'legacy of conflict; segregation in housing, education, health and leisure services; very high levels of child poverty; low levels of family support services; inadequate provision of services for young people with particular needs; and the relationship between poverty, segregation and conflict' (Horgan and Kilkelly 2005, p.3). Children have experienced state and non-state violence including paramilitary punishment attacks, bombings, shootings, sectarianism, house-raids and exile and forced removal from home. Harland's (2011, p.429) recent research concludes that violence and 'violence-related issues' remain a 'normal part of marginalized young men's everyday lives and experiences', young men being drawn to and yet afraid of conflict. As Horgan (2011, p.464) warns, 'there is a real danger that the level of exclusion faced by such young people makes them prey to those – whether drug dealers or paramilitaries – who offer to give them a role in the community'. There is deep trauma at community level, and in the most deprived communities 'rising levels of emotional and psychological stress among children and young people, manifesting as anxiety, depression, deliberate self-harm and escalating suicide rates, are collateral damage following years of civil strife' (health professional, Kilkelly *et al.* 2004, p.112). Despite the extent of mental health needs and inter-generational trauma, mental health services are under-developed. McClelland (2006) notes 'major deficits' in child and adolescent mental health services and the 'high price' that society pays for this in terms of 'social disruption, education failure, ill health, anti-social behaviour, and hard cash' (p.79).

Muncie (2011, p.46) observes that 'the "troubled", dynamic and complex political context in Northern Ireland has had a unique effect on its youth justice system' with the unexpected consequence of providing a 'range of potentially progressive responses to youth crime' including restorative justice initiatives at both statutory and community level, and lower rates of youth detention than in England. Since the multi-party Belfast Agreement of 1998, which formalised the peace process and established a devolved power-sharing political administration, developments aimed at producing a human rights-centred criminal justice system have included independent reviews of policing, criminal justice, the prison system and youth justice, and establishment of a range of monitoring and accountability bodies. Despite many positive initiatives, the evidence from *Still in Our Care* and subsequent statutory and non-statutory reports suggests persistent breaches of rights regarding children's custodial detention.

Children's rights and custody in Northern Ireland

Northern Ireland has two custodial institutions for children: the Juvenile Justice Centre (JJC) run by the Youth Justice Agency and Hydebank Wood Young Offenders Centre, a Northern Ireland Prison Service establishment. Situated near Bangor, about 10 miles out of Belfast, the JJC (known as Woodlands) has accommodation for 48 boys and girls aged 10 to 17, remanded or sentenced by the courts under the Criminal Justice (Children) (Northern Ireland) Order 1998 (CJCO) or remanded under the Police and Criminal Evidence (Northern Ireland) Order 1989 (PACE). The central plank of the CJCO is the Juvenile Justice Centre Order (JJCO), for children aged 10 to 17, a determinate sentence of between six months and two years, half of which is spent in the JJC and half under supervision in the community. In recent years, no child under 12 has been detained in the JJC, and the average population of around 27 children (YJA 2010) are mostly boys aged 15 and 16. Woodlands comprises six house units, each with a social-work-trained house manager and staffed by care workers. It has a school, health centre and leisure facilities including a swimming pool. Despite the domestic-style environment, the JJC is a highly secure establishment.

Hydebank, situated on the outskirts of Belfast, is a medium to low security prison with capacity to accommodate up to 306 prisoners (including adult women). Northern Ireland's only women's prison is within the Hydebank complex, which creates a myriad of problems for boys and women. The Willow House unit has provision for up to 19 boys aged 15 to 17. The imprisonment of children alongside young adults aged up to 23 is in breach of CRC Article 37c. Due to legislative restrictions on the detention of 17-year-olds in the JJC, Hydebank is the primary place of detention for boys of this age. The CJCO provides for children as young as 15, deemed likely to injure themselves or others, to be remanded or committed to detention in a young offenders' centre. This results in the most vulnerable boys with the most complex needs being detained in Hydebank. Yet, serious deficiencies in children's care there have been identified by a succession of official and independent reports.

The Criminal Justice Inspection Northern Ireland (CJINI 2010a, p.36) found there was 'no routine provision for the treatment of mental health illness among the juveniles'. The Independent Monitoring Board (2010) reported on a punitive regime based on the routine use of solitary confinement. Children and young people told Include Youth (2009) about lengthy lock-ups, varying staff attitudes from helpful to abusive, fear of placement in the isolation cells, inadequate opportunities for education and training and reluctance to make complaints for fear of reprisals. The legacy of conflict was understood by the boys: 'Some twisted ones [prison officers] work here – they've been in with Provies [Provisional IRA] and all, used to high security, they're not used to working with 15 to 16-year-olds' (Include Youth 2009, p.7).

An independent review of the prison system (PRT 2011, pp.23–25) concludes that 'we do not believe that Hydebank is, or can ever be, an appropriate environment for children', particularly when compared with the JJC where review team members were 'impressed with the quality of care, the relaxed atmosphere, the social work approach and culture, and the wide range and quality of activities available'. However, the Hydebank regime is 'extremely poor' and 'entirely inappropriate' for children, and ironically the most 'difficult, damaged or needy children' may end up in the institution 'least able to cope with them'. There is a 'residual belief' among staff in Hydebank that 17-year-olds are 'not really children'.

On 4 May 2011, Samuel Carson (aged 19) and Frances McKeown (a young woman prisoner aged 23) were found dead in their cells in Hydebank, in separate and apparently unrelated incidents. Ligatures were removed from both cells. Their deaths underscored long-standing concerns about the care of troubled children and young people.

The analysis below focuses on the care of children in the JJC, where our primary research was focused. The fieldwork was carried out in 2006, prior to the centre's move to a new building on the same site and rebranding as 'Woodlands'. Evidence from recent inspection and other reports discussed below demonstrates that, despite improvements to the physical environment, many of the issues we identified as breaches of rights persist.

Contrary to the principle of custody as a last resort, most children in the JJC are on remand, some for relatively minor offences, and most of those remanded do not subsequently receive custodial sentences. As a member of JJC care staff (Convery and Moore 2006, p.31) explained:

> You could have a boy in because he's broke[n] windows and you could have a boy in because he's attempted murder. And that's a fault.

Figures from 2009/2010 show that of a total of 475 admissions to the JJC, 199 receptions were under PACE and 238 under pre-trial remand. Only 38 receptions were for committal (sentenced children). The high ratio of children detained for short periods under PACE or on remand limits the support which can take place. An inspection (SSI 2005, p.8) noted that:

> the psychologist and staff have found that often a young person on admission is ready and willing to discuss their offence and the impact it has had on the victim, but by the time the case comes to court this has often changed to resistance and denial.

Delays in the criminal justice system have also been identified as a serious problem, contributing to over-use of remand (CJINI 2010b).

Our research (Convery and Moore 2006) found an over-representation of care-experienced children (children who have been looked after outside of the parental home):

> He was in and out of the [children's home] consistently... He's in for nuisance offences... He has serious learning difficulties and there's a concern that this may lead to serious harm. (JJC care staff, Convery and Moore 2006, p.35)

> We had a boy who'd been in over 210 homes in 10 years... That was horrendous...and then you wonder why he offends? (JJC care staff, Convery and Moore 2006, p.35)

Recent reports confirm the continued over-use of pre-trial detention and over-representation of care-experienced children. The CJINI (2008, p.vii) reports that:

> Many of the children whom Inspectors met were neither serious nor persistent offenders. They were troubled children whose JJC placements often resulted from benign intent on the part of courts or police. When unsure about how to deal with them, they were placed in custody as much for their own safety as in response to their offending behaviour.

The Voice of Young People in Care, which represents care-experienced children in Northern Ireland, documents their frustrations at being criminalised for behaviour which would be dealt with differently within a family setting. Quotes from two care-experienced children are instructive:

> Children in care are targeted over every stupid incident that happens in their children's home compared to young people who live at home with their families.
>
> Too many young people in care have criminal records for stupid things because they're in a children's home. It's not fair. (VOYPIC 2011, p.28)

The significance of the state's failure to protect the rights of children in custody is evidenced in children's descriptions of their experiences of detention. During interviews for *Still in Our Care*, children reported feelings of fear, uncertainty, isolation, loneliness, frustration, anxiety and depression. The first days and nights in the JJC were anxiety-filled and care staff were agreed that 'all kids are scared… They all need reassurance, they're still kids.' The following comments from teenage boys in the JJC (Convery and Moore 2006, p.42) provide insight into the anxieties of being locked up for the first time:

> It was a bit scary because all I done was sat and stared at the ceiling until about two or three in the morning.
>
> When you're in your room…you can think about things. You can think about strange things so you can…like hanging yourself or something. Thought about it a few times.

Another boy explained, 'my mates told me, whenever you're inside it'll be easy. One of my mates told me all, but I just stayed in my cell and other young people were running around slabbering [talking] about what to do' (Convery and Moore 2006, p.42). Anger and self-blame were experienced; 'you would wake up angry some mornings. Angry at yourself for being here' (boy in JJC, Convery and Moore 2006, p.111).

Detention is a particularly isolating experience for girls who usually come to custody from looked-after care backgrounds, often distressed and with histories of abuse. Care staff commented on the particular vulnerability of girls, and boys revealed that girls' distress was an extra stress for them: 'some of the wee girls do your head in...they just cry. Everything they do' (boy in JJC, Convery and Moore 2006, p.65). Separation from family caused distress, and although regular visiting was facilitated, a small number of children refused visits, finding them too upsetting:

> I don't really like visits. Just do without them. Seen my ma and dad once, but they leave and you don't. I don't like when you're sitting here and they go. (Boy in JJC, Convery and Moore 2006, p.72)

International standards require appropriate training for staff working with children in custody (UN Rules for the Protection of Juveniles Deprived of their Liberty, part V). In the JJC, all six unit managers and 11 team leaders were social-work qualified and care staff had a range of lower-level qualifications (CJINI 2008). These levels of training are in contrast to those in Hydebank staffed predominantly by prison officers with very limited training in working with children, undoubtedly a significant factor in explaining the different ethos in the two establishments.

Daily life in the JJC was structured and busy. Children have a right to effective education (CRC Article 28), and at the JJC school a broad range of subjects were studied in small class groups. Many children had been out of education prior to admission but most were enthusiastic about their educational experience in custody:

> School in here is far better than the ones outside. There's less classes but less people are in the class, so you learn more. (Girl in JJC, Convery and Moore 2006, p.122)

> I'll be doing cartooning, art and design, maths, geography. There's so many classes I haven't done yet. I've done business

> studies and I've done swimming. I ended up swimming in here and I haven't swum for about three years. I was sitting around and I says, 'I'll try it'. I went and got in and all, and was swimming up and down the very best. I thought, 'I can't believe I've just done that'. (Boy in JJC, Convery and Moore 2006, p.121)

Despite the successes of the school, the high levels of short-term placements and unpredictability of pre-trial remand made it difficult for teachers to plan for children's needs. Staff liaised with education authorities, schools and alternative providers to try to ensure that children continued their education on release; however, this was often difficult as some children had been previously suspended or excluded from school, and appropriate community resources were not always available.

Children in custody have the right to appropriate health and mental health care (CRC Article 24; UN Rules Section H). Children in the JJC had access to a full-time on-site psychologist, in marked contrast to the lack of adolescent mental health provision in the community (Kilkelly *et al.* 2004). While children may engage with mental health services while in custody, legal considerations regarding pre-trial remand restrict the work which can take place and there is no guarantee that the child will continue the treatment on release, especially in the context of limited services. Care staff interviewed (Convery and Moore 2006, p.114) considered that specialist training was essential for dealing with a complex range of mental health issues: 'I would plead for more training and more specialised staff'; 'I think staff should have more training re dealing with young people with mental health problems: basic counselling course, body language, how to listen.' A 'snapshot' of children in the JJC on one day in November 2007 (CJINI 2010a) found that, of 30 children, 20 had a diagnosable mental disorder, 17 a history of self-harm and eight had previously attempted suicide. Fourteen of the children had a statement of special educational needs and indicated learning difficulties or disabilities.

Despite the emphasis on domesticity and 'normality', the JJC operated on a high-security basis, and regardless of risk assessment, children were subject to a high level of supervision. Some staff maintained that children who had experienced few boundaries in family or community welcomed this highly structured and secure regime. For others the lack of privacy and space proved claustrophobic:

> Staff have to watch you no matter where you turn. You can't open doors and you can't do anything, so you can't. [At the

> start] it was stressing, stressing so it was. (Boy in JJC, Convery and Moore 2006, p.58)

The significant emphasis on security was further evidenced by the routine handcuffing of children during transportation to and from the centre by a commercial security firm. The 'pat down' body search on admission, although leaving young people fully clothed, was distressing for some, not surprising given histories of abuse:

> I hate other men touching my body. I hate people touching my body...they touch you there [points to top of legs], search you and you feel like hitting them. (Boy in JJC, Convery and Moore 2006, p.40)

During the research for *Still in Our Care*, use of physical restraint emerged as an issue of concern. Although the figures for levels of restraint were reducing over time, it was still used on a regular basis and all of the young people interviewed had witnessed a restraint. The method employed, physical control in care (PCC), involved children being held but not brought to the ground. Staff worried about the technique's safety, while children found it degrading:

> It's not fair...it shouldn't take six people to hold a wee boy down. They got a shield and made his nose bleed. Bent his fingers back. It's supposed to calm you down, but it makes you more angry. (Boy in JJC, Convery and Moore 2006, p.89)

> When I first saw someone else getting restrained, I felt like helping the other wee lad instead of helping staff. This wee lad, a wee small thing, not even five foot and these men about six foot, and he was just getting jumped over...it looked like they nearly killed him; he couldn't breathe or nothing. He's going, 'I can't breathe, I can't breathe', and staff didn't listen to him. (Boy in JJC, Convery and Moore 2006, p.89)

JJC records documented each incident, giving examples of children being restrained in response to violence against staff or other children. However, the researchers also witnessed a child threatened with restraint for refusing to go to bed when staff refused his request for juice. Through continued use of crisis intervention training for all staff there has been a continued reduction, with recent figures showing that restraint was used on 58 occasions in 2009/2010 (a reduction from 172 in 2007/2008).

Staff and children mutually lacked conviction that the rehabilitation programs provided would prove effective, especially given the problems faced on release. The reality of the 'revolving door' is that many children returned to custody soon after release, often 'graduating' to Hydebank on turning 17 years. Children were returning to lives characterised by family difficulties, limited education and work opportunities, lack of mental health provision and communities suffering multiple deprivation. A 15-year-old boy spoke of losing his father and two friends through bereavement and witnessing paramilitary violence. Staff were understandably pessimistic about children's chances of staying out of the justice system:

> We're not sending them back to a nice loving family; we're sending them back to 10 mates who all steal cars every night and take joints every night. That peer pressure is massive. (JJC care staff, Convery and Moore 2006, p.99)

Conclusion

The experiences of custody for children in Northern Ireland demonstrate the state's failure to adequately protect children's rights in law, policy and practice. The CRC has not been incorporated into domestic law, nor is the principle of the primacy of the best interests of the child included within youth justice legislation. The low age of criminal responsibility (10 years) represents an ideology of criminalisation, holding children individually responsible for their actions, rather than realising the state's responsibility for meeting their needs. The detention of children along with adults in Hydebank remains an egregious breach of rights.

Research demonstrates the strong links between poverty, deprivation, learning difficulties and disabilities, mental health problems, abuse, and pathways to custody. In Northern Ireland, experiences of violence, conflict and sectarianism further compound children's marginalisation and exposure to risk of harm. Yet children are treated as having brought their situation upon themselves, their disadvantage punished through criminal justice responses (Jacobson *et al.* 2010). This is not to suggest that children have no individual agency and are simply passive victims of their circumstances, but to acknowledge the importance of the broader structural contexts on children's daily lives, which in Northern Ireland include high levels of social exclusion, sectarianism and violence (McAlister *et al.* 2009). Lack of transparency within the justice system, and prioritisation of other security-focused issues during the conflict, may underpin the lack of progress in addressing the rights-abuse of children in custody. However, this lack of progress also reflects the global tendency towards punitive measures and criminal justice responses which require that children take personal responsibility for their crimes (Muncie 2007). Garland (2001, pp.198–199) describes how incarceration is used to mask need and negate the need for effective state welfare:

> The sectors of the population effectively excluded from the worlds of work, welfare and family – typically young minority males – increasingly find themselves in prison or in jail, their social and economic exclusion effectively disguised by their criminal status. Today's reinvented prison is a ready-made penal solution to a new problem of social and economic exclusion.

The criminalisation of socially excluded children, and the prioritisation of responsibility over rights, negates pressure on state agencies to respond to children in conflict with the law by identifying and meeting their complex needs. Despite consistent research findings that custody is harmful, hugely expensive and relatively ineffective, state-sanctioned exclusion of some of the most vulnerable children in society prevails, with children selected for custody in Northern Ireland sharing many of the characteristics of incarcerated children worldwide.

Custody has been described as providing a 'short window of opportunity' by the Chief Inspector of Prisons (England and Wales), Nick Hardwick (HMCIP/YJB 2010, p.8). Research for *Still in Our Care* found positive aspects of the JJC regime, and subsequent inspections support this, for example regarding the provision of education, health care and the supportive approach of many professional staff. The tragedy is that appropriate levels of support are not available in the community.

The Youth Justice Agency and the Department of Justice celebrate Woodlands JJC as a 'centre of national and international excellence' (Youth Justice Agency website); however, the JJC's achievements must be seen within the totality of custodial arrangements for children in Northern Ireland. The Inspectorate's (CJINI 2008, p.3) comment is instructive that 'while Woodlands has a strong childcare ethos, it is fundamentally a custodial facility for children who are charged with criminal offences'. Further, children deemed to be persistent offenders, or at risk of self-harm or harm to others, may be placed or transferred to Hydebank, a wholly inappropriate facility for children. So long as the most vulnerable, damaged and sometimes dangerous children are sent to Hydebank then the youth justice system must be judged to have fallen short of meaningful rights-compliance.

The devolution of criminal justice offers an opportunity to develop rights-based and needs-led responses to children in conflict with the law. At the very least, the imprisonment of all children in the adult penal system should be abolished, custody restricted to a last resort and the age of criminal responsibility be increased. In place of criminal justice responses, adequate child-centred provision within communities should be made available with the capacity to address the complex and multiple needs of children in conflict with the law, and through this laying the foundation for a rights-based response to some of our most vulnerable children.

Acknowledgements

Dr Una Convery and Dr Linda Moore would like to thank the Northern Ireland Human Rights Commission for its support; they wish it to be known, however, that the conclusions expressed herein are their own and should not be attributed to the Commission or any other organisation. They wish to thank all the children, staff and managers in the Juvenile Justice Centre and the Youth Justice Agency for their participation in the research.

References

Byrne, J. and Jarman, N. (2011) 'Ten years after Patten: Young people and policing in Northern Ireland.' *Youth and Society 43*, 2, 433–452.

Carlile, Lord (2006) *An Independent Inquiry into the Use of Physical Restraint, Solitary Confinement and Forcible Strip Searching of Children in Prisons, Secure Training Centres and Local Authority Secure Children's Homes.* London: The Howard League for Penal Reform.

Convery, U. and Moore, L. (2006) *Still in Our Care: Protecting Children's Rights in Custody in Northern Ireland.* Belfast: NIHRC.

Criminal Justice Inspection Northern Ireland (CJINI) (2008) *Inspection of Woodlands Juvenile Justice Centre, May 2008.* Belfast: CJINI.

Criminal Justice Inspection Northern Ireland (CJINI) (2010a) *Not a Marginal Issue: Mental Health and the Criminal Justice System in Northern Ireland.* Belfast: CJINI.

Criminal Justice Inspection Northern Ireland (CJINI) (2010b) *Avoidable Delay, June 2010.* Belfast: CJINI.

Edwards, A. and McGrattan, C. (2010) *The Northern Ireland Conflict: A Beginner's Guide.* Oxford: OneWorld Publications.

Farrant, F. (2001) *Troubled Inside: Responding to the Mental Health Needs of Children and Young People in Prison.* London: Prison Reform Trust.

Garland, D. (2001) *The Culture of Control: Crime and Social Order in Contemporary Society*. Chicago: University of Chicago Press.
Goldson, B. (2009) 'Child Incarceration: Institutional Abuse, the Violent State and the Politics of Impunity.' In P. Scraton and J. McCulloch (eds) *The Violence of Incarceration*. Oxon: Routledge.
Harland, K. (2011) 'Violent youth culture in Northern Ireland: Young men, violence and the challenges of peacebuilding.' *Youth and Society 43*, 2, 414–432.
Her Majesty's Chief Inspector of Prisons (England and Wales)/Youth Justice Board (HMCIP/YJB) (2010) *Children and Young People in Custody 2009–2010: An Analysis of 15–18 Year Olds in Prison*. London: HMCIP.
Hollingsworth, K. (2008) 'Protecting rights at the margins of youth justice in England and Wales: Intensive fostering, custody and leaving custody.' *Youth Justice 8*, 3, 229–244.
Horgan, G. (2011) 'The making of an outsider: Growing up in poverty in Northern Ireland.' *Youth and Society 43*, 2, 453–467.
Horgan, G. and Kilkelly, U. (2005) *Protecting Children and Young People's Rights in the Bill of Rights for Northern Ireland*. Belfast: Save the Children and Children's Law Centre.
Include Youth (2009) *Young People's Response to the Independent Monitoring Board Annual Report: Hydebank Wood 2007/8*. Belfast: Include Youth.
Independent Monitoring Board (IMB) (2010) *Hydebank Wood Prison and Young Offenders Centre Independent Monitoring Board's Annual Report for 2009/10*. Belfast: IMB.
Jacobson, J., Bhardwa, B., Gyateng, T., Hunter, G. and Hough, M. (2010) *Punishing Disadvantage: A Profile of Children in Custody*. London: Prison Reform Trust.
Kilkelly, U., Kilpatrick, R., Lundy, L., Moore, L. *et al.* (2004) *Children's Rights in Northern Ireland*. Belfast: Northern Ireland Commissioner for Children and Young People.
Lyon, J., Dennison, C. and Wilson, A. (2000) *'Tell Them So They Listen': Focus Group Research for Young People in Custody*. Home Office Research Study No. 201. London: Home Office.
McAlister, S., Scraton, P. and Haydon, D. (2009) *Childhood in Transition: Children and Young People Experiencing Marginalisation in Northern Ireland*. Belfast: Queens University of Belfast/Save the Children/Prince's Trust.
McClelland, R. (2006) *The Bamford Review of Mental Health and Learning Disability (Northern Ireland): A Vision of a Comprehensive Child and Adolescent Mental Health Service*. Belfast: DHSSPSNI.
Muncie, J. (2007) 'The responsibilised child.' *Safer Society: The Journal of Crime Reduction and Community Safety 32*, 2–4.
Muncie, J. (2008) 'The punitive turn in juvenile justice: Cultures of control and rights compliance in Western Europe and the USA.' *Youth Justice 8*, 2, 107–121.
Muncie, J. (2011) 'Illusions of difference: Comparative youth justice in the devolved United Kingdom.' *British Journal of Criminology 51*, 1, 40–57.
Ng, I., Shen, X., Sim, H., Sarri, R., Stoffregen, E. and Shook, J. (2011) 'Incarcerating juveniles in adult prisons as a factor in depression.' *Criminal Behaviour and Mental Health 21*, 1, 21–34.
Pinheiro, P.S. (2006) *World Report on Violence Against Children*. Geneva: United Nations Secretary-General.
Prison Review Team (PRT) (2011) *Review of the Northern Ireland Prison Service: Conditions, Management and Oversight of All Prisons. Interim Report, February 2011*. Belfast: PRT.

Scraton, P. (2004) 'Streets of terror: Marginalization, criminalization and authoritarian renewal.' *Social Justice 31*, 1, 130–158.
Scraton, P. and McCulloch, J. (eds) (2009) *The Violence of Incarceration.* Oxon: Routledge.
Smyth, M., Fay, M.T., Brough, E. and Hamilton, J. (2004) *The Impact of Political Conflict on Children in Northern Ireland.* Belfast: Institute for Conflict Research.
Social Services Inspectorate (SSI) (2005) *Unannounced Inspection Visit to the Juvenile Justice Centre (Northern Ireland) Friday 12 August 2005 Between 8.30 am and 7 pm.* Belfast: DHSS.
United Nations Committee on the Rights of the Child (UNCRC) (2007) *Forty-fourth Session: General Comment No. 10 (2007) Children's Rights in Juvenile Justice.* CRC/C/GC/10. 25 April 2007.
United Nations Committee on the Rights of the Child (UNCRC) (2008) *Forty-ninth Session: Consideration of Reports Submitted by States Parties under Article 44 of the Convention. Concluding Observations: United Kingdom of Great Britain and Northern Ireland.* CRC/C/GBR/CO/4. 3 October 2008.
United Nations General Assembly (UNGA) (2009) *Interim Report of the Special Rapporteur on Torture and Other Cruel, Inhuman or Degrading Treatment or Punishment,* UN Reference A/64/215.
United Nations Standard Minimum Rules for the Administration of Juvenile Justice (The Beijing Rules) adopted by General Assembly Resolution 40/33 of 29 November 1985.
Voice of Young People in Care (VOYPIC) (2011) *'Because I'm a Kid…and I'm in Care': VOYPIC's Response to the Department of Justice Review of the Youth Justice System, March 2011.* Belfast: VOYPIC.
Volz, A. (2010) *Stop the Violence! The Overuse of Pre-trial Detention or the Need to Reform Juvenile Justice Systems. Review of Evidence.* Geneva: Defence for Children International.
Youth Justice Agency (YJA) (2010) *Annual Report 2009–2010.* Belfast: YJA.

PART II

Indigenous and Non-national Children and Vulnerability

Chapter 7

The Victimisation of Indigenous Children

Suzanne Oliver

A 2010 report of the Australian Institute of Criminology titled *Indigenous Perpetrators of Violence: Prevalence and Risk Factors for Offending* (Wundersitz 2010) noted that there is growing evidence in the general literature that children who experience or witness violence have a greater risk of becoming perpetrators of violence. The report comments that one of the explanations for this link between childhood violence and subsequent offending may be that there is an effect on the child's cognitive and emotional development and that the child may grow up believing that violence is normal (Wundersitz 2010). Moreover, as is underlined by the theory of learned helplessness, children maltreated or exposed to violence during childhood may be more likely to be victimised as adults. They may model or learn victim behaviours as opposed to behaviours associated with the perpetration of maltreatment (Renner and Slack 2004).

With those views in mind, findings that there are extremely high levels of neglect and abuse of Aboriginal children would suggest that there is an increased risk of intergenerational offending and victimisation in communities in which high levels of violence and child abuse exist (*Little Children are Sacred Report*, Northern Territory Government Australia 2007; *Growing Them Strong, Together*, Bath and Roseby 2010).

This chapter considers the background to the Emergency Response strategy of the Federal Government of Australia to a report in 2007 on the abuse of children in the Northern Territory and the elements of the strategy that address dysfunction and may bring about a reduction in an offender/victim cycle. It considers how effective these changes have been in terms of child protection and decreasing offending and whether gaps will remain.

The *Little Children are Sacred Report*

On 30 April 2007 the *Little Children are Sacred Report* (*Ampe Akelyernemane Meke Mekarle*) was released in the Northern Territory of Australia. The report chronicled widespread violence and sexual abuse of both women and children in the Northern Territory. The report was the outcome of a board of inquiry established by the Northern Territory Government in 2006 to inquire into concerns about the protection of Aboriginal children from sexual abuse.

Amongst its findings, the board concluded that the combined effects of poor health, alcohol and drug abuse, unemployment, gambling, pornography, poor education and housing, and a general loss of identity and control had contributed to violence and to sexual abuse in many forms in Aboriginal communities across the Northern Territory of Australia.

The findings did not come as a surprise to those involved in the justice or health and welfare systems in the Northern Territory. As the report noted, the view expressed in a submission from the Crimes Victims Advisory Committee to the inquiry was mirrored by most individuals and organisations that participated in the inquiry. The Committee wrote:

> No member of CVAC doubts that sexual abuse of aboriginal children is common, widespread and grossly underreported. None of us claims a precise grasp of the extent of the abuse, but the working experiences of the committee members – whose backgrounds include police work, victim's support, health services and legal practice in criminal law and crimes compensation – uniformly persuade us that abuse is rife. (*Little Children are Sacred Report* 2007, p.17)

A finding that there was extensive violence and dysfunction in aboriginal communities together with a high level of sexual abuse of children was not unique to the Northern Territory. Earlier inquiries into child sex offences in other jurisdictions had produced similar findings (Aboriginal Child Sexual Assault Taskforce 2006; Gordon Hallahan and Henry 2002; Victorian Law Reform Commission 2004). However, the response of the Federal Government to these reports was nowhere near as dramatic nor immediate as it was to the *Little Children are Sacred Report* (2007).

Within weeks, the Federal Government in power at the time announced – and began to implement – a package of reforms within the Northern Territory. The response was said to reflect the first recommendation of the *Little Children are Sacred Report* which asked that 'Aboriginal child sexual abuse in the Northern Territory be designated as an issue of urgent national significance by both the Australian and Northern Territory governments' (*Little Children are Sacred Report* 2007, p.22). However, it may be noted that whilst the first recommendation did indeed call for Aboriginal child sexual abuse to be designated as an issue of urgent national significance by both the Australian and Northern Territory Governments, the governments were actually called upon to 'immediately establish a collaborative partnership with a Memorandum of Understanding to specifically address the protection of Aboriginal children from sexual abuse' (*Little Children are Sacred Report* 2007, p.22).

The response of the Federal Government at the time was however a unilateral one, implemented by the *Northern Territory National Emergency Response Act 2007* and associated legislation passed by the Australian Parliament in August 2007 (referred to here as the NTER).[1] Although said to be 'an emergency response', the action was almost immediately and has since been more commonly referred to as the 'Federal Intervention', characterising the unilateral nature of the federal response, even though the unilateral character of the strategy has since moved to a joint approach under *Closing the Gap* in the Northern Territory National Partnership Agreement. *Closing the Gap* in the Northern Territory provides for a continuation of the 2007 core measures of the NTER. *Closing the Gap* is a national strategy agreed through and monitored by the Council of Australian Governments (COAG) in March 2008. It aims to reduce Indigenous disadvantage by achieving targets focused on health, housing, early childhood, education, economic participation, and remote service delivery (*Closing the Gap*, Department of FaHCSIA 2011).

The emergency response ('Federal Intervention')

The NTER created a package of changes to welfare provision, law enforcement, land tenure and other measures. The operation of the *Racial Discrimination Act 1975* was suspended in order to achieve these changes, as was the application of anti-discrimination law in the Northern Territory.

Section 5 of the *Northern Territory National Emergency Response Act 2007* states the object of the Act is 'to improve the well-being of certain communities in the Northern Territory'. The Act has a sunset provision that unless amended will mean that that the majority of measures enacted (other than Parts 4, 6 and 8 and Schedule 1 to the Act)[2] cease to have effect at the end of the period of five years beginning on the day after the day on which the Act received the Royal Assent.

In order to appreciate the nature of the Federal Intervention and the degree of difficulty in the implementation of its measures, it is necessary to understand the demographics and geography of the Northern Territory. The Northern Territory is geographically large (over 1,349,129 square kilometres/520,902 square miles). A comparison with Italy (116,000 square miles), France (212,935 square miles) or Germany (138,000 square miles) gives perspective to the vast land areas; however, the population is small and sparse, with only 221,100 inhabitants (based on the national census, 2006). The majority of the population live in the main or regional cities and townships. Darwin and surrounds has a population of around 121,000 and Alice Springs approximately 26,000, representing around 1 per cent of the Australian population as a whole. The number of people identified as being of Aboriginal and/or Torres Strait Islander origin in the 2006 Census as a whole was 455,028, representing 2.3 per cent of the total Australian population. In stark contrast, in the Northern Territory around 31 per cent of the Northern Territory population is identified as Aboriginal. Many Aboriginal communities are remote, and for considerable parts of the year, particularly in the Northern and Gulf region, are inaccessible by road. Even when roads are open there are communities that can only ever be accessed by four-wheel-drive vehicles. Communities vary in size and are constituted by many different language groups. In addition, there are 'town camps' associated with the major cities and towns in which many people have resided for some generations. The Alice Springs town camps in particular have attracted considerable attention because of the high level of social problems associated with them, which so far appear to have continued largely unabated by the intervention strategies.

The application of the NTER reforms was achieved by the designation of vast areas of land within the Northern Territory as 'prescribed areas'. Prescribed areas include all land held under the *Aboriginal Land Rights Act (Northern Territory) 1976*, all Aboriginal community living areas and all Aboriginal town camps. In total this is an area of over 600,000 sq km, approximately half the total land mass of the Territory.

More than 500 Aboriginal communities are situated in prescribed areas, with the result that the NTER applies to around 70 per cent of Aboriginal people in the Northern Territory. In terms of numbers, this is around 45,500 people.

One of the more controversial aspects of the NTER was the removal of the operation of the *Racial Discrimination Act 1975* (RDA). The operation of the RDA in the Northern Territory was suspended in order to be able to implement a system of income management that was a key component of the NTER package. Income management did not reduce the amount of welfare payments received by individuals, but rather 'quarantined' half of those payments onto a 'Basics Card', which could then be utilised on goods and services such as food, housing, clothing, education and health care. It could not be used to purchase alcohol, tobacco, pornography, gambling products or gambling services with income-managed money. It is this measure that has largely consumed a public debate around civil rights impacted by the NTER measures against the need for extraordinary measures to address disadvantage.

Although initially income management applied only to Aboriginal people living in prescribed areas, the measure has been expanded to roll out from 1 July 2010 to particular categories of non-indigenous welfare benefit recipients. The system now applies in the Northern Territory to people in receipt of specified welfare payments (Youth Allowance, Job Seeking Allowance, Special Benefit or Parenting Payment (Partnered or Single)) and to people referred for income management by child protection authorities or a Centrelink (Social Security) social worker. Other welfare recipients may volunteer for income management. Applications for exemption from the system can be made. There is an evaluation being undertaken with a view to the eventual roll out of income management on a national basis.

Offending in the Northern Territory

The courts in the Northern Territory are constantly faced with cases that illustrate the degree of dysfunction both in communities and in urban areas of the Territory and create a high risk for violent offending including sexual violence.

The establishment of the inquiry that resulted in the *Little Children are Sacred Report* had its impetus in an interview given by the Crown Counsel in Alice Springs on Australian Broadcasting Corporation

(ABC) national television, in which she highlighted an appalling degree of violence against women and children that showed no sign of abatement. In particular she highlighted two cases in which very small children had been the victim of sexual assaults, one a baby and the other a toddler of two years.

In the first case (*Inkamala v The Queen* [2006] NTCCA 8), the 18-year-old offender was found guilty of sexual intercourse without consent of a baby of seven months. The baby had been removed from the house in which she had been sleeping with another adult female. Earlier in the night the offender had been thwarted in that attempt by a female occupant. The baby's mother was away from the house drinking. The baby was digitally penetrated by the offender with such force that she required surgery. Her injuries were life-threatening due to loss of blood. The offender had been found by another male from the house on the verandah with the baby who was naked from the waist down. He persuaded the offender to give the baby to him and took her back inside where he placed her between himself and his girlfriend and they went to sleep. In the morning the mother, who was still drunk, returned, found the baby dressed her in clothes with no nappy and left again. An older female asked her daughter to get the baby after the mother left and she noticed the bleeding from the vaginal cavity. The baby was taken to the clinic and then hospital.

At 15 years the offender had attempted to rape a woman on a street in Alice Springs. In early childhood he was exposed to domestic violence, sniffed petrol from a young age and used alcohol and other drugs. He had attempted self-harm in custody. His cognitive capacity was in the borderline range, possibly as a result of petrol sniffing and alcohol abuse.

In *The Queen v Riley* ([2006] NTCCA 10) the victim was two years old. Her mother had left her with her mother (the child's grandmother) and gone into town. The offender, who had been drinking, woke and saw the child playing. He carried her away into the bush where she was digitally penetrated both vaginally and anally. He attempted penile penetration but was unable to achieve a full erection. He took the child, now naked, back to the tin sheds at Dump Camp. His father told him to take the child home but he handed the child to his father and went off to sleep. The father simply carried the child to her house, put her on a mattress outside and left her there. The next day, the child's mother noticed blood on her vagina and down her leg when showering her. She required surgery to repair her injuries.

The offender was 26 years old. He spoke English well, but his literacy and numeracy skills were almost non-existent. He had an extensive history of alcohol and cannabis abuse and was a long-term petrol sniffer. His cognitive capacity appeared to be in the normal range although 'hindered by alcohol abuse' ([2006] NTCCA 10 at [41]).

The cases are themselves shocking in terms of appalling attacks on completely defenceless infants. But what is further apparent is the level of neglect by the mothers of the infants who left their children in vulnerable circumstances to go and drink, and the lack of concern displayed by other adults where it might be expected that immediate alarm would be raised. This, taken together with what is apparent about the offenders' personal circumstances, including, as the reports indicate, no empathy or understanding of the seriousness of their actions, illustrates why children will remain at risk unless and until the risk factors for violent offending are addressed and an intergenerational cycle of abuse brought to an end.

Intergenerational trauma and dysfunction

The *Little Children are Sacred Report* noted that a theme presented by both men and women during consultations was that it was young people who were often sexually abusing other children. The inquiry concluded that this was due to the combination of intergenerational trauma, the breakdown of cultural restraints and the fact that many of these children (if not all) had themselves been directly abused or exposed to inappropriate sexual activity (through exposure to pornography or observing others in both consensual and non-consensual sexual acts).

The inquiry concluded that child sexual abuse has led to intergenerational cycles of offending such that victims had subsequently become offenders and, in turn, were creating a further generation of victims and offenders.

Two recent cases in the Youth Justice Court demonstrate how intergenerational abuse and dysfunction may create an offender/victim cycle.

Case of 'F'

In an unreported matter before the author, the defendant F pleaded guilty to a charge of being a male who had sexual intercourse (mutual masturbation and oral sex) with another male who was not an adult when the defendant was around 14–15 years of age and the victim, his cousin, around eight years of age. Although only one instance was identified, it was clear that there had been sexual encounters over some period. Both lived in one of the Alice Springs town camps. The town camps exist on special purpose leases and are home to around 1800 Aboriginal families, some of whom come in and out of remote desert communities and some who have lived there for generations. They and other children were constantly exposed to alcohol abuse and violence and were victims of sexual abuse by adults. Both thought that their own behaviour with each other was 'normal'. F could identify at least three adults who had sexually assaulted him from the age of five years to around 15–16 years and four other juveniles with whom he engaged in sexual acts he (and they) thought 'was normal and happened all the time'.

Around 15, F's parents gave up a lifestyle of drinking and the family moved interstate. Later F moved to Darwin and began training for the Ministry. He attended a seminar on sexual offending at which someone asked whether sexual acts between adolescents would be sexual offences and, when the presenter said they were, F, now 24 years old, was shocked. After talking to his minister he reported himself to the police. His cousin gave a statement and he too had not considered that his sexual conduct with F was anything other than 'normal'.

This account may lead to a conclusion that almost every child in that community was either subject to sexual abuse by an adult/s and/or engaged in sexualised behaviour with other children, either consensual or coercive. It is true that F had grown into adulthood without offending, but this might be attributed to his parents' reform and relocation whilst he was still relatively young. The fate of the other children who grew up in that town camp is unknown.

A further case that illustrates how growing up in a community where resort to weapons to settle disputes, assaults that are sparked by 'jealousy' and domestic violence are a commonplace may establish a belief that such conduct is the acceptable social norm.

Case of 'J'

J was 13 years old when he struck his 15-year-old girlfriend with a machete after being told she had been seeing other boys. The tendons in her hand were severed and she was evacuated for medical treatment. In J's family, violence was a constant feature of the relationship between his parents. His mother and older male siblings had committed recent violent offences and his father had an extensive history of violence. Offences involving the use of weapons, primarily machetes and spears, to either physically harm or to threaten and intimidate people, are a constant feature of J's small community, often committed in the public view of children. Alcohol is generally not a factor. J did not report any personal physical abuse and appeared as a bright and healthy teenager who had never been in trouble. His school principal described him as being capable of becoming a leader of his people. His mother and aunt wanted him to go to boarding school to remove him from the environment which they identified and agreed had harmed his upbringing. Orders were made for Corrections' supervision and for arrangements to be made for boarding school, but his father undermined compliance. Before action could be taken, J attacked the same girl, having been told by a brother that she was again seeing other boys. She was stabbed twice in the back with a small knife and fortuitously did not suffer a serious or life-threatening injury. The case illustrates how a young person may develop a distorted view of acceptable responses from an environment where violence of a particular kind appears as a social norm.

The case examples given are illustrative of multiple factors that are associated with the high levels of Indigenous violent offending and the victimisation of children. In his sentencing remarks in *Taylor et al. v The Queen*,[3] Riley J (as he then was) referred to many of the factors that influence the high rate of violent and sexual offending. These factors, and others such as the relationship of health and disability to violent offending, are also extensively discussed in the 2010 Australian Institute of Criminology Report *Risk Factors for Indigenous Violent Offending* (AIC Reports Research and Public Policy Series 105). Many of these factors are ones that are targeted under the NTER and subsequent *Closing the Gap* strategies.

Disadvantaged living standards arising out of a chronic lack of housing

The Strategic Indigenous Housing and Infrastructure Program (SIHIP) is one of the major initiatives of the Australian and Northern Territory Governments coming out of the NTER. The program aims to deliver 750 new houses, 250 rebuilds of existing houses and 2500 refurbishments out of a budget of around $700 m. Few communities could be said to have sufficient and adequate housing. Already crowded circumstances are often compounded by relatives coming from outstations or to town camps from bush communities. They may expect to be accommodated for lengthy periods of time. A housing situation which is ordinarily bad is made worse. Three bedroom houses may have 20 people living in them. The health and hygiene issues raised by such cramped circumstances are obvious. There are significant impacts on children living in these conditions. They may not be able to get sufficient rest for good school attendance and they may be exposed to pornography and sexual conduct between adults from a very early age. They may witness or be involved in family violence.

Improving the living circumstances of people in communities and town camps is clearly a critical step in providing greater protection for children and advancing their ability to obtain a good education. Although considerable criticism has been aimed at SIHIP, principally at the time taken to start construction and at the level of refurbishments, it is in its scope a program of immense complexity, given the number of communities and town camps involved across a vast geographical area. As at April 2011 work was complete in 31 communities and under way in 17 more, with 232 new houses built and 161 more under construction. A total of 1381 rebuilds and refurbishments were complete. Of significance, 300 Indigenous people (or 32%) were employed on the projects, well exceeding the target for Indigenous employment that had been set at 20 per cent (Department of Housing, Local Government and Regional Services in conjunction with the Australian Government 2011).

Alcohol and substance abuse

The *Little Children are Sacred Report* noted that the level of consumption of alcohol in the NT was extraordinary. In a 2009 Report of the South Australian Centre for Economic Studies (Harms from and Costs of Alcohol Consumption in the Northern Territory, Final Report, September 2009) the rates of alcohol consumption in the Northern Territory were significantly higher than the rest of Australia, with 17 per cent of the adult population drinking at a risky or high risk rate in terms of long-term harm and 18 per cent of the population consuming alcohol at a rate that risks short-term harm on at least one occasion each month. The report states: 'Aboriginal consumption in 2004/2005 is estimated to have been 16.9 litres and non-aboriginal consumption 14.5 litres. If the Northern Territory were a country then it would have the second highest rate of per capita alcohol consumption in the world' (2009, p.i).

It is a common misconception that Aboriginal people as a group consume alcohol in greater proportion to non-indigenous people. The proportion of Aboriginal persons who consume alcohol is no different from non-indigenous persons.

The NTER made illegal the possession or consumption of alcohol in prescribed areas. However, many prescribed areas already had liquor management plans in place or had been long-term 'dry' communities under declaration powers in the *Liquor Act*. It is not the case that there was no control on alcohol prior to the Federal Intervention; indeed a number of liquor management plans had been very effective in reducing problems in some communities. The liquor management plan at Groote Eylandt, for example, has reduced violent offending by around 30 per cent. The overlay of the prescribed areas ban has not produced any significant change in alcohol consumption. A deficiency of the prescribed area or 'dry community' approach is that people can simply consume alcohol on the boundary and when intoxicated enter the community and cause havoc.

The Northern Territory Government has recently passed legislation which enables the police to issue a ban on the purchase, possession or consumption of alcohol by someone taken into protective custody because of their level of intoxication three times in three months, by certain drink drivers or where alcohol is involved in domestic violence incidents. A tribunal is established with power to mandate treatment for alcohol and drug abuse as part of the *Enough is Enough* Alcohol Reform Package (*Alcohol Reform Prevention of Alcohol-Related Crime and Substance Misuse Act 2011*).

There are also problems of substance abuse. Volatile substance use (petrol, paint, glue) has not been eliminated, although the rollout of the unleaded fuel 'Opal' has brought about a significant reduction under the Petrol Sniffing Strategy (Department of FaHCSIA 2008).

Anecdotally, an outcome of tighter alcohol management may be an increase in cannabis use. The high cost of cannabis in communities ($AUS100/g) creates an attractive source of income for suppliers and removes large amounts of money from communities. As with alcohol misuse, there is an emerging picture of child neglect and violence. In court, many defendants admit, and even more victims assert, that cannabis had been smoked at the time of the (violent) offence or that violence occurred as a result of withdrawal effects.

Even if the measures now in place and about to be embarked on by the NT Government result in a dramatic lowering of the alcohol consumption rates, the cumulative and ongoing effects of dysfunction caused by decades of alcohol abuse will take much greater time to address. An emerging issue will be the number of people with foetal alcohol spectrum disorders and their management in the community.

Pornographic material

An issue raised in the *Little Children are Sacred Report* was that children were being exposed to pornographic material that may be causing early sexualised behaviour and have adverse consequences. In *Taylor* (unreported sentencing remarks, Northern Territory Supreme Court, 19 December 2007) during one of the assaults on the 13-year-old boy, a pornographic DVD was being watched. The NTER has made illegal the possession of pornographic material within prescribed areas. This is material that may be lawfully possessed elsewhere in Australia. There is no empirical evidence that exposure to pornographic material increases the risk of sexual offending. The measure is largely reported to have caused immense shame and embarrassment to Aboriginal people in prescribed areas and, although the restriction remains, the signs used to advise of entry to a prescribed area are no longer required to carry the warning about possession of pornographic material being an offence.

Other factors

There are other matters that may affect the offender/victim cycle that are not directly related to the dysfunctional issues mentioned above but which are likely to have a direct and sustained effect. They are not susceptible to change by regulation and greater resources. These matters require attitudinal change, and unless and until community members are willing to accept that change, the ability of the criminal justice system to deal with offenders and protect victims will remain difficult.

Pressure not to disclose or give evidence

The *Little Children are Sacred Report* recognised that certain aspects of Aboriginal culture discourage some Aboriginal people from disclosing abuse, in particular obligations under the kinship system. This problem is by no means confined to sexual offending against children. It is a strong and ever present feature across the Northern Territory in cases of violence against women. There is enormous pressure on victims not to report violence or, if reported, not to give evidence in court. There may be retribution when a child or young woman reports, and they may not be supported by the mother or other female relatives. This may be due partly to intimidation, partly to reluctance for the offender to be imprisoned, and partly due to kinship obligations.

Downgrading of charges

Downgrading of charges is common because of the reluctance or inability of the victim to give evidence. The difficulty generally faced by victims of sexual offences in giving evidence in court is well recognised. Legislatures, including the Northern Territory, have put in place laws that seek to minimise the trauma by allowing for recorded statements of children to be given as their evidence in chief and for all victims' evidence to be given outside the court room by closed circuit television. Even with those measures Aboriginal victims face additional difficulties because of language barriers and because their culture generally embraces a conservative attitude to discussing sexual matters, particularly in mixed company. Shyness and embarrassment and the language barrier are all factors in the reluctance to give evidence or the failure to give evidence in accordance with earlier statements. Many Aboriginal people in the Northern Territory only speak limited English as a second, third or fourth language. Some will have no English language. There is not easy access to interpreters. Interpreters themselves sometimes face difficulties in assisting in court because people may see them as 'siding' with the victim. Even with an interpreter the difference in cultural concepts may be a barrier to a person being able to fully explain what has happened. The prosecuting authorities face the dilemma of either accepting a plea to a downgraded charge or risking that, because of the factors mentioned above, of not being able to prove the more serious offence.

Ostracism of the victim and family

In *Taylor* it was not the offenders but the young victim who was unable to return to the community. This is not an uncommon feature of offences of this nature. The victim is blamed for the trouble that has been brought to the offender and his family and the victim is forced to live elsewhere. The dislocation may have a profound effect on the young person's continuing development. It may prevent the victim from undergoing the appropriate ceremonies to progress to adulthood. The sentencing remarks illustrate this attitude and the dislocation caused to the victim:

> The community and identified members of the community are willing to support each of the prisoners on their return to the

> community. I have borne these matters in mind in determining how I am best to deal with the individual prisoners.
>
> The position of the victim within the community is not so clear. While some members of the community consider it will be safe for him to return, that is not the view of all. The family of the victim is sufficiently concerned to only contemplate returning to an outstation. Regrettably, that will keep the victim away from his community and from the schooling available within that community. His dislocation is set to continue. (Sentencing Remarks, Northern Territory Supreme Court 2007)

Has the Federal Intervention improved child protection?

As has been noted earlier in this chapter, the need for greater child protection is not an issue confined to the Northern Territory.

Indeed, although the NTER commenced in 2007, by December 2009 a further Board of Inquiry was established in the Northern Territory following adverse publicity and public concern after a number of tragic deaths of children and public complaints about the adequacy of child protection. Clearly none of the NTER measures have had an immediate impact on levels of abuse and neglect or child protection. The child protection system was found to be in crisis, described as a 'tsunami of need'. The report *Growing Them Strong, Together* (Board of Inquiry into the Child Protection System in the Northern Territory Report, Bath and Roseby 2010) made 147 recommendations for the improvement of the child protection system in the Northern Territory, ranking the urgency of their implementation from urgent (immediate to less than six months), semi-urgent (within 18 months) to important but not urgent (within two to three years).

In brief summary, and without listing all the findings, the system was found to be in crisis because of insufficient resources to deal with the number of interventions required and the issues integral to case management, a backlog of uninvestigated children at risk (870 children identified as at risk receiving no support or investigation and the likelihood of many unreported cases), a failure to monitor children in out-of-home care or provide appropriate support to foster parents, workforce issues around recruitment and retention of staff and a lack of support and therapeutic services for protected young people in the Northern Territory, who were at risk of adverse mental health outcomes, relationship difficulties and becoming clients of the youth and adult justice systems.

Encouragingly the first progress report (Department of Children and Families, Northern Territory Government 2011) on the urgent recommendations indicates that substantial gains have been made, including that the backlog of investigations has been reduced from 870 to 17 as at 14 April 2011.

Conclusion

This chapter has canvassed a range – though by no means all – of the factors that have been identified as creating a risk for child abuse and/or offending. Others such as physical and mental health, education and employment, and access to services to address trauma are all equally relevant and interrelated to disadvantaged living standards and substance abuse, both of which have created and contributed to an environment of violence, abuse and neglect in some communities.

It is not suggested that all communities have these problems or that all families within communities have these problems. However, the prevalence is high, and these issues are ones which have been sought to be addressed by the Intervention and the *Closing the Gap* strategies.

The *Little Children are Sacred Report* found that there were no quick fixes. The best that could be hoped for was improvement over a 15-year period (which they described as an Aboriginal generation, shorter indeed than most would regard a generation within non-Aboriginal families, but reasonably accurate taking into account the young age of many mothers and fathers in Aboriginal communities and shortened life expectancy). It is significant to note that it was 'improvement' that was hoped for, not elimination.

If anyone anticipated that the strategies of the Federal Intervention would bring immediate change to the circumstances of children and young persons in the Northern Territory, they would have been both extraordinarily optimistic and totally divorced from reality. If nothing else, the NTER has focused public attention on the dire circumstances of many Aboriginal people and their children, and caused awareness of the need for assistance across governments by a sustained and practical approach. The continuation of many of those strategies under the *Closing the Gap* initiative shows progress in addressing disadvantaged living standards and other risk factors and, as a consequence, the potential to overcome the chronic victim/offender cycle, but the time has been short and sustained effort is required.

Endnotes

1. Northern Territory National Emergency Response Act 2007; Social Security and Other Legislation Amendment (Welfare Payment Reform) Act 2007; Families, Community Services and Indigenous Affairs and Other Legislation Amendment (Northern Territory National Emergency Reponse and Other Measures) Act 2007.
2. Part 4 and Schedule 1 to the Act deal with the granting of five-year leases and the acquisition of an estate in fee simple in land. Part 6 deals with bail and sentencing and removes the ability of a court in the Northern Territory to take into account any form of customary law or cultural practice as either an aggravating or mitigating circumstance of the offence when sentencing, when considering a grant of bail. Part 8 contains miscellaneous provisions including the suspension of the *Racial Discrimination Act* and a declaration that the measures in the Act are special measures for the purposes of the *Racial Discrimination Act.*
3. NT Supreme Court, 19 December 2007. This case too attracted wide attention. Five offenders (two adults and three youths) pleaded guilty to various charges of sexual intercourse with an 11-year-old boy and acts of gross indecency or indecent conduct on him. The offending had come to light when during treatment for a painful and swollen elbow the young boy was found to have gonorrhoea. None of the offenders were ultimately identified as being responsible for transmission of the disease to the young boy. The offences occurred on separate days in 2006. The offenders were aged 19, 18, 16, 15 and 13 at the date of offending.

References

Aboriginal Child Sexual Assault Taskforce (2006) *Breaking the Silence, Creating the Future: Addressing Child Sexual Assault in Aboriginal Communities in NSW.* Sydney: NSW Attorney General's Department.

Bath, H. and Roseby, R. (2010) *Growing Them Strong, Together: Promoting the Safety and Wellbeing of the Northern Territory's Children.* Report of the Board of Inquiry into the Child Protection System in the Northern Territory. Available at www.childprotectioninquiry.nt.gov.au/__data/assets/pdf_file/0011/49781/CPI_Cover_Volume_1.pdf, accessed on 28 October 2011.

Department of Children and Families, Northern Territory Government (2011) *Child Protection Reform Progress Report Volume 1.* Available at www.childrenandfamilies.nt.gov.au/ChildProtectionSystemReform/Reform_Progress_Reports/index.aspx, accessed on 28 October 2011.

Department of Families, Housing, Community Services and Indigenous Affairs (FaHCSIA) (2008) *Petrol Sniffing Strategy: Review of the First Phase.* Available at www.fahcsia.gov.au/sa/indigenous/pubs/evaluation/petrolsniffing/Documents/default.htm, accessed on 28 October 2011.

Department of Families, Housing, Community Services and Indigenous Affairs (FaHCSIA) (2011) *Closing the Gap – Prime Minister's Report 2011: The Third Report on Closing the Gap in Indigenous Disadvantage.* Available at www.fahcsia.gov.au/about/news/2011/Pages/2011_ctg_pm_report.aspx, accessed on 28 October 2011.

Department of Housing, Local Government and Regional Services in conjunction with the Australian Government (2011) *Strategic Indigenous Housing and Infrastructure Program (SIHIP).* Available at www.dhlgrs.nt.gov.au/housing/remotehousing/sihip, accessed on 28 October 2011.

Gordon, S., Hallahan, K. and Henry, D. (2002) *Putting the Picture Together: Inquiry into Response by Government Agencies to Complaints of Family Violence and Child Abuse in Aboriginal Communities.* Western Australia: Department of Premier and Cabinet.

Northern Territory Government Australia (2007) *Ampe Akelyernemane Meke Mekarle: Little Children are Sacred.* Inquiry into the Protection of Children from Sexual Abuse. Available at www.inquirysaac.nt.gov.au/pdf/bipacsa_final_report.pdf, accessed on 28 October 2011.

Renner, L.M. and Slack, K.S. (2004) *Intimate Partner Violence and Child Maltreatment: Understanding Co-occurrence and Intergenerational Connections.* Madison, WI: Madison Institute for Research on Poverty.

South Australian Centre for Economic Studies (2009) *Harms from and Costs of Alcohol Consumption in the Northern Territory, Final Report.* Adelaide: The South Australian Centre for Economic Studies Centre.

Victorian Law Reform Commission (2004) *Sexual Offences: Final Report.* Melbourne: Victorian Law Reform Commission.

Wundersitz, J. (2010) *Indigenous Perpetrators of Violence: Prevalence and Risk Factors for Offending.* Reports Research and Public Policy Series 105. Canberra: Australian Institute of Criminology.

Chapter 8

Non-national Children and Vulnerability

The Child Protection Context

Goos Cardol

Introduction

UNICEF describes Dutch children as doing very well; in fact, most children in the Netherlands are perceived as very happy (UNICEF 2007). UNICEF examined the dimensions of child wellbeing: material wellbeing, health and safety, educational wellbeing, family and peer relationships, behaviour and risks, and subjective wellbeing. These six dimensions, when applied to children in the Netherlands, reveal how well they are faring (Rispens, Hermanns and Meeus 1996; van der Laan 2008; Weijers 2008).

The majority of children in the Netherlands (85%) require negligible support negotiating the stages of child development (Hermanns 2009). What support they do need comes largely from family and relatives. The 15 per cent of children who do need outside help in order to prevent more serious problems will predominantly be assisted by minimal intervention; for some children this may include however a protection order or perhaps an out of home placement for a short period of time. Very few of these children will need intensive treatment, but some will need ongoing statutory intervention. It is youth care and child protection organisations which provide this external and statutory support when indicated. There is considerable confidence in these approaches, and it is felt that, on the whole, whilst treatment agencies and interventions are helpful, what the youth care and child protection organisations put in place for children supports them to resolve both developmental and family problems.

This degree of confidence, however, is challenged by recent societal shifts and emerging problems. Poverty among certain groups is increasing, the political landscape is changing, and children in the Netherlands now include those seeking asylum as well those who have come with their families as migrants. These children do not always enjoy the same rights and protection as other children in the Netherlands, and their marginalisation is across the board: in access to education, health care, social services and to child protection services.

This chapter examines the way the Child Protection Board addresses the concerns raised by these groups of children by describing who comprises these new groups of children and how the system of youth care in the Netherlands is organised. Particular attention is given to non-national children (and non-nationals in the Netherlands are often described as alien) and the operation of the Child Protection Board in terms of its interaction with these new groups of children and the problems they bring with them. It is debated whether or not the Child Protection Board adequately meets the needs of these children and, if they do not, what constitutes a better and more effective response.

Vulnerable children

Over the past few decades the Netherlands has been confronted by significant social changes and it is now a multicultural country, although some sections of the population try to deny this fact. As a result of these changes, the Netherlands has become less tolerant of 'incomers', especially refugees and asylum seekers, in part because these new arrivals bring with them different habits, unfamiliar religions and differing values and standards, and they are unfamiliar with Dutch norms and mores, which all contributes to feelings of uncertainty amongst the Dutch community (Cardol 2006). These new citizens have become part of the society: they marry, have children, develop lives, travel, attend school, work and come in conflict with the law. Their children as they grow may also have pedagogical needs and developmental problems which their parents cannot meet; problems which are often influenced by culture, trauma, war experiences, the loss of family members, separation from loved ones, and/or the consequences of victimisation from trafficking.

The children and families who have come to the Netherlands seeking asylum form the largest group of newcomers who have come to the attention of the Child Protection Board. In addition, problems presented by Roma children remain an ongoing concern for the Board; so too are girls affected by female genital mutilation or honour-related violence. Whilst some details about these groups of children will be provided in this chapter, most attention is given to children referred to as 'minor aliens', children residing illegally in the Netherlands and who have become clients of the Child Protection Board.

Over recent decades, children described as 'minor aliens' have arrived in the Netherlands, sometimes with their family, but also as separated minors, very often as trafficked children, all searching for work, the opportunity to study and to have a better life. They have fled their home countries because of natural disasters, war, internal conflicts and poor economic conditions. These children sometimes seek asylum or they reside with relatives without requesting legal status, thus remaining in the Netherlands illegally. Of the children who seek legal status, a significant number leave the reception centres before a decision is made about their status; they are forced to work in restaurants and sweatshops, as houseboys or in prostitution. Some will travel to another European country to live with family or relatives. Those who remain in the Netherlands are there illegally.

The numbers of children in this situation arriving in the Netherlands varies from year to year. The largest group of separated children arrived in 2000, when 6705 children sought asylum. The number decreased in 2006, when just 410 children requested legal status. However, in 2009, 1039 children were seeking asylum (Immigration and Naturalisation Services 2010).

It is difficult to establish the exact number of minors residing in the Netherlands illegally, although it is estimated to be 30,000 children. In the Bijlmer, the most multicultural district in Amsterdam, it is estimated around 10,000 people living there are illegal immigrants; how many of these are children is not known. It is estimated that in Amsterdam and in Rotterdam 1 to 3 per cent of all children are illegal immigrants (Defence for Children 2006). Their situation is vulnerable, they are less likely to use youth care services than others (Hermanns 2009). They are not entitled to work, or access to housing, health care or social security. They are children who very often have limited school opportunities, have come from rural areas, with little experience of the world, and often feel lost and alienated in their new country. If they are unaccompanied minors they are even more vulnerable, living in the Netherlands without their parents and extended family. The lack of opportunities they have in the Netherlands, with lack of access to basic rights as just described, means they are not provided with the adequate standard of living they should have, as outlined in Article 27 of the UN Convention on the Rights of the Child.[1]

As well as this group of children, who are very diverse, are children from the new EU member states who wish to settle in the Netherlands. Roma children are part of this group, who come with their families to the Netherlands to earn money. Numbers of these children will live alone, but more often they will live with relatives. They are vulnerable children because of the uncertainty which surrounds them in terms of their care, their housing and their engagement with education. The precise numbers of children in this group are unknown; very few come to the attention of the Child Protection Board, which would deal with only about ten Roma children each year. Most Roma children will avoid contact with the Child Protection Board and with youth care organisations.

Dutch society is particularly confronted by female genital mutilation, by forced marriages for children, and by cultural or honour-related violence. Young girls continue to be circumcised in the Netherlands, although it is expressly forbidden under Dutch law, or they are sent abroad for this procedure; on occasion they do not return after a holiday in their country of origin. Victims of female genital mutilation are amongst the illegal immigrants who flee to the Netherlands, but feature also in migrant groups who have settled in Holland from the 1970s. Figures indicate that at least 50 girls resident in the Netherlands are circumcised every year (Raad voor de Volksgezondheid en Zorg 2005). The Child Protection Board has had referred to it at least six cases over recent years, but it is assumed there is a significant unknown number of cases. Most of the cases are not dealt with by the Child Protection Board.

Female genital mutilation, forced marriage and honour-related violence have become very political issues, and this has raised awareness amongst child care workers and others who have looked to interventions and prevention methods, although their effectiveness is still to be realised.

Recently, UNICEF and Defence for Children published for the first time a report on the state of children's rights in the Netherlands (Defence for Children 2008; UNICEF 2007). They reported the findings of a panel of five experts who examined the way in which the Netherlands responds to matters such as child abuse, child healthcare, care and welfare provision for children and young people, and how young people who come into contact with the criminal justice system are managed (Defence for Children 2008). In three of these fields (minor aliens, youth care and juvenile justice) the Netherlands has been judged to be failing in some way. The criticism mainly targets the country's treatment of children who are living in the Netherlands illegally. As this is the largest group of newcomers, this group will be the focus of this chapter, but first I will briefly describe the position, tasks and procedures of the Child Protection Board.

Child Protection Board

The mission of the Child Protection Board is to ensure that children's rights are protected, most particularly when the development of a child is jeopardised and/or their parents are incapable of providing stability of care and the means for them to achieve their childhood development (Cardol and Theunissen 2007; Klein 2007). The mission of the Child Protection Board is derived from the provisions in the UN Convention on the Rights of the Child which require nation states to take responsibility for a child when there is a threat to their health and human development and their parents are failing to provide for this. This responsibility has been confirmed by the European Court of Human Rights (ECHR), which stresses the state must take positive action in such circumstances and act without undue delay (Forder 2007). The Child Protection Board, as part of the Ministry of Justice, is required to meet these obligations.

The Child Protection Board is however not the first point of contact when there is concern about a child's care and their development being jeopardised. Dutch legislation has established the Youth Care Office as the first contact when concerns about a child are raised; concerns may range from issues about child development and educational problems to concerns about child abuse and neglect, physical assault and poor parenting. Any concerned person can contact the Youth Care Office about these problems and Youth Care attempts to put in place voluntary measures for assistance where necessary. If Youth Care is unable to solve the problem together with the parents and/or the child and the development of the child is still in danger, then the Child Protection Board is notified by the Youth Care Office.

The Child Protection Board then conducts an inquiry in order to seek a solution that is in the best interests of the child. Three outcomes are possible as a result of the inquiry. *First,* the parents are seen to be able to resolve their difficulties without assistance. *Second,* the parents can manage their responsibilities but need voluntary assistance. *Third,* the children's judge is requested to impose a child protection order, which puts in place compulsory interventions in the family, and parents will be required to work with authorities to improve the care of their children. Currently, there are 40,000 children on child protection orders in the Netherlands, out of a total of 3.5 million children. This is the highest number of children on child protection orders since the end of the Second World War. The Child Protection Board's methods and procedures are laid down in a Quality Standard (Kwaliteitskader); these are directives of the Ministry of Justice and define how to conduct an inquiry, which information is to be included in a report and what parents and families can expect from the Child Protection Board. The framework for dealing with non-resident and illegal children is outlined in the next section.

Non-resident and illegal status children and the Child Protection Board

As a state organisation, an important directive to the Child Protection Board is the political view that the development of any new childcare policy for 'minor aliens' will not lead to a higher influx of such children as refugees to the Netherlands. Another directive is that any new policy is not to involve greater expense than that currently allocated. Yet at the same time the Child Protection Board is required to guarantee children's rights as embodied in the CRC and in national legislation. These competing political directions create limits for child protection agencies, raise questions about the nature of their role and who they serve, and forces them to be creative in how they respond to the needs of this group of children.

The challenge for the Child Protection Board is whether or not the standards that have been put in place to deal with children and their families are sufficient or whether they should be changed. Should non-resident and illegal status children be treated as aliens or simply as children? In this context it is important to know how child protection organisations meet the needs of these children when they become clients of Dutch child protection organisations. Does the Youth Care Office have the legal knowledge it needs in order to adequately respond to these children? It is central to child welfare responses to children in the Netherlands, although it may not be formally noted, that agencies are to respond to children's needs as early as possible, before their developmental problems escalate. So it is important that youth care organisations act quickly without waiting until there are new policies developed around working with children residing illegally in the Netherlands – 'minor aliens'.

Until recently, there was little formal policy for responding to the needs of non-resident children, residing in the Netherlands illegally, to discourage an influx of children from this group into the country. It was government policy to decrease the number of such children from entering the Netherlands. The reality however was that these children were in the Netherlands and youth care organisations did need to take action when they were notified about child maltreatment concerns. Childcare workers sought knowledge and information about how to respond to these children. Child protection workers were very aware of the political constraints on them and on how these children should be managed. They found it difficult to know what they should do and were mindful that they could be overruled by politicians in this politically sensitive area. The only guideline child protection workers had in this regard, although this was not universally known, was that a child protection order could be imposed on any child within the borders of the Netherlands, irrespective of their legal status. However, there was negligible policy developed for these children because they were perceived as aliens, rather than as children, in the eyes of the government.

Child protection workers are left to respond to children perceived as 'minor aliens', without adequate formal policy and without enough knowledge about the needs of these children and what are effective responses. They have little guidance about what they are permitted to do and what is possible for these children; for example, can such children be placed with a foster family, or a child without formal documents (birth certificate, residence documents, etc.) attend school, or have access to psychological services?

The legislation known as the Right to Public Provisions (Koppelingswet) explicitly states that an individual has to be in the Netherlands legally; if not, they are not entitled to provisions (www.rechtspraak.nl). However, exceptions can be made for children with respect to health care, education and legal assistance. Children living in the Netherlands without legal resident status are allowed to attend school (until they reach the age of 18 years or finish their education which they commenced prior to turning 18); however, on a day-to-day basis, this can be difficult to achieve. Schools may not accept a child's attendance if these children do not have residence status. Schools are often not aware of the fact as to whether or not they will be compensated equally for enrolling resident children and children without the necessary documents. It is often difficult to provide children who have attended school, but have no formal documentation and uncertain legal status, the usual diploma received when completing school, because the child is not registered in public records. This creates difficulties for the child, who may wish to go on to a traineeship, but has no working permit. These limitations stand in the way of these children having a right to education.

As well as the Right to Public Provisions legislation there is the Youth Care Act which allows non-resident children to have access to youth care services (voluntary individual and family support).[2] However, there are some differences in the nature of access to services when compared with children who are legal citizens. Non-resident children can receive assistance for only six months instead of the usual 12 months, as these children's situations may change very quickly (with respect to a change of housing or school); it is possible however to seek a six-month extension. Youth Care support terminates when the child turns 18 years. An important objective is that the support offered is not to assist parents, but to provide for the children, which is not a problem with children who are not in this category. There is ambivalence about placing non-resident children in foster families; it is understood that the child might become attached to their foster parents and, in terms of Article 8 of the ECHR, this becomes an obstacle to remove the child from the country (Breen 2002). It is only when there appear to be no other options that placement in a foster family becomes a last resort to help the child. This ambivalence infringes the principle of continuity, enshrined as vitally important for the development of children; it also is not observant of the principles of the CRC. It is understood that the more changes for children in their housing and schooling, the more obstacles they experience as they grow up, and the more risks there are for them in terms of healthy development.

Discussion

Identity is multi-layered, although government policy constrains it to whether or not an individual has the correct form of documentation that can grant them legal residence in the Netherlands. Amartya Sen (2006), the Indian Nobel Prize winning economist, addresses the multi-faceted nature of identity. Whilst a child living in the Netherlands might not have legal status, s/he might also be, for example, a citizen of Burundi with South African ancestors and Chinese genes. S/he may also be good at computer games, be highly intelligent, enjoy watching television, be good at percussion, have sleeping problems and bad teeth, and be an orphan as well as a teenager. Yet for years Dutch policy has targeted this group of children as 'illegal' aliens; the policy is that they are not permitted to be in the Netherlands and thus have no rights as citizens. Sen (2006) outlines the hierarchy that there is in the construction of identities. A child must have the capacity for optimal human development which allows them to develop their core identity. The development of this identity is fundamental and of paramount importance in terms of developing other identities. If the child's development is thwarted or harmed this has a major impact on the child, with consequent negative effects for the child as they grow older, as well as a negative impact on their capacity to participate in society.

Two major themes derive from this which challenge the Child Protection Board when dealing with children described as 'minor aliens', children residing in the Netherlands illegally. The first challenge is grounded in the legal standard needed for requesting a child protection order. The second challenge arises when a child is removed from their parents' care in order to persuade the parent to leave the country.

Article 1:254 in the Civil Code legislation states that a child protection order may be imposed if there is a threat to the moral or physical development of the child. These are the most common grounds on which a child protection order is made in the Netherlands. The legal standards by which this harm to a child is likely to occur or has occurred is flexible in its interpretation. This flexibility means that individual solutions can be achieved for each child and their family; however, this very flexibility can create uncertainty for parents and children (Bruning 2001). The main aim of such an order is to provide help for the child and family when voluntary measures do not work. The object of the order is to restore relationships between the parents and their child so the family can function without statutory intervention.

The broad interpretation allowed by the legal standard required to achieve a child protection order must focus however on the social, moral, emotional and/or physical development of the child. Whether or not the child protection concerns are to do with the child themselves or with their parents is not relevant. Where there is parental drug abuse, domestic violence, poverty, mental illness, parental inability to care for their child or help them grow and develop, parental cognitive problems or parental problems in dealing with authority, all are reasons why a child protection order can be imposed, whenever voluntary measures have not led to sufficient change or they are not appropriate. Child protection orders can be made even when there is likelihood of a threat to the development of the child but it is clear there are concerns held for the child.

A child protection order can be made for any child on Dutch territory, so the residence status of the child is not important. However, it is problematic imposing a protection order for children without legal resident status. Child protection orders in the Netherlands focus attention on the child only, and measures needed to assist them are also thus focused. The orders are not intended to provide supports for parents and the orders do not extend beyond the child's 18 years.

The measures put in place by child protection orders do not focus on parental material problems which may affect the development of the child. This is considered quite problematic, most particularly for children who are residing in the Netherlands illegally and often lack continuity in their life. They are without a stable home, often move around, and may have little continuity in school attendance. Families often have marginal or irregular income, and struggle to provide children with food and clothing, as well as toys, a quiet space to study and opportunities for leisure. The families often hide away from the community because they fear expulsion. As a result these children do not receive, for example, medical help when they need it, until problems are serious, for all the reasons just stated. They are children whose material needs are poorly met, which is detrimental to their individual development (Cardol 2005). They are children already vulnerable because of their previous life experiences, and when they are separated from their families and living alone even more vulnerable. They have to work to earn a living, although most of them fear the police and being caught, and this has major consequences for school attendance, as well as any time for leisure activity. They are also dealing with the trauma of loss, separation, war and natural disaster experienced in their country of origin as well as the pressure to earn money in order to support their family.

Where a child has no parents available, or their parents cannot provide for their basic needs, the state is obliged to do so, according to the CRC. In Article 6.2 of the CRC the state and its agencies are required to ensure to the maximum extent possible the survival and development of the child. Article 6 is one of the four most important articles in the CRC. Together with Article 2 (non-discrimination), Article 3 (best interest of the child) and Article 12 (right to be heard), these articles are the umbrella articles of the CRC, and derogation from these is not easily allowed, leaving the state and its agencies with little room for deviation.

The rights laid down in Article 27 of the CRC elaborate on the general principle of Article 6: the principle that development is important for children and this has to be secured. Article 27 emphasises the obligation for state parties to recognise the right of every child to enjoy a standard of living that is adequate for the child's physical, mental, spiritual, moral and social development. Parents are ultimately responsible for this, but the Article also refers to caregivers who are not the child's parent. The parent or caregiver has to secure, within their abilities and financial capacities, the conditions of living necessary for the child's development. This obligation for parents was not a new obligation in Dutch law, because Article 1:245 of the Civil Code already stated that parents are responsible for taking care of their children.

The UN Committee on the Rights of the Child that supervises the implementation of, and compliance with, the provisions of the Convention on the Rights of the Child interprets the development of children as a holistic concept: the child's development goes further than solely preparing the child for adulthood. It also includes the creation of conditions for the child's current life. Food and water are basic physical needs for all children; Maslow reminds us that physical needs are basic human needs in his typology of human motivation (Maslow 1981). Basic needs are not limited to physical needs but to other elementary needs such as shelter and clothing; the importance of these is highlighted by children who, in the absence of shelter, risk becoming victims of sexual exploitation and abuse as well as the risk of child labour.

If parents cannot meet these basic needs of their children then state parties are obliged to fulfil their responsibility as *parens patriae* and protect the child when the parents fail in this primary responsibility, for whatever reason. The state has to meet this obligation by taking appropriate measures to assist parents or caregivers to meet these responsibilities either by facilitating services or by their direct provision. The state is obliged to provide material assistance and support programs, particularly with regard to housing, when the child has these needs.

This obligation is interpreted in a restrictive way in the Netherlands. Material problems may lead to a protection order, but only when there are developmental problems as well. However, this approach fails to fit with the needs of children increasingly referred to the Child Protection Board. Children's rights appear to be not being served as they ought, and needs to be taken up as a concern by the Youth Care Office, children's judges and politicians. The restrictive interpretation of the legal basis for a protection order is in conflict with international standards; there is a need for a shift in political thinking and provision for a wider interpretation of child protection.

Another major challenge arises from the separation of parents from their children. In order to compel parents residing in the Netherlands illegally and who could not be expelled, it had been practice until recently to separate them from their child. The parent was detained and the child was brought into custody and placed in a foster family or in residential care. In this way the immigration services tried to 'motivate' parents to take action and leave the country.

Alternatively, when internal legal procedures are exhausted and parents and children have to leave the country, they can stay at a reception centre for a maximum period of 12 weeks in order to facilitate their departure. However, when expulsion is not possible because the parent will not cooperate or it is impossible to arrange documents, the immigration services may require the parent and the child to leave the reception centre and live on the streets. However, since the child's rights are at stake if they have to live on the streets, the Child Protection Board is requested to place the child in residential care or with a foster family. This will be intended to be for only a short period; the aim is that ultimately the whole family will leave the country.

Whilst the immigration services implemented this practice seemingly without discussion, child lobby organisations have been highly critical of this practice. For the Child Protection Board, which is part of the Ministry of Justice – also responsible for immigration services – this has created a significant dilemma. What has happened is that the Child Protection Board acts as it thinks is proper, even if the Ministry of Justice acts differently. It is generally understood that, from a child's perspective, the separation of parents and children is harmful and detrimental for their development when parents are generally capable parents and there are no concerns about the parent–child relationship. In cases of parents and children who are illegal residents, separation may cause even more harm as parents and children may depend strongly on each other and 'only have each other'.

Recently several innovative legal decisions have forced this policy to be revised, after Defence for Children International Netherlands (DCI), UNICEF Netherlands and some other organisations brought this situation to the European Committee of Social Rights. It was argued that sending children out to live on the streets because they do not have a residence permit constitutes a violation of the CRC and of the European Social Charter (Defence for Children vs the Netherlands 2008). The DCI sued the Netherlands government because this violated

Article 31 of the European Social Charter (the right to housing).[3] The Committee concluded on 27 October 2009:

> ...the right to shelter is, according to the Committee, closely connected to the right of life and is crucial for the respect of every person's human dignity... Children would adversely be affected by a denial of the right to shelter... Eviction from shelter should be banned as it would place the persons concerned, particularly children, in a situation of extreme helplessness which is contrary to the respect for their human dignity. (Defence for Children vs the Netherlands 2008)

On the basis of the above, the Committee concluded that state parties are required, under Article 31.2 of the Revised Charter, to provide adequate shelter to children unlawfully present in their territory for as long as they are in their jurisdiction. Any other solution contradicts respect for human dignity and fails to take due account of the particularly vulnerable situation of children.

Following this decision, an application was lodged at the Court of Appeal in The Hague, where the court was asked to decide if terminating the stay at the asylum centre of an Angolan woman and her three children was legal and not in conflict with the law, as this was the intention of the Ministry of Justice (www.rechtspraak.nl). The Minister of Justice argued that the state has the right to decide who may enter and reside in the Netherlands and who is granted residency permits. The Angolan mother would not cooperate in leaving the Netherlands and therefore the Minister argued entitlement to end her stay. This would mean the mother and her children would live on the streets. As this would infringe children's rights, the Minister requested that the Child Protection Board place the children in a foster home or in residential care, in order to respect the children's rights.

However, the Child Protection Board stated that separation of mother and children was not in the best interests of the children. Moreover, placement would only be an option if the children's judge imposed a protection order to provide shelter for the children (see the previous discussion above), so long as the mother did not disappear with her children before this ministerial decision could be executed and before the Youth Care Office acted on the decision.

The court took a firm decision. The right to family life is an important right, and given this fundamental right the Minister was not allowed to separate the mother from her children in order to force them to leave the country. The state had to provide shelter for the mother and children until another solution could be remedied. Although this decision was good news from the perspective of children's rights, the Minister decided to appeal this decision in the Supreme Court. As yet this has not been decided by the Supreme Court. However, the Minister has agreed to not separate children from their parents in order to persuade illegal adults to leave the country until the Supreme Court gives its decision.

Conclusion

What urgently needs to change in order to improve the situation of children residing in the Netherlands illegally is a change of political attitude. Children's rights must be taken seriously, and there needs to be a less defensive and a more courageous approach to their recognition. The child's development must always be paramount whatever is the legal status of the child. Separation of children from their parents, without proper cause, cannot be an option.

Moreover there needs to be an urgent review of existing policies on child protection matters in terms of observing children's rights. Do existing policies do what they have to do for all children in the Netherlands? What this chapter demonstrates is that current policy does not protect children who are illegal residents in a proper way; changes are necessary as Dutch society has become a multicultural society. There needs to be a shift in thinking about the legal basis of a child protection order to address not only when psychological problems occur, but also when basic needs are lacking. Article 27 of the CRC requires that an adequate standard of living be provided for all children. Housing is one of the basic needs. The need for these changes needs to be taken up and recognised, not only by the Child Protection Board, but also by children's judges, youth care organisations and politicians. This is the only way to guarantee children who are illegal residents living in the Netherlands their safe and healthy development.

Endnotes

1. Convention on the Rights of the Child, United Nations, November 1989 (Resolution 44/25). In force in the Netherlands March 1995.
2. Youth Care Act 2005, TK 2002–2003, 28 168.
3. European Social Charter, 18 October 1961, Torino, Italy (Trb. 1963, 90; Trb. 1962, 3).

References

Breen, C. (2002) *The Standard of the Best Interests of the Child.* The Hague/London/New York: Martinus Nijhoff Publishers.

Bruning, M.R. (2001) *Rechtvaardiging van kinderbescherming.* Amsterdam: Kluwer Law.

Cardol, G. (2005) *Ontheemd, Vreemd en Minderjarig.* Tilburg: Wolf Legal Publishers.

Cardol, G. (2006) 'In de schaduw van de samenleving.' *Journaal Vreemdelingenrecht 5*, 4, 255–266.

Cardol, G. and Theunissen, W. (2007) *Het Kind: Bijzonder Belangrijk.* Amsterdam: SWP Uitgevers.

Court of Appeal, The Hague, 11 January 2011, www.rechtspraak.nl, LJN BO9924.

Defence for Children (2006) *Jeugdzorg Voor 'Illegale' Kinderen.* Amsterdam: Defence for Children. Available at www.illegaalkind.nl.

Defence for Children (2008) *Jaarbericht Kinderen 2008.* The Hague/Amsterdam: Defence for Children/UNICEF Netherlands, www.defenceforchildren.nl/jaarbericht.

Defence for Children vs the Netherlands, 4 February 2008, Complaint 47/2008. See: www.coe.int, decision European Committee of Social Rights, 20 October 2009.

Forder, C. (2007) 'Child Protection in Accordance with Human Rights and Children's Rights.' In S. Meuwese, S. Detrick and S. Jansen (2006) *100 Years of Child Protection.* Tilburg: Wolf Legal Publishers.

Hermanns, J. (2009) *Het Opvoeden Verleerd.* Amsterdam: Vossiuspers.

Immigration and Naturalisation Services (2010) www.ind.nl

Klein, H. (2007) 'Participation of Ethnic Parents by the Child Protection Board.' In S. Meuwese, S. Detrick and S. Jansen (2006) *100 Years of Child Protection.* Tilburg: Wolf Legal Publishers.

Maslow, A.H. (1981) *Motivatie en Persoonlijkheid.* Rotterdam: Lemniscaat. (Original work published 1954.)

Raad voor de Volksgezondheid en Zorg (2005) *Bestrijding Vrouwelijke Genitale Verminking.* Rijswijk: Quantes.

Rispens, J., Hermanns, J. and Meeus, W. (1996) *Opvoeden in Nederland.* Assen: Uitgeverij van Gorcum.

Sen, A. (2006) *Identity and Violence.* London: W.W. Norton.

UNICEF (2007) *Child Poverty in Perspective: An Overview of Child Well-being in Rich Countries.* Florence: UNICEF.

van der Laan, P. (2008) 'De meeste jongeren zijn niet crimineel.' *Jeugdbeleid 2*, 1, 75–85.

Weijers, I. (2008) 'Het gaat niet slecht met de Nederlandse jeugd.' *Justitiele Verkenningen 34*, 8, 38–48.

Chapter 9

Mana Tamariki, Takahi Tamariki – Māori Child Pride, Māori Child Abuse

Rawiri Taonui

Introduction

Māori are experiencing a four-decade cultural renaissance marred by several horrific Māori child homicides. Each new incident raises the question of whether that flowering of culture is making a difference. Debate has raged around causes and solutions. Led by columnist and former Mayor of Whanganui, Michael Laws, some non-Māori commentators assert the violence derives from inadequate Māori parenting, and the warlike and backward nature of Māori society (Laws 2009a, 2009b; 2010). This view has sympathy in a wider non-Māori audience that perceives cultural icons such as the haka (war dances) as evidence of a culture preoccupied with violence (TV3 NZ 2005). Most Māori commentators believe the violence stems from colonisation and argue that the media exaggerates Māori child abuse. While that view has substance, Māori rates of abuse are disproportionately high. This chapter examines: how much worse Māori child homicide is than for non-Māori; media reporting; pre-European Māori parenting; the impact of colonisation, postcolonial assimilation, cultural alienation, urbanisation and intergenerational poverty on Māori child abuse; the contribution of the renaissance; systemic impediments to progress; and the place of Māori culture.

Colonisation

Māori are the indigenous people of New Zealand whose Austronesian ancestors migrated through Oceania, Micronesia, Melanesia and Polynesia, arriving in New Zealand about 1000 years ago (Howe 2006). Britain colonised New Zealand for its resources, signing the Treaty of Waitangi with Māori in 1840, after which Māori were subjected to war, confiscation and forced sale of land. Between 1840 and 2000 Māori lost 96 per cent (63.4 million acres) of their land (New Zealand History Online 2009). During the wars colonial cavalry murdered Māori boys aged eight to ten years at Handleys Shed; bounties were paid for the heads of Māori, Apartheid-type laws passed and detention without trial applied in Taranaki (Simpson 1979); surrendering Māori were shot dead at Rangiaowhia (Cowan 1922); there were scorched earth campaigns and summary killings of prisoners and non-combatants at Kōpani, Onepoto and Ngātapa in the Urewera Forest (Waitangi Tribunal 2009, 2010); and Auckland Māori were expelled, interned or forced to wear coloured armbands (Sorrenson 1959). Demographic decimation by disease, dispossession, disenfranchisement and dismemberment of culture caused the population to drop 70 per cent, from up to 150,000 in 1769 to 42,000 in 1896 (Poole 1991). Māori were expected to become extinct (Belich 2001); in the words of politician Issac Featherston government policy should 'smooth…their dying pillow' (Foster 1966).

Generations later, Māori were urbanised as unskilled labour, moving from 89 per cent rural in 1936 to 83 per cent urban in 1986. In the cities, Māori faced systematic economic, political, social and cultural marginalisation, cultural alienation, assimilation, racism, structural institutional prejudice and intergenerational impoverishment. Māori language was banned, with the number of speakers declining from 95 per cent in 1900 to just 5 per cent in 1980 (Waitangi Tribunal 1986). Housing was advertised as 'Europeans only' and hotels refused reservations from Māori; Māori could not tour with the All Blacks National Rugby Team to South Africa. In South Auckland Māori were discriminated against in movie theatres, swimming pools and barber shops and a separate school established when Pākehā (New Zealander of European descent) parents protested about Māori children mixing with their own (Belich 2001).

Renaissance

Māori have rebuilt to 565,000 or 14.6 per cent of the population (Statistics New Zealand 2006). Led by radical Māori youth protest in the 1970s (Walker 1991), Māori became an official language in 1987; 24 per cent of Māori can speak te reo (Māori language) (Statistics New Zealand 2006). Māori have 25 radio stations and two TV channels. Many tribes are powerful economic units; the Māori economy is worth $36 billion. Twenty-two Māori sit in the 120-member Parliament, seven from dedicated Māori seats. There are significant efforts to address youth issues in health, education, unemployment, justice, violence, suicide, and alcohol and substance abuse.

Māori-led initiatives in education under the maxim 'Māori do not fail in education; education fails Māori' have been a flagship, with the phenomenon of brown people failing in white education changing under Māori advocacy. There are 491 kohanga reo and kohungahunga (immersion pre-schools up to five years old) (Ministry of Education 2009), over 150 kura kaupapa, kura teina and whare kura (primary and secondary immersion schools up to 17 years old) (Ministry of Education 2008), over 91 tikanga reo rua (bilingual units in mainstream primary and intermediate schools up to 12 years), 90 schools with immersion classes (Maxim Institute 2006), and three whare wānanga (Māori universities). Most other state tertiary institutions teach Māori language. Most importantly these initiatives are successful because they are Māori led via devolution of resources from the system that created the problems Māori now address.

The result is progress at all levels. Māori pre-school entrants have increased to 91.4 per cent (Ministry of Education 2009). Māori leaving school with university entrance qualifications doubled between 2001 and 2006 (Ministry of Education 2007). The proportion of Māori adults with a high school qualification has risen from 39 to 54 per cent, and those with post-school qualifications from 18 to 25 per cent. Enrolments in tertiary education rose from 38,000 to 91,000 between 1994 and 2003 (Ministry of Education 2005a); Māori are now the highest percentage participating ethnic group (Ministry of Education 2005b). The number of Māori with PhDs and other doctoral-level qualifications has grown from about 30 in 1993 to over 500 in 2007 (Walker 2010). Gaps between Māori and non-Māori linger in all areas of education, but under Māori leadership there is change.

High-profile cases of Māori child abuse

Despite recent social progress, Māoridom has been stunned by successive high-profile child homicides. The torture to death of three-year-old Nia Glassie evokes a litany of such incidents. Nia was subjected to extensive abuse for weeks before being admitted to hospital and dying of brain injuries on 3 August 2007. She had been kicked, beaten, slapped, jumped on and held over a fire; she had had wrestling moves practised on her; and she had been placed in a clothes dryer and spun at top heat for up to 30 minutes, folded into a sofa and sat on, shoved into piles of rubbish, dragged through a sandpit, flung against a wall, dropped from a height onto the floor, and whirled rapidly on a rotary clothes line until thrown off.

Two-year-old Jhia Te Tua was killed during a drive-by shooting between two Māori gangs – gangs that formed in the late 1960s and early 1970s after Māori were urbanised. Karl Perigo-Check, the two-year-old son of her killer, now in jail, was later kicked to death by his step-father after wetting his pants.

Three-month-old twin brothers, Christopher and Cru Kahui, died in 2006 of serious head injuries. Their father was charged with the killings but later acquitted. Some evidence suggested that he was 'profiled' into the charges. Serious questions were raised about the mother who, among other things, stopped for a meal at McDonald's on the way to the hospital (leaving the twins in the car) before dropping them at the emergency ward asking staff to phone about the outcome.

The dreadful toll includes too many other children. Every new report brings dread among Māori that it is one of their own. This raises several questions.

How bad is Māori child abuse?

In 2003, the Māori child homicide rate was double that for non-Māori (Ministry of Social Development 2004), which contributed disproportionately to New Zealand ranking third highest for child abuse deaths in 27 OECD countries. At 1.2 deaths per 100,000 children under the age of 15 years, against an OECD median of 0.6 deaths per 100,000, only Mexico and the United States (both 2.2 per 100,000) had higher child maltreatment death rates (UNICEF Innocenti Research Centre 2003). Māori comprise 50 per cent of babies under one-year-old taken into State care and 46 per cent of 2000 critical and 25,000 general child abuse cases reported annually (Ministry of Social Development 2007).[1] At 55 per 100,000, the Māori rate of abuse-related head injuries to children under two is amongst the highest in the world (Taonui 2007). Māori child intentional harm-related admissions to hospital were more than double all other ethnic groups between 1994 and 2004 (Department of Child, Youth and Family Services 2006). Māori boys are those most at risk of homicide (Doolan 2004).

Violence in Māori homes not only occurs at a higher rate but is more likely to be serious; Māori women experience considerably more serious and much greater levels of domestic violence than non-Māori (Newbold 2000). Fifty per cent of those sentenced for the offence of 'male assaults female' in 2004 and 2005 were Māori, and 42 per cent of Māori women report a partner had abused them physically, compared to only 20 per cent of white women (Ministry of Justice 2007).

Do the media over-report Māori child abuse?

Although the rate of Māori violence against children is high, the work of Hirsch and Spoonley (1990); McCreanor (1989); Nairn and McCreanor (1990, 1991); and Rankine *et al.* (2008) underlines that Pākehā-dominated media represents Māori as inferior, negative, extreme and threatening and promotes the idea that Māori (men especially) seek out and enjoy violence. The media also portray Māori as unfairly privileged by Treaty of Waitangi settlement processes and affirmative action policies while characterising them as an indigent source of societal conflict that is a drain on the taxpayer. These perceptions were exacerbated by the *Once were Warriors* film (Scholes and Tamahori 1994), which while portraying the vivid reality of the domestic violence among the Māori urban underclass also reinforced negative stereotypes about Māori. This caricature received further impetus from the 'Warrior Gene' research (Lea 2007) claiming Māori had a genetic tendency to negative behaviour – later discredited for sensationalising the findings from too small a sample in order to obtain more funding (Hook 2009). More recently, historian Paul Moon's *This Horrid Practice* (2008) used the example of pre-European Māori infanticide as evidence that Māori were inherently violent and therefore cannibalistic. Interestingly, *This Horrid Practice* missed the fact that the highest rate of infanticide during the 1800s was in Britain where legal changes removing support for single mothers gave rise to a factory system, starving infants to death on 'baby farms' (Rose 1986), which, using the thesis proffered, would mean that the British, rather than Māori, were the 'savages'.

Child homicide is not just a Māori problem; it is a New Zealand problem. Although Māori at 14.6 per cent of the population accounted for 28 or 32 per cent of the 88 children killed between 1993 and 2003, 48 or 55 per cent were non-Māori Pākehā children of European descent (Pacific Island or Asian comprised 12 deaths or 13.6%).[2] Between 2001 and 2005, Māori children under 15 were 28 per cent or 17 of 61 child homicides; 44 were non-Māori (Ministry of Social Development 2008). The majority of children killed were European; the question arises: are Māori child victims deemed more newsworthy? The names and photos of Māori victims are widely known; the names of Pākehā children less so. Merchant (2010), in a study tracking eight years of reporting, demonstrated that: only 30 per cent of homicides and 3 per cent of child abuse cases are reported – nearly all Māori; non-Māori cases are not ethnically signified as European, Pacific Island or Asian; Māori child homicide and abuse is 42 per cent more reported than non-Māori cases; and of the 21 most high-profile cases over half are Māori (13), who are written about more than twice as often as non-Māori children. Reporters interviewed for the study stated that media organisations preferred publicising Māori cases.

It is therefore simplistic to blame Māori or label child homicide as solely a 'Māori problem'. We do not condemn all white men because they have the highest incidence of child pornography and paedophilia, vilify all Christians because of sexual and physical abuse by Catholic nuns and priests, judge all mental health workers for 30 years of institutionalised torture of young patients in the psychiatric hospitals at Lake Alice and Porirua, or reject the work of all social workers working with indigenous communities because of the horrors of the Residential Schools in Canada, the Stolen Generations in Australia and Residential Homes in New Zealand. Racist stereotyping and scapegoating do not solve issues they do not try to understand. The abusive 'Once Were Warriors Syndrome' we have today did not exist in pre-European times; it is part of a colonial legacy that afflicts colonised indigenous minorities the world over. Further, it is ignorant and arrogant to blame the Māori leaders of decimated communities, who work hard for their communities for little or no recompense. The Māori Party, Māori Council and Māori Women's Welfare League have shown regular commitment to this issue. Māori leaders were amongst the staunchest supporters of New Zealand's recently introduced anti-smacking legislation.

Was pre-European Māori parenting violent?

Māori believe pre-European society was not as violent as Pākehā writers suggest. Appeals to tikanga (customary beliefs and practices) such as aroha (compassion and love), whanaungatanga (family) and whakapapa (genealogy) support this. Traditional whakataukī (aphorisms expressing values and codes of conduct) speak of the importance of children. The bond between mother and child was valued – 'he aroha whāereere, he pōtiki piri poho' (a mother's love, a breast-clinging child). 'tāku hei piripiri, tāku hei mokimoki, tāku hei tāwhiri, tāku kati taramea' referred to children cherished as 'my pendant of scented fern, fragrant fern, scented gum, sweet-scented speargrass'. Children were 'te tau o te ate', literally the 'string of the heart'. 'He kai poutaka me kinikini atu, he kai poutaka me horehore atu, mā te tamaiti te iho' (pinch off a bit of the potted bird, peel off a bit of the potted bird, but leave the substantial part for the child) iterated that the welfare of the children ensured the future of the tribe.

Grieving parents were 'me he rau i peke i te haupapa' (leaves shrivelled by frost). A mother's grief was expressed as 'ka whati rā ia tāku māhuri tōtara' (my broken tōtara sapling). Parents were to provide initial welfare and the other members broader life: 'nāu i whatu te kahu, he tāniko tāku' (you the parents wove the cloak; we provide the fine border). The extended tribe cared for children: 'te parahako o te koekoeā' (the egg of the long-tailed cuckoo raised in the nest of others), 'he tamaiti i aitia ki te takapau wharanui' (children conceived upon the broad mat), and 'ka mahi koe, e te tamariki moe pori' (children who sleep near their relatives). When parents might be lost, children would be cared for by the 'matua pou whare rokohia ana; matua tangata e kore e rokohia' (the ancestral carvings are eternal; the parent is not) – carvings represented the tribe.

Other sayings cautioned to protect children: 'māku e kapu i te toiora o ā tāua tamariki' (by my hand will our children be kept unharmed). 'Ko te rātā te rākau i takahia e te moa' refers to the rātā sapling that when trodden on cannot grow straight. 'Ngā huka kokoti kōmata' means 'just as frosts (huka) will cut down young shoots (kōmata) so too will the ill-treatment of children disrupt their life'. Parents were to instruct children and children to take their guidance – 'kia mau ki te kupu a tōu matua' (children, listen to the words of your parents). However, the young were also encouraged to speak their mind: 'ka mahi te tamariki wāwāhi tahā' (well done children who break calabashes, meaning who challenge the status quo). Exuberance was encouraged: 'he ahi tawa ki uta, he kumu tarakihi ki te moana' (children are like the noisy popping of roasting tawa berries, and the noisy feeding of large shoals of the tarakihi fish) (whakataukī from Mead and Grove 2007).[3]

While whakataukī are insightful, there are no extant Māori accounts from the early contact period about their parenting. The observations of early European explorers, traders, missionaries, settlers and administrators made at different places and independently of each other between 1814 and 1868 are therefore useful. Given there were few Europeans in New Zealand in 1814 and no more than 2000 in 1840, we can assume the parenting they observed are a fair indication of practice before contact.

Samuel Marsden, the first missionary to New Zealand, arrived in 1814, 45 years after first contact. Reflecting that Māori men commit most Māori child homicides today, Marsden made the critical observation that Māori men engaged in little violence against women and children:

> I saw no quarrelling while I was there. They are kind to their women and children. I never observed either with a mark of violence upon them, nor did I ever see a child struck. (Elder 1932, p.128)

> The chiefs take their children from their mother's breast to all their public assemblies, where they hear all that is said upon politics, religion, war etc. by the oldest men. Children will frequently ask questions in public conversation and are answered by the chiefs. I have often been surprised to see the sons of the chiefs at the age of four or five years sitting amongst the chiefs and paying close attention to what was said. (Elder 1932, p.193)

Joel Polack (1838) supports Marsden's comments regarding Māori fathers, which he contrasts with European views of punishment:

> The New Zealand father is devotedly fond of his children, they are his pride, his boast, and peculiar delight; he generally bears the burden of carrying them continually within his mat… The children are seldom or never punished; which consequently, causes them to commit so many annoying tricks, that continually renders them deserving of a sound, wholesome castigation. The father performs the duty of a nurse; and any foul action the embryo warrior may be guilty of, causes a smile rather than a tear from the devoted parent. (Polack 1838, p.374)

George Angas's (1847) observations emphasise the positive care of both parents:

> Both parents are almost idolatrously fond of their children; and the father frequently spends a considerable portion of his time in nursing his infant, who nestles in his blanket... The children are cheerful and lively little creatures, full of vivacity and intelligence. They pass their early years almost without restraint... (Angas 1847, pp.91–92)

William Colenso (1868) also wrote about extended family parenting:

> Their love and attachment to children was very great, and that not merely to their own immediate offspring. They very commonly adopted children; indeed no man having a large family was ever allowed to bring them all up himself – uncles, aunts and cousins claimed and took them, often whether the parents were willing or not. They certainly took every physical care of them; and as they rarely chastised (for many reasons) of course, petted and spoiled them. (Colenso 1868, p.30)

Edward Shortland's observations about Māori parenting, published in 1856, explains the Māori view against physical punishment:

> Curbing the will of the child by harsh means was thought to tame his spirit, and to check the free development of his natural bravery. The chief aim, therefore, in the education of children being to make them bold, brave, and independent in thought and act... (Shortland 1856, p.156)

Swainson (1859) bespeaks the effectiveness of non-physical parenting:

> Considering how little the Māori children are subject to restraint, their quiet and orderly conduct is especially remarkable. In bringing them up, the parents seldom have recourse to personal chastisement, believing that it has the effect of damaging the spirit of the child. At an early age, the Māori children acquire great self-respect... (Swainson 1859, p.10)

Polack (1840) explains the role women performed in protecting children and the sense that children belonged to the tribe:

> The wife almost invariably opposes the husband in favour of her children, and the former dares not assume any superiority,

> as the relatives of his wife are ever ready to avenge, even with his blood, any unkindness shown to her or the children, the latter being regarded as less belonging to the parents than to the tribe in general. (Polack 1840, Vol. 1, pp.32–33)

Shortland also observed how the extended family acted as a check against over-chastisement:

> ...a parent is seldom seen to chastise his child, especially in families of rank. Were he to do so, one of the uncles would probably interfere to protect his nephew, and seek satisfaction for the injury inflicted on the child by seizing some of the pigs or other property of the father. (Shortland 1856, p.156)

These observations accord with others in the Pacific. Malinowski (1929), for example, gave a seminal description of the child-raising practices of the Trobriand Islanders in Melanesia including rejecting his advice to physically punish:

> Children...enjoy considerable freedom and independence... there is no idea of a regular discipline, no system of domestic coercion... The parents would either coax or scold or ask as from one equal to another...the idea of a definite retribution, or of coercive punishment, is not only foreign, but distinctly repugnant...several times when I suggested, after some flagrant infantile misdeed, that it would mend matters for the future if the child were beaten or otherwise punished in cold blood, the idea appeared unnatural and immoral to my friends, and was rejected with some resentment. (Malinowski 1929, pp.52–53)

In summary, violence toward children in pre-European times was the exception rather than the rule. Shared parenting by the extended family was an important check against violence. This suggests that contemporary high child abuse rates have their genesis in the post-contact period.

Is there a link between colonisation and the intergenerational impacts of colonisation and Māori child abuse?

The post-colonial physical maltreatment of children has several strands. Māori inherited the British education corporal punishment tradition that hitting children was acceptable and good for them via education (see Chandos 1984; Quigly 1984) (New Zealand abandoned corporal punishment in 1990). There is also a connection between Māori child abuse, cultural alienation and intergenerational impoverishment. The key ingredients can be traced to the period after the colonial wars of the 1860s when increasing landlessness impacted on the cohesion of Māori society. As the *New Zealand Herald* observed:

> ...men and women have abandoned all work and all industrious occupation. They can scarcely be said to have had a home...for the most part they have for years past lived in tents or slept on the ground with the shelter merely of a wind break. They have been made to do this by having to run from one part of the country to the other end after land courts. They have had to live on wretched watery foods and the only relief from the utter misery of their surroundings is in getting drunk. What wonder is it that they should die like rotten sheep and the children borne to them should linger out a short life. (*New Zealand Hearld* 1885)

And as the Member of Parliament Robert Bruce said:

> I believe we could not devise a more ingenious method of destroying the whole of the Māori race than by these land courts. The natives come from the villages in the interior, and have to hang about for months in our centres of population... They are brought into contact with the lowest classes of society, and are exposed to temptation, the result is that a great number contract our diseases and die. (Bruce 1885)

Contemporary domestic abuse and child violence began between 1950 and 1980 when 60 per cent of Māori were urbanised as cheap unskilled labour (Belich 2001). This brought forth new generations of doubly-alienated Māori: rejected by the dominant culture and at distance from their ancestral culture, concentrated in poor housing, working for low wages or on welfare, and subject to across-the-board racism and assimilation. A generation of urban Māori parents who had been born in the 1970s, 1980s and 1990s entered an intergenerational cycle of poverty, alcohol, drugs, gang culture, single-parent families, domestic violence, hopelessness and frustration, dislocating and isolating families from the traditional contexts and the extended networks that protected children. By 2001, 20 per cent or 120,000 of Māori people did not know their tribe (Statistics New Zealand 2001). Māori have the highest rate of solo parent families: 41 per cent of Māori children compared to 17 per cent of European children live in single parent families mainly headed by women (Families Commission 2008).

The post-contact dislocation of families is directly or indirectly a history of the application of colonial violence. That experience creates anger that is turned inward, manifesting in violence and abuse which spikes when the vulnerability of Māori families is exposed during economic downturns. Thirty-year figures show that after the 1984 to 1990 economic restructuring, which impacted more on poor Māori than poor non-Māori (Minto 2007), the Māori child homicide rate, which had been only 10 per cent higher than that for non-Māori between 1978 and 1987, more than doubled between 1991 and 2000 (see Table 9.1).

TABLE 9.1 Changes in rates of Māori and non-Māori child homicide: 1978–1987 and 1991–2000 (rate per 100,000 for children aged 0–14 years)

	MĀORI	NON-MĀORI
1978–1987	1.05	0.92
1991–2000	2.40	0.67

Source: Connolly 2012

The connection between economic restructuring leading to greater alienation and then more violence is further supported by the fact that most *prima facie* reports suggest Māori child homicide occurs in culturally less robust families. This supports the argument that it is not the inherent nature of indigenous culture that causes cyclic child maltreatment but rather the proximal removal from culture. One of the highest rates of cyclic poverty and of alcohol, drug and child abuse in Western Europe is in the Glaswegian south-west of Scotland – amongst the descendants of *white* Highlanders urbanised after Culloden, who had lost their lands, language and culture (BBC 2010; Keystone 2008; *Herald Scotland* 2012). This cultural alienation is also why, in New Zealand, Māori child abuse rates currently outstrip those for Pasifika. Samoan and Tongan populations remained a majority in their own countries during colonisation; they retained more land and their languages stayed intact. Culturally stronger Pasifika communities were more successful at transferring their communities from Apia and

Tongatapu to Auckland than Māori were at transporting them from Ahipara and Te Tai. However, Pasifika now living as minorities within a dominant culture are a ticking time bomb in places such as South Auckland, as gradually, three or more generations of re-settlement have begun to erode the cultural cohesiveness of those communities (Taonui and Newbold 2011).

Is the Māori renaissance making a contribution?

Thirty-year figures show that the renaissance period is having a positive impact. In fact, the rate of Māori child homicide is decreasing at more than twice the rate of that for non-Māori (see Table 9.2).

TABLE 9.2 Changes in rates of Māori and non-Māori child homicide 1991–2005 (rate per 100,000 for children aged 0–14 years)

	MĀORI	NON-MĀORI
(i) 1991–2000	2.40	0.67
(ii) 1996–2000	1.90	0.90
(iii) 1999–2003	1.50	0.70
(iv) 2001–2005	1.50	0.60

Sources: (i) Doolan 2004, p.10; (ii) and (iv) Ministry of Social Development 2008, p.7; (iii) Ministry of Social Development 2006, p.5

When compared another way, the rate of Māori child homicide has been improving steadily, both in terms of the reduction in the number killed (see Figure 9.1) and, as shown in Figure 9.2, as a percentage of all child homicides.

The mid-2000s percentage of non-Māori child homicides (including Pākehā European, Pasifika and Asian) was increasing as a proportion of all homicides as Māori child homicide decreased (see Figure 9.2). Meanwhile, the rate of reported Māori child abuse, although still twice that for non-Māori (11.9 compared with 5.9 per 1000, 1998–2003), is also decreasing. Together this suggests the Māori renaissance is making a difference. Furthermore, the greater rapidity of the decline intimates that long-term the Māori child homicide could track lower than Pākehā rates. Notwithstanding that trend, there is a concern of Māori child abuse re-increasing with the current economic downturn 2008–2010; there were four new Māori child homicides in 2010.

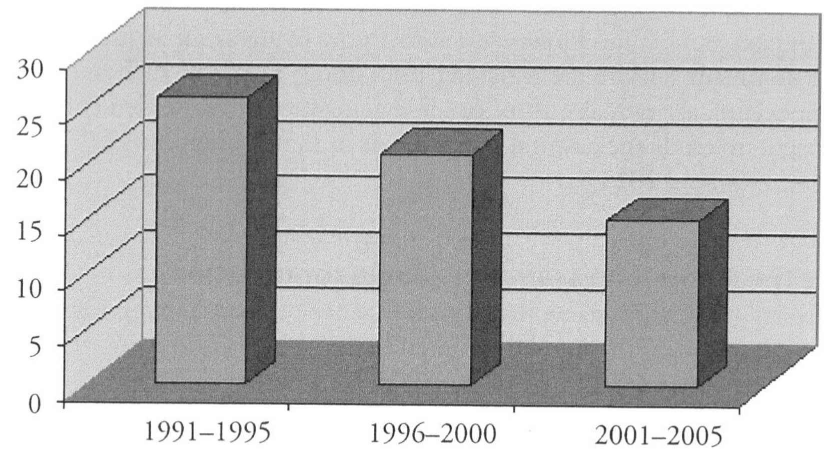

FIGURE 9.1 Number of Māori child homicides
Source: Connolly and Doolan 2007, p.42

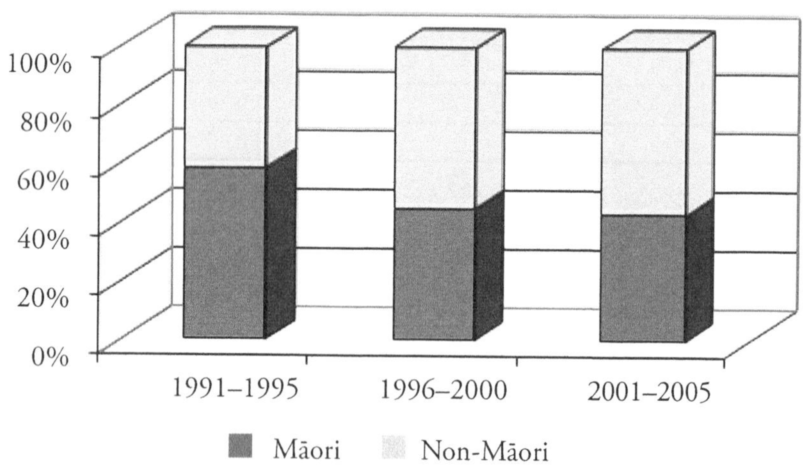

FIGURE 9.2 Māori child homicides as a percentage of all child homicides
Source: Connolly and Doolan 2007, p.43

What will help?

The majority of the measures currently in place address symptoms rather than causes. Moreover, the structures and organisations that address the issue derive from the structures that created the problem. The Māori revolution in education was predicated on across-the-board Māori presence: in teaching, administration, policy, leadership and decision making. Māori-designed and led initiatives in other areas such as health areas have also proved more successful with Māori communities (Durie 2005). The same needs to happen in child welfare. There are many Māori working in social work and support services; however, more Māori with strong cultural skills and requisite professional qualifications are required in decision-making. They need to be properly resourced. A steady devolution of resources will allow Māori-led programs to succeed. The new suite of Whānau Ora policies promoted by the Māori Party and the Māori-led Paiheretia whānau (family) restoration programs need resourcing.

The current government has called for a white paper on mandatory reporting of child maltreatment. There is a need for anti-silence awareness-raising initiatives, although these can generate many petty or false complaints that traumatise families (O'Donahugh 2011), particularly where racial profiling occurs. In 2009 a senior nurse from New Zealand's largest children's hospital, Starship, said at the Good Fellow Symposium that 'all parents were liars until proven otherwise'. Starship introduced internal mandatory reporting in 1995. The hospital has since been the subject of numerous complaints, such as professionals jumping to conclusions. A judge has also criticised the hospital for this. A former Health and Disability Commissioner, whose own daughter was wrongly accused, described the remark as 'hyperbole that suggests phobia and zealotry beyond reason' (Wall 2010). Given Māori are disproportionately represented in this area as clients and Europeans over-represented as professionals, there is a risk of racial profiling if reporting is to a monocultural system; not all brown people are child abusers and not all Māori are child abusers – the majority patently are not. Pākehā health workers, administrators and decision makers need cultural re-training similar to the successful Kotahitanga Programme in education not only to understand Māori but also to understand the assumptions Pākehā decisions make about them. Devolution of reporting to Māori-centred or Māori-sensitive organisations is also required.

The place of culture

We rarely recognise that colonisation and its concomitant intergenerational impacts constitute violence – colonisation is the application of anger upon vulnerable peoples. Cultural alienation, forced assimilation and cumulative marginalisation create a reciprocal reaction within the indigenous societies upon which it is inflicted. Where this anger is not understood, it is internalised by the colonised society and inverts upon itself. The indigenous oppressed attack each other. In families the violence expresses itself by seeking out the innocent, the vulnerable and the weak in the form of mothers and children. Re-enculturalisation can emancipate individuals, families and tribal groups. Case histories about perpetrators and victims need not only to trace the circumstances of the individual concerned but also their parents and wider family, because the journey of the many in the past shapes the life of the one in the present. Promoting the rebuilding of culture within the perpetrator not only includes the beliefs and values of the ancestors but also the history of the people, including colonisation. At an individual level this knowledge has the ability to dissipate anger by raising consciousness. Positive enculturation enhances a sense of belonging, rebuilds identity and promotes self-worth. This facilitates the healing of relationships within families. At its best expression this allows perpetrators to reconnect both with the honour of traditional whakapapa (genealogy) and the dishonour of colonisation to find meaning and place in terms of honouring their ancestors and working for the good of current and future generations. Māori culture is not a problem; it is a solution.

Conclusion

Child violence in pre-European Māori society was much less than today. Māori child murder, although still higher than that for non-Māori, has been decreasing at twice the rate as that for non-Māori as part of the wider Māori renaissance. The current crisis derives from cumulative intergenerational experiences of colonisation, alienation and impoverishment. Culturally strong families are less violent. Culturally based programs for Māori are more likely to be successful. These programs need the devolvement of resources from non-Māori-dominated systems that created the problems they now seek to solve.

E ngā taonga iti, moe mai i waenganui i ngā mātua tūpuna, ma rātou koutou e tiaki. Moe marie. Kei a mātou te whakamā, kia kaua anō – rest with the ancestors, they will care for you. Find peace. The shame of your suffering rests with us, may there be no more.

Endnotes

1. Figures released in June 2007 show that, in the year to 30 June 2007, a total of 4672 cases of child abuse – 46 per cent of the overall total – came from Māori households, compared with 27.8 per cent (2828 cases) from Pākehā families. In 2006, the number for Māori was 45.1 per cent, and the figure for Pākehā was 30.7 per cent. Only 2.8 per cent were Asian and 16.4 per cent were Pacific Island.
2. Interview by Steve Braunias of Dr Cindy Kiro, New Zealand Commissioner for Children, published in the *Sunday Star Times* (5 Aug 2007, p.A18). Dr Kiro said that 88 died between 2003 and 2006. More precisely, it was 50 between 1993 and 1998 and 38 between 1999 and 2003 (Ministry of Social Development 2006, p.v).
3. See pp.64, 66, 81, 119, 164, 167, 198, 258, 287, 288, 297, 319, 322, 379, 384 and 391 – index available by first word.

References

Angas, G.F. (1847) *Savage Life and Scenes in Australia and New Zealand.* London: Smith, Elder and Co.

BBC (2010) 'Big rise in Scottish unemployment.' *BBC Online – News Scotland Business,* 15 September. Available at www.bbc.co.uk/news/uk-scotland-scotland-business-11310730, accessed on 25 January 2012.

Belich, J. (2001) *Paradise Reforged.* Auckland: Penguin.

Bruce, R. (1885) In *New Zealand Parliamentary Debates.* Wellington: Government Printer.

Chandos, J. (1984) *Boys Together: English Public Schools 1800–1864.* London: Hutchinson.

Colenso, W. (1868) 'On the Māori races of New Zealand.' *Transactions and Proceedings of the New Zealand Institute 1.*

Connolly, M. (2012) Personal communication.

Connolly, M. and Doolan, M. (2007) *Lives Cut Short: Child Death by Maltreatment.* Wellington: Dunmore.

Cowan, J. (1922) *New Zealand Wars: A History of the Maori Campaigns and Pioneering Period (1922–23).* Wellington: Government Printer.

Department of Child, Youth and Family Services (2006) *Children at Increased Risk of Death from Maltreatment and Strategies for Prevention.* Wellington: Ministry of Social Development.

Doolan, M. (2004) 'Child death by homicide.' *Te Awatea Review – Te Awatea Violence Research Centre's Newsletter 2,* 1.

Durie, M. (2005) *Ngā Tai Matatū – Tides of Māori Endurance.* Melbourne: Oxford.

Elder, J.R. (1932) *The Letters and Journals of Samuel Marsden 1765–1838.* Dunedin: A.H. Reed.

Families Commission (2008) *The Kiwi Nest – 60 Years of Change in New Zealand Families.* Wellington: Families Commission.

Foster, B.J. (1966) 'Dr Isaac Featherston.' *New Zealand Online Encyclopaedia.* Available at www.teara.govt.nz/en/1966/featherston-dr-isaac-earl/1, accessed on 19 December 2011.

Herald Scotland (2012) 'Scotland among world's worst for drug abuse.' *Herald Scotland*, 26 January. Available at www.heraldscotland.com/news/scotland-among-world-s-worst-for-drug-abuse-1.1045274, accessed on 2 February 2012.

Hirsch, W. and Spoonley, P. (1990) *Between the Lines: Racism in the New Zealand Media*. Auckland: Heinemann Reid.

Hook, G.R. (2009) 'Warrior genes and the disease of being Māori.' *MAI Review 2*. Available at www.review.mai.ac.nz, accessed on 19 December 2011.

Howe, K.R. (2006) 'The Last Frontier.' In K.R. Howe (ed.) *Vaka Moana*. Auckland: Dunmore.

Keystone, R. (2008) 'Child abuse on the rise in Scotland.' *The Journal*, Issue 14, 23 November. Available at www.journal-conline.co.uk/article/5120-child-abuce-on-the-rise-in-scotland, accessed on 23 January 2012.

Kiro, C. (2007) Interview by Steve Braunias of Cindy Kiro, New Zealand Commissioner for Children, published in *Sunday Star Times*, 5 August, p.A18.

Laws, M. (2009a) 'Māori racism creates culture of failure we should not accept.' *Sunday Star Times*, 25 October. Available at www.stuff.co.nz/blogs/opinion/2998771/Maori-racism-creates-culture-of-failure, accessed on 28 October 2011.

Laws, M. (2009b) 'Sterilise the underclass to stop child abuse.' *Dominion Post*, 30 October. Available at www.stuff.co.nz/national/crime/3012655/Sterilise-underclass-to-stop-child-abuse-Michael-Laws, accessed on 28 October 2011.

Laws, M. (2010) 'Sterilising scumbags saves our children.' *Sunday Star Times*, 3 July. Available at www.stuff.co.nz/sunday-star-times/columnists/3414027/Sterilising-scumbags-saves-our-children, accessed on 28 October 2011.

Lea, R. (2007) 'Monoamine oxide, addiction, and the "warrior" gene hypothesis.' *The New Zealand Medical Journal 120*, 1250, 5–9.

Malinowski, B. (1929) *The Sexual Life of Savages in North-Western Melanesia*. Whitefish, MT: Kessinger.

Maxim Institute (2006) *Policy Paper – Current Issues in Māori Schooling*. Available at www.maxim.org.nz/files/pdf/policy_paper_maori_education.pdf, accessed on 28 October 2011.

McCreanor, T. (1989) 'Talking about Race.' In H. Yensen, K. Hague and T. McCreanor (eds) *Honouring the Treaty: An Introduction for Pākehā*. Auckland: Penguin.

Mead, H. and Grove, N. (2007) *Ngā Pēpeha a ngā Tīpuna*. Wellington: Victoria University Press.

Merchant, R. (2010) *Who are Abusing our Children?* Master of Social Work thesis. Palmerston North: Massey University.

Ministry of Education (2005a) *Tertiary Sector Performance Analysis and Reporting: Profiles and Trends*. Wellington: Ministry of Education.

Ministry of Education (2005b) *Ngā Haeata Mātauranga – The Annual Report on Māori Education 2004*. Wellington: Ministry of Education.

Ministry of Education (2007) *Ngā Haeata Mātauranga – The Annual Report on Māori Education 2006–2007*. Wellington: Ministry of Education.

Ministry of Education (2008) *Ngā Haeata Mātauranga – The Annual Report on Māori Education 2007–2008*. Wellington: Ministry of Education.

Ministry of Education (2009) *Ngā Haeata Mātauranga – The Annual Report on Māori Education 2008–2009*. Wellington: Ministry of Education.

Ministry of Justice (2007) *Victims of Crimes Report*. Wellington: Ministry of Justice.

Ministry of Social Development (2004) *Report – Child Abuse and Neglect*. Wellington: Ministry of Social Development.

Ministry of Social Development (2006) *Children at Increased Risk of Death and Strategies for Protection*. Wellington: Ministry of Social Development.
Ministry of Social Development (2007) Official Information Act release. See S. Cook. 'CYF seized Nia's sibling after injuries.' *Herald on Sunday*, 5 August. Available at www.nzherald.co.nz/nz/news/article.cfm?c_id=1&objectid=10455891&ref=rss, accessed on 19 December 2011; and L. Mitchell (2009) *Te Oranga o te Iwi Māori: A Study of Māori Economic and Social Progress: Māori and Welfare*. Wellington: Business Round Table.
Ministry of Social Development (2008) *Children and Young People – Indicators of Wellbeing in New Zealand – Safety*. Wellington: Ministry of Social Development.
Minto, J. (2007) 'Restructuring of the 1980s sowed the seeds of child abuse.' *The Press*. Available at www.stuff.co.nz/the-press/opinion/columnists/john-minto/25571, accessed on 28 October 2011.
Moon, P. (2008) *This Horrid Practice: The Myth and the Reality of Traditional Maori Cannibalism*. Auckland: Penguin.
Nairn, R.G. and McCreanor, T. (1990) 'Sensitivity and insensitivity: An imbalance in Pākehā accounts of Māori/Pākehā relations.' *Journal of Language and Social Psychology 9*, 293–308.
Nairn, R.G. and McCreanor, T. (1991) 'Race talk and commonsense: Ideological patterns in Pākehā talk about Māori/Pākehā relations.' *Journal of Language and Social Psychology 10*, 245–262.
Newbold, G. (2000) *Crime in New Zealand*. Palmerston North: Dunmore.
New Zealand Herald, 1 August 1885.
New Zealand History Online (2009) *Māori Land Loss*. Wellington: Ministry of Culture and Heritage. Available at www.nzhistory.net.nz/media/interactive/maori-land-1860-2000, accessed on 28 October 2011.
O'Donahugh, E. (2011) 'Overseas experience with mandatory reporting.' *Radio New Zealand News (Morning Report)*, 18 April.
Polack, J. (1838) *New Zealand: Being a Narrative of Travel and Adventures*. London: R. Bentley.
Polack, J. (1840) *Manners and Customs of the New Zealanders*. London: J. Madden.
Poole, I. (1991) *Te Iwi Māori*. Auckland: Auckland University Press.
Quigly, I. (1984) *The Heirs of Tom Brown: The English School Story*. Oxford: Oxford University Press.
Rankine, J., Nairn, R., Moewaka-Barnes, A., Gregory, M., Kaiwai, H. and Borell, B. (2008) *Media and te Tiriti o Waitangi*. Auckland: Kupe Taea.
Rose, L. (1986) *Massacre of the Innocents: Infanticide in Great Britain 1800–1939*. London: Routledge and Kegan Paul.
Scholes, R. (Producer) and Tamahori, L. (Director) (1994) *Once were Warriors* [Motion Picture]. New Zealand: Communicado Productions.
Shortland, E. (1856) *Traditions and Superstitions of the Māori*. Christchurch: Capper Press.
Simpson, T. (1979) *Te Riri Pākehā – The White Man's Anger*. Auckland: Hodder and Stoughton.
Sorrenson, M.P.K. (1959) 'The Māori people and the city of Auckland.' *Te Ao Hou 27*, 8–13.
Statistics New Zealand (2001) *Census of Populations and Dwellings*. Available at www.stats.govt.nz/Census/2001-census-data.aspx, accessed on 28 October 2011.
Statistics New Zealand (2006) *Census of Populations and Dwellings*. Available at www.stats.govt.nz/Census/2006CensusHomePage.aspx, accessed on 28 October 2011.

Swainson, W. (1859) *New Zealand and its Colonisation*. London: Smith, Elder and Co.
Taonui, R. (2007) 'Not a race issue.' *New Zealand Sunday Star Times*, 5 August, p.A10.
Taonui, R. and Newbold, G. (2011) 'Gangs in New Zealand.' *Te Ara – New Zealand Online Encyclopaedia*. Wellington: Ministry of Culture and Heritage.
TV3 NZ (2005) *A Maori Challenge – 60 Minutes*. 18 April, Auckland.
UNICEF Innocenti Research Centre (2003) *A League Table of Child Maltreatment Deaths in Rich Nations*. Florence, Italy: UNICEF.
Waitangi Tribunal (1986) *Wai 11 Te Reo Māori Report*. Wellington: Department of Justice.
Waitangi Tribunal (2009) *Urewera Report – Part I*. Wellington: Waitangi Tribunal.
Waitangi Tribunal (2010) *Urewera Report – Part II*. Wellington: Waitangi Tribunal.
Walker, M. (2010) 'Māori Research – The National Picture.' In R. Taonui (chief ed.), H. Kahi, C. Deeming, K. Kururangi, G. Cooper *et al.* (eds) *Ngā Kete a Rēhua Inaugural Māori Research Symposium Te Waipounamu 4–5 September 2008 Conference Proceedings*. Christchurch: University of Canterbury.
Walker, R. (1991) *Ka Whawhai tonu matou – Struggle without End*. Auckland: Penguin.
Wall, T. (2010) 'All parents lie declares Starship nurse.' *Sunday Star Times*, 19 December.

Chapter 10

International Human Rights Law and the Needs of Indigenous Children

Terri Libesman[1]

Introduction

This chapter explores some of the ways in which international human rights law offers a framework within which Indigenous children and young people's welfare can be addressed. It considers how the re-characterisation of international law, from universal and transcendental to pluralising and inclusive, has been theoretically and practically relevant to Indigenous children and young people's rights. It focuses on Indigenous peoples' engagement with the United Nations in the context of evolving understandings of principles of self-determination as they relate to Indigenous children and young people.[2] It explores these issues through two Australian-based case studies: the implementation of the Aboriginal and Torres Strait Islander Child Placement Principle (ATSICPP), with particular reference to the State of Victoria, and the Northern Territory Emergency Response (NTER) in the Northern Territory.

While international law is often referred to as a higher law which by its nature is universal and general, contemporary human rights committees attempt to establish standards and monitoring mechanisms which respond in a culturally and historically sensitive manner and in this way are inclusive of Indigenous communities' aspirations. This chapter suggests that the greater the reflective engagement with

Indigenous peoples at both an international and national level, the more human rights frameworks are able to understand, transform and serve Indigenous children's wellbeing.

Colonial context

Many of the barriers to Aboriginal and Torres Strait Islander children's wellbeing are founded in historical injustices and associated social and economic inequities which weigh on Aboriginal and Torres Strait Islander communities.[3] Indigenous peoples have higher levels of contact with child welfare systems in Australia than any other group. They are placed in out of home care at a rate nine times higher than all children (AIHW 2010). Indigenous families and communities have protested and responded to the removal of their children at a local level from the time of colonisation. The formation of national Indigenous organisations in Australia in the 1960s and 1970s led to political advocacy for greater cultural control over child welfare, and the first Aboriginal and Torres Strait Islander Child Care Agencies (AICCAs) were established in the 1970s in the same period that Indigenous peoples were advocating for recognition in the United Nations (UN).

The importance of Indigenous agencies and cultural recognition has been an ongoing theme, with incremental legislative and policy changes being made from the 1970s onwards (Libesman 2008). In 1992, *Bringing Them Home*, the report of the National Inquiry into the Separation of Aboriginal and Torres Strait Islander children from their families, recommended that a negotiated transfer of responsibility for child welfare from government agencies to Aboriginal and Torres Strait Islander organisations take place in accordance with their capacity and desire to assume this responsibility (NISATSIC 1997, recommendation 43c). While this recommendation is yet to be fully implemented, legislative reform has taken place which facilitates greater control by Indigenous organisations over their children's wellbeing. For example, legislative recognition of ATSICPP (discussed below) acknowledges the importance of cultural security and identity rights in a limited self-determination framework. Recommendations with respect to and reforms of Australian child welfare legislation have been influenced by the ongoing advocacy by Indigenous children's organisations for greater control over child welfare and reflect an interactive relationship between Indigenous advocacy for reform at a local level and advocacy and engagement in international forums which have sparked local Indigenous children's organisations, such as the peak Indigenous children's organisation the Secretariat of National Aboriginal and Torres Strait Islander Child Care (SNAICC), to frame their claims in terms of human rights principles, with particular reference to the right to self-determination.

To address Indigenous children's wellbeing requires responses which also address the structural and systemic inequality and poverty which is embedded in their communities. While there has been incremental, if at times tenuous, recognition of the principle of cultural safety as reflected in legislative reforms embodied in the ATSICPP, there has been a failure to apply principles of self-determination or cultural recognition to reforms addressing structural poverty and inequality. This is most sharply illustrated with the paternalistic Northern Territory Emergency Response. The inconsistent recognition of cultural rights and principles of self-determination reflects both the depth of colonial understanding which pervades responses to Indigenous children's wellbeing and the tension between homogeneous Western ways of framing responses to Indigenous children's welfare and more inclusive pluralised understandings.

Indigenous peoples' engagement with the United Nations

Indigenous peoples have exercised enormous imagination and innovation in negotiating colonial powers. When outranked in might they have exercised ingenuity in responding to injustice through the political and legal forums of colonisers and in some ways transforming these forums to incorporate a greater understanding of Indigenous claims to justice. Aboriginal and Torres Strait Islander peoples from the time of colonisation, when local political institutions failed them, looked for a more just response to their plight outside of national borders. William Cooper, a Yorta Yorta man from Victoria, who spent most of his life in the Cummeragunja community living under oppressive Victorian 'protection' legislation, collected over 1800 signatures on a petition to King George V. The petition, which was reported in the *Melbourne Herald* in September 1933, complained that the lands of the Indigenous peoples had been appropriated and their legal status has been denied. In more recent times, engagement with Indigenous peoples in comparable situations such as in Canada, New Zealand and the USA, and with UN forums, has afforded the inspiration and opportunity to transform understandings of law in ways which have incrementally incorporated or recognised Indigenous peoples' claims to justice.[4]

While minority Indigenous peoples from Australia and elsewhere were left out of UN processes of decolonisation in the 1960s, they saw the potential for change which the human rights framework – and what the principle of self-determination in particular – could offer.[5] Indigenous peoples have subsequently pushed the statist boundaries of the UN to not only recognise their individual claims but also to recognise group rights, their position as separate peoples, and to carve out a body of Indigenous-specific international law.[6]

The transformation in international understanding is evident in the change from the first UN-affiliated instrument to address Indigenous issues specifically – the International Labour Organisation Convention 107 of 1957, which was framed in terms of protecting vulnerable Indigenous minorities and promoting their economic and social progress within the mainstream community – to the Declaration on the Rights of Indigenous Peoples, adopted by the General Assembly in September 2007, which recognises Indigenous peoples' cultural rights and their right to self-determination. With the establishment of the Permanent Forum for Indigenous peoples in 2000, Indigenous peoples' inclusion in a specific UN forum is no longer ad hoc (*UN Economic and Social Council Resolution 2000/22*). In addition, the Human Rights Commission appointed a Special Rapporteur on Indigenous peoples' human rights and fundamental freedoms (*UN Commission on Human Rights Resolution 2001/57*). The Rapporteur, Professor James Anaya, visited Australia in 2008 and reported on breaches of Indigenous Australians' rights, with specific reference to the Northern Territory Emergency Response, which is discussed below (Human Rights Council 2010).

What is perhaps more remarkable than the specific instruments and forums established to address Indigenous peoples' rights is the influence which Indigenous participation in the UN has had on the treaty system. It is this influence which is evident in the jurisprudence of the Convention on the Rights of the Child (CROC) and these ideas which have circulated through Aboriginal and Torres Strait Islander children's organisations and are evident in Australian law reform with respect to Indigenous children's welfare and wellbeing. The legitimacy and prominence of Indigenous peoples' claims within the UN system has influenced how Australian Governments have responded to Indigenous peoples' claims of discrimination, cultural rights and more broadly the right to participate in decisions which impact on them. These responses, in particular the formalisation of inclusion of Indigenous peoples in decision-making within child welfare legislation, as discussed below with respect to the ATSICPP, in turn influences and affects non-

Indigenous understandings at local and regional levels, transforming mainstream understandings and giving substance and legitimacy to law reform with respect to the wellbeing of Indigenous children. The increased prominence and recognition given to Indigenous rights and advocates within the UN system, although the extent of these rights and recognition may be contested, has changed both the landscape of international human rights law and the space for contestation and recognition of Indigenous children's rights more locally.

Self-determination

The principle of self-determination is found in Article 1 in the two main human rights treaties: the International Covenant on Civil and Political Rights (ICCPR) and the International Covenant on Economic, Social and Cultural Rights (ECOSOC). It remains unclear whether this article includes Indigenous peoples. However, statements by the Human Rights Committee (HRC) in the context of country reports with respect to compliance with ICCPR, including Australia's country report, indicate that an internal form of self-determination, without prescriptive requirements, is expected if countries are to fulfil their obligations under ICCPR.[7] The ICCPR and ECOSOC definition of self-determination is mirrored in Article 3 of the Declaration on the Rights of Indigenous Peoples.

Established and developing norms with respect to Indigenous peoples' self-determination are impacting on the interpretation of many articles in human rights treaties. The relationship between the right to one's culture and collective rights has been recognised by the Human Rights Committee with respect to complaints brought under the optional protocol with respect to Article 27 of ICCPR.[8]

Article 27 of ICCPR provides:

> In those States in which ethnic, religious or linguistic minorities exist, persons belonging to such minorities shall not be denied the right, in community with the other members of their group, to enjoy their own culture, to profess and practice their own religion, or to use their own language.

Despite not referring to Indigenous peoples, Article 27 has been used by Indigenous authors who have brought individual complaints under the Optional Protocol. These address denials of the right to group membership, identity and the state's responsibility with respect to persons who share cultural rights.[9] Article 30 of CROC is framed in similar language to Article 27 of ICCPR but makes specific reference to Indigenous peoples.

Article 30 provides:

> In those states in which ethnic, religious or linguistic minorities or persons of Indigenous origin exist, a child belonging to such a minority or who is Indigenous shall not be denied the right, in community with other members of his or her group, to enjoy his or her culture, to profess and practice his or her own religion, or to use his or her own language.

While individual complaints cannot be brought with respect to CROC, the jurisprudence of the Human Rights Committee with respect to Article 27 is relevant to interpretations of CROC.[10] These developments reflect a growing understanding of the relationship between collective and individual rights, the recognition of rights which are specific to an Indigenous way of life and the requirement to balance the rights of a vulnerable Indigenous minority against the many competing interests of the majority and other minorities.[11] The jurisprudence of CROC has developed from the spectrum of the Committee on the Rights of the Child's activities, including examination of options to address specific problems, undertaking studies of special problems facing particular groups of children, holding discussion days and the Committee's reporting on countries' compliance with CROC (Article 45). While a primary method for elaborating on the CROC articles is through countries which have acceded to the treaty reporting on their compliance,[12] the Committee has demonstrated an openness to receipt of information and understandings from a range of sources including non-government organisations (NGOs). Indigenous organisations have actively contributed to these reports.

The Aboriginal and Torres Strait Islander Child Placement Principle, Australia

The ATSICPP has been one of the remarkable achievements of Aboriginal and Torres Strait Islander children's organisations. The principle is an acknowledgment of the importance of culture and family connection for Indigenous children and young people and it is also recognition of the destructive impact the history of policies of assimilation and forced and unjustified removal of children has had on Indigenous peoples.[13] The ATSICPP has developed from a principle applied when children need to live in out of home care to a foundation for legislative inclusion of Indigenous families and organisations in decisions with respect to a child or young person's wellbeing from the time they have contact with a child welfare system (Libesman 2008). This reflects the growing recognition within the UN human rights framework of the centrality of the principle of self-determination, which at minimum encompasses the right to participation in decisions which impact on Indigenous peoples' lives and recognition of their cultural rights (Anaya 2004).

In each jurisdiction the ATSICPP has been embedded in legislation and has a similar descending order of placement for children who need to be in out of home care:[14] the first preference being with the child's extended family or kinship group, the second preference with their local community and the third preference with another Aboriginal or Torres Strait Islander family in the area. If these preferences are not practicable or in the best interests of the child, then they will be placed with a non-Aboriginal or Torres Strait Islander family. There is also a requirement in each jurisdiction that relevant Aboriginal or Torres Strait Islander organisations (and in some jurisdictions, the extended family) be consulted about the child's placement. In each jurisdiction children who are placed with non-Indigenous carers are to be assisted to keep in contact with their family, language and culture, and in most jurisdictions the aim is to reunite children who are placed in non-Indigenous care with their families and communities. The principle is established in a more or less rigorous form in legislation in all states and territories in Australia.[15]

In four Australian jurisdictions (Queensland, South Australia, Victoria and Western Australia) there is legislative provision for the gazetting or designating of Aboriginal and Torres Strait Islander organisations, which has formalised their role in decision-making. Designated or gazetted organisations such as the Victorian Aboriginal Children's Service (VACCA) have developed into large organisations, which are highly respected by all stakeholders in child welfare, including government departments and non-Indigenous NGOs, and which have transformed non-Indigenous understandings of Indigenous children and young people's experience of child welfare and their broader needs. Indigenous organisations have also changed through the roles and responsibilities which they have assumed, many attaining capacities and skills related to assessing and addressing child welfare needs, providing out of home care services, training and educating non-Indigenous organisations in cultural care, providing cultural advice to governments and advocating and negotiating with government agencies, amongst other responsibilities.[16] Legislation in some jurisdictions, such as New

South Wales, include explicit reference to Indigenous organisations' participation in decisions with respect to Aboriginal and Torres Strait Islander children with as much 'self-determination' as is possible (*Children and Young Persons (Care and Protection) Act 1998*, s. 12). While the wording in this legislation is inherently contradictory, providing that the extent of self-determination is constrained by the extent to which the Department of Community Services (NSW) will exercise its discretion to allow it, it is reflective of changing normative values and understandings with respect to differences between Indigenous and non-Indigenous children and young people and how these differences are relevant in understanding the nature of abuse and neglect and what is required to address their wellbeing.

A memorandum of understanding between VACCA and the Department of Human Services (in which the child protection service is located) has set a precedent for the kind of cultural understanding and respectful relationships between Indigenous children's organisations and government departments which should be aspired to (DHS 2002). The *Children, Youth and Families Act 2005* (Vic) and memorandum of understanding establish VACCA's jurisdiction with respect to Aboriginal and Torres Strait Islander children and young people. This is a sphere of influence which has expanded as understandings and more subtle nuances with respect to cultural difference have been established. Lakidjeka Aboriginal Child Specialist Advice Support Service (ACSASS) is a service within VACCA which provides advice and contributes to the case planning and decision-making for all Aboriginal and Torres Strait Islander children who have contact with child protection services in Victoria. ACSASS is involved from the point when DHS is notified about a child to involvement in compliance with the ATSICPP if the child needs to be placed in out of home care.[17] ACSASS case workers are cultural consultants who provide an Indigenous perspective on risk and safety assessments and who work as partners with DHS, involving family and community in the case management of Indigenous children who have contact with the Victorian child protection system. While ACSASS makes an enormous contribution to children's wellbeing, its impact is limited by the lack of culturally appropriate services for referral purposes and measures to address the systemic disadvantage which Indigenous people in Victoria face.

Despite enlarged consciousness within government departments and amongst non-government child welfare organisations, bureaucratic and conceptual barriers persist in preventing a more complete implementation of the ATSICPP and, more broadly, cultural care for Indigenous children in out of home care. A participant in recent research with respect to the provision of cultural care to Indigenous children in out of home care commented with respect to the Victorian Department of Human Services Cultural Care Plans:

> They just want to put it in a box, put a boomerang on it and call it culture. Cultural care is more complex than this. (Libesman 2011, p.11)

This statement encapsulates the contradictory attitude of DHS; on the one hand Victoria is the only jurisdiction where cultural care plans are legislatively mandated for Aboriginal and Torres Strait Islander children on guardianship orders, while on the other the ongoing awareness and resources required to substantially implement these is lacking. The anomalous situation of support for cultural care but a lack of either resources or understanding to effectively implement this requirement is indicative of the transitional consciousness which greater influence and contact with Indigenous organisations such as VACCA creates. The pluralisation of child welfare is a process rather than something that can or has been implemented at a point in time.

Despite VACCA's expanded role and the shift in consciousness which engagement with VACCA has facilitated, the organisation looks after a relatively small number of children in out of home care and has not been able to impact on the systemic factors which result in the disproportionate contact which Indigenous children from Victoria have with the child welfare system. These systemic factors require a culturally embedded approach to community development which redresses poverty, intergenerational trauma, racism and marginalisation from the services and opportunities which are available to other sections of the community. For this to occur there needs to be broader participation by and recognition of Indigenous organisations and communities across housing, education, employment, health and in all spheres of social inclusion. A structural approach to children's wellbeing, however, as the Northern Territory Emergency Response discussed below illustrates, must be founded on the same human rights principles which have transformed Indigenous peoples' engagement with international law over the past decades and which has provided the foundation for legislative reform to child protection legislation. While reform to child protection legislation has been incremental and the process of legislative inclusion transforming bureaucratic and dominant Anglo-understandings is slow and ongoing, it nonetheless has brought about positive change. The culturally infused micro-experiences, which saturate difference between mainstream and Indigenous organisations and personal interactions, push against and challenge dominant language, resources and personal interactions and bring Indigenous understanding, albeit incrementally, to the jurisprudence of child welfare at a national and international level.

The Northern Territory Emergency Response

The Northern Territory has a history of neglect of Aboriginal and Torres Strait Islander children in the area of child welfare (Pocock 2010). It is the most overt colonial frontier in contemporary Australia. While Aboriginal people have retained or attained parts of their traditional lands,[18] and in many communities speak their own language and practise ceremonies as a central part of their belief system, they have also been impacted by the worst of Western culture, with a loss of traditional food sources and the introduction of alcohol and other drugs, gambling and pornography and, related to this, high levels of violence, in particular against women and children. The trauma of past colonial policies is often compounded by current and repeated traumatic experiences (Aboriginal Child Sexual Assault Taskforce 2006; Atkinson 2002; Board of Inquiry into the Child Protection System in the Northern Territory 2011; Robertson 2000). Indigenous communities have faced an incursion of the worst of Western culture with little support to address the problems related to this. They have advocated that supporting their culture serves to strengthen their communities and that culture provides a buffer against social breakdown. The research which has looked at the impact of culture on social breakdown, for example suicide rates amongst Indigenous youth and engagement in risky behaviour, suggests that cultural strength does serve as a buffer against the social breakdown ushered in by colonialism.[19]

In the course of 2006 and 2007, considerable publicity focused on child sexual assault in Aboriginal communities in the Northern Territory, particularly after the revelation of horrific cases, by public prosecutor Nanette Rogers, on a current affairs program (Australian Broadcasting Corporation 2006). While these 'revelations' shocked many, the issues had been raised over decades with few effective responses (Board of Inquiry into the Protection of Aboriginal Children from Sexual Abuse 2007). Just prior to the 2007 election, the Commonwealth Government, under Prime Minister John Howard, with no notice, consultation, forward planning or evidence base, made the astounding decision to use the Australian Army to seize prescribed Aboriginal communities in the

Northern Territory, to suspend the *Racial Discrimination Act 1975* (Cth) and 'roll out' a more than billion dollar project of 'measures' collectively called the Northern Territory Emergency Response (NTER). This affected at its peak over 500 Aboriginal settlements in the Northern Territory ranging from large towns to town camps and outstations (NTER Review Board 2008). The NTER was ostensibly in response to the *Little Children are Sacred* report which was commissioned by the Chief Minister of the Northern Territory in response to the publicity surrounding child abuse in Aboriginal communities in the Northern Territory (Board of Inquiry into the Protection of Aboriginal Children from Sexual Abuse 2007). The NTER, commonly known as 'The Intervention', created enormous fear and disquiet in communities, and, with a veil of sanctity created through the proclaimed objective of child protection, attracted much attention but very little critical scrutiny from the media or the wider community.

The level of neglect experienced by Aboriginal communities in the Northern Territory warranted and continues to warrant urgent measures. Further, as discussed with respect to the Aboriginal and Torres Strait Islander Child Placement Principle above, addressing identity and cultural concerns without changing the systemic and structural factors which corrode Indigenous children's wellbeing, and which make them susceptible to abuse and neglect, cannot fundamentally change their life chances. However, it is not surprising that four years after the initiation of the intervention, as the Government's monitoring reports attest, very little has been achieved (Department of Families, Housing, Community Services and Indigenous Affairs 2010). It is remarkable that measures which were described as an emergency response are continuing despite a change of Federal Government from Liberal (conservative) to Labor and despite, as discussed below, the Intervention's assimilationist and neo-liberal ideological framework. While reforms to child protection legislation have adopted human rights principles of cultural recognition and participation by Aboriginal and Torres Strait Islander organisations, the Intervention has adopted a paternalistic approach, which heavy-handedly attempts to impose Eurocentric and punitive measures to 'clean up' Aboriginal communities.

The Intervention ushered in a regime of control which for many is reminiscent of the Protectionist era, when the Chief Protector was the guardian of all Aboriginal children and police officers could remove children at their discretion, when all aspects of Aboriginal peoples' lives, from who they could associate with, what medical treatment they received and where they lived, were regulated and controlled under the Act (Markus 1990). Reminiscent of the Protection era, the Intervention saw:

- the introduction of Mission Manager-styled business managers who were responsible for coordinating all aspects of the Intervention
- the requirement that traditional and other land owners sign mandatory five-year and subsequently 40-year leases handing broad control over their land to the Government
- the permit system which communities used to control who entered their land removed
- half of welfare income quarantined, to be spent on a 'basics card', which required the recipient to spend the money at designated stores on food and specified essential items, regardless of the recipient's conduct
- other benefits such as family payments dependent on compliance with sending children to school, even in communities where no functioning school existed.

Punishing financially deprived families, in communities where malnutrition is already a significant problem, and where many people live chaotic lives marked by crisis, which makes compliance with rules often difficult, will inevitably bring about greater hardship and suffering for some of the most disadvantaged children. This coercive measure contrasts with programs such as those initiated by Dr Chris Sarra, former principal of Cherbourg school, a former Aboriginal Reserve in Queensland, who turned non-attendance and poor achievement for Aboriginal children around with his *Stronger and Smarter* program which made school attractive and relevant for Aboriginal and Torres Strait Islander children.[20] The Intervention also brought in police officers to assist with law and order issues in communities, health workers to perform health checks on children, alcohol and pornography bans in communities and increased other services such as child welfare workers. These are services which have been abysmally lacking in Indigenous communities and which did not need the composite raft of legislation which enabled the Intervention to be given effect. Other aspects of the Intervention included the removal of customary law defences from the criminal code and new powers provided to the Australia Crime Commission allowing access to children and young people's medical records to investigate child abuse.[21]

With the change of Federal Government, a complaint to the United Nations and a report by the Special Rapporteur on Indigenous Affairs, some changes have been made to the Intervention in order to technically comply with the *Racial Discrimination Act 1975* (Cth). The major change is that welfare quarantining will now be extended to all welfare recipients, not just Indigenous people in the prescribed areas, and compensation will be paid for the acquisition of leases. However, these changes do not reform the fundamentally paternalistic values driving the Intervention.

Four years on, the NTER and the billion dollars plus spent appear to have made very little impact on Indigenous children's welfare (Board of Inquiry into the Child Protection System in the Northern Territory 2011). Whilst debates in the international arena persist with respect to how to most effectively address developmental needs of communities which have been beset by conflict and poverty, there is a level of consensus with respect to the need for community development to be participatory (Hunt 2005). The Intervention is founded on Western economic values, which have no embedded significance within communities and which have in more dilute forms in comparative international contexts proven to be counter-productive and destructive of Indigenous peoples' culture and community (Hepburn 2006). The compulsory acquisition of land through leases, which under the original Intervention was not negotiated and did not attract compensation, was plainly a discriminatory derogation from Aboriginal peoples' property rights. The justification provided for compulsory acquisition of land is twofold. The Government claims that it needs to secure control of areas to facilitate major investments such as housing and then to implement market rents for housing which it provides. The idea of a market regulated economy within remote communities and town camps defies the reality of the situation – there is little commercial opportunity in these communities and the idea is in stark contradiction with the competing value system in place that emphasises land and community relations.

Prior to the implementation of the Intervention, the Howard Government already had a longstanding agenda of mainstreaming Aboriginal affairs. In 2006, a year prior to the Intervention, the Commonwealth Government enacted controversial reforms following the Reeves Review of the *Aboriginal Land Rights (Northern Territory) Act 1976* (Cth) (Reeves 1998), including reforms which enabled the lease arrangements which underpin the Intervention's land reforms.[22] These reforms, together with others which were recommended by John Reeves QC, would break down Aboriginal decision-making bodies, including the land councils in the Northern Territory, and dilute Aboriginal control over land (Reeves 1998). There is no mention of child abuse in the Reeves Review. It is curious that Mr Reeves QC was one of the eight members of Mr Howard's emergency response taskforce appointed to oversee the Intervention. It is more curious that nowhere in the text of the legislation which enabled the Intervention are children mentioned.

The innovation of the Intervention was the inclusion of a massive project of structural reform to address children's welfare. Its tragedy, in addition to leaving vulnerable people feeling further shamed and disempowered, is that the opportunity to harness structural reform to address systemic disadvantage in a manner which respects Aboriginal peoples' human rights has been squandered on an ideological experiment. It is doubtful whether the audacious implementation of the Intervention, which lacks an evidence base or precedent anywhere in the world, could have avoided the scrutiny which it did if it had not been implemented in the name of child protection. The robust element of contest in media, amongst advocacy groups and more broadly in the community, with respect to the Howard Government's rejection of principles of self-determination and adoption of a 'One Australia' policy, largely evaporated in the less than transparent cloud of child protection which enveloped the Intervention.

Conclusion

A human rights approach to Indigenous children and young people's wellbeing has at its core participation and engagement with Indigenous peoples and communities. In this way the experience of Indigenous peoples is incorporated into measures to address their wellbeing whether it be at an individual family level or with respect to the systemic and structural issues which underpin their disproportionate rate of contact with child protection systems. It is ironic that homogeneous and paternalistic understandings lie at the core of the colonial violence which grounds current inequities and yet a commitment to this frame of reference is evident in the Northern Territory Intervention. The opportunity exists to bring pluralised human rights understandings, which have incrementally developed in child protection through legislative reforms such as those discussed with respect to the ATSICPP, to projects with resources on the scale of the NTER and thereby initiate reforms which address the ongoing, devastating and routine breaches of Australian Indigenous children's human rights.

Endnotes

1. Thank you to Costa Avgoustinos for his research assistance work on this chapter. The sections of this chapter which assess the Aboriginal and Torres Strait Islander Child Placement Principle draws on research on cultural care prepared by the author for the Secretariat of National Aboriginal and Torres Strait Islander Child Care (SNAICC) and Barnardo's Australia. The report from this research (Libesman 2011) is available on the SNAICC website at www.snaicc.asn.au/_uploads/rsfil/02727.pdf.
2. For an analysis and review of UN Treaty jurisprudence with respect to Indigenous children see Libesman 2007.
3. The inequities between Indigenous and non-Indigenous Australians are evident in all spectrums of wellbeing: health, life expectancy, education, employment, income, housing. See, for example, the Australian Bureau of Statistics 2010.
4. For example, several of the influential recommendations of NISATSIC's *Bringing Them Home Report* in 1997 were inspired by the US *Indian Child Welfare Act 1978*. Further, Australian Indigenous organisations such as SNAICC have close relations with Canadian Indigenous organisations such as the First Nations Child and Caring Society of Canada. For a review of comparative legislative and policy frameworks see Libesman 2004.
5. General Assembly Resolution 1514 (xv), 14 December 1960, facilitated international decolonisation measures.
6. For a discussion of the influence of Indigenous peoples in international law see Anaya 2001 and Thornberry 2002.
7. See Thornberry 2002, p.128.
8. However, the Human Rights Committee has clearly differentiated between the right to self-determination in Article 1 and minority group rights in Article 27. See *General Comment No. 23: The rights of minorities* (Art. 27): 08/04/94. CCPR/C/21/Rev.1/Add.5, paras. 2–3.1.
9. See, for example: *Sandra Lovelace v Canada*, Communication No. 24/1977; *Ilmari Lansman et al. v Finland*, Communication No. 511/1992, views adopted on 30 July 1981; *Jouni E. Lansman et al. v Finland*, Communication No. 167/1995, views adopted on 30 October 1996; *Ominayak v Canada*, Communication No. 167/1984. For discussion of these cases see Libesman 2007.
10. For example, general comments by the HRC were acknowledged by the Committee on the Rights of the Child in their recommendations made at the Day of General Discussion on the Rights of Indigenous Children. They noted, '...the enjoyment of rights under Article 30, in particular the right to enjoy one's culture, may consist of a way of life which is closely associated with territory and use of its resources. This may be particularly true of members of Indigenous communities constituting a minority.' The Committee on the Rights of the Child, 34th session, Day of General Discussion on the Rights of Indigenous Children, Recommendation 4, 3 October 2003.

11. See Libesman 2007 for more detailed discussion of the jurisprudence of CROC and ICCPR.
12. The Committee on the Rights of the Child (at the 34th session, Day of General Discussion on the Rights of Indigenous Children, 3 October 2003) reaffirmed its commitment to promote and protect the human rights of Indigenous children by addressing more systematically the situation of Indigenous children when reviewing periodic state reports; see Recommendation 2.
13. See NISATSIC 1997 and Cunneen and Libesman 2002 for further discussion on the destructive impact of child removal and assimilationist government policies.
14. *Children and Young People Act* (2008). Canberra: Australian Capital Territory Legislative Assembly. ss.10, 513; *Children and Young Persons (Care and Protection) Act* (1998). Sydney: New South Wales Parliament. s.13; *Care and Protection of Children Act* (2007). Darwin: Northern Territory Legislative Assembly. s.12(3); *Child Protection Act* (1999). Brisbane: Queensland Parliament. s.83; *Children's Protection Act* (1993). Adelaide: South Australia Parliament. s.4(5); *Children's Protection Regulations* (2006). Adelaide: South Australia Parliament. reg. 4; *Children, Young Persons and their Families Act* (1997). Hobart: Tasmanian Parliament. s.9 (the principle is more clearly stated as policy of the Department of Health and Human Services); *Children, Youth and Families Act* (2005). Melbourne: Victoria Parliament. s.13; *Children and Community Services Act* (2004). Perth: Western Australia Parliament. s.12.
15. Ibid.
16. See VACCA's official website for the range of services which this organisation provides: www.vacca.org.
17. *Children, Youth and Families Act 1995*, s.12.
18. This has been achieved via various pieces of legislation such as the *Aboriginal Land Rights (Northern Territory) Act 1976* (Cth).
19. For example, research suggests that Aboriginal and Torres Strait Islander youth in remote areas who speak an Indigenous language are less likely to engage in risky behaviour (for example, alcohol or substance abuse): Australian Bureau of Statistics 2011. Also see Chandler and Lalonde 1998.
20. See the official website of the Stronger and Smarter Institute, which has been established to replicate and develop Dr Sarra's work: www.strongersmarter.qut.edu.au/profiles/index.jsp.
21. This has been controversial as doctors have been concerned the breach of privacy will inhibit patients from seeking medical treatments which they need. For discussion on this point, see *Crikey* 2010.
22. The removal of the permit system was only given legislative effect in 2007 with the implementation of the Intervention; reforms were rejected by the Senate in Parliament when the *Aboriginal Land Rights (Northern Territory) Act 1976* was amended a year earlier, in 2006.

References

Aboriginal Child Sexual Assault Taskforce (2006) *Breaking the Silence: Creating the Future; Addressing Child Sexual Assault in Aboriginal Communities*. Sydney: Attorney General's Department.

Anaya, J. (2001) 'The Influence of Indigenous Peoples on the Development of International Law.' In S. Garwkawe, L. Kelly and W. Fisher (eds) *Indigenous Human Rights*. Sydney: Federation Books.

Anaya, J. (2004) *Indigenous Peoples in International Law*. Sydney: Oxford University Press.

Atkinson, J. (2002) *Trauma Trails: Recreating Song Lines*. Melbourne: Spinifex Press.

Australian Broadcasting Corporation (2006) 'Prosecutor reveals sexual abuse and violence in NT Indigenous communities.' *Lateline*, television broadcast transcript, 15 May. Available at www.abc.net.au/lateline/content/2006/s1639133.htm, accessed on 5 May 2011.

Australian Bureau of Statistics (2010) *National Aboriginal and Torres Strait Islander Social Survey: Users' Guide 2008*. Canberra: ABS. Available at www.abs.gov.au/ausstats/abs@.nsf/mf/4720.0, accessed on 5 May 2011.

Australian Bureau of Statistics (2011) *Aboriginal and Torres Strait Islander Wellbeing: A Focus on Children and Youth*. Canberra: ABS. Available at www.abs.gov.au/ausstats/abs@.nsf/Lookup/4725.0main+features1Apr%202011, accessed on 5 May 2011.

Australian Institute of Health and Welfare (AIHW) (2010) *Child Protection Australia 2008–2009: Child Welfare Series No 47*. Canberra: AIHW.

Board of Inquiry into the Child Protection System in the Northern Territory (2011) *Growing them Strong, Together*. Darwin: Northern Territory Government.

Board of Inquiry into the Protection of Aboriginal Children from Sexual Abuse (2007) *Little Children are Sacred*. Darwin: Northern Territory Government.

Chandler, M. and Lalonde, C. (1998) 'Cultural continuity as a hedge against suicide in Canada's First nations.' *Transcultural Psychiatry 35*, 2, 191–219.

Convention on the Rights of the Child (CROC) (1989) New York: United Nations.

Crikey (2010) 'The latest on the Australian Crime Commission's invasion of medical records and patient privacy.' 12 February. Available at http://blogs.crikey.com.au/croakey/2010/02/12/the-latest-on-the-australian-crime-commissions-invasion-of-medical-records-and-patient-privacy, accessed on 5 May 2011.

Cunneen, C. and Libesman, T. (2002) 'Removed and discarded: The contemporary legacy of the stolen generations.' *Australian Indigenous Law Reporter 7*, 4, 1–26.

Department of Families, Housing, Community Services and Indigenous Affairs (2010) *Closing the Gap in the Northern Territory Monitoring Report January–June 2010*. Canberra: Australian Government. Available at www.fahcsia.gov.au/sa/indigenous/pubs/nter_reports/ctg_monitoring_report_jan_Jul10/Pages/default.aspx, accessed on 5 May 2011.

DHS (Department of Human Services) (2002) *The Protocol between the Department of Human Services and the Victorian Aboriginal*. Melbourne: DHS. Available at www.cyf.vic.gov.au/__data/assets/pdf_file/0004/15979/dhs-vacca-protocol-2002.pdf, accessed on 5 May 2011.

Hepburn, S. (2006) 'Transforming customary title to individual title: Revisiting the Cathedral.' *Deakin Law Review 11*, 1, 64–88.

Human Rights Council (2010) *Report of the Special Rapporteur on the Situation of Human Rights and Fundamental Freedoms. Addendum: The Situation of Indigenous Peoples in Australia, James Anaya.* UN Doc A/HRC/15/37Add.4. Available at www2.ohchr.org/english/issues/indigenous/rapporteur/docs/ReportVisitAustralia.pdf, accessed on 5 May 2011.

Hunt, J. (2005) *Capacity Development in the International Development Context: Implications for Indigenous Australia.* Canberra: Centre for Aboriginal Economic Policy Research. Available at https://digitalcollections.anu.edu.au/bitstream/1885/43047/2/2005_DP278.pdf, accessed on 3 February 2012.

Libesman, T. (2004) *Child Welfare Approaches for Indigenous Communities: International Perspectives.* Melbourne: Australian Institute of Family Studies. Available at www.aifs.gov.au/nch/pubs/issues/issues20/issues20.pdf, accessed on 3 February 2012.

Libesman, T. (2007) 'Can international law imagine the world of indigenous children?' *International Journal of Children's Rights 15*, 2, 283–309.

Libesman, T. (2008) 'Aboriginal and Torres Strait Islander Children and Contemporary Child Welfare.' In G. Monahan and L. Young (eds) *Children and the Law in Australia.* Sydney: LexisNexis Butterworths.

Libesman, T. (2011) *Culture Care for Aboriginal and Torres Strait Islander Children in Out of Home Care.* Melbourne: The Secretariat of National Aboriginal and Islander Child Care (SNAICC). Available at www.snaicc.asn.au/_uploads/rsfil/02727.pdf, accessed on 3 February 2012.

Markus, A. (1990) *Governing Savages.* Sydney: Allen and Unwin.

Melbourne Herald, The (1933) 'Petition to the King.' 15 September.

NISATSIC (National Inquiry into the Separation of Aboriginal and Torres Strait Islander Children from their Families) (1997) *Bringing Them Home: Report of the National Inquiry into the Separation of Aboriginal and Torres Strait Islander Children from their Families.* Sydney: Human Rights and Equal Opportunity Commission.

NTER Review Board (Northern Territory Emergency Response Review Board) (2008) *Report of the NTER Review Board.* Canberra: Australian Government. Available at www.nterreview.gov.au/docs/report_nter_review/appendix-10.htm, accessed on 5 May 2011.

Pocock, J. (2010) *State of Denial: The Neglect and Abuse of Aboriginal and Torres Strait Islander Children in the Northern Territory.* Melbourne: The Secretariat of National Aboriginal and Islander Child Care (SNAICC).

Reeves, J. (1998) *Building on the Land Rights for the Next Generation: Report of the Review of the Aboriginal Land Rights (Northern Territory) Act 1976.* Canberra: Aboriginal and Torres Strait Islander Commission.

Robertson, B. (2000) *The Aboriginal and Torres Strait Islander Women's Task Force on Violence Report.* Brisbane: Department of Aboriginal and Torres Strait Islander Development.

Thornberry, P. (2002) *Indigenous Peoples and Human Rights.* Manchester: Manchester University Press.

UN Commission on Human Rights Resolution 2001/57. New York: United Nations.

UN Economic and Social Council Resolution 2000/22. New York: United Nations.

PART III

Child Welfare and Family Identity

Chapter 11

High Frequency Parental Contact for Infants in Care

Whose Rights are Being Served?

Cathy Humphreys and Meredith Kiraly

Introduction

Family contact for babies in care is not a new issue. However, there is some new territory in the 21st century. This includes the developing body of knowledge on neurobiology and attachment between infants and their carers; the changing nature of foster care whereby parents (at least in some jurisdictions) rarely visit their children in the home of the foster carer; and the assertion of children's rights under the UN Convention on the Rights of the Child (United Nations 1989). There is also a trend in some jurisdictions to move decision-making about abused children into inquisitorial or consensus-building processes through the child protection system and Children's Court. These changes in policy and practice provide the backdrop for a discussion about babies in care and the extent to which their best interests are understood and served, in relation to contact with their mothers and fathers. The issue of high frequency contact which is currently being ordered by the Children's Court of Victoria (Australia) is outlined in Vignette 1. It is a particularly vexed issue and one which provides the focus for this chapter.

Vignette 1

Tom was born substance affected. He spent the first three weeks in hospital and then moved to a foster care placement. The Children's Court ordered supervised access with his mother five days per week involving 50-minute journeys each way. The Department of Human Services, Victoria, contested this, but failed in their attempt to gain a less intensive parental contact arrangement. The foster care agency reported that, in a week, usually five different people supervised contact visits. Sometimes visits went well, but other times Tom's mother slept through the visit. Her attendance was inconsistent. Tom is reported to be having difficulty establishing a sleep routine and is suffering from frequent colds.

This chapter draws from a research study which explored the issue of infants and high frequency contact (defined as contact from four to seven times per week between infants and family members). It arose initially from concerns by foster carers and child protection workers about the impact of such orders of the Children's Court of Victoria.

A number of different aspects of the literature are relevant to this research, in particular issues in relation to attachment and neurobiology; the changing nature of parental contact in relation to children in foster care; and interpretation of the UN Convention in relation to infants.

Neurobiology and attachment issues

The turn of the century has brought increased interest in the social nature of brain development (Shonkoff and Phillips 2000). While the early attachment theorists (Ainsworth 1967; Bowlby 1969, 1982) understood the significance of infants' relationships with primary carers and their distress when these relationships were disrupted through their research and clinical observation (Winnicott 1960), it was not until some time later that the links between neurological development and attachment to consistent caring adults was established (Perry 1997).

The neurobiology and attachment literature draws attention to the first year of life as critical. Massive brain development occurs, which is directly related to the infant's attachment experience (Perry 1997). While brain development begins in utero, it is only 25 per cent of its adult size at birth, but by three years it is 90 per cent of adult size. Within that time, the density of the brain also increases with extraordinary development of the interconnections between different parts of the brain (RACP 2006, cited in Jordan and Sketchley 2009). This critical cognitive, behavioural and emotional development occurs in the context of infants' attachment relationships (functional and dysfunctional) with their primary caregivers (Steele 2002).

The research on attachment is not without controversy. Feminist and cross-cultural researchers have queried the over-riding importance of a primary attachment figure and have looked to evidence which suggests that multiple attachments are possible (Hazan and Shaver 1994). Some clarity is emerging that infants require a parental figure who has the capacity to create a safe, predictable and secure psychological and physical space, and that without this adult the infant's capacity to grow and explore the world is limited. Within the infant's world there is a hierarchy of attachment relationships, with empirical evidence consistently showing that, even when a range of safe, caring figures are available, infants show clear discrimination and consistent preferences (Jordan and Sketchley 2009). Multiple relationships are clearly possible though not limitless, and support for quality and consistency in these relationships is important for infant development that is not undermined by distress (Beek and Schofield 2006).

Family contact in out of home care

The entry of a baby into care creates myriad issues in relation to the development of key relationships. The maintenance of the infant's relationship with their mother and/or father may be critical if reunification is to remain a possibility. At the same time the infant needs to settle into a predictable environment with a carer who is highly attuned to their needs, in order to ameliorate the destructive effects of disrupted relationships in this earliest period of life (Dozier *et al.* 2002).

The first year of life encompasses a wide developmental range. While infants between six months and three years may show the strongest indications of separation anxiety and stranger anxiety (American Academy of Pediatrics 2000; Bowlby 1982), the work of Dozier *et al.* (2002) measuring levels of cortisol ('the stress hormone') showed that younger infants were stressed by separation from their carer even when external signs of distress were not apparent.

In a retrospective study of 26 families where high frequency contact (up to five days per week) occurred with parents while infants were in foster care (Kenrick 2009), significant levels of distress in infants were reported. In this study it was the carer who was taking the infant to contact visits. The research found disruption for infants associated with: leaving their foster carer at significant points in their development; the extent of commuting; and the level of disruption to routines. Continuing effects were evident in such areas as joining playgroups and starting school, long after children were established in permanent care. The research pointed to particular concerns which lay with infants moving rapidly into the high frequency contact regime before they had time to settle and get to know their carer. It was a particular issue for infants coming to the carer direct from hospital, and for infants from five to eight months of age when there appeared to be greater sensitivity and anxiety about separation (Kenrick 2009).

The Kenrick (2009) study is one of the few to explore the impact of high frequency contact on infants who are travelling to visit parents. There is little research evidence on the effects of different patterns and intensities of family contact for very young children in care (Haight, Kagle and Black 2003; Monck, Reynolds and Wigfall 2005). In particular, frequency of family contact for infants who are being transported away from a significant (and often primary) attachment figure by a number of different workers has not been directly addressed.

Infants and the Convention

The UN Convention provides principles, but not specific guidelines, about how competing clauses should be realised (Kelly and Mullender 2000). A number of articles are relevant in understanding and responding to children's needs at the individual, institutional and societal level. Rights to good care and protection (Article 3) and participation in decision-making as appropriate to maturity (Article 12) sit alongside the rights to protection from violence and abuse (Article 19) and to family life (Article 7). This is a landmark document in asserting that children are the bearers of human rights, not just the recipients of welfare and protection (Tsantefski, Humphreys and Jackson forthcoming 2012) with separate interests to their parents (Schoeman 1980).

Where there is tension between articles in the Convention, such as when the infant's right to protection and safety, and the parent's rights and duties regarding guardianship and custody of their child, are unable to be simultaneously realised, adherence to Article 3(1) requires this conflict to be resolved according to the child's best interests (Tsantefski *et al.* forthcoming 2012). In an adversarial system, each side will argue vehemently that they represent the 'best interests of the child' and this clearly occurs over parental contact where there is a history of child abuse or neglect. It is therefore unsurprising that the primary critique of the Convention turns on this issue of 'best interests', which is both difficult to interpret and to implement in practice (Bessell and Gal 2009; Musgrove and Swain 2010).

Potentially, the development of an evidence base to inform an understanding of the 'best interests of infants' may assist in taking the discussion beyond adversarial point-scoring between lawyers. The literature to date highlights a set of complexities for infants in out of home care and their contact arrangements, which warrant further exploration in relation to the impact on infants' wellbeing, the development of attachments, brain development and family reunification. A research project was developed as the first stage in a complex area of work.

Description of the study

A multi-methods study was undertaken to explore the issues arising where family contact at different levels of frequency was being ordered for infants in protective care. The study addressed the following questions. *First*, what are the current arrangements for infants' contact with their family members in Victoria? *Second*, what are the issues which impact on the infant's experience of contact with their family members? *Third*, what are the directions for good practice in this area? The study had ethics approval from both the Department of Human Services (DHS) Human Research Ethics Committee and the University of Melbourne. A reference group was established to oversee the research. The Victorian Child Safety Commissioner, President of the Children's Court, infant mental health specialists, representatives from foster care organisations, DHS senior policy workers, and academics from the University of Melbourne brought different perspectives to review the study in progress.

The multi-methods utilised were three-fold. *First*, there was data mining of the electronic child protection files (Epstein 2001) to explore the patterns of court-ordered family contact, the extent of high frequency family contact orders, related demographic data, and some detail about the implementation of these arrangements. Files were examined for all infants 12 months of age or less who were in care on 1 August 2007. Frequent family contact was defined as four to seven visits per week with family members. Infants were mainly in foster care or kinship care, with some newborns in hospital at the time contact orders were commenced.

Second, focus groups, interviews and brief case studies were recorded to provide a rich understanding of the patterns and impact of arrangements on infants, their parents and caregivers (Patton 2002). Eleven focus groups involving 118 participants and five interviews with relevant stakeholders were undertaken. The groups comprised foster carers and managers; child protection workers; case support workers involved in transporting and supervising contact visits; high-risk-infant specialists; legal representatives for parents; Department of Human Services (DHS) lawyers (who present matters at Court); and Children's Court Clinic staff (who undertake assessments for the Children's Court). The focus groups and interviews were audio-recorded and the records transcribed and coded using NVivo (QSR 2010).

Third, 30 brief case studies were collected opportunistically using a semi-structured approach in response to requests from foster carers and DHS and foster agency case managers who wished the researchers to know details of cases where high frequency contact had been ordered.

A set of themes emerged from the coded data, and analysis continued until no new themes emerged (Garrison *et al.* 2006). Themes were generally strong and consistent; however, there was intense disagreement between many legal advocates for parents, and human services staff and foster carers involved directly with infants (Humphreys and Kiraly 2009).

The study findings

The data mining of the case files brought several important issues to light. One-third of all cases (40 out of 119) had a high frequency family contact Court Order at some stage of the infant's life. In this group, substance abuse was evident in the majority of cases: usually involving both parents (29 mothers and 23 fathers out of 40 cases). Domestic violence and mental health problems were also significant issues. In many cases, contact between infants and their parents occurred only infrequently in spite of the high frequency contact order. Reasons evident from the files included parental illness; financial and other difficulties with transport; being in jail; and, other reasons not articulated, presumably related to parents' social issues and circumstances. Rarely did contact not occur due to an infant's illness, and even more rarely because DHS had been unable to provide a worker to support the contact.

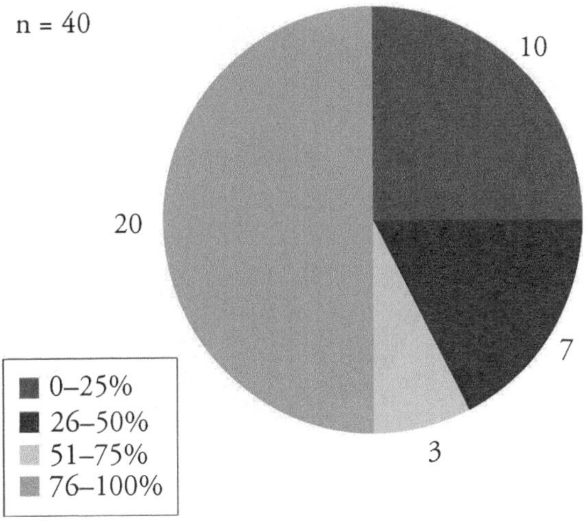

FIGURE 11.1 Number of high frequency contact ordered visits, by proportion of visits that actually occurred

Figure 11.1 shows that half of the parents (20) for whom high frequency contact was ordered (mainly but not exclusively mothers) attended for more than 75 per cent of the contact visits, while for the other half of the parents, contact visits occurred much less frequently than ordered.

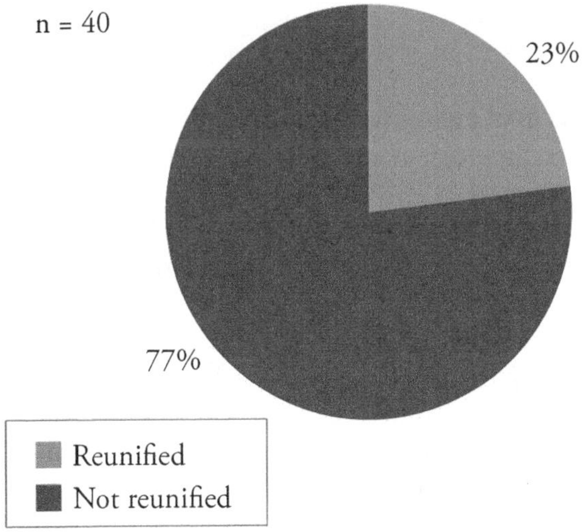

FIGURE 11.2 Reunification of infants and parents with one or more orders for high frequency family contact (one year on)

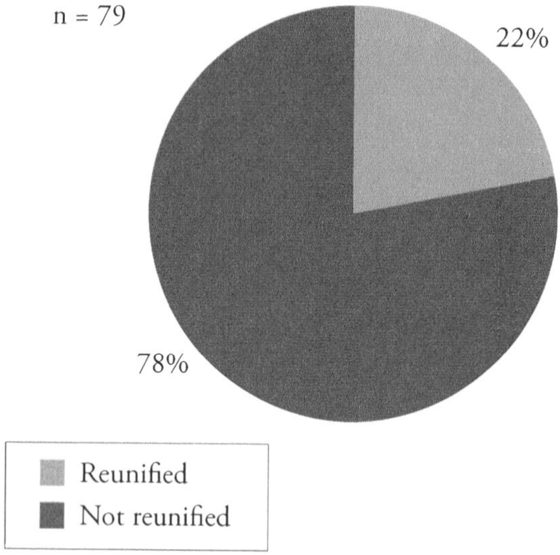

FIGURE 11.3 Reunification of infants and parents without an order for high frequency family contact (one year on)

The ordering of high frequency family contact did not contribute to a greater rate of family reunification (Figures 11.2 and 11.3). At the end of one year, the reunification rate for infants with high frequency contact and those with a lesser level of contact were virtually the same (23% and 22% respectively).

Focus group and case study data

The focus group and case study data indicated that all the stakeholder groups were generally positively disposed to family contact for infants in care, despite the inherent challenges. However, regarding the appropriate frequency of parental contact for infants, opinion was generally sharply divided between parents' lawyers and those who worked with infants (foster carers, child protection workers, foster care managers, high-risk-infant specialists), with views from Children's Court Clinic staff straddling both sides of the argument. Concerns pertained particularly to infants travelling away from the home in which they were trying to settle, not to situations seen more frequently in kinship care when infants were visited by their parents in the carer's home. Those who were directly involved with infants were strongly of the view that high frequency contact was unmanageable for the infants involved. However, many parents' lawyers were equally strong in their view that parents had a right to see their baby as frequently as possible and argued for up to seven days a week of contact visits. Both sides felt that their view was in the best interest of infants. There were, however, points of commonality; these are articulated below.

Attachment

Significantly, both groups saw the infant's attachment issues as important. The lawyers for the parents saw this in relation to the infant's connection to their parent, while those working with infants prioritised the need for them to become settled and stabilised with their carer to promote their wellbeing and relationship development:

> The important thing for a baby and their future emotional health is how well they're responded to and looked after by a constant carer...because we all know that children, if they get that really good, solid response and care in those first six months whilst their parents do whatever work they need to be able to care for them safely, they will be able to form an attachment with their parents if we do return them home. (Case support worker 1)

The relationship between the infant's attachment relationship and brain development was a theme among many infant workers, as many had training input on this. By contrast, some parents' lawyers were less convinced about the role of neurological development, and a few spoke strongly against its significance.

A problem for attachment identified by those looking after infants was the multiple strangers involved in their handling and care during contact visiting arrangements. Few carers were involved in providing parental contact in their own homes or driving infants to visits in Victoria. Infants are therefore often involved with an 'army' of support workers transporting them. The more frequent the visits, the more difficulty there seemed to be in keeping any regularity with support workers, particularly when the Court had ordered parental contact on weekends when workers were not on duty. It was felt that this was distressing for infants; observations of highly emotional reactions, and conversely, dissociating or 'freezing' (Bowlby 2007), were reported:

> Now, the older babies get, the harder it gets for them to leave us to go and see their birth parents. And we literally have to pass

> over screaming babies to the worker that might not be the same worker as yesterday. (Foster carer A)

A worker expressed concern that, in amongst the multiple adults involved, an infant may not have known who his mother was; the baby's mother had actually asked him if this was the case. Many parents' lawyers were less concerned about this and saw the issues largely as a resourcing problem for DHS. One lawyer expressed nostalgia for the days when children were in institutions, and therefore (allegedly) more accessible for parents to visit. These advocates were concerned that current resource difficulties in arranging frequent visits were seriously interfering with parents' rights for contact with their children.

Transportation

Numerous concerns were expressed about the amount of time infants spent travelling in cars to visits. Both frequency and lengths of trips were seen as problems. In rural areas, distances were often described as being excessive; in the city, traffic congestion was noted as adding time and making it more difficult to attend to care needs during travel. Exposure to undue temperatures was raised by some participants, especially frequent exposure to excessive heat in summer:

> I just think, even for your own children you would not expect to give your own infants that experience really, of that level of transport and that number of people. (Case support worker 2, rural Victoria)

Distress and disrupted routines

The distress associated with infants being unsettled and having disrupted routines was a dominant theme for those working with them. Indicators of stress following visits with parents were frequently mentioned, including unduly wakeful nights, sobbing to sleep, being tired and grizzly, and being clingy:

> Of course, going to an access involves possibly waking them up; they go in the car, they fall asleep again, they get woken up again, they're in the access. They go back in the car, they fall asleep again, and they get woken up again… It is quite traumatic. Then, of course, if they are cranky and unsettled it is harder on us as well. (Foster carer B)

In situations where there had been abuse, older infants at times were reported to show anxiety or fear directly – crying or pulling away from parents. Infants were also reported as sometimes becoming passive or 'floppy' on visits. These behavioural manifestations are symptomatic of trauma in infants (Jordan and Sketchley 2009).

A couple of carers spoke of differences they had experienced in infants' behaviour when high frequency parental contact shifted to lower frequency visits of longer duration. Vignette 2 provides an example.

Vignette 2

James came to us at five weeks with his two-year-old brother Frank. There were two siblings in care elsewhere. At first, the access visit was four days per week for one hour, at the departmental office. They would go at 1 pm and return about 6 pm. The worker would pick up the other children after these two, as we were the furthest away. Returning was in peak-hour traffic. James was really unsettled; his routine was out. But they were both much more settled when access changed to twice a week, and for longer; the new travel time was only twenty minutes each way. At that stage, they went to their paternal grandfather's home, and he supervised access. Circumstances caused the change – the father died of a drug problem. So after that, less supervision was needed for the mother. I think that if ever it is possible to have access in a more natural environment, for longer and less often, it is better. In a six-hour access, they can have a bath and a nap. I thought it was brilliant. (Foster carer C)

Environments for visits

A point of agreement in all focus groups was the unsuitability of DHS offices for visits. Rooms were often described as being too small and lacking needed equipment. The environment was described as being threatening to parents, representing the authority that had removed the child – with the presence of a security guard as a visible reminder of this:

> Clients tell us about their experiences all the time. They hate supervised access at departmental offices. (Lawyer representing parents 1)

> I had a client whose access was facilitated by their foster care service and, at that stage, things improved dramatically. Until then, there'd actually been a cessation of access, which is very unusual. But that was a reflection of the fact that the client found the experience of access in the department's premises just unsupportable. (Lawyer representing parents 2)

Alternative venues that were also seen as unsuitable included shopping centres and fast food outlets. Many participants offered ideas about better environments for family visiting. Critical factors were seen as a friendly, informal atmosphere, and sufficient space and facilities for feeding, sleeping and play. It was understood that security arrangements needed to be in place for particular families, and that this might entail some compromise with an ideal environment, but it was also seen that many families did not need security guards present.

Support and communication between foster carers and parents

While not a common feature of current practice in Victoria, a number of participants commented on the value to both parents and infants of a supportive relationship between foster carers and parents:

> I think we could, with the magic wand approach…just let the carers work with the parents and, through education, break down that fear that's been drummed up over the last 20 years… Like when the extended family look after kids who go and visit auntie. (Case support manager 1)

> The children have gone home… We will build our relationship with the mother and be some sort of support, sort of like a grandparent. I've seen a few carers build relationships with mothers and help them – it's good for them. In the past it was not encouraged, but I think that's changing a little. (Foster carer C)

The adversarial court system

> The adversarial system prevails. [The parties' legal advocates], like I, are prisoners of the grossly wasteful processes of the adversarial system with their concomitant negative impact on the efficient, timely and economical disposition of proceedings

> in the Family Division of this Court. (Magistrate in *DOHS v Ms B & Mr G*, Children's Court of Victoria, 2008)

There was much concern expressed in the focus groups by those involved with infants about the overly adversarial nature of the court system. Legal advocates for parents were seen as arguing for very frequent parental contact, not necessarily because it was seen as desirable in its own right, but to maximise the chance of family reunification (a relationship with reunification not borne out by the case file data in this study). Some participants suggested that such arguments may take place even when parents themselves do not want high frequency visits:

> It commonly happens that we'll have a client [DHS child protection worker] saying, 'What do you mean the mother is not agreeing to reducing from five times weekly to three times weekly access? She was the one who asked for it, and now the lawyer is telling her that she's not agreeing to it. What's going on?' We're in a litigation field. Often a client's [parent's] mind will be changed once they've had discussion with their lawyer, which might go something like: 'Ms Brown, I'm not going to advise you to agree to reducing your frequency of access, because that might compromise your chances of having the child reunified with you'... Then we have to take it off to a contest if we want to get that reduction. (DHS lawyer 1)

On the other hand, many lawyers for parents saw the adversarial process as a protection for their clients and were mistrustful of the commitment of child protection workers to actively work with parents and support reunification:

> So I don't think there can be a Best Interests Plan until a court has made a decision about whether the parent is going to be able to be with the child. And I think that's part of the problem; that the department [workers] don't like having courts, they don't like other people interfering with their decision-making process. (Lawyer representing parents 2)

In summary, grave concerns about the policy of high frequency contact for infants emerged around a number of issues, not the least of which was using court battles to resolve such a sensitive matter.

Discussion and conclusion

The issues of attachment, infant distress and its causes, and the way in which the human rights of infants are approached through decision-making in an adversarial court system, frame discussion of the findings regarding infants in care and parental contact.

At the heart of this contentious issue lies the question of whether a context can be established which supports the 'capacity of the infant and caregiver to develop a positive interactive relationship' that will ensure appropriate brain development (Perry 2008). Babies are not objects that can simply be passed about to meet the needs of adults and comply with legal orders and the demands of complex organisational arrangements. Holding the infant's needs at the heart of arrangements for parental contact means that all parties (mothers, fathers, caregivers, lawyers, child protection workers and magistrates) need to have some awareness of infant development and its intimate connection to secure attachment relationships.

Our findings suggest that *quality* of contact may be more important than *frequency* of contact, and that parents may need much greater therapeutic and basic parenting support during visits with their children. Many mothers and fathers may also have been 'set up to fail' by having contact regimes that were impossible for them to maintain when they were struggling with substance abuse, mental health issues and domestic violence.

When infants are in care, they need to have time to settle, attune to their caregiver and establish a predictable and safe routine. This is difficult territory, as when an infant is in care for a significant time, it is likely to mean conceptualising the primary attachment as the person with 24-hour care. The separation process involves grief for the mother and father, and also for the infant if they have lived with their parent(s) prior to care. Without time to settle each day and particular nurturing through the separation process, the infant will be in an attachment vacuum, with no one fully attuned to their needs for much of the time. It is dangerous in both the short and long term. Mothers and fathers also clearly need support. To date this has received little recognition and poor service development. We would argue that continuing family contact is important, but not with arrangements that undermine the infant's ability to settle with their caregiver.

A further issue which to date has received little attention by the Court and policymakers is the changing practice of foster care. For better or worse, few foster carers in Victoria are prepared to host parents in their own home or drive the infant to parental contact visits. Foster carers are volunteers who receive minimal reimbursement for looking after children; many have jobs and other children; and many hold grave concerns about the drug abuse and violence which have brought infants into their care. In this context, orders for high frequency parental contact involve infants being transported considerable distances, often by multiple different workers. Foster carers were unconvinced that these orders benefited babies; their experience and descriptions of infant distress were palpable. Foster care organisations are now reporting increased difficulty recruiting carers who are prepared to be involved in these arrangements. However, these issues are not seen to be the concern of the Children's Court, even though they impact profoundly on infants.

Within the adversarial court system, it is difficult to hear infants' distress. Parents' lawyers argue that carers' reports of infant distress are self-interested. Reports from DHS workers that contact arrangements are not child-centred are dismissed as inappropriately bringing Departmental resource concerns to the Court. Rulings by Magistrates suggest they find the arguments from parents' lawyers more convincing than those of the Departmental lawyers, who consistently argue against high frequency parental contact.

Ongoing arguments about these issues in the Children's Court suggest a circuit breaker is needed. In some other jurisdictions, issues of parental contact for children are case planning decisions agreed through less adversarial processes (Goldsmith, Oppenheim and Wanlass 2004; Zero to Three 2005); more support is provided for parents and children during visits (Cleaver 2000; Miller *et al.* 2000; Pine, Warsh and Maluccio 1993). The details of parental contact are essentially case planning decisions which require an understanding of infants' needs in relation to the significant adults in their lives, and flexibility. There is little to suggest that court battles contribute to a nuanced understanding of infants' needs. Our research provided no evidence to suggest that high frequency parental contact provided a route to family reunification for these infants.

Interestingly, a one-day conference in the UK in late 2010 brought together researchers, child psychiatrists and judges to discuss the high frequency parental contact for infants in care (Family Justice Council 2010). The findings outlined in this Victorian research study were used alongside other evidence in presentations. Justice Munby, LJ, who made the daily parental contact decision for an infant in the UK, recanted his original judgment and pressed for further research on impact to help inform future decision-making. This is an illuminating example of the way in which social science research may be used to alert the judiciary to practices which are not aligned with the best interests of infants (Ministry of Justice 2011).

The struggle for the recognition of infants' rights requires that, where specific rights under the Convention are in tension, there should be an appropriate resolution of the paramount human right to provision of security and a nurturing environment. Adherence to Article 3 to address the best interests of the child only makes sense when seen in context of other Articles, in particular Article 19 (protection from abuse or maltreatment) (Tsantefski *et al.* forthcoming 2012). The Convention asserts that the right to family life (Article 7), while important, is qualified by the phrase 'as far as possible'. It is therefore not an unqualified parental right, but rather one in which other forms of family may also need to be considered. The highest priority needs to be given to the establishment of processes by the state which provide the most vulnerable babies in society with the best opportunities for their growth and development. The vignette about Tom at the start of this chapter, which was typical of the case studies, suggests that there is a long journey ahead in the adversarial jungle of Court and child protection processes.

References

Ainsworth, M.D.S. (1967) *Infancy in Uganda: Infant Care and the Growth of Love.* Baltimore: Johns Hopkins University Press.

American Academy of Pediatrics (2000) 'Developmental issues for young children in foster care.' *Pediatrics 106*, 1145–1150.

Beek, M. and Schofield, G. (2006) *Attachment for Foster Care and Adoption: A Training Programme.* London: British Association for Adoption and Fostering (BAAF).

Bessell, S. and Gal, T. (2009) 'Forming partnerships: The human rights of children in need of care and protection.' *International Journal of Children's Rights 1*, 17, 283–298.

Bowlby, J. (1969) *Attachment and Loss, Vol. 1: Attachment.* New York: Basic Books.

Bowlby, J. (1982) *Attachment and Loss, Vol. 1: Attachment* (2nd edition). New York: Basic Books.

Bowlby, R. (2007) 'Babies and toddlers in non-parental daycare can avoid stress and anxiety if they develop a lasting secondary attachment bond with one carer who is consistently accessible to them.' *Attachment and Human Development 9*, 4, 307–319.

Cleaver, H. (2000) *Fostering Family Contact.* Studies in Evaluating the Children Act 1989. London: The Stationery Office.

Dozier, M., Higley, E., Albus, K.E. and Nutter, A. (2002) 'Intervening with foster infants' caregivers: Targeting three critical needs.' *Infant Mental Health Journal 23*, 5, 541–554.

Epstein, I. (2001) 'Using available clinical information in practice based research: Mining for silver while dreaming of gold.' *Social Work in Health Care 33*, 3/4, 15–32.

Family Justice Council (2010) *Transcript of UK Family Justice Council Conference*. United Kingdom. Available at www.family-justice-council.org.uk/docs/Transcript_of_baby_contact_debate.pdf, accessed on 9 April 2011.

Garrison, D., Cleveland-Innes, M., Koole, M. and Kappelmann, T. (2006) 'Revisiting methodological issues in transcript analysis: Negotiated coding and reliability.' *Internet and Higher Education 9*, 1–8.

Goldsmith, D.F., Oppenheim, D. and Wanlass, J. (2004) 'Separation and reunification: Using attachment theory and research to inform decisions affecting the placements of children in foster care.' *Juvenile and Family Court Journal Spring 2004*, 1–14.

Haight, W.L., Kagle, J.D. and Black, J.E. (2003) 'Understanding and supporting parent–child relationships during foster care visits: Attachment theory and research.' *Social Work 48*, 2, 195–207.

Hazan, C. and Shaver, P. (1994) 'Deeper into attachment theory.' *Psychological Inquiry 5*, 1, 68–79.

Humphreys, C. and Kiraly, M. (2009) *Baby on Board: Report of the Infants in Care and Family Contact Research Project*. Melbourne: University of Melbourne.

Jordan, B. and Sketchley, R. (2009) *A Stitch in Time Saves Nine: Preventing and Responding to the Abuse and Neglect of Infants*. Melbourne: Australian Institute of Family Studies, Australian Government.

Kelly, L. and Mullender, A. (2000) 'Complexities and contradictions: Living with domestic violence and the UN Convention on Children's Rights.' *International Journal of Children's Rights 8*, 229–241.

Kenrick, J. (2009) 'Concurrent planning: A retrospective study of the continuities and discontinuities of care, and their impact on the development of infants and young children placed for adoption by the Coram Concurrent Planning Project.' *Adoption and Fostering 33*, 4, 5–18.

Miller, P.M., Gorski, P.A., Borchers, D.A., Jenista, J.A. *et al.* (2000) 'Developmental issues for young children in foster care.' *Pediatrics 106*, 1145–1150.

Ministry of Justice (2011) *UK Family Justice Review Interim Report*. United Kingdom: Ministry of Justice, the Department of Education and the Welsh Assembly Government. Available at www.justice.gov.uk/publications/family-justice-review.htm, accessed on 9 April 2011.

Monck, E., Reynolds, J. and Wigfall, V. (2005) 'The role of contact in concurrent planning: The experiences of birth parents and carers.' *Adoption Quarterly 9*, 1, 13–34.

Musgrove, N. and Swain, S. (2010) 'The "best interests of the child": Historical perspectives.' *Children Australia 35*, 2, 35–37.

Patton, M.Q. (2002) *Qualitative Research and Evaluation Methods* (3rd edition). Thousand Oaks, CA: Sage Publications.

Perry, B. (1997) 'Incubated in Terror: Neurodevelopmental Factors in the "Cycle of Violence".' In J. Osofsky (ed.) *Children, Youth and Violence: The Search for Solutions*. New York: Guilford Press.

Perry, B. (2008) *Bonding and Attachment in Maltreated Children: Consequences of Emotional Neglect in Childhood*. Available at http://teacher.scholastic.com/professional/bruceperry/index.htm, accessed on 25 January 2010.

Pine, B.A., Warsh, R. and Maluccio, A.N. (1993) *Together Again: Family Reunification in Foster Care*. Washington, DC: Child Welfare League of America.

QSR (2010) *NVivo 9*. Doncaster, Australia: QSR International Pty.

Schoeman, F. (1980) 'Rights of children, rights of parents and the moral basis of the family.' *Ethics 91*, 6–19.

Shonkoff, J.P. and Phillips, D.A. (2000) *From Neurones to Neighborhoods: The Science of Early Childhood Development.* Washington, DC: National Academy Press.
Steele, H. (2002) 'State of the art: Attachment.' *The Psychologist 15*, 10, 518–523.
Tsantefski, M., Humphreys, C. and Jackson, A. (forthcoming 2012) 'Engaging substance-dependent mothers in the perinatal period.' *Child Welfare 90*, 4.
United Nations (1989) *Convention on the Rights of the Child.* New York: Office of the United Nations High Commissioner for Human Rights.
Winnicott, D. (1960) 'The theory of the parent–child relationship.' *International Journal of Psychoanalysis 41*, 585–595.
Zero to Three (2005) *Assuring the Safety, Permanence and Well-Being of Infants and Toddlers in the Child Welfare System.* Washington DC: National Center for Infants, Toddlers and Families.

Chapter 12

Maternal Incest

Challenges for Child Protection

Jackie Turton

Introduction

> Children are sometimes hopeless because there is no hope, helpless because there is no help and compliant because there is no alternative. (Kitzinger 1997, p.181)

Child sexual abuse is a worldwide problem. It is an emotive crime that often provokes a strong media response and is high on the agenda of child protection professions and the public more generally. Although we have evidence of female perpetrators (Bunting 2005; Finkelhor and Williams 1988; Ford 2006; Saradjian 1996), child sexual abuse is generally considered a 'male' crime, a perspective that can cloud investigations. For instance, despite recent legal changes in England and Wales[1] and the robust revamping of the 'Working Together to Safeguard Children'[2] (Her Majesty's Government 2006) policy, which cites the investigative responsibility of different professional groups, there remain barriers in the understanding and recognition of women who sexually abuse children. As the quote above suggests, it is these barriers that can silence the child victims. This chapter presents an overview of some of the issues that arise in practice when confronted by victims of female perpetrators. The primary data used in this discussion come from a series of qualitative interviews conducted with professionals,[3] female perpetrators and adults who reported childhood victimisation.

In order to make sense of the findings discussed here and some of the difficulties in understanding the sexual abuse of children by women, there are a number of key underlying factors that require brief consideration. As suggested, child sexual abuse is perceived as a male crime, encouraging gendered assumptions that create gaps in our knowledge concerning both male and female perpetrators. While there is very strong evidence to suggest that the perpetrators are in the main male, such a focus works to conceal sexually abusive women behind the veil of social stereotypes of masculinity and femininity. The impossibility of the female abuser is further reinforced by the media impressions of a masculinised 'stranger danger', removing the abuse away from the home and away from the feminised site of mothering and nurturing. Crucially, when faced with a female perpetrator, the child victim may have fewer opportunities to disclose and thus remain silent for longer about their abuse.[4] So we have four key inhibiting factors when we attempt to unravel the problem of understanding responses to the female abuser: the low recorded prevalence rate; the discursive removal of the site of abuse to outside of the home (stranger danger); stereotypical notions of women and mothering; and the limited voice of the child victim.

Prevalence of women who sexually abuse children

Estimating rates of child sexual abuse has always been complex. Even when the abuser is male, cases of sexual abuse may not reach the criminal court, through lack of evidence or the judicial difficulties of very young child witnesses; and these are just the cases where the abuser has been identified. Using the statistical data from criminal justice systems is clearly an underestimate, especially for female abusers. The research so far offers a wide range of estimated figures partly affected by variable definitions of abuse and methodologies (Strickland 2008). For instance Kite and Tyson (2004) state that the offending rate for female sexual abusers varies from 4 per cent to 24 per cent, with retrospective reports offering rates in the higher ranges. Kemshall (2004) found that, every year, between 50 and 100 women were convicted of sexual offences against children in England and Wales, and conservative estimates suggest between 4 and 5 per cent of all (known) cases of sexual abuse against children have female perpetrators (Bunting 2005; Cortoni and Hanson 2005; Logan 2008; Russell and Finkelhor 1984).

However, as Kite and Tyson (2004) recognised, estimates are challenged by figures that emerge from victim surveys. In 1990 Kasl found therapists who worked with survivors reported that 10–39 per cent had been abused by women and perhaps more importantly 'the highest incidence of people surviving female sexual abuse occurred in male perpetrators' (Kasl 1990, p.259). A more recent survey of victims in the UK comes from ChildLine.[5] In the year ending April 2009, ChildLine counselled 12,268 children about sexual abuse. Although some children did not disclose their abuser, 54 per cent (6623) stated that their abusers were males and 17 per cent (2142) identified their abusers as female. Further analysis of this latter group showed that '1311 children (11%) cited their mother as the perpetrator, making mothers the main female perpetrators. Mothers were perpetrators for four per cent of girls and 20 per cent of boys' (ChildLine 2009, section 3.3.2).

Despite any shortcomings, the statistics do offer us some gender comparisons of the problem, indicating that, whilst we are not talking about many women, the numbers are large enough to 'give a clear indication that the sexual abuse of children by female perpetrators does occur and is not limited to a few "dysfunctional" women' (Turton 2008, p.11).

That said, we do need to treat these figures, and research focused on prevalence rates, with some caution. Russell and Finkelhor (1984) hinted that studies focused on prevalence rates might hide ulterior motives as some researchers find it difficult to accept a male preponderance of perpetrators. Peter (2008) also encourages a cautious approach to the statistics, 'especially where "iceberg" arguments are seen as the primary motive [to prevalence studies], because it succeeds in propagating moral panics, which inevitably become appropriated into truth claims' (p.1035). Some of this we can observe within the media reporting of the few female perpetrators who reach the public domain. Furthermore there is always the danger that by recognising female perpetrators 'men will attempt to assuage their guilt and obscure the preponderance of male sexual abuse by saying "but women do it too"' (Kasl 1990, p.261). This situation creates opportunities for feminist backlash and political gain, rather than obscuring the need to develop approaches to protect children. Even if there is one child victim then in many ways the number of male or female perpetrators is irrelevant (Kelly 1996), and these women cannot be ignored if we are to further our understanding of child sexual abuse (Turton 2008). 'Ignoring their crime...is analogous to trying to put a puzzle together with pieces missing' (Jennings 1993, p.244).

Stranger danger

It seems appropriate at this point to reflect on the influence of the media attention given to child sexual abuse and how it has been instrumental in shaping the social narratives of this particular problem (Kitzinger 2004). The sexual abuse of children is largely a domestic crime (Young 1993) and yet the stock framework used by journalists paints a picture that perpetuates the image of the psychotic stranger (Kitzinger 2004), often othering the abuser as a 'sub-human monster'. Thus we move away from the more common domestic site of child abuse and distance ourselves from the dominant abuser, the ordinary man – the familial male. The fixation on the psychopathic stranger also reinforces the ideal, nuclear, family structure (Jenkins 1998) confirming the protection, power and control of parents, despite the evidence that home is the most dangerous place for the young child (Jenks 1996). In terms of child protection work, abuse that occurs outside of the domestic environment is easier to manage. 'Dangerous outsiders have attracted a vastly disproportionate share of official attention, precisely because they represent the easiest targets for anyone wishing, however sincerely, to protect children' (Jenkins 1998, p.238).

The recognition of sexual abuse within the home thus remains difficult for public and media to contemplate within the framework of stranger danger. It remains emotionally and practically complicated to move beyond the male stranger-danger model. Difficulties in locating the familial, female abuser are further inhibited by our stereotypical notions of femininity.

Women and mothering

Given the data, the most obvious risk to become a child sexual abuser is being male (Seto 2008). Sexual abuse of children by women, though unusual, has been documented within the criminal justice system since the 19th century (Jackson 2000); however, it is not uncommon for their behaviour to be minimised and justified (Denov 2004; Strickland 2008; Turton 2008). It is not just the focus on the male crime that inhibits the recognition of female perpetrators but a 'cultural resistance has hindered the identification of sex crimes committed by women' (Strickland 2008, p.474) and particularly those committed by mothers or mother figures.

Glenn (1994) suggests that all women are structured in terms of the maternal and are thus assumed to share a universal nurturing role. Women, especially those in the mothering role, are presumed to have 'special', asexual relationships with children and are encouraged to be emotionally intimate and physically close (Saradjian 1996). As Plummer (1981) recognised, this intimacy has often been socially denied to men and even to fathers, and in part this indicates the different social perceptions of masculinity and femininity and what this means in relation to the child. 'Mothers are perceived as nurturing and asexual to their children...at worst their behaviour is labelled as seductive...not harmful. The same behaviour in a father is labelled child molestation' (Banning 1989, p.567).

For some, any maternal idealisation can create complications as it excludes those women with ambivalent feelings towards their children. Mothers who dare to discuss such feelings can have these concerns minimised. Welldon's early work found that when seeking help such women were ignored. 'People simply don't want to know. I see women who have been to all kinds of agencies to try and get help and they are simply not taken seriously' (Welldon, cited in Search 1988, p.83). Furthermore, mothers may feel failures if they are unable to reach the high standards of excellence set by health and welfare agencies and society more generally. This was a problem highlighted by one abuser. 'Once I had Richard I knew I wasn't capable of looking after children... basically no mothering instincts' (Janet).[6] Thus some mothers may be silenced since it is presumed that all mothers love their children – or at least can be helped to do so (Parker 1997).

There are not just difficulties in dealing with the mothers who appear different. Social assumptions about the maternal figure sometimes extend to child victims and affect the responses to disclosures. For example, Penny[7] was sexually abused by her mother, and on the one occasion she tried to disclose she was told 'but she's your mother dear, of course she wants a cuddle'. Thus her 'secret' remained with her throughout her childhood.

So it appears that traditional sexual scripts act to deter recognition of female perpetrators (Denov 2004; Mellor and Deering 2010; Strickland 2008) because 'abuse – particularly sexual abuse – does not fit the cultural construction of femininity' (Mendel 1995, p.27) and because 'to be feminine means to be nurturing, protecting, caring, non-aggressive and non-sexual' (Denov 2003, p.308). Thus idealisation of the mother on the one hand fails to account for those who find their relationships with children difficult or different and on the other opens the opportunity to ignore or minimise any possibly abusive behaviour.

The child

As the above example of Penny indicates, for victims there are disclosure difficulties in cases of female perpetrators as it is the social model of the maternal that silences the child for a number of reasons.

First, the child fears that his/her story will be discredited. Choosing whom to tell, and how to find the safe and empathetic adult, is often a carefully contrived moment for victims and always carries the risk of shame, ridicule and disbelief, even more so in cases of maternal incest (Denov 2004; Elliott 1993; Saradjian 1996). Thus it appears that sexual abuse by a mother may be experienced as more shameful than male abuse (Sgroi and Sargent 1993). Rosencrans (1997) clearly defines the difficulty in her research on mother/daughter incest.

> If abused children reveal the sexual abuse by their mothers too freely, they risk not being seen as victims but as so strange that even their mothers didn't love them. They risk making others uncomfortable by challenging the stereotypes and that social mantra that 'mothers love their children, mothers love their children'. (Rosencrans 1997, p.33)

There are further complexities to disclosing sexual abuse since some revelations are more readily received than others. Plummer (1995) discusses this very issue in some depth, suggesting that the time has to be right and society prepared to listen to sexual 'stories'. Although most victims are granted some space to disclose their child sexual abuse, survivors of female perpetrators have more problems being heard.

The second inhibiting factor relates to male survivors. A number of studies have suggested that boys who suffer sexual abuse by women go unrecognised (Allen 1991; Denov 2004; Mendel 1995). Mendel revealed this problem in his seminal work discussing the plight of male victims:

> Male survivors of child sexual abuse constitute an extremely under-identified, underserved, and, all too often, misunderstood population. The lack of recognition of this phenomenon is... determined largely by a constellation of societal myths or beliefs regarding what it means to be male and by complementary myths or beliefs regarding what it means to be female. (Mendel 1995, p.1)

There is little doubt that disclosure is often emotionally traumatic. But, as Mendel (1995) suggests, boys have additional problems since the cultural norms of masculinity are expressed as active, powerful and competent, which downgrades the attached notions of risk for male victims. More recent examples from Denov's (2004) research indicate that despite the increase in knowledge and training of specialist police officers many stereotypical responses remain:

> You want to know what happens when a case of [sexual assault] comes forward involving a female suspect and a male victim at our office? The entire office breaks out in laughter. Lots of snickering. It's not taken seriously. (Female detective cited in Denov 2004, p.81)

The assumption that sexual abuse by a female is harmless titillation, a rite of passage (Mellor and Deering 2010), leads to the rather envious 'lucky dog' reaction of some of the police in Denov's study. This response is reinforced by other research findings highlighting the variety of responses to abuse by male survivors:

> Looking back it seemed no great drama. Even though I was only seven years old, I knew how to fondle her and suck her breasts. Oral sex led to full intercourse with my mother. We had sex until I left home at the age of eighteen. (Male survivor, cited in Elliott 1993, p.6)

In a study on male victims of childhood sexual abuse conducted by Woods and Dean (1984), 30 per cent were abused by women and 50 per cent of these identified their sexual experiences as non-abusive. But although not all victims recognise the behaviour as abuse in the first instance, such results do not necessarily mean the experience was atraumatic for the male child – effects may emerge later in adulthood. For instance, Groth (1979), Petrovich and Templar (1984) and Briere and Smiljanich (1993) found over 50 per cent of the sexually aggressive men in their studies reported sexual abuse in childhood by a female. Furthermore, the feminisation of victimisation, as Sepler (1990) calls it, and the masculinisation of aggression (Mendel 1995), can silence the male victim, reinforcing confusion concerning masculine identity.

> I was not only a victim, but a victim of a woman – a weaker gender…it makes you a much lesser man. I was asking myself what kind of man was I. I didn't feel very comfortable with my manliness. I didn't feel like a man. (David,[8] cited in Denov 2004, p.157)

The maternal/child bond or attachment can present a further barrier for victims. Psychologists have described the attachment process (Bowlby 1988; Salter-Ainsworth 1991) as an internal psychological response to the maternal relationship. But there do seem to be two forces at play here. The internal psychological desire for an intimate relationship with the maternal figure is closely linked with the socially idealised notion of mother. The end result is that mothering that falls outside of the social norms has a detrimental impact on victims, leaving them with feelings of helplessness and loss of identity.

Penny, a survivor of maternal incest, took on the burden of responsibility and guilt for the abuse she suffered at the hands of her mother. And while she wanted it to stop she did not want to let her mother down, so accepted the abuse:

> She passed on huge clouds of guilt to me. I remember her blaming me for what went on at times. I remember her being very angry with me, she was dangerous when she was angry… and I remember her looking at me with disgust and contempt. She could also behave in a very hurt way, which made me feel terrible and made me want to do what she wanted me to do. (Penny)

This desire to please the offending mother is reflected in other research.

> I've never blamed my mother. Consequently, I have no reason to forgive her. My entire life has been spent hypervigilant of my mother's moods and needs. (Lynne's[9] story in Elliott 1993, p.136)

Victims of maternal incest are not just faced with a sceptical world if they tell their tale but remain silent because of a very strong desire to retain the mother/child relationship:

> Mothers have enormous power to validate the lovableness and value of children. This child within us as adults seems to believe that, more than any other person, mother can convince the world that we are worthwhile human beings. Mothers can convince us of that…abused children want it. (Rosencrans 1997, p.33)

As a consequence even as adults, some victims find it difficult to de-attach from their abusing mothers (Elliott 1993; Turton 2008) and disclose the sexual abuse. Even if they are courageous enough to tell, there are other problems to overcome within the child protection system.

Professional denial

It is important to understand professional responses to female perpetrators as these can generate formidable barriers for child victims. There is no doubt that child protection is a difficult business regardless of the gender of either perpetrator or victim. Since 1989[10] the focus in the UK has been on 'working together' within multi-agency partnerships, but the differing professional agendas, training and resources have often inhibited best practice (Laming 2003) by reinforcing agency boundaries (Payne 2000; Witz 1992). For the purposes of this chapter what is interesting is that research suggests women who sexually abuse children are less likely than their male counterparts to be identified by professionals and more likely to have their behaviour adjusted to fit gender stereotypes (Denov 2004; Hetherton and Beardsall 1998; Turton 2008). Explanations for female sexual abuse come from two main sources, the acquired knowledge of child sexual abuse and the gender identity of the person involved. These used together form the perception of the situation. The sound base knowledge that men are the perpetrators and the antithesis of the stereotypical woman as nurturing, caring and sexually passive means that 'when a woman sexually abuses a child it conflicts with society's gender schema' (Kite and Tyson 2004, p.310). As a consequence gender emphatically affects the ways in which cases are handled (Bunting 2005), influencing the responses of child protection workers. Apart from outright denial (Denov 2004; Turton 2008), explanations of the behaviour may take a variety of forms, as the following examples reveal.

Over-enthusiastic mothering

We have suggested the notion that mothers 'must fall in love with their babies as well as serving them' (Morss 1996, p.45). As a consequence the expectations that professionals have of mothers can romanticise the maternal role as a 'natural' bond:

> ...by presuming women are natural mothers and by maintaining an image of what it is to be a mother...we collude with some abusive mothers by excusing their behaviour as lack of ability. (Turton 2008, p.31)

Thus the actions of some perpetrators may be disguised as childcare, as mothers are able to hide any sexual meaning to their behaviour within the ordinary and everyday care of the child victim. Such behaviour may go unnoticed by adults outside of the relationship; alternatively it may be minimised by professionals and others as over-enthusiastic childcare or in some cases a very strong attachment to the child (Turton 2008).

Janet, mentioned earlier, admitted her inadequate mothering skills but used this 'fault' to justify the abuse of her victims as clumsiness or ineptitude. 'I had to get them clean. You have to get in all the creases.' The case of Deena[11] offers a further example of professional minimisation where even quite extreme abuse can be misaligned when mothers are involved.

> We had quite a lot of argument about whether [it] was abusive or…actually something more natural…whether [it] was a sexual need being gratified or whether it was some other instinct, like a maternal one, which was becoming confused with sexual gratification no-one got to the root of. (Family lawyer)

The masculinised woman

In cases where abuse is beyond doubt, professionals may attempt to explain the behaviour by asserting that female perpetrators are more male-like than other women. Such a woman is not considered female enough, not a real woman, which is the opposite of the male perpetrator who may be considered too aggressively masculine. The following quote from a child protection social worker suggests that this can be the case.

> …she was quite a masculine woman; quite…again I can picture her. She had long hair and was much bigger than them [her two male co-offenders] much…physically stronger than them and she ruled the roost…and she was clearly, noticeably different from the rest of them [the family]. She had long hair, but with all due respect there was nothing feminine about her…always wore trousers…very dowdy looking…a bit smelly…there was nothing feminine about her at all. (Sue, social worker)

Consequently professionals sometimes explain women who sexually abuse by suggesting 'they become sociological males' (Heidensohn 1981, p.30), since this may be the only way to acknowledge such anti-feminine behaviour. When faced with the undeniable fact that some women abuse children, it is just easier to interpret them as different. By doing so this distances the abuser, as 'them', from us.

Women as victims

These gender stereotypes can also interfere with perception when working with abusive women.

Delia[12] (counsellor/therapist) suggested that it was easy to move from talking about the 'abuser' to using the word 'survivor' especially when working with female offenders who suffered abuse as children. This moves the concern away from the child victim, focusing on the offences as actions of a victim rather than actions of an abuser. While recognising that therapeutically counsellors may need to address past experiences, there is a real danger here of absolving the abuser of responsibility, while ignoring the child victim and minimising the sexual offences. Another example from a family lawyer further indicates the gendered response from professionals.

> ...and again I can't condone or in any way defend an adult who treats a child like that. But she didn't have a chance. Her own emotions were so screwed up. She loved her children...she worshipped them...it destroyed her to lose them. She wasn't doing it because she was predatory like this scout...who has just got eighteen years...she wasn't that sort of abuser...she was a victim turned abuser in the classic sense. (Family lawyer)

It is difficult to imagine a response like this to a case of paternal incest and perhaps the question to ask in any of these cases is, what message does this send out to the child?

Conclusion

Within the emotive and complex child protection process the presence of a female perpetrator creates difficulties and dilemmas for all involved. This chapter suggests that many of these problems are closely linked with our social and cultural perceptions of what it is to be a woman. Consequently professionals may draw upon gendered assumptions about femininity and victimhood when confronted with female perpetrators. Identifying responses of professionals not only illuminates the particular difficulties for child protection workers, but also for child victims who find it difficult or impossible to tell their stories. We need to use these revelations to analyse our gendered responses to cases of child abuse and develop a framework for understanding the social context in which women operate and offend.

The final word must be for the child:

> I was 30 years old when I talked [disclosed abuse]...before that you know for the first 16 years there was sexual abuse...it was my model. (Petra)[13]

> I wanted me mum but not the mum I got. (Louise)[14]

Endnotes

1. The Children Act (England and Wales) 1989 was updated in the new Children Act 2004 – making the responsibilities and roles of key professions much more explicit. The Sexual Offences Act 2003 revised much of the old legal framework around incest and added some new offences such as grooming on the internet. It also attempts to create a gender-neutral approach to the identification of offenders.
2. Working Together to Safeguard Children was initiated following the Butler-Sloss report on the Cleveland child sexual abuse scandal in 1989. It was last updated in March 2010 and sets out how organisations should use the above Acts to safeguard children.
3. Professional respondents included health workers, lawyers, social workers, probation officers and police.
4. O'Leary and Barber (2008) found in their research that of those that do disclose some male victims took in excess of 20 years.
5. ChildLine is a free confidential 24-hour helpline for children and young people. It was set up as a registered UK charity in 1986 and is now part of the National Society for the Prevention of Cruelty to Children (NSPCC).
6. Janet was convicted of sexually abusing her partner's son. Police suspected that she had also abused her own two children and her partner's daughter but there was insufficient evidence to take this to criminal court.
7. Penny suffered sexual and emotional abuse at the hands of her mother from about the age of two until she reached puberty when the sexual abuse stopped. The emotional abuse continued until her mother died.
8. David was abused by a female babysitter between the ages of three and six years.
9. Lynne is a survivor of maternal incest and physical abuse. The abuse started in infancy and continued until she was a teenager.
10. In 1989 the inquiry into the Cleveland scandal – a case where numerous children were removed from their homes and taken into care as they were 'diagnosed' as victims of child sexual abuse – was published, suggesting that professionals failed to piece together the evidence to ensure safe decisions. The Butler-Sloss report challenged the child protection system in England and Wales, influencing both the law (the Children Act 1989) and the subsequent procedural documentation – 'Working Together'.
11. Deena sexually abused both of her two sons and they went on to display extremely overt sexualised behaviour with any female adults they met.

12. At the time of the interview Delia was working with a woman who had been sexually abused by her mother and then went on to abuse her own daughter.
13. Petra was sexually abused by her mother and father from the age of three until she was 14.
14. Louise was sexually and physically abused by her mother from an 'early age' until she was 16.

References

Allen, C. (1991) *Women and Men who Sexually Abuse Children: A Comparative Analysis.* London: Safer Society Press.

Banning, A. (1989) 'Mother–son incest: Confronting the prejudice.' *Child Abuse and Neglect 13*, 563–570.

Bowlby, J. (1988) *A Secure Base: Clinical Applications of Attachment Theory.* London: Routledge.

Briere, J. and Smiljanich, K. (1993) *Childhood Sexual Abuse and Subsequent Sexual Aggression Against Adult Women.* Paper presented at 101st annual conference of the American Psychological Association, Toronto, Canada.

Bunting, L. (2005) *Females who Sexually Offend Against Children: Responses of the Child Protection and Criminal Justice Systems.* London: NSPCC.

ChildLine (2009) *Children Talking to ChildLine about Sexual Abuse: Case Notes.* London: NSPCC. Available at www.nspcc.org.uk/Inform/publications/casenotes/children_talking_to_childline_about_sexual_abuse_wda69414.html, accessed on 23 March 2010.

Cortoni, F. and Hanson, R.K. (2005) *A Review of Recidivism Rates of Adult Female Sexual Offenders.* Ottawa: Correction Service of Canada. Available at www.csc-scc.gc.ca/text/rsrch/reports/r169/r169_e.pdf, accessed on 28 October 2011.

Denov, M. (2003) 'The myth of innocence: Sexual scripts and the recognition of child sexual abuse by female perpetrators.' *Journal of Sex Research 40*, 3, 303–314.

Denov, M. (2004) *Perspectives on Female Sex Offending: A Culture of Denial.* Aldershot: Ashgate.

Elliott, M. (ed.) (1993) *Female Sexual Abuse of Children: The Ultimate Taboo.* London: Longman.

Finkelhor, D. and Williams, L.M. (1988) *Nursery Crimes: Sexual Abuse in Day Care.* Newbury Park, CA: Sage.

Ford, H. (2006) *Women who Sexually Abuse Children.* Chichester, UK: Wiley.

Glenn, E. (1994) 'Social Constructions of Mothering.' In E. Glenn, G. Chang and L.R. Forcey (eds) *Mothering: Ideology, Experience and Agency.* London: Routledge.

Groth, N. (1979) *Men who Rape.* New York: Plenum.

Heidensohn, F. (1981) *Women and Crime.* London: Macmillan.

Her Majesty's Government (2006) *Working Together to Safeguard Children: A Guide to Inter-Agency Working to Safeguard and Promote the Welfare of Children.* London: The Stationery Office (TSO).

Hetherton, J. and Beardsall, L. (1998) 'Decisions and attitudes concerning child sexual abuse: Does the gender of the perpetrator make a difference to child protection professionals?' *Child Abuse and Neglect 22*, 1265–1283.

Jackson, L. (2000) *Child Sexual Abuse in Victorian England.* London: Routledge.

Jenkins, P. (1998) *Moral Panic: Changing Concept of the Child Molester in Modern America.* New Haven, CT: Yale University Press.

Jenks, C. (1996) *Childhood.* London: Routledge.

Jennings, K. (1993) 'Female Child Molesters: A Review of the Literature.' In M. Elliott (ed.) *Female Sexual Abuse of Children: The Ultimate Taboo.* London: Longman.

Kasl, C.D. (1990) 'Female Perpetrators of Sexual Abuse: A Feminist View.' In M. Hunger (ed.) *The Sexually Abused Male: Prevalence, Impact and Treatment, Vol. 1.* Lexington, MA: Lexington Books.

Kelly, L. (1996) 'When Does the Speaking Profit Us? Reflections on the Changes of Developing Feminist Perspectives on Abuse and Violence by Women.' In M. Hester, L. Kelly and J. Radford (eds) *Women, Violence and Male Power: Feminist Activism, Research and Practice.* Buckingham: Open University Press.

Kemshall, H. (2004) 'Risk, Dangerousness and Female Offenders.' In G. McIvor (ed.) *Women who Offend.* London: Jessica Kingsley Publishers.

Kite, D. and Tyson, G.A. (2004) 'The impact of perpetrator gender on male and female police officers' perceptions of child sexual abuse.' *Psychiatry, Psychology and Law 11*, 2, 308–318.

Kitzinger, J. (1997) 'Who Are You Kidding? Child, Power, and the Struggle Against Sexual Abuse.' In A. James and A. Proud (eds) *Constructing and Reconstructing Childhood.* Beverly Hills, CA: Routledge Falmer.

Kitzinger, J. (2004) *Framing Abuse: Media Influence and Public Understanding of Sexual Violence Against Children.* London: Pluto Press.

Laming, Lord (2003) *The Victoria Climbié Inquiry.* Available at www.publications.parliament.uk/pa/cm200203/cmselect/cmhealth/570/570.pdf, accessed on 28 October 2011.

Logan, C. (2008) 'Sexual Deviance in Females: Psychopathology and Theory.' In D.R. Laws and W.T. O'Donohue (eds) *Sexual Deviance: Theory, Assessment and Treatment.* New York: Guilford Press.

Mellor, D. and Deering, R. (2010) 'Professional response and attitudes toward female-perpetrated child sexual abuse: A study of psychologists, psychiatrists, probationary psychologists and child protection workers.' *Psychology, Crime and Law 16*, 5, 415–438.

Mendel, M.P. (1995) *The Male Survivor: The Impact of Sexual Abuse.* London: Sage.

Morss, J. (1996) *Growing Critical: Alternatives to Developmental Psychology.* London: Routledge.

O'Leary, P. and Barber, J. (2008) 'Gender differences in silencing following childhood sexual abuse.' *Journal of Child Sexual Abuse 17*, 2, 133–143.

Parker, R. (1997) 'The Production and Purposes of Maternal Ambivalence.' In W. Holloway and B. Featherstone (eds) *Mothering and Ambivalence.* London: Routledge.

Payne, M. (2000) *Teamwork in Multiprofessional Care.* Basingstoke: Macmillan.

Peter, T. (2008) 'Speaking the unspeakable: Exploring the impact of mother–daughter sexual abuse.' *Violence Against Women 14*, 9, 1033–1053.

Petrovich, M. and Templar, D. (1984) 'Heterosexual molestation of children who later become rapists.' *Psychological Reports 54*, 810.

Plummer, K. (1981) 'Pedophilia: Constructing a Sociological Baseline.' In M. Cook and K. Howells (eds) *Adult Sexual Interest in Children.* London/New York: Academic Press.

Plummer, K. (1995) *Telling Sexual Stories.* London: Routledge.

Rosencrans, B. (1997) *The Last Secret: Daughters Sexually Abused by Mothers.* Brandon, VT: Safer Society Press.

Russell, D. and Finkelhor, D. (1984) 'Women as Perpetrators.' In D. Finkelhor (ed.) *Child Sexual Abuse: New Theory and Research*. New York: The Free Press.
Salter-Ainsworth, M. (1991) 'Attachments and Other Affectional Bonds Across the Life-Cycle.' In C. Murray-Parkes, J. Stevenson-Hinde and P. Marris (eds) *Attachments Across the Life-Cycle*. London: Routledge.
Saradjian, J. (1996) *Women who Sexually Abuse Children: From Research to Clinical Practice*. London: Sage.
Search, G. (1988) *The Last Taboo: Sexual Abuse of Children*. London: Penguin.
Sepler, F. (1990) 'Victim Advocacy and Young Male Victims of Sexual Abuse: An Evolutionary Model.' In M. Hunter (ed.) *The Sexually Abused Male: Vol. 1. Prevalence, Impact and Treatment*. Lexington, MA: Lexington Books.
Seto, M.C. (2008) 'Pedophilia: Psychopathology and Theory.' In D.R. Laws and W.T. O'Donohue (eds) *Sexual Deviance: Theory, Assessment and Treatment*. New York: Guilford Press.
Sgroi, S. and Sargent, N. (1993) 'Impact and Treatment Issues for Victims of Childhood Sexual Abuse by Female Perpetrators.' In M. Elliott (ed.) *The Last Taboo*. London: Longman.
Strickland, S.M. (2008) 'Female sexual offenders: Exploring issues of personality, trauma and cognitive distortions.' *Journal of Interpersonal Violence 25*, 4, 474–489.
Turton, J. (2008) *Child Abuse, Gender and Society*. London: Routledge.
Witz, A. (1992) *Professionals and Patriarchy*. London: Routledge.
Woods, S.C. and Dean, K.S. (1984) *Final Report: Sexual Abuse of Males Research Project (90 CA/812)*. Washington, DC: National Center on Child Abuse and Neglect.
Young, V. (1993) 'Women Abusers: A Feminist View.' In M. Elliott (ed.) *The Last Taboo*. London: Longman.

Chapter 13

Lost Identities

Denying Children their Family Identity

James Reid

Introduction

There is a rich literature on the benefits to children of both mother and father involvement, but the experience for many children in contested contact and residence proceedings in the UK is denied familial and cultural experiences and lost identity. The public discourse on separated families has included the stereotypes of 'deadbeat dads' and 'obstructive mums' and such stereotypes continue to be common in social work with families (Trinder 2007). This is in part encouraged by conflicting messages in policy and uncritical approaches to practitioner utility – defined as subjectivities influenced by agency, social structures and culture – perpetuated particularly in assessment by mandated tools such as the *Framework for the Assessment of Children in Need and their Families* (Department of Health 2000) (hereinafter the 'Assessment Framework'). This chapter considers the impact of practitioner utility in characterising many childhoods through minimised or ignored opportunities for a broader and inclusive familial, community and cultural experience and makes recommendations for a framework for intervention that enables social work practitioners to be open to a wider range of ideas, including considering at least the need for contact between the children, their non-resident parent and the wider family network, and to be more secure in explaining and defending their decision-making.

Fathers out of the assessment process

At a time when the benefits to children of father involvement including the accompanying social and cultural opportunities are undisputed, there is ongoing concern that social work practice does not engage sufficiently with many fathers. Indeed there are significant levels of non-resident father dissatisfaction with social work intervention, which is unsurprising since the details of fathers and the wider paternal family are not always fully recorded by practitioners on their child's file or such information is minimal or not easily accessible. Additionally, beyond the possibility of the child being looked after by the local authority or where there are safeguarding concerns, fathers are not consistently consulted during routine assessments (Ashley *et al.* 2006; Roskill *et al.* 2008). The outcome of this for many children is denied access to their full identity and the social inclusion in community that is core to their relational networks.

Such experiences occur in a period when social work practice in the UK is replete with guidance and tools designed to aid the practitioner in achieving best outcomes for children. Of the most widely used assessment tools, the 'Assessment Framework' is notable as it is based upon a holistic approach to assessment of need across three interrelated domains: the child's developmental needs, parenting capacity, and family and environmental factors. Significantly the guidance for the 'Assessment Framework' requires practitioners to engage with 'each parent or caregiver', including 'fathers and father figures' (Department of Health 2000, p.20). As such, assessment practice and subsequent intervention should be inclusive and support a child's development in a context of dynamic family and community structures except where the safety of the child demands otherwise.

Whilst there is some evidence that when used inclusively the 'Assessment Framework' is an aid to greater partnership with parents and carers (Cleaver and Walker with Meadows 2004) and consequently can produce a therapeutic impact (Millar and Corby 2006), there has been consistent evidence of fathers being dealt with less favourably, with practitioner attitudes stereotypically defining many fathers as a threat, of no use, irrelevant, as absent and dead-beat (Daniel and Taylor 1999; Featherstone 2003; Roskill *et al.* 2008; Scourfield 2006). Significant barriers to father engagement include gender differences between father and practitioner, lack of time or resources to identify non-resident parents, fear of aggression or violence and a lack of training in dealing with this (Broadhurst *et al.* 2010). As a consequence 'father engagement was unimportant and practice was orientated towards the most accessible parent, the mother' (Page, Whitting and McLean 2008, pp.88–89), a situation that is potentially discriminatory to both fathers and mothers and ultimately to the child. Utility is favoured over inclusive practice, and the prospects offered to the child by the direct involvement of the father and importantly the father's wider family, community and culture are being ignored. For numerous children, childhood is being defined in a context of lost or denied opportunities.

Family identity

Ironically the importance of family and ancestry is recognised by government for those who have lost contact through fostering or adoption, or through gamete donation. This is also in a context where the internet, through the availability of genealogy search sites and social networking sites, and popular television programs, have fuelled an explosion of interest across Europe and former European colonies in particular in answering questions of heritage, identity and belonging. Whether individual interest in ancestry is reflexive, that is a matter of personal meaning making and cultural capital, or defensive, a guard against utilitarian or racialised approaches to belonging at local, national or transnational levels, there can be little argument about the importance of family identity to the human psyche.

Ancestry and identity however are not a simple matter of linear biological relationships or normative definitions of family but necessarily involve consideration of kinship – the dual role of blood ties and social structures. That the anthropological concern of 'who is related to whom?' is understood in a context of place, difference and social and cultural practices is carefully explored by Nash (2005). She cites the analysis from an ethnography undertaken by Jeanette Edwards in the north of England, which illustrates the manner in which blood ties were mediated through 'a constant process of including and excluding persons from social categories which are, in turn, reproduced in the process' (Edwards 2000, p.28). Edwards and Strathern (2000) further explore how immutable biological relationships are indeed shaped by social and cultural considerations so that:

> a person who could be claimed in terms of blood ties may be disowned through lack of social interest, which might or might not be a matter of consequence. Conversely, someone who was forgotten may be claimed back through resurrected biological links. (Edwards and Strathern 2000, p.160)

So it is with practitioners. Since both definitions and enactment of identity are mediated through social structures, these structures must also inevitably have an effect on the work of social work practitioners. Indeed this point was emphasised by Jan Howarth (2007), a key contributor in the development in the UK of the 'Assessment Framework', who, in her critique of practitioner judgements when undertaking an assessment, discusses how outcomes for children are impacted by practitioner, personal, professional and organisational beliefs. This point was later reiterated by Howarth (2010, p.14):

> If we are really going to achieve child-focused assessments, it is necessary not only to 'see' the child, but also to 'see' the practitioner. Just as for the child this means understanding the child's lived experience and consulting with the child to identify ways of improving life in order to ensure that their needs are met, the same is true for practitioners.

Utility and assessment practice

Practitioner utility is inevitably of 'consequence' to children in contested contact or residence proceedings if the practitioner does not seek to define, analyse or evaluate what they bring to a situation (their personal, professional and cultural mores, values and experience), nor their impact on assessment, how they set goals and subsequently act. This is because the practitioner's own experiences can affect judgements; their experience can create bias, which in turn can influence decisions about what is normal or acceptable. Consequently personal, professional and cultural mores, values and experience have a role in quality assessment practice.

However, the 'Assessment Framework' and accompanying documentation do not require the practitioner to consider the 'lens' through which they view the child. Since the practitioner does not systematically consider what about them helps or hinders their assessment practice, intuitive reasoning is encouraged above analytic reasoning and as such the 'Assessment Framework' is structurally dissonant to many children's needs.

Assessment practice is much more than a cerebral process or task; it is also responsive to external demands that shape and influence practitioner action. Structural concerns include the temporal dimension of assessments, repetition and information being gathered because the system requires it, a cut and paste approach to recording that prevents a holistic view of the child and family, and an approach to supervision that continues to focus on managerialist and bureaucratic requirements above others. Fear and the prevailing culture of blame, both through the popular media and in the system of inspection and regulation of practice, are also relevant, as is the consequent high-blame working environment (Bell *et al.* 2007; Bradley and Höjer 2009; Broadhurst *et al.* 2010; Munro 2005, 2010).

Review of child protection

Many of the above concerns are being recognised in the current review being undertaken by the 'Munro Review of Child Protection' in the UK. In June 2010 the Secretary of State for Education, whose department has responsibility for social work, asked Eileen Munro, Professor of Social Policy at the London School of Economics, to undertake a review of the child protection system, 'with a focus on strengthening the social work profession, to put them into a better position to make well-informed judgements based on up-to-date evidence in the best interests of children and free from unnecessary bureaucracy and regulation' (Department of Education 2010). The review comes on the back of growing public and political concern about the quality of social work practice following a number of high profile child deaths which led to the introduction of further mandated assessment practices.

In her interim report Eileen Munro (2011) recognises the need for less bureaucracy and therefore greater practitioner autonomy in the exercise of professional judgements. One of her major criticisms has been the focus of practitioners on targets and rules at the expense of time spent on establishing inclusive practice with children and their families. She is also cognisant of the assessment system being inefficient and not therefore facilitating effective decisions about risk. Whilst the review will have lessons for all social work practice, it is focused on child protection, thus exposing the societal and cultural concern for risk and in particular an aversion to risk.

A focus on risk

That children in the UK are systematically measured and classified throughout their lives is consistent with the contemporary focus on risk. In the accompanying plethora of policy and legislation that deals with the dichotomy of risky children or children at risk, a father's risk to – or ability to – protect a child is of central concern to practitioners undertaking an assessment of parenting (Woodcock 2003). Indeed, despite evidence of the benefits to a child of father involvement, much of the contemporary social work discourse has continued to concentrate on fathers as a risk (Clapton 2009). Scourfield's (2003) finding of the predominant construction of men as a threat continues to resonate, and many practitioners continue to adopt an approach that is wary or at least hesitant of fathers. Research, of course, does not straightforwardly conclude that perpetrators are likely to be fathers. This gives rise to the potential influence of the availability heuristic – the tendency of people to take into account, over other potentially relevant issues, those matters which are called to mind most readily within a situation (Middleton, Clyne and Harris 1999; O'Connor *et al.* 2006 – so that, for example, the risk presented by some fathers can lead some practitioners to perceive all fathers in a context of risk.

For some practitioners, therefore, assessment of a father's capacity, when it does occur, is affected by risk as a social phenomenon, and subsequently their wariness and perception of threat, either towards the child or to themselves, is exacerbated by a lack of departmental or managerial guidance or training on how to deal with fathers and/or aggression. Interestingly Peacey and Hunt, in their study of the extent and nature of contact problems among separated families in the UK (for both resident and non-resident parents), found that all but one of the parents interviewed in their sample reported bad feeling or conflict with their ex-partner (Peacey and Hunt 2009). Almost all of their respondents reported angry exchanges or verbal abuse from their ex-partner, with a few describing harassment or even violence. Given the nature of social work, it is likely that the practitioner is involved with the family at a time of particular tension. However, Peacey and Hunt (2009) show that resident and non-resident parents are equally as likely to have concerns about the welfare of a child based on a range of issues from abuse to substance misuse to derogatory comments. Despite this, and acknowledgement of the benefits to children of father contact, practitioners can follow the path of least resistance – particularly when faced with barriers or reluctance for contact from the resident parent – that minimises father involvement and maximises the expectations of mothers to safeguard and protect the child from actual or perceived risk from the father.

Practitioner influences

Concern about the impact of social and cultural phenomena on assessment practice however does not deal with agentic influences. Agentic practice or practitioner agency refers to the practitioner's engagement with social and cultural phenomena and subsequently how these phenomena are construed and constructed by the practitioner to direct action or practice. For example, practice in light of the following gives rise to the influence of agency:

- fear of certain fathers (Smith and Nursten 1998)
- the resistance or aggression of some fathers (Ryan 2000)
- a working environment that is more readily orientated towards mothers (Ghate, Shaw and Hazel 2000; Moran, Ghate and Van der Merwe 2004)
- practitioners who have beliefs that mothers provide better care than fathers
- the impact of the practitioner's own experience of fathers (Daniel and Taylor 1999; Ghate *et al.* 2000; O'Hagan and Dillenburger 1995).

It is unlikely that the Munro Review will directly address practitioner subjectivities that involve emotions and prejudices in this regard.

Of course, it is difficult to work inclusively with both parents when one is accusing the other of harming the child, where the practitioner has fear of conflict, or where the situation conforms to established practice wisdom and gender stereotypes. Affect and the availability heuristic play a role in heightening the practitioner's perception of risk (Keller, Siegrist and Gutscher 2006), which in turn increases the likelihood that intervention is based upon the power, duties and utility of the practitioner rather than equity and empowerment. It is also difficult to conduct or be part of an assessment when definitions and variation in understanding of the concept of 'parenting' are not systematically debated by practitioners, nor is guidance always available from managers in supervision despite 'definitional clarity' being fundamental to effective parenting capacity assessments (White 2005). Definitions of parenting, for example, range from: parenting capacity, which is 'good enough' parenting over a sustained period; 'parenting ability', which is the capacity to meet a child's needs over a short period or in specific circumstances (Conley 2003); and parenting style, including authoritative or authoritarian parenting, and parenting practice that is culturally specific (Stewart and Bond 2002). Questions can consequently be raised about the cultural relativity of some parenting assessments not helped by inconsistent use of the parenting assessment tools accompanying the 'Assessment Framework', especially when a tick box approach is adopted with little consideration to the relative nature of identified strengths or weaknesses (Donald and Jureidini 2004).

Statutory intervention in family life

It is also worthwhile taking some time to consider the wider landscape in which social work is situated. There are continuing debates, just as there have been over previous decades, about the point at which the state should intervene in family life and about the extent to which the workplace remains gendered both in terms of the make-up of the workforce and in the expectations placed on mothers in intervention. The practitioner is affected by and shapes the meanings, practices and policies that are the heart of the middle-class ideology of government (Morgen 2001; Walkowitz 1999). Assessment and intervention are holistically focused, but are invariably outcome based. There are for example 198 national indicators of child wellbeing in England. Children have become objects of measurement. Parenting support has come to be a main facet of family support, but this has led to a blame culture where practitioners can attribute fault to parents, or parents to each other. A sustained period of social investment (Jenson 2009) is now threatened by a change in economic and political ideology.

Tensions in policy are common, so despite an acknowledgement by government that investment in children and in breaking the cycle of disadvantage is crucial, many policies are short-term, for the life of a parliament or tenure of the supporting Minister of State. Many contradictions are apparent:

- Successive governments have been criticised by the European Court of Human Rights for allowing physical chastisement of children in England.
- Asylum-seeking children are incarcerated.
- Young people are the largest unemployed group.
- Libraries are closing despite seven out of the ten most borrowed titles being children's books.

- According to UNICEF (2007), children in the UK experience greater deprivation, worse relationships with their parents and are exposed to more risks from alcohol, drugs and unsafe sex than those in any other wealthy country in the world.

These tensions and contradictions and similar conflicts in legislation and guidance make the social work task more difficult. Section 1 of the *Children Act 1989*, for example, asserts that the welfare of the child is paramount, but Article 3 of the UN Convention of the Rights of the Child (UNCRC) expresses welfare as a 'primary' consideration. Article 9(3) of the UNCRC declares that:

> States Parties shall respect the right of the child who is separated from one or both parents to maintain personal relations and direct contact with both parents on a regular basis, except if it is contrary to the child's best interests.

Contact is therefore understood by practitioners as a qualified right, with such qualifications within their discretion to determine. Of particular interest in this regard is the concept of parental responsibility, defined by s3(1) of the *Children Act 1989* as: 'all the rights, duties, powers, responsibilities and authority which by law a parent of a child has in relation to the child and his property'. If not married at the time of the child's birth, a father has to do something to gain parental responsibility; a mother does not. This and other legislative provision, such as s52(9) of the *Adoption and Children Act 2002*, which allows that a father without parental responsibility is deemed to have consented to the placement even if he later obtains parental responsibility and objects, mean that parental responsibility is a contentious concept, as Evans and Harris (2004, p.885) when referring to Handler (1973, p.138) point out:

> ...rules, even though we often think of them as unambiguous, can contribute to the uncertainty that creates discretion. He [Handler] noted the imprecision of statute law and the inability of policy makers to make clear rules stemming from statutes. Instead, law and policy are expressed in vague phrases, which are open to interpretation, and this creates wide discretion for the interpretation or generation of policy in the absence of guidance from managers.

There are clear indications that contradictions will continue to be a feature of the assessment landscape in the UK. There are, for example, proposals to cut back on expenditure on housing benefit that will impact upon many non-resident parents. At present it is possible to claim financial help for a property that enables contact including overnight stays for children with the non-resident parent. If adopted, the proposal would see the removal of this benefit to a level where the non-resident parent could only seek accommodation in a shared property. Such a move is likely to have an effect on the outcome of contact and residence decisions.

The situation is exacerbated by 'the normal chaos of family law', that is:

> The extent that family law deals in ideas of what families are, how their members should deal with each other, and what the role of law and the state should be with regard to them, it is not coherent at all. Instead...many contemporary developments in family law can be characterised as chaotic, contradictory or incoherent. (Dewar 1998, pp.467–468)

Such fragmentation of legal norms allied to the practitioner's power in deciding risk, need and the rights of fathers, including the need and right for contact between a father and child, can lead to an outcome where the acknowledged possibilities offered by broad familial and community contact lose emphasis.

Contested contact or residence

It is already evident from the discussion that, in situations of contested contact or residence, the father and wider familial involvement can be minimal or non-existent, never mind genuine or inclusive. As a holistic tool, the 'Assessment Framework' lacks substance as it does not include a practitioner domain to consider the impact of agency, social structures and culture on outcomes (Howarth 2010). Currently the 'Assessment Framework' is too prescriptive (Corby, Millar and Pope 2002) and is used descriptively; it does not always balance intuitive reasoning with analytical reasoning and therefore does not encourage the practitioner to include in the assessment all of the potentially relevant features within a situation.

Analytic reasoning is characterised as 'a step-by-step, conscious, logically defensible process', whereas intuitive reasoning typically means the opposite: 'a cognitive process that somehow produces an answer, solution or idea without the use of a conscious, logically defensible, step-by-step process' (Hammond 1996, p.60). His argument however is not that intuitive reasoning should be expunged and that analytical reasoning favoured but that each should be employed as part of a continuum. If used solely, intuitive reasoning can be criticised for its implicitness, low-level theorising, subjectivity, inconsistency and biases towards the emotive and availability heuristic (Kahneman and Frederick 2002).

In a situation involving contested contact or residence, reliance on intuitive reasoning can lead the practitioner to believe that the needs of the child are wholly met in the care of the resident parent, whereas a balance involving analytical reasoning would include consideration of the child's full identity and the social inclusion in community that is core to their wider relational networks. For many non-resident fathers in particular, the opportunity to define their needs and potential solutions within an assessment that explicitly evaluates the assumptions and reasoning on which decisions are based is indicative of the practitioner's concern that practice is inclusive and reflects the circumstances in which children and parents feel genuine partnership and empowerment (Millar and Corby 2006).

Howarth's (2010, p.14) call 'to *see* the child [and] also to *see* the practitioner' (author emphasis) is apt, and an approach is required that encourages genuineness, recognises the competing and conflicting demands facing practitioners, and enables them to develop child-centred assessments that take into account all factors in a situation, including the strengths and possibilities offered by the non-resident parent. It is unlikely that any framework would be able to account fully for agency, social structures and culture, including: affect, the social construction of children or childhood and the range of, at times, competing and contradictory policy and legislation. What is possible however is a framework that enables practitioners to be explicit about their practice whatever their level of knowledge or competence, including appropriate tools and practices that make explicit their thinking and reasoning, both intuitive and analytical, for pursuing a particular model or method of intervention. Such a framework for intervention needs to be much more than a vehicle for recording information but also, essentially, an aid to analysis of information, for example through explicit reference to empirical research or the development of more than one hypothesis based on a number of possibilities and cognisant of both parents.

The New Zealand perspective

A framework for intervention exists in New Zealand where three sets of philosophical perspectives – child-centredness, family-led and culturally responsive, and strengths and evidence-based – are interwoven with three phases of practice – assessment and engagement, finding solutions, and securing safety and belonging (Connolly 2007). Importantly, in her discussion of the New Zealand framework, Connolly also provides a series of trigger questions for practice to ensure that the philosophical perspectives are interwoven through each phase of the intervention. These are not repeated here but point to the need for appropriate tools or practices, such as supervision, that make explicit the practitioner's thinking and reasoning, both intuitive and analytical, for pursuing a particular model or method of intervention.

Likewise, a hypothesis tree is one method of demonstrating explicit reasoning in analysis, with the potential for the practitioner to develop not one but a number of hypotheses to explain a situation. The tree is an approach that enables the practitioner to break down each hypothesis into key elements and to analyse and compare each hypothesis in turn in order to arrive at an assessment that is least likely to be wrong. Doing so increases the likelihood of an appropriate outcome for the child and better information and involvement of both parental families. Comparative hypotheses are important in developing depth and rigour within analysis (Sheppard *et al.* 2001) and in enabling evaluation by the practitioner and others of the rigour of the approach used in the assessment. The practitioner is much more likely to seek empirical research and less likely to rely on only one parent or source for information – both current issues in assessment (Cleaver *et al.* 2008).

Conclusion

Comparative hypotheses are therefore important for the considerable number of children in the UK for whom contact is an issue. In a survey of separated families for Gingerbread, the UK charity for single parent families, Peacey and Hunt (2009) found that 29 per cent of respondents reported no current contact with their previous partner, of which 63 per cent claimed no contact whatsoever with the non-resident parent since separation. A further 6 per cent said that the father was not aware of the child's existence (Peacey and Hunt 2009). Social work practice needs to rise to the challenge of inclusive parental involvement and analytical reasoning in assessment. Where this does not occur, the outcome for fathers is that they feel disenfranchised, invisible or irrelevant to the development of their child. The outcome for the mother is that she is perceived as wholly responsible for parenting and all that that entails. The outcome for children is that their development is affected and access to a range of economic and socio-cultural opportunities is restricted.

References

Ashley, C., Featherstone, B., Roskill, C., Ryan, M. and White, S. (2006) *Fathers Matter: Research Findings on Fathers and their Involvement with Social Care Services.* London: Family Rights Group.

Bell, M., Shaw, I., Sinclair, I., Sloper, P. and Rafferty, J. (2007) 'The integrated children's system: An evaluation of the practice, process and consequences of the ICS in councils with social services responsibilities (full report).' *A Report to the Department for Education and Skills/Welsh Assembly Government.* May 2007. York: University of York.

Bradley, G. and Höjer, S. (2009) 'Supervision reviewed: Reflections on two different social work models in England and Sweden – Granskad handledning: Reflektioner från två olika handledningsmodeller i England och Sverige.' *European Journal of Social Work 12,* 1, 71–85.

Broadhurst, K., Wastell, D., White, S., Hall, C. *et al.* (2010) 'Performing initial assessment: Identifying the latent conditions for error in local authority children's services.' *British Journal of Social Work 40,* 2, 352–370.

Clapton, G. (2009) 'How and why social work fails fathers: Redressing an imbalance, social work's role and responsibility.' *Practice 21,* 1, 17–34.

Cleaver, H. and Walker, S. with Meadows, P. (2004) *Assessing Children's Needs and Circumstances: The Impact of the Assessment Framework.* London: Jessica Kingsley Publishers.

Cleaver, H., Walker, S., Scott, J., Cleaver, D. *et al.* (2008) *The Integrated Children's System: Enhancing Social Work and Inter-Agency Practice.* London: Jessica Kingsley Publishers.

Conley, C. (2003) 'A review of Parenting Capacity Assessment Reports.' *OACAS Journal 47,* 3, 16–22.

Connolly, M. (2007) 'Practice frameworks: Conceptual maps to guide interventions in child welfare.' *British Journal of Social Work 37,* 5, 825–837.

Corby, B., Millar, M. and Pope, A. (2002) 'Assessing children in need assessments – a parental perspective.' *Practice 14,* 4, 5–15.

Daniel, B. and Taylor, J. (1999) 'The rhetoric versus the reality: A critical perspective on practice with fathers in child care and protection work.' *Child and Family Social Work 4,* 209–220.

Department of Education (2010) *The Munro Review of Child Protection.* London: Department of Education. Available at www.education.gov.uk/munroreview/background.shtml, accessed on 27 April 2011.

Department of Health (2000) *Framework for the Assessment of Children in Need and their Families.* London: The Stationery Office.

Dewar, J. (1998) 'The normal chaos of family law.' *The Family Law Review 61,* 4, 467–485.

Donald, T. and Jureidini, J. (2004) 'Parenting capacity.' *Child Abuse Review 13,* 5–17.

Edwards, J. (2000) *Born and Bred: Idioms of Kinship and New Reproductive Technologies in England.* Oxford: Oxford University Press.

Edwards, J. and Strathern, M. (2000) 'Including our Own.' In J. Carsten (ed.) *Cultures of Relatedness: New Approaches to the Study of Kinship*. Cambridge: Cambridge University Press.

Evans, T. and Harris, J. (2004) 'Street-level bureaucracy, social work and the (exaggerated) death of discretion.' *British Journal of Social Work 34*, 871–895.

Featherstone, B. (2003) 'Taking fathers seriously.' *British Journal of Social Work 33*, 239–254.

Ghate, D., Shaw, C. and Hazel, N. (2000) *Fathers and Family Centres: Engaging Fathers in Preventative Services*. York: Joseph Rowntree Foundation.

Hammond, K. (1996) *Human Judgement and Social Policy*. Oxford: Oxford University Press.

Handler, J. (1973) *The Coercive Social Worker*. Chicago: Rand and McNally.

Howarth, J. (2007) 'The missing assessment domain: Personal, professional and organizational factors influencing professional judgements when identifying and referring child neglect.' *British Journal of Social Work 37*, 1285–1303.

Howarth, J. (2010) 'See the practitioner, see the child: The Framework for the Assessment of Children in Need and their Families ten years on.' *British Journal of Social Work*, 1–18 (advanced access published 29 November 2010). Available at doi:10.1093/bjsw/bcq137, accessed on 22 February 2011 [subscription access only].

Jenson, J. (2009) 'Lost in translation: The social investment perspective and gender equality.' *Social Politics 16*, 4, 446–484.

Kahneman, D. and Frederick, S. (2002) 'Representativeness Revisited: Attribute Substitution in Intuitive Judgment.' In T. Gilovich, D. Griffin and D. Kahneman (eds) *Heuristics and Biases: The Psychology of Intuitive Judgment*. New York: Cambridge University Press.

Keller, C., Siegrist, M.L. and Gutscher, H. (2006) 'The role of the affect and availability heuristic in risk communication.' *Risk Analysis 26*, 3, 631–639.

Middleton, W., Clyne, A. and Harris, P. (1999) 'Risk Assessment and Decision Making.' In D. Messer and F. Jones (eds) *Psychology and Social Care*. London: Jessica Kingsley Publishers.

Millar, M. and Corby, B. (2006) 'The Framework for the Assessment of Children in Need and their Families – a basis for a "therapeutic" encounter?' *British Journal of Social Work 36*, 6, 887–899.

Moran, P., Ghate, D. and Van der Merwe, A. (2004) *What Works in Parenting Support? A Review of the International Evidence*. London: Policy Research Bureau.

Morgen, S. (2001) 'The agency of welfare workers: Negotiating devolution, privatization, and the meaning of self-sufficiency.' *American Anthropologist 103*, 3, 747–761.

Munro, E. (2005) 'Improving practice: Child welfare as a systems problem.' *Children and Youth Services Review 27*, 375–391.

Munro, E. (2010) 'Learning to reduce risk in child protection.' *British Journal of Social Work 40*, 4, 1135–1151.

Munro, E. (2011) *The Munro Review of Child Protection. Interim Report: The Child's Journey*. Nottingham: Department for Education.

Nash, C. (2005) 'Geographies of relatedness.' *Transactions of the Institute of British Geographers 30*, 4, 449–462.

O'Connor, I., Hughes, M., Turney, D., Wilson, J.E. and Setterlund, D.S. (2006) *Social Work and Social Care Practice*. London: Sage. (First published 1996.)

O'Hagan, K. and Dillenburger, K. (1995) *The Abuse of Women within Childcare Work*. Buckingham: Open University Press.

Page, J., Whitting, G. and McLean, C. (2008) *A Review of How Fathers Can Be Better Recognised and Supported Through DCSF Policy*. Research Report DCSF-RR040. Nottingham: DCSF.

Peacey, V. and Hunt, J. (2009) *I'm Not Saying it was Easy: Contact Problems in Separated Families*. London: Gingerbread.

Roskill, C., Featherstone, B., Ashley, C. and Haresnape, S. (2008) *Fathers Matter Volume 2: Further Findings on Fathers and their Involvement with Social Care Services*. London: Family Rights Group.

Ryan, M. (2000) *Working with Fathers*. Oxford: Department of Health, Radcliffe.

Scourfield, J. (2003) *Gender and Child Protection*. Basingstoke: Palgrave Macmillan.

Scourfield, J. (2006) 'The challenge of engaging fathers in the child protection process.' *Critical Social Policy 26*, 2, 440–449.

Sheppard, M., Newstead, S., DiCaccavo, A. and Ryan, K. (2001) 'Comparative hypothesis assessment and quasi triangulation as process knowledge assessment strategies in social work practice.' *British Journal of Social Work 31*, 6, 883–885.

Smith, M. and Nursten, J. (1998) 'Social workers' experiences of distress – moving towards change?' *British Journal of Social Work 28*, 351–368.

Stewart, S.M. and Bond, M.H. (2002) 'A critical look at parenting research from the mainstream: Problems uncovered while adapting Western research to non-Western cultures.' *British Journal of Developmental Psychology 20*, 379–392.

Trinder, L. (2007) 'Dangerous Dads and Malicious Mothers: The Relevance of Gender to Contact Disputes.' In M. Maclean (ed.) *Parenting after Partnering*. Oxford: Hart.

UNICEF (2007) 'Child poverty in perspective: An overview of child well-being in rich countries. A comprehensive assessment of the lives and well-being of children and adolescents in the economically advanced nations.' *Innocenti Report Card 7*. Florence: UNICEF Innocenti Research Centre.

United Nations Convention on the Rights of the Child (1989) New York: United Nations.

Walkowitz, D.J. (1999) *Working with Class: Social Workers and the Politics of Middle-Class Identity*. Chapel Hill: University of North Carolina Press.

White, A. (2005) *Assessment of Parenting Capacity: Literature Review*. Ashfield, NSW: Centre for Parenting and Research, NSW Department of Community Services.

Woodcock, J. (2003) 'The social work assessment of parenting: An exploration.' *British Journal of Social Work 33*, 87–106.

Chapter 14

Should Adoption Be an Option?

Greg Kelly and Chaitali Das

Introduction

The purpose of this chapter is to explore the use of adoption as a placement for children who are in state care because they have been abused or neglected, whose families cannot offer them the care they need and who are often adopted against their parents' wishes. Adoption is used in this way extensively in the United States of America (USA) and the United Kingdom (UK) but scarcely at all in other countries. The chapter will set out the arguments proffered for this development in the UK and the USA and ask why these arguments do not hold sway elsewhere.

Adoption as a placement for children in state care developed first in the USA in the 1970s and this was subsequently taken up by UK theorists and practitioners in the adoption field. There were two key influences at work in both countries. First, adoption services were facing a crisis as the supply of children of unmarried mothers to be placed for adoption diminished rapidly in the face of changing social attitudes to single parents and the increased availability of contraception (Kelly 1998). Second, there was widespread unease at the quality of the care offered to children who were in long-term state care (Rowe and Lambert 1973) and adoption was seen as a possible route to provide better care for these children. At the root of many of these problems was the instability of long-term placements, so the call of the American theorists for 'permanence' for children held (and still holds) a great attraction. Permanence in this context has been defined:

> The child will grow up with a family (whether birth family or substitute family) which offers continuity of relationships with nurturing parents or caretakers and the opportunity to establish lifetime relationships. (Maluccio, Fein and Olmstead 1986, p.11)

The preferred means of providing this permanence was and remains the child's birth parents and, where they are unable to, the child's extended family. This is reflected in the legislation in the UK where the threshold for a Care Order is that the child has or is likely to suffer 'significant harm'. The average time taken to bring and test the evidence to achieve a Care Order, where the state is granted parental rights, is over 12 months (Ministry of Justice 2010; Northern Ireland Guardian Ad Litem Agency 2010). Where a Care Order is granted it will be with a court-agreed 'care plan', and care outside the family will not be approved unless the birth and the extended family options have been explored and found wanting. The singular contribution of the permanence theorists was to argue that adoption should be considered preferable to long-term state care as a means of providing these children with the stability and permanence they need. This emphasis on permanence was based on a critical acceptance of the work of Bowlby (1953) and the attachment theorists, supported by practice and clinical experience indicating that those children who do not enjoy stable attachments in their childhood struggle to adjust to the demands of adolescence and beyond (Goldstein, Freud and Solnit 1973).

The principle of seeking stable attachment figure/s, usually foster parents, as an alternative to institutional care for children for short periods of separation (Robertson and Robertson 1989) blossomed into the search for stable or 'permanent' long-term family placements for children who could not return to their birth families. These developments have been subsequently supported by research evidencing the highly negative impact of early institutionalisation on children's health, development and wellbeing (European Commission – Daphne Programme 2007). In many countries this acceptance of the inadequacies of institutional care has led to the development of extensive foster family services. For example, in Spain and Romania where children in care were previously cared for in institutions, there is movement towards the development of foster care and consequent reduction of the institutionalisation of children (Dickens 1999; Palacios and Amorós 2006). The questions posed by the permanence theorists and discussed in this chapter are: Is foster care always adequate to the task of providing the stability children need? Why is the use of adoption for children who would otherwise remain in state care not developed, particularly as it has long been known that adoption can deliver very satisfactory outcomes for children (Triseliotis 1989 and 2002)?

Different approaches to childcare planning and permanence are, of course, to be understood as the products of different social contexts. Thus, for example, in the collective community context of New Zealand, a more embedded partnership approach is evident, leading to a greater capacity to find wider family-based solutions. While in the UK, where the dominant conceptualisation of the family is 'nuclear', there is a tendency to seek alternative nuclear families (Parkinson 2003). This is true of many countries of Western Europe (Dumaret and Rosset 2005; Palmer 1989; Parkinson 2003; Rushton 2003; Sargent 2003). In many Western European countries, barring the UK, domestic adoption without parental consent is rare, and it is not pursued for children in state care unless it can be shown that their parents have abandoned them (Bainham 2009; Dumaret and Rosset 2005; Bunkers, Groza and Lauer 2009). Thus, while many of these countries widely employ alternative nuclear families, such as foster families, it is curious as to why they do not also promote the use of adoption for the children in care who need alternative families. These same countries do, however, permit and often provide services to facilitate their citizens to parent children needing families from foreign countries through the route of intercountry adoption.

On the other hand, the USA and the UK have recently enacted laws that reaffirm their commitment to adoption in child welfare policy: the *Adoption and Safe Families Act 1997* in the USA and the *Adoption and Children Act 2002* in England and Wales. Both these Acts reinforce the policy of promoting the adoption of children who would otherwise remain in care and commit resources to the pursuit of this goal. The White Paper on which the legislation was based set out the Government's proposals to encourage wider use of adoption, particularly of children looked after by local authorities (Department of Health 2000). The purpose of legislation for England and Wales is 'to improve the performance of the adoption service and promote greater use of adoption and to ensure that the child's welfare is the paramount consideration in all decisions relating to adoption' (*Adoption and Children Act 2002*, s.38).

We will set out four arguments to justify adoption for children who face many years in public or state care and consider whether it is a legitimate response to the needs of these children.

1. ADOPTION CAN BE MORE SUCCESSFUL THAN FOSTER CARE IN PROVIDING CHILDREN WITH A STABLE PLACEMENT AND A 'FAMILY FOR LIFE'

Adoption can be a remarkably successful intervention in the lives of abandoned and neglected children. Sir Michael Rutter and colleagues (1998) in their study of Romanian adoptees have demonstrated this to spectacular effect. Children who spent their early months in extremely deprived conditions in the Romanian orphanages showed marked developmental delay. However, children who were adopted within six months of their birth, on adoption, predominantly achieved remarkable catch-up in terms of overcoming these developmental and cognitive deficits by the age of four years. These improvements continued into adolescence for the early adopted children and there were very few placement breakdowns. However, those who had spent more than six months in the Romanian orphanages were more likely to have ongoing cognitive and behavioural problems. These findings are replicated in many studies of baby adoptions, both domestic and intercountry. A major Swedish study of 6000 intercountry adoptees who had reached young adulthood found that they had reached the same educational levels as the general population, but did not achieve the level of those raised in similar circumstances of affluence (Lingblad, Hjern and Vinnerjung 2003). In a review of outcome studies, Howe concluded:

> Their [adopted children's] levels of psychosocial functioning tend, on the whole, to be much more favourable than those for children raised in adversity by biological parents and children looked after in foster and residential care. (Howe 1998, p.8)

Studies of adopted children generally find them functioning well within the normal range of functioning but more vulnerable to emotional, behavioural and academic problems compared to non-adopted children living in intact homes with their biological parents (Brodzinsky 1993). Hoksbergen's (1999) review paper concludes that adopted children seem to function better than children in institutions or children in care restored to their birth families.

For those planning child placement, a great strength of adoption is its 'stickability'. Very few placements of young children break down even in potentially troubled populations like the Romanian adoptees. However, as older children with more difficulties consequent to their longer exposure to abuse, neglect and instability are placed, they present greater needs that adoptive parents and support services have to meet. Placements of older children, especially over eight years of age, are more likely to break down, although most studies report a 'success rate' of around 80 per cent even for children with special needs[1] (Triseliotis 2002).

This stability of placement is one of the key issues in the choice of adoption or foster care as a placement for a child who needs permanent substitute care. Research over the last 40 years and across many jurisdictions, in general, has highlighted the instability of foster family placements and of children's careers in care. In a recent study in England, Harriet Ward (2009) summarised this:

> One factor, however, which is likely to impact on the life trajectories of children in care is the unstable nature of placements, again a common problem, both in the United Kingdom, North America, Australia, and in much of Europe (Stein and Munro 2008; Unrau, Seita and Putney 2008). English children move home on average three times before reaching adulthood (Moyers and Mason 1995), whereas it is not unusual for those in the care system to experience the equivalent level of change in the course of a year (Department for Children, Schools and Families 2008). (Ward 2009, p.1)

Perhaps the most depressing finding in Ward's work is that most of these moves were not because of placement breakdown but occurred due to administrative reasons and took place within a culture of change and mobility where social workers were changing every few months and children were moved from one team to another according to the organisational structure of the local authority.

It is difficult to make exact comparisons of disruption rates in foster and adoptive placements because of the impossibility of achieving matched samples (Brodzinsky 1993; Triseliotis 2002). The closest to achieving a matched sample is the work of Selwyn and Quinton (2004) in England. They followed a sample of 130 children in care for whom the plan was adoption. However, adoption was not achieved for all of them and 46 were placed in long-term foster care. This allowed for a comparison between those placed in long-term foster care and those adopted. At follow-up, on an average of seven years later, 83 per cent of the adopted children were still in their adoptive homes compared to 54 per cent of the fostered children who remained in their original planned long-term foster homes. The authors concluded as others have done:

> This study provides evidence that there is a link between insecurity felt by the carers and the child and the development of close, trusting relationships and adoption had advantages in providing this security. (Selwyn and Quinton 2004, p.14)

Thus in terms of providing permanent placements for children, adoption has two key and linked advantages. First, it provides the conditions that permit parent and child to commit wholly to the relationship and, second, it appears less likely to break down. This is not to say that foster care cannot and does not provide excellent and stable care for many children and enable them to develop their potential. Studies of surviving, successful placements (Festinger 1983; Schofield 2000) demonstrate this. Indeed long-term foster care can provide permanence, particularly when the placement is intended to be permanent from the start (Parkinson 2003; Sinclair 2000; Ward 2004). However, instability in foster care is rife and exposes children to the most damaging elements of being in state care. Indeed, Sinclair's research found that, for most children in the UK, the system did not provide this stability and most long-stay children wanted to move less often than they did (Sinclair 2000).

2. FOSTER CARE RETAINS CHILDREN IN THE DOMAIN OF STATE CARE WHICH IS ASSOCIATED WITH A HIGH RISK OF POOR OUTCOMES

There is little uniformity in the organisation of state care of children. It is very much dependent on national histories and traditions. In many countries, there is little or no research on the outcomes for children. It is therefore difficult to generalise, and it is for each jurisdiction to judge their performance. Nonetheless, it is hard to find any country that believes its services to children in care are satisfactory. In the UK, there has been a 'hue and cry' about the perceived poor outcomes for children who have been in care (for example, children in care are 60 times more likely to be homeless and 50 times more likely to be sent to prison, compared to the general population) and this material was used directly by the Government to promote adoption of children out of care (Performance and Innovation Unit 2000). These figures have, in turn, been criticised principally on the grounds that they compare children in care with the average of the population and not children from the disadvantaged sections of society from which they are taken into care. They attribute all the problems to the children having been in care when much of the 'damage' may have been inflicted either before they came into care or after they left care.

However, more balanced research in a range of countries indicates that children in care are at considerable risk of a range of poor outcomes even when compared with peers from their community who have not experienced care. A Swedish study by Hoger reported in Stein and Munro (2008) compared young people from adverse circumstances and indicated that care leavers showed elevated risk of early mortality, mental health problems, suicide attempts, poorer educational attainments and higher rates of teenage pregnancy. They pointed out that these findings were generally consistent with small-scale studies in Canada, Australia and most European countries where care leavers show difficult transitions and poor outcomes. This is not to say that foster care and residential care do not provide a valuable service for very many children, particularly when compared to the circumstances and situations that led to their admissions. The argument for adoption is that it can provide these benefits but also remove children from the care population and minimise the risk of very poor and damaging outcomes.

An additional disadvantage of remaining in care is the bureaucracy that surrounds the parenting of the child. Key decisions are often not taken by those caring for the child on a day-to-day basis but by professionals who change from year to year, and the professionals too are subject to extensive bureaucratic accountability. Efforts have been made to decrease this bureaucracy and depersonalisation of parenting for foster children in the UK. However, if parental rights are vested in the public authority, this bureaucracy is always likely to remain to a greater or lesser extent.

3. ADOPTION CAN INCORPORATE SOME OF THE FEATURES OF FOSTER CARE AND BRIDGE THE DIVIDE BETWEEN THE TWO

The history of adoption is complex and there is great variation across time within countries and between different countries. In the UK, until the 1970s, adoption was essentially a service to provide childless couples (usually middle class) with the healthy white babies they could not have. It was based on 'consent' from the child's mother that was virtually assured in a society where having a child outside wedlock was the ultimate disgrace. Birth parents were encouraged to forget their child and 'get on with their lives', not knowing if their child was alive or dead. Much of the pain this caused has been revealed in work done with adult adoptees and their birth parents (Kelly 2005). Adoption began to change when the supply of children born out of wedlock rapidly diminished in the 1970s and its advocates argued for its incorporation within wider child welfare provision and its use for children who needed long-term substitute family care (Kelly 1998).

If adoption was to provide families for this new population of children in care, it had to change. Essentially, it has moved from being a service to infertile couples and the expression of society's disapproval of extramarital pregnancy to one that prioritises the needs of children who need families. It demands of those who would adopt that they can meet the complex and varied needs of the children for whom placements are being sought. Most adopters still come to adoption because of their infertility (Selwyn *et al.* 2006) but many do so also for reasons of altruism. In addition, within this new context of adoption, adopted children often retain contact in some form with their birth family relatives or parents. The key challenges for adoptive parents are to also develop the capacity to parent the child inclusive of his/her past and associated relationships. Brodzinsky and Schechter (1990) stressed this openness as an important feature and quality in adoptive families that permits a freedom to discuss these issues of adoption. Indeed, the great majority of children adopted from care have some contact with their birth families (Kelly *et al.* 2007; Young and Neil 2009). Incorporating this into family life requires adoptive parents to stretch their original views of the family they were seeking. It also requires an acknowledgment from adoption services to support and provide adequate training to adopters who are willing and have the capacity to move in this direction. There is a lot of evidence that it is possible to recruit adopters who can grow into these parenting roles (Kelly *et al.* 2007). In the UK, the authorities may also award an adoption allowance and provide post-adoption services.

So, although the fundamentals of adoption remain (that is, the child is no longer a member of their birth family and is now wholly and completely a member of the adoptive family with no mandatory state involvement), the surrounding practice has been very much modernised to take account of the needs of children who may have spent some time with their birth families. This can be characterised as adoption drawing on the essentials of foster care in terms of the assessment, training and post-placement support of adoptive parents. It could be said that it incorporates many of the advantages and safeguards of foster care without its key disadvantages: the child remaining in public care and the child not being wholly the responsibility of those who care for him/her. As we have seen above, while exact comparisons are not possible, researchers and commentators appear in general agreement that this 'modern' adoption offers children a better chance of the stability and commitment of family life than long-term foster care.

4. THERE IS, POTENTIALLY, A STEADY SUPPLY OF CHILDLESS COUPLES WHO ARE KEEN TO ADOPT YOUNG CHILDREN

In the UK, it is estimated that one in seven couples have difficulty conceiving naturally (*BBC News* 2005). It is from this group that adopters are predominantly drawn. Only a proportion of these couples will seek to adopt. Many will not progress when confronted with the reality of the children needing adoption and some will opt for intercountry adoption. Nonetheless, Social Services in the UK have been very successful in recruiting adoptive parents assessed as suitable for children in care from this population. They are, typically, highly motivated. They have had many disappointments in their quest for children and they see adoption as their last chance to have the family they have longed for. It is this motivation, commitment or 'stickability' in the face of the considerable difficulties that adopted children often present that makes them such a valuable resource. There is much evidence of their capacity, with support and training, to adapt and stretch their expectations of adoption to meet the special needs of children adopted from care (Selwyn *et al.* 2006). Despite the possibility of long-term options within foster care, adoption is still often their preferred option because of its permanence, and the legal rights it affords to them. They and their adopted children are legally a 'real' family.

It is one of the surprising aspects of reviewing international child welfare policy that so many states provide services and assist couples and individuals to adopt from abroad, but severely limit their doing so for children in care in their own countries. In Greene *et al.*'s (2008) study of intercountry adoption in Ireland, 70 per cent of the adoptive parents gave 'the unavailability of Irish children' as a reason for adopting from abroad. Thus, for many countries there is an untapped resource of potential parents for children in long-term state care, particularly for those who enter care at a very young age and cannot return to their birth families.

Is adoption a 'proportionate' response?

Having children adopted against their parents' wishes by 'dispensing with their consent' is a draconian step and severs their previous identity (Parkinson 2003). It is in this sense an extreme intervention in the life of both child and parent (European Commission – Daphne

Programme 2007). It is also associated with much undesirable historical baggage. It can be seen as the descendant of various forms of social engineering and racist policies that were prevalent in many parts of the former British Empire – for example, Australia's 'stolen generation';[2] it is insensitive to the histories and cultures of Indigenous Australians such as the Aboriginal and Torres Strait Islander communities in Australia (Parkinson 2003), First Nation communities in Canada, as well as the Native Americans in the USA (Lazarus 1997). It can be seen as a punishment for families unable to parent their children (Cardarello 2009; Guggenheim 2000). The courts in the UK are in no doubt as to the gravity of an adoption order. Dispensing with parents' consent to adoption has always been subject to protracted proceedings and is among the most difficult issues that courts have to adjudicate on. In Northern Ireland, for instance, it has to be shown that adoption is not only in the child's best interests but also that the parent is withholding their consent unreasonably. Recent legislation in England has relaxed this condition and now consent can be dispensed with if adoption can be shown to be in the child's best interests (*Adoption and Children Act 2002*). However, the incorporation of the European Convention of Human Rights into the domestic legislation in the UK through the *Human Rights Act 1998* has meant that decisions have to be compliant with its Articles. Chief among these is Article 8: 'Everyone has the right to respect for his private life and family life, his home and his correspondence', and this should be protected against arbitrary action by the state. The European court has, however, clearly recognised public authorities' responsibility to pursue the welfare of the child. Where there is a need to balance the competing rights of parent and child, 'the Court will attach particular importance to the best interests of the child, which may override those of the parent' (O'Halloran 2009, p.122). In addition, case law has also ruled that, 'If any balancing of welfare is necessary, the interests of the child must prevail' (O'Halloran 2009, p.122). Every application involves a court balancing the rights of the participants to the application (including the children who are the subject of it) and arriving at a result which is in the interests of those children and proportionate to the legitimate aim being pursued (O'Halloran 2009).

The contention of this chapter is that it is legitimate to regard adoption without parents' consent as a 'proportionate' response to the legitimate aims of protecting children from persistent abuse and neglect and meeting their need for a stable family life and a home environment. The discussion above has attempted to use the existing knowledge base to set out the advantages of adoption over the principal alternative: long-term foster care.

A potential problem with these arguments is that they compare adoption with a foster care and a childcare service that are socially constructed. Many of the faults in both that make them relatively poor in providing children with security and satisfactory outcomes could and should be addressed. Foster care could learn from adoption and develop placements that mirror many of the qualities that make adoption successful. Greater efforts could be made to plan and deliver 'permanent' foster placements and to reduce the bureaucratic infrastructure that detracts from the experience of normal family life. It is difficult to base arguments for adoption solely on weaknesses of the foster care and childcare services that could and should be remedied.

The argument for adoption is ultimately only sustainable if we are convinced that it is intrinsically better than foster care, not just in keeping children safe but in allowing them to develop to their full potential. This is the position of those who argue for it (Goldstein *et al.* 1973; Katz 1996). They argue that adoption, with its clear and unequivocal transfer of parental rights to the adoptive family, provides the foundation on which the essential commitment of parent to child and child to parent can most readily develop. On the other hand, the essential nature of foster care, with the parenting of the child shared between the foster parent, the birth parent and the state, inhibits the development of this commitment. This is not to say, of course, that all adoptions are better than all foster care placements or that all children in long-term care should be adopted. For example, older children may already have a well-developed identity with their birth family they want to maintain. It is to argue for adoption to be available as a 'proportionate response' to the child's needs where the following conditions are met:

- the child has suffered or is likely to suffer extensive abuse or neglect and the evidence of such is subject to rigorous examination in the courts with parents and child legally represented
- all available efforts have been made and opportunities given to remedy the problems in the child's family
- there is no prospect in the foreseeable future of the child returning to his birth family
- adoptive parents can be recruited, trained and supported to meet the child's particular needs; this will often include continued relationships with his birth family.

Adoption should be available as a last resort when children's families cannot care for them. It should not be seen as a panacea to be ruthlessly pursued. It is the gravest infringement of parents' rights in relation to their children, and in a balanced child welfare policy will only be sought for a small minority of children whose families cannot be resourced and supported to care for them.

Conclusion

It is difficult to understand why so few countries make provision for the use of the very limited and circumscribed adoption as described above, particularly when it has been evidenced to have successful outcomes for children and is often superior to other care options. It is doubly perplexing when these same states permit intercountry adoption where there is evidence that many of the children have living parents and extensive birth families and where there are many issues surrounding the circumstances of their parents' consent to adoption (Saclier 2000; Triseliotis 2000). It may be that other countries are more successful in their support for families and preventive measures and they are more confident that their services for children in care are delivering satisfactory outcomes for children. It is difficult to find the evidence for this, with most jurisdictions apparently struggling with poor outcomes for their children leaving care. The reluctance to develop adoption as an alternative to children remaining in state care appears grounded in a wide range of different histories and traditions which are fearful of state interference in family life. These fears may spring from religious principles or from long discredited policies towards the disadvantaged and their children. It is perhaps time to reconsider adoption in the light of current evidence of what best enables children to achieve their potential where, with all available assistance and safeguards, their birth families are unable to parent them.

Endnotes

1. Children with special needs indicate children who have past experiences of disadvantage, abuse and neglect and show emotional, behavioural and/or learning problems (McKenzie 1993; Rees and Selwyn 2009).
2. Stolen generation refers to the removal of Aboriginal and Torres Strait Islander children from their families. The National Inquiry into the Separation of Aboriginal and Torres Strait Islander Children from their Families, 'Bringing Them Home', provides detailed analysis of the legislative history of State, Territory and Commonwealth laws applying specifically to Indigenous children,

as well as general child welfare and adoption laws. The inquiry estimates that in the period 1910–1970 between 1 in 10 and 1 in 3 Indigenous children were forcibly removed from their families (Commonwealth of Australia 1997).

References

Bainham, A. (2009) 'The politics of child protection in Romania.' *International Journal of Children's Rights 17*, 527–542.

BBC News (2005) '"Infertility time bomb" warning.' 20 June. Available at http://news.bbc.co.uk/1/hi/health/4112450.stm, accessed on 28 October 2011.

Bowlby, J. (1953) *Child Care and the Growth of Love*. Baltimore, MD: Pelican Books.

Brodzinsky, D.M. (1993) 'Long-term outcomes in adoption.' *The Future of Children 3*, 1, 153–166.

Brodzinsky, D.M. and Schechter, M. (eds) (1990) *The Psychology of Adoption*. Oxford: Oxford University Press.

Bunkers, K.M., Groza, V. and Lauer, D.P. (2009) 'International adoption and child protection in Guatemala: A case of the tail wagging the dog.' *International Social Work 52*, 5, 649–660.

Cardarello, A. (2009) 'The Movement of the Mothers of the Courthouse Square: "Legal child trafficking", adoption and poverty in Brazil.' *Journal of Latin American and Caribbean Anthropology 14*, 1, 140–161.

Commonwealth of Australia (1997) *Bringing Them Home: National Enquiry into the Separation of Aboriginal and Torres Strait Islander Children from their Families*. Sydney: Human Rights and Equal Opportunity Commission.

Department for Children, Schools and Families (2008) *Children Looked After in England (Including Adoption and Care Leavers): Year Ending 31 March 2007 (SFR27/2007)*. London: Department for Children, Schools and Families.

Department of Health (2000) *Adoption: A New Approach*. A White Paper. London: DoH.

Dickens, J. (1999) 'Family support in Romania and the UK: Different circumstances, similar challenges.' *Children and Society 13*, 155–166.

Dumaret, A.C. and Rosset, D.J. (2005) 'Adoption and child welfare protection in France.' *Early Child Development and Care 175*, 7, 661–670.

European Commission – Daphne Programme (2007) *De-institutionalising and Transforming Children's Services: A Guide to Good Practice*. Birmingham: University of Birmingham.

Festinger, T. (1983) *No One Ever Asked Us: A Postscript to Foster Care*. New York: Columbia University Press.

Goldstein, J., Freud, A. and Solnit, A.J. (1973) *Beyond the Best Interests of the Child*. London: Burnett Books.

Greene, S., Kelly, R., Nixon, E., Kelly, G. *et al.* (2008) *A Study of Intercountry Adoption Outcomes in Ireland*. Republic of Ireland: The Adoption Board and Trinity College, Dublin.

Guggenheim, M. (2000) 'Review. Somebody's children: Sustaining the family's place in child welfare policy.' *Harvard Law Review 113*, 7, 1716–1750.

Hoksbergen, R.A.C. (1999) 'The importance of adoption for nurturing and enhancing the emotional and intellectual potential of children.' *Adoption Quarterly 3*, 2, 29–41.

Howe, D. (1998) 'Adoption outcome research and practical judgment.' *Adoption and Fostering 32*, 2, 6–15.

Katz, L. (1996) 'Permanency action through concurrent planning.' *Adoption and Fostering 20*, 2, 8–13.

Kelly, G. (1998) 'The Influence of Research on Child Care Policy and Practice: The Case of "Children Who Wait" and the Development of the Permanence Movement in the United Kingdom.' In D. Iwaniec and J. Pinkerton (eds) *Making Research Work: Promoting Child Care Policy and Practice*. Chichester: Wiley Publications.

Kelly, G., Haslett, P., O'Hare, J. and McDowell, K. (2007) 'Permanence planning in Northern Ireland: A development project.' *Adoption and Fostering 31*, 3, 18–27.

Kelly, R. (2005) *Motherhood Silenced: The Experiences of Natural Mothers on Adoption Reunion*. Dublin: The Liffey Press.

Lazarus, K.B. (1997) 'Adoption of Native American and First Nations children: Are the United States and Canada recognizing the best interests of the children?' *Arizona Journal of International and Comparative Law 14*, 1, 255–284.

Lingblad, F., Hjern, A. and Vinnerjung, B. (2003) 'Intercountry adopted children as young adults – A Swedish cohort study.' *American Journal of Orthopsychiatry 73*, 2, 190–202.

Maluccio, A.N., Fein, E. and Olmstead, K.A. (1986) *Permanency Planning for Children: Concepts and Methods*. London: Tavistock Publications.

McKenzie, J.K. (1993) 'Adoption of children with special needs.' *The Future of Children: Adoption 3*, 1, 62–76.

Ministry of Justice (2010) *Establishment of a System-Wide Target for Reducing Unnecessary Delay in Care and Supervision Proceedings*. London: Ministry of Justice.

Moyers, S. and Mason, A. (1995) 'Identifying Standards of Parenting.' In H. Ward (ed.) *Looking after Children: Research into Practice*. London: The Stationery Office.

Northern Ireland Guardian Ad Litem Agency (2010) *Annual Report*. Belfast: NIGALA.

O'Halloran, K. (2009) *The Politics of Adoption*. Vienna: Springer Publications.

Palacios, J. and Amorós, P. (2006) 'Recent changes in adoption and fostering in Spain.' *British Journal of Social Work 36*, 921–935.

Palmer, M.J.E. (1989) 'Civil adoption in contemporary Chinese law: A contract to care.' *Modern Asian Studies 23*, 2, 373–410.

Parkinson, P. (2003) 'Child protection, permanency planning and children's right to family life.' *International Journal of Law, Policy and the Family 17*, 147–172.

Performance and Innovation Unit (2000) *Prime Minister's Review of Adoption*. London: Cabinet Office.

Rees, C.A. and Selwyn, J. (2009) 'Non-infant adoption from care: Lessons for safeguarding children.' *Child: Care, Health and Development 35*, 4, 561–567.

Robertson, J. and Robertson, J. (1989) *Separation and the Very Young*. London: Free Association Books.

Rowe, J. and Lambert, L. (1973) *Children Who Wait*. London: Association of British Adoption and Fostering Agencies.

Rushton, A. (2003) *Knowledge Review 2. The Adoption of Looked After Children: A Scoping Review of Research*. London: Social Care Institute for Excellence.

Rutter, M. and the English and Romanian Adoptees Study Team (1998) 'Developmental catch-up and deficit following adoption after severe global early privation.' *Journal of Child Psychology and Psychiatry 39*, 465–476.

Saclier, C. (2000) 'In the Best Interests of the Child?' In P. Selman (ed.) *Intercountry Adoption: Developments, Trends and Perspectives*. London: BAAF.

Sargent, S. (2003) 'Adoption and looked after children: A comparison of legal initiatives in the UK and the USA.' *Adoption and Fostering 27*, 2, 44–52.

Schofield, G. (2000) 'Resilience and family placement: A lifespan perspective.' *Adoption and Fostering 25*, 3, 6–19.
Selwyn, J. and Quinton, D. (2004) 'Stability, permanence, outcomes and support: Foster care and adoption compared.' *Adoption and Fostering 28*, 4, 6–15.
Selwyn, J., Sturgess, W., Quinton, D. and Baxter, C. (2006) *Costs and Outcomes of Non-Infant Adoptions.* London: BAAF.
Sinclair, I. (2000) 'Residential Care.' In M. Davies (ed.) *Encyclopaedia of Social Work.* Oxford: Basil Blackwell.
Stein, M. and Munro, E. (2008) *Young People's Transitions from Care to Adulthood: International Research and Practice.* London: Jessica Kingsley Publishers.
Triseliotis, J. (1989) 'Foster care outcomes: A review of key research findings.' *Adoption and Fostering 13*, 3, 5–17.
Triseliotis, J. (2000) 'Intercountry adoption: Global trade or global gift?' *Adoption and Fostering 24*, 2, 45–54.
Triseliotis, J. (2002) 'Long term foster care or adoption? The evidence examined.' *Child and Family Social Work 7*, 1, 23–33.
Unrau, Y.A., Seita, J.R. and Putney, K.S. (2008) 'Former foster youth remember multiple placement moves: A journey of loss and hope.' *Children and Youth Services Review 30*, 11, 1256–1266.
Ward, H. (2009) 'Patterns of instability: Moves within the care system, their reasons, contexts and consequences.' *Children and Youth Services Review 31*, 10, 1113–1118.
Ward, P. (2004) 'Achieving permanence for looked after children through special guardianship: A study of the experience of New Zealand guardians with implications for special guardianship in England.' *Adoption and Fostering 28*, 4, 16–26.
Young, J. and Neil, E. (2009) 'Contact after Adoption.' In G. Schofield and J. Simmonds (eds) *The Child Placement Handbook: Research, Policy and Practice.* London: BAAF.

PART IV

Child Welfare and Legal Intervention

Chapter 15

Child Protection and Family Law

The Australian Experience

Lisa Young

Introduction

The difficulties of protecting children from violence is a longstanding theme in Australian family law. Modern policy debates have seen increasing concern about child protection juxtaposed with the fear of strategically false allegations of child abuse and an overwhelming desire to try to maintain and foster father/child bonds. While the competing interests may be predictable, Australian family law has undergone very radical reforms in recent years, which have failed to appreciate the potential dangers children face if those interests are not balanced in favour of child protection.

This chapter traces the background to the 2006 family law reforms in Australia, outlines those reforms in so far as they relate to child protection, and briefly identifies the critique that attended their introduction. It then considers the impact of those reforms on the protection of children from family violence, using a case example to support its argument that legislative reform, including increasing emphasis on shared parenting, has fostered a decision-making approach that minimises issues of child protection in favour of parental contact. Recent research and evaluations of the 2006 reforms are then considered; so too is whether or not current proposals for further legislative reform are likely to improve the protection of children in separated families.

The legislative background

In Australia, contested disputes between parents about the care of their children are heard in the federal family courts: the Family Court of Australia and the Federal Magistrates Court. The law governing such disputes (*Family Law Act 1975* (Cth), Part VII) requires the courts to regard the child's best interests as the paramount consideration when deciding orders about care arrangements. Until 2006, Australian family courts had to decide parenting disputes on the basis that the child's best interests were the paramount consideration and, in determining that, were required to have regard to a list of mandatory considerations, none of which was stated to take priority over the other. This 'best interests checklist' did not include any specific mention of violence until 1996 (see *Family Law Reform Act 1995* (Cth)), though it was able to be considered under other provisions, in particular the final catch-all consideration 'any other relevant matter'. Thus, some early parenting decisions evidenced little judicial appreciation of the significance of child abuse (Rhoades, Frew and Swain 2010), in particular where the child witnessed violence to other family members, as opposed to being the direct victim. By 1996 judicial opinion on the matter had shifted considerably and legislative reform followed with the introduction of mandatory considerations relating to 'family violence'. At the same time political demands for a 'shared parenting' presumption had gained momentum in Australia (Kaye and Tolmie 1998) and there were other, contemporaneous, legislative amendments designed to promote greater paternal involvement in post-separation parenting through greater shared care.

While the 1996 reforms may not have been as effective as some had hoped in producing an increase in shared care arrangements, research confirmed an increasingly 'pro-contact' culture within the family courts, and it was suggested this development had overwhelmed the new violence provisions; only in cases of extremely severe violence would a decision-maker even question whether contact should take place (Kaspiew 2005). Conversely, however, it was claimed that the increased focus on protection of children from violence had resulted in an explosion of false claims of violence, for strategic purposes, and that such allegations could now effectively be used to exclude fathers from the lives of their children (Parkinson, Cashmore and Webster 2010). Claims about false violence allegations and a concern to promote shared parenting were significant factors in the decision of the Australian government to introduce further, and more radical, reforms in 2006: *Family Law Amendment (Shared Parental Responsibility) Act 2006* (Cth).

For present purposes, the key elements of the 2006 reforms were:

(a) Creating two tiers of mandatory best interests considerations, 'primary' and 'additional'. The 'primary' considerations are (in this order) (i) the benefit to the child of promoting a meaningful relationship between the child and both parents and (ii) the need to protect children from violence (s 60CC(2)).

(b) In the remaining 'additional' considerations (which otherwise largely reflected the best interests checklist prior to the reforms), introducing a 'friendly parent' provision (s 60CC(3)(c)), namely the requirement that the court take into account the extent to which a parent promotes the relationship of the child with the other parent.

(c) Providing that costs orders *must* be awarded against parties who make 'false allegations' (s 117A); while broadly worded, it was clear from parliamentary debate that this was specifically aimed at false allegations of child abuse.

(d) Requiring decision-makers, when deciding precisely what parenting orders to make where there is to be joint responsibility for major long-term issues (what was once known as 'guardianship'), to consider a hierarchy of shared parenting orders, *starting with* equal shared parenting (s 65DAA).

Commentators immediately predicted that the combined effect of these reforms would be to increase the risk of children being exposed to violence (Banks *et al.* 2005). In short, it was argued that the deliberate focus on increasing shared parenting outcomes would work to encourage decision-makers to under-rate issues of protection from violence in favour of trying to find a shared parenting solution; and threats of costs orders and the need to appear 'friendly' would discourage parents from bringing forward valid claims of violence. Friendly parent provisions had, after all, been the subject of much criticism in other jurisdictions (de Simone 2008). In relation to the costs order provision, there was no evidence to support an assumption that false allegations were a pervasive, or increasing, problem (Moloney *et al.* 2007), whereas the evidence was clear on the high rates of actual family violence. Given the difficulty of establishing violence, there was concern the fear of a costs order would discourage real victims of violence from voicing their safety concerns for both themselves and their children.

It was technically possible these fears would not be realised. For example, the substance of the family-friendly provision had long been considered relevant in Australian family law decision-making. Further, the primary considerations can be read in a way that allows for protection from violence to have primacy over shared parenting. For example, the violence consideration is expressed in more mandatory and precise terms (the 'need'), whereas the terms 'benefit' and 'meaningful' used in the other primary consideration are more elastic and allow for interpretations which accommodate recognition that where violence is a significant factor it may outweigh the other primary consideration (Explanatory Memorandum, *Shared Parental Responsibility Bill 2006*). On the other hand, it could also be argued that a clear legislative push towards greater shared care was destined to weaken judicial resolve to take strong measures to protect children from violence.

The impact of the 2006 reforms: Case examples

What then can be garnered from the case law as to how decision-makers have been applying these provisions? In many parenting cases the question of whether there actually was, or is, any violence remains unresolved. Determining such questions is not, of course, the central purpose of the proceedings (*M v M* (1988) 166 CLR 69). It seems appropriate therefore to take by way of example cases where the violence is either acknowledged or established in court, and to see how decision-makers are applying the new provisions against the backdrop of recognised serious violence. If the application of the new provisions appears to undermine the protection of children even where serious violence is established, it seems fair to assume that in other cases, where violence is present but harder to establish, children will be at even greater risk of exposure to harm.

A case in point: Mills v Watson *(2008) 39 FamLR 52*

This decision stands out as exemplifying the dangers of the 2006 amendments, and when one reads many cases there is reason to believe it is not atypical. The case involved a child who was seven years old at the time her mother relocated her away from their home state, away from the child's father; he then started proceedings to secure the return of both mother and child. The father admitted to having been very violent towards the mother since the start of their relationship. He suffered from a mental illness, had refused for many years to take any medication, was found not to be trustworthy to take his medication and used marijuana daily, even though it exacerbated his illness. Nonetheless, the mother, believing it to be her duty to foster contact, did precisely that after separation, moving from initially supervised contact to unsupervised contact including overnight contact. However, the father regularly missed contact visits, on two occasions failed to return the child after contact and was violent to his new partner in front of the child. As a result, the mother became increasingly concerned about the child's welfare when in the care of the father.

The mother stopped contact; however, the father obtained an order for supervised contact. At the same time, the father began to harass the mother and her new partner at their joint place of work. The mother took the child to another state and refused to comply with orders requiring her to return the child to their home state. An Independent Children's Lawyer for the child was appointed and a Family Report was prepared by a psychologist. While the mother was not ultimately ordered to return to her previous home state, the father succeeded in obtaining orders that he have supervised contact with the child and joint responsibility for long-term decision-making.

There are some disconcerting features to this case and it is not unique in terms of the way the new provisions are used as a lens through which to view the parties' conduct. Before turning to the Federal Magistrate's decision, let us look at what will be a common feature of such cases: the recommendations of the Independent Children's Lawyer and the psychologist.

The role of the Independent Children's Lawyer is to advocate for the best interests of the child. No doubt because of the very strong statements in the Family Law Act about the need to build meaningful relationships between children and both parents, the Independent Children's Lawyer in this case came to the view that the mother ought to be required to return to her previous abode, so that 'one last effort' (paragraph 49) could be made at promoting a meaningful relationship between father and child. The mother in this case appears to have made reasonable efforts to build that relationship; rather it seems it was the behaviour of the father that had sabotaged those efforts. And yet, despite the impact on her and risk to the child, the *mother* should, in the Independent Children's Lawyer's view, be forced to make this 'one last effort'. This was against a backdrop that suggested there was little likelihood that the father could be relied upon to take steps that would facilitate this relationship; he had totally failed to do so thus far.

The conclusions of the psychologist are no less disturbing. There is little doubt that expert witnesses routinely reporting in these cases will be influenced by the way the legislation is now written; indeed, that is the intent: to influence all the professionals in the process in terms of how they look at parenting arrangements post-separation. During interviews the mother admitted she removed the child from the home state because she was afraid the court would ultimately require the child to have unsupervised contact with the father. The psychologist concluded that the child had no independent memory of violence, but had been told of it by the mother. Focusing on these matters, and essentially ignoring the father's role in this state of affairs, the psychologist concluded the estrangement of child and father was the mother's fault. The mother's removal of the child was characterised as being a self-interested move addressing her fears of the father, and she was advised to have counselling for this. The psychologist considered the mother to have employed violence as a convenient tactic to justify her departure and considered these actions were more detrimental to the child than the father's violent behaviour!

Despite acknowledging that, when unwell (and do not forget the father took no steps to ensure his own 'wellness'), the father presented a serious risk to the child, the psychologist concluded that he could have a positive impact on the child's life, if 'appropriate safeguards' were in place. It was also suggested that, in future, this responsibility could be shifted to the child, as by the age of about 10 to 12 years she would be 'better able to control her relationship with her father and manage her own safety' (at paragraph 209).

Although unimpressed by some of the findings of this expert, the negative characterisation of the mother's behaviour by the psychologist is echoed in some of the findings of the Federal Magistrate, notwithstanding the following findings about the father:

- He was the cause of serious family violence during the relationship.
- He behaved in a threatening way post-separation.
- He had neither the capacity, attitude nor will to comply with court orders and could not be trusted to follow through with the regular commitment necessary to re-establish his relationship with his child.

Nonetheless, the Federal Magistrate concluded:

- The mother's relocation reflected in part her unwillingness to 'allow the father to have a meaningful relationship with the child' (at paragraph 242).
- The mother's decision to leave the state, though explicable, was 'unjustified and inappropriate' (at paragraph 245).

- The child was being exposed to 'psychological harm as a result' of her actions (at paragraph 283).

Ironically, the Federal Magistrate also concluded that, unlike the father, the mother had seen the error of her ways, and by the time of trial accepted the need for the child to have the best possible relationship with her father. In reading this decision, the far more likely reality seems that the mother appreciated her actions in trying to protect the child had seriously harmed her chances in any parenting dispute and she now understood her only option was to appear to have 'recanted'. In other words, to be the 'friendly parent' notwithstanding she had every reason to fear for her child's, and her own, safety.

The pervading impression from this decision is that all three professionals considered the law imposed on them a responsibility to find a way to maintain the child/father relationship and that the mother should be judged on this basis also; that is, that she should be voluntarily and happily prepared to do this, regardless of the father's own responsibility in creating this situation or the impact on her of having to do so. When the Family Law Act places such significance on shared parenting, it seems little room is left for decision-makers to recognise protective parenting and to allow such parents, when behaving reasonably, to be given the responsibility to decide how best to parent their children.

There are some predictable themes of decision-making apparent in *Mills v Watson*. First, suspension of contact is extremely rare, notwithstanding findings of extremely serious abuse. Almost all children are considered to be better off having contact, regardless of how violent a parent may be. Second, violence is mutualised; that is, a mother's response to a violent father can attract equivalent approbation, regardless of the circumstances. This can occur even in cases of quite severe and persistent marital violence. In that context, violence is equated to other poor parental behaviour, notwithstanding it is a *primary* consideration. Indeed, some decision-makers have in fact ignored the significance of violence now being a 'primary' consideration. Third, there continues to be judicial misunderstanding of how victims of violence would reasonably behave and a lack of understanding of the research on violence and its impacts on children. Finally, it would also seem that the inclusion of the friendly parent provision is being used adversely against mothers taking steps to protect their children; little attention is given, as in *Mills v Watson*, to the link between the violent parent's behaviour and the mother's response. Thus, it is simply not open to a parent in family court to present their case on the basis that a violent parent have no, or very limited, contact with their child(ren). Moreover, children could be expected to rely very heavily on Independent Children's Lawyers and experts preparing Family Reports to ensure their protection and yet the impact of the reforms on how those professionals understand their responsibilities raises concerns about their attention to this issue.

Many of these criticisms are not new and have been identified in a considerable body of research on how family courts deal with violence allegations. Further, if one considers that nearly half of all cases that get to court involve violence allegations (Kaspiew *et al.* 2009) and that decision-makers in cases like *Mills v Watson* are routinely dealing with this as their core business, then it is difficult not to conclude that violence is being poorly addressed in too many cases. These concerns are being echoed in research emerging about the impact of the reforms.

The impact of the 2006 reforms: The responses and the research

As indicated above, the 2006 reforms require decision-makers when deciding parenting disputes to give first consideration to equal shared physical care: s65DAA. The incidence of shared care has increased since the reforms (Cashmore *et al.* 2010), particularly in disputes that are judicially determined (Kaspiew *et al.* 2009). This may be underpinned by a common (if mistaken) perception that courts must order shared care, and so in matters resolved by negotiation it seems more likely now that shared care may be agreed on the understanding that this will be forced on parents anyway in court (Bagshaw *et al.* 2010; Kaspiew *et al.* 2010). If the impact of the new provisions is to under-rate violence, and also to increase the incidence of shared care, then there is a danger that the intersection of these outcomes will present real dangers for children.

If there is any doubt that, within a few years of the introduction of the reforms, there was growing concern that they were compromising the protection of children from violence, one has only to note that, by 2009, the Chief Justice of the Family Court was prepared to express publicly her concerns in this regard (Pelly 2009). Public awareness of the issue was also heightened by the sad death, in 2009, of four-year-old Darcey Freeman, who was thrown by her father from a bridge; the parents were involved in a parenting dispute in the Family Court and the incident occurred the day after consent parenting orders were made. In the wake of these events, Australia saw increasing demands for further legislative reform, including calls for a legislative direction that decision-makers must give priority to child safety over contact.

The result of concern over the reforms has been a number of important reports which have, in different ways, confirmed that the 2006 reforms need to be reconsidered (Australian Institute of Family Studies 2009; Australian Law Reform Commission and New South Wales Law Reform Commission 2010; Bagshaw *et al.* 2010; Chisholm 2009; Family Law Council 2009). The Australian Institute of Family Studies (2009), which undertook a review of 17 studies on the impact of the reforms, concluded:

- Professionals in the legal system consider the reforms have promoted a focus on parental rights over children's needs and are much more satisfied that 'meaningful' relationships are being prioritised than is safety of children.
- Advice giving to parents is now more focused on shared care rather than protection from violence.
- Reduced child wellbeing is linked with 'the presence of ongoing safety concerns', with children in shared care suffering the most where this exists.
- Concerns about child safety are reported as frequently by parents in shared care arrangements as in other parenting arrangements.
- Shared care arrangements are just as common in cases where there are violence concerns as in cases where there are no such concerns.
- The family law system is not succeeding in being able to identify where shared care is best for children.
- The 2006 reforms are creating impediments to the proper resolution of disputes where violence is a factor; one reason for this is a lack of awareness of some professionals as to the significance of violence in parenting arrangements for separated parents.
- The costs order provision and friendly parent provision were both identified as factors that may inhibit the disclosure, and use, of allegations of violence; these provisions were also seen to compromise the way in which the protective provisions in the FLA were applied.

The Australian Institute of Family Studies report included a review of the work of McIntosh and Chisholm, which is particularly significant in this regard. In reviewing mental health outcomes of children post-resolution of a dispute, they have found children in shared care (unlike those with a primary carer) did not experience a decline in conflict. Fathers with shared care, who also reported high levels of conflict, were, unlike their children, nonetheless very satisfied with the parenting arrangement. Substantially shared care was found to be a predictor of high degrees of emotional stress for children, and families were emerging from Family Court with 'shared care arrangements that occurred in an atmosphere that placed psychological strain on the children' (McIntosh and Chisholm 2008, p.4). This, together with other research (see, for example, the emerging results of the Longitudinal Study of Separated Families being carried out by the Australian Institute of Family Studies (Weston and Kaspiew 2011)), supports the notion that children's wellbeing is at greater risk where a pro-contact/shared care agenda fails to pay due regard to the impact of violence on children.

The latest government response: The way forward?

In response to the various reports, and at the same time as releasing the Australian Law Reform Commission report, the Australian government has introduced the *Family Law Legislation Amendment (Family Violence and Other Measures) Bill 2011* (Cth) (the Family Violence Bill), with the express aim (amongst other things) of prioritising children's safety. Significantly, the Family Violence Bill proposes the repeal of the costs order provision for false allegations and the friendly parent provision. An expanded definition of family violence is proposed, as is a provision that requires decision-makers to ask parties about violence and child abuse. In relation to the difficult issue of the interaction of the two primary considerations, the suggested solution is the insertion of a new s60CC(2A) in the legislation which will require the courts to give greater weight to the protection of children from violence where there is 'any inconsistency in applying' the two primary considerations.

There are clearly some positives to be taken from the latest proposals. It is heartening, and historically surprising, that the government has been so quick to respond to calls for a reconsideration of laws that were so recently enacted. Although it has in fact been little used, abandoning the false allegations costs order would be a step in the right direction, as would excising the friendly parent provision (see, for example, Behrens and Fehlberg 2011).

However, while there is much consensus that the 2006 provisions are compromising the protection of some children from violence, it seems that not all commentators are convinced that the proposals will effect the positive change needed in this area. Rhoades *et al.* (2010) argue that the proposed s60CC(2A) 'will not alter what Professor Chisholm has called the "common view that the court is required to order that the children spend equal or near-equal time with each parent except where there is family violence"' (p.310). This is particularly concerning given that violence can be so difficult to establish. They also question the failure to provide any guidance to decision-makers as to appropriate parenting regimes where violence is an issue, and argue that the government should support the Family Law Council's recommendation of developing a common knowledge base about family violence for use by all professionals in the family law system, including judicial decision-makers. This will also be crucial they say to give effect to the proposed requirement that judges ask about family violence.

The utility of a provision such as s60CC(2A) might indeed be questioned if decision-makers harbour doubts as to the general veracity of violence claims. Studies support the conclusion that many of those working in the field of family law subscribe to the view that violence restraining orders are used tactically by women in family law disputes (Carpenter, Currie and Field 2001; Parkinson *et al.* 2010). If a decision-maker's starting position is one of scepticism, and they are not required to give real consideration to an agreed body of research on violence, it is difficult to see how they will alter their views as to the general veracity of violence claims, and this may influence their application of the provisions. The Family court does not necessarily require any legislative directive to take better account of relevant research. Were the court to establish its own database of accepted research there is no impediment to the court adopting its use by way of judicial education. However, as the Family Law Council has suggested, it would be preferable to permit judges to be able to take judicial notice of that research in particular cases (Family Law Council 2009). While an individual judge may not be bound to consider such evidence, it would provide an appellate court with opportunities to reconsider whether discretion had been properly exercised and so encourage the use of the database and thus help to change attitudes and improve the knowledge base of judges.

As a number of submissions in response to the Family Violence Bill have argued, the new 'tie-breaker' provision will not be without its problems in application. The new section will only apply where there is 'any inconsistency in applying' the two primary considerations. How will this work? Violence is difficult to prove and is often unproven; this does not mean there was no violence, nor that there is no further risk of violence to a child. How will this provision guide decision-makers where violence is not definitively established? Even where violence is proved, cases such as *Miller v Watson* call into question the ability of those in the system to pay proper regard to its significance. The Explanatory Memorandum to the Family Violence Bill says of this new provision: 'Where child safety is a concern, this new provision will provide the courts with clear legislative guidance that protecting the child from harm is the priority consideration.' It is difficult to see from the statute or the explanation how this section might be interpreted; how much evidence leads to child safety being a concern, or to there being an inconsistency in application of the primary considerations? For example, does this leave open the possibility of the court deciding that, because it believes it can adequately protect a child from violence, there is no inconsistency or that child safety is not a concern? Indeed, some have argued that, where child safety is a concern, building parental bonds should cease to be a primary consideration; that is, protection from violence should become the overriding consideration (Behrens and Fehlberg 2011). It is possible the unclear terms of this provision will be as difficult to interpret as many of the other provisions in the 2006 reforms proved to be. Moreover, what of the concern that, even if a child may be protected from violence or violence is not proved, we have evidence that suggests wellbeing outcomes for children are worst where there is shared care and 'ongoing concerns' about violence in the family? How does this new provision direct decision-makers to account for unsubstantiated allegations of violence when considering shared care more generally; if there is a high level of conflict and allegations of violence, will shared care be an optimal outcome for children and should it be the primary goal? It must be remembered that the two tiers, as well as the other provisions in the Family Law Act promoting shared care, have not been repealed and will continue to operate.

Conclusion

Cases where violence is contested will always be problematic and they form a core part of the Family Court's work. False allegations *will* be made, and no one wishes to see a child deprived of beneficial paternal contact on that basis. Yet it must be remembered that false denials will also be made, and the statistics on the prevalence of familial violence suggest that much violence in separated families is unlikely to be established. Presently, it seems far more likely that actual violence will be not be proved and contact will continue than that contact will be seriously impeded on the basis of a false allegation. Is this the appropriate policy objective?

We need a legislative framework that encourages true disclosures, and works against a starting position of judicial scepticism, which then provides robust processes to investigate such claims. Where violence is not contested, it is arguable that a failure to be more directive in the legislation indicates an unwillingness by the government to stand up and be counted on the matter of violence in family disputes, and so to drive change in the way the research would indicate is necessary. Drafting appropriate provisions may be challenging, but where the court is satisfied there is serious violence, what is the case for not having provisions which state that a shared care regime should not be ordered and which shift the burden to the violent parent to establish safety before contact is ordered?

After all, the dispute before the court is in essence about with whom a child should live and interact and the extent to which you give one parent, or both, the right to make such decisions. The legislative provisions should have the effect that, in a case like *Mills v Watson*, the mother's protective behaviours should be acknowledged, the father's inability to parent effectively should be recognised, as should the risk he poses to both mother and child, and a decision should be made to choose the mother to parent that child unhindered by the views of a few legal and social science professionals who happen to interact with the case for a brief period. This, of course, is anathema in the current climate; the possibility that the mother would stop contact *for whatever reason* runs counter to the primacy placed on shared parenting and the legislative imperative to build 'meaningful' relationships. It remains to be seen whether the latest reforms will at least shift this balance in a positive way from shared parenting to protection of children from violence.

References

Australian Institute of Family Studies (2009) *Evaluation of the 2006 Family Law Reforms.* Available at www.aifs.gov.au/institute/pubs/fle/summaryreport.html, accessed on 19 May 2011.

Australian Law Reform Commission and New South Wales Law Reform Commission (2010) *Family Violence: A National Legal Response.* Available at www.alrc.gov.au/sites/default/files/pdfs/publications/ALRC114_WholeReport.pdf, accessed on 19 May 2011.

Bagshaw, D., Brown, T., Wendt, S., Campbell, A. and McInnes, E. (2010) *Family Violence and Family Law in Australia: The Experiences and Views of Children and Adults from Families who Separated Post-1995 and Post-2006.* Canberra, ACT: Attorney-General's Department.

Banks, C., Bagatol, B., Carson, R. and Fehlberg, B. (2005) 'Review of Exposure Draft of the Family Law Amendment (Shared Parental Responsibility Bill).' *Australian Journal of Family Law 19*, 2, 75–93.

Behrens, J. and Fehlberg, B. (2011) *Submission on the Family Law Legislation Amendment (Family Violence and Other Measures) Bill 2011.* Available at www.aph.gov.au/senate/committee/legcon_ctte/family_law_familyviolence/submissions.htm, accessed on 19 May 2011.

Carpenter, B., Currie, S. and Field, R. (2001) 'Domestic violence: Views of Queensland magistrates.' *Nuance 3*, 16–30.

Cashmore, J., Parkinson, P., Weston, R., Patulny, R. *et al.* (2010) *Shared Care Parenting Arrangements Since the 2006 Family Law Reforms: Report to the Australian Government Attorney-General's Department.* Sydney, NSW: Social Policy Research Centre, University of New South Wales.

Chisholm, R. (2009) *Family Courts Violence Review.* Available at www.ag.gov.au/www/agd/rwpattach.nsf/VAP/(3273BD3F76A7A5DEDAE36942A54D7D90)~Chisholm_report.pdf/$file/Chisholm_report.pdf, accessed on 19 May 2011.

de Simone, T. (2008) 'The friendly parent provisions in Australian family law – how friendly will you need to be?' *Australian Journal of Family Law 22*, 1, 56–71.

Family Law Council (2009) *Improving Responses to Family Violence in the Family Law System: An Advice on the Intersection of Family Violence and Family Law Issues*, December 2009. Available at www.ag.gov.au/www/agd/agd.nsf/Page/FamilyLawCouncil_Publications_ReportstotheAttorney-General_FamilyViolenceReport, accessed on 19 May 2011.

Kaspiew, R. (2005) 'Violence in contested children's cases: An empirical exploration.' *Australian Journal of Family Law 19*, 2, 112–143.

Kaspiew, R., Gray, M., Weston, R., Moloney, L. *et al.* (2009) *Evaluation of the 2006 Family Law Reforms.* Melbourne: Australian Institute of Family Studies.

Kaspiew, R., Gray, M., Weston, R., Moloney, L. *et al.* (2010) 'The Australian Institute of Family Studies Evaluation of the 2006 family law reforms: Key findings.' *Australian Journal of Family Law 24*, 1, 5–33.

Kaye, M. and Tolmie, J. (1998) 'Fathers' rights groups in Australia.' *Australian Journal of Family Law 12*, 1, 19–68.

McIntosh, J. and Chisholm, R. (2008) 'Shared care and children's best interests in conflicted separations: A cautionary tale from current research.' *Australian Family Lawyer 20*, 1, 1–11.

Moloney, L., Smyth, B., Weston, R. and Richardson, N. (2007) 'Allegations of family violence and child abuse in family law children's proceedings: Key findings of Australian Institute of Family Studies Research Report No. 15.' *Family Matters 77*, 8–15.

Parkinson, P., Cashmore, J. and Webster, A. (2010) 'The views of family lawyers on apprehended violence orders after parental separation.' *Australian Journal of Family Law 24*, 3, 313–336.

Pelly, M. (2009) 'Fathers misread "joint parenting".' *The Australian*, 27 July, p.3.

Rhoades, H., Frew, C. and Swain, S. (2010) 'Recognition of violence in the Australian family law system: A long journey.' *Australian Journal of Family Law 24*, 3, 296–312.

Weston, R. and Kaspiew, R. (2011) *Submission to the Senate Standing Committee on Legal and Constitutional Affairs Inquiry into the Family Law Legislation Amendment (Family Violence and Other Measures) Bill 2011.* Available at www.aph.gov.au/senate/committee/legcon_ctte/family_law_familyviolence/submissions.htm, accessed on 19 May 2011.

Chapter 16

The Police Role in Identifying and Responding to Children Experiencing Domestic Violence

Nicky Stanley, Pam Miller, Helen Richardson-Foster and Gill Thomson

This chapter examines the police role in relation to children and young people experiencing domestic violence. In particular, we draw on research undertaken in England between 2007 and 2009 to consider police practice in respect of providing immediate protection for children and victims, police communication with children, domestic violence victims and perpetrators and the police's role in linking those involved in domestic violence incidents to specialist domestic violence support services.

In England and Wales, campaigning by women's organisations has contributed to a raft of policy from central government which has included the *Crime and Disorder Act 1998*, the *Protection from Harassment Act 1997*, the *Domestic Violence, Crime and Victims Act 2004*, the 2009 Strategy to End Violence Against Women and Girls (HM Government 2009) and the inclusion of arrests at domestic violence incidents in police performance measures. These measures are generally agreed to have had the effect of improving police practice in relation to domestic violence (Applegate 2006; Richards, Letchford and Stratton 2008). Policy and practice developments have been boosted by research, and the British Crime Survey (BCS) has played a key role in setting domestic violence in the context of all violent crime and so making a case for prioritising police intervention in domestic violence; for instance, the BCS 2007/2008 identified domestic violence as the crime with the highest rate of repeat victimisation (Povey *et al.* 2009).

The police are increasingly being required to focus on the needs of children at domestic violence incidents (Burton 2000; Shields 2008). In England and Wales, the definition of significant harm was amended by the *Adoption and Children Act 2002* to include 'impairment suffered from seeing or hearing the ill-treatment of another' (*Adoption and Children Act 2002*, s.120), and a substantial body of guidance obliges the police to communicate with children's social services in respect of children in the household at a domestic violence incident (ACPO 2004, 2008; HM Government 2010a). This has produced a deluge of notifications of families experiencing domestic violence from the police to children's social services (Cleaver *et al.* 2007; Rivett and Kelly 2006); the majority of these do not reach the threshold for a service response from social services (Stanley *et al.* 2011a). A comparable overloading of child protection services with domestic violence referrals is evident in North America (Edleson 2004; Jaffe, Crooks and Wolfe 2003). Humphreys (2008) paints a similar picture of the system in Australia where the requirement for mandatory reporting in some states augments the volume of such referrals. She argues that a statutory child protection response to notifications of incidents of domestic violence is 'not effective, efficacious, efficient or ethical' (p.237) and suggests that resources for responding to the needs of children exposed to domestic violence should be diverted to the community sector.

The inability of child protection services to respond to this volume of notifications means that the frontline response to such incidents provided by the police is crucial for the welfare of children experiencing domestic violence. The police role in relation to children exposed to domestic violence is myriad and complex. The Association of Chief Police Officers (ACPO) (2008) guidance defines police priorities in responding to domestic violence thus:

- to protect the lives of both adults and children who are at risk as a result of domestic abuse
- to investigate all reports of domestic abuse
- to facilitate effective action against offenders so that they can be held accountable through the criminal justice system
- to adopt a proactive multi-agency approach in preventing and reducing domestic abuse.

(ACPO 2008, p.7)

This definition embraces a range of tasks – protection, criminal investigation, prevention, multi-agency collaboration – and requires a focus on different family members whose interests may diverge. In relation to women and children, police intervention aims at securing the immediate and longer-term safety of the victim (usually the mother) and this is the primary goal of police intervention as it is currently conceived. However, protection of any children in the household is also emphasised and the ACPO (2008) guidance draws attention to the links between domestic violence and child abuse. The police are expected to undertake an assessment of risks to the victim, which should also include consideration of risks to children, and to direct victims and children to relevant support and protection services. In relation to perpetrators, police intervention is directed towards collecting evidence to support prosecution and immediate removal where possible.

The research discussed here was undertaken in two English local authorities and used police and social services records to track 251 incidents of domestic violence occurring in the month of January 2007 from the point of police intervention through to children's social services over a period of 21 months. Young people's, domestic violence survivors' and perpetrators' views of services were captured through a series of focus groups, and interviews and the perspectives of police and social workers were also collected through individual interviews. Findings concerning the practice of children's social services and risk assessment have been reported elsewhere (Stanley *et al.* 2011a, b); here, the focus is on police practice with parents and children at the scene of the incident and their role in directing families to domestic violence support services.

Immediate protection

In common with other research with children and mothers experiencing domestic violence (Mullender *et al.* 2002), young people and survivors interviewed were explicit that they wanted the police to use their powers to remove perpetrators from the family home following an incident of domestic violence:

> Like get your dad away from the house and like not be there shouting. (Jackie, Young People's Focus Group 5)

While a speedy response was appreciated, a slow response from the police was seen as evidence of a failure to take domestic violence seriously:

> Personally, I think that they don't take it as something serious. It's like a slow…response, or even a casual… But it's just you know, it's not something deep. It's just something superficial. (Denise, Survivor of Domestic Violence)

Likewise, young people who made the call to the police themselves (11 did so in sample cases) felt that immediate removal of the perpetrator demonstrated that the police had taken their request for help seriously:

> When they come straight away, they could like take him away straight away, instead of waiting around and everything and listening to sides, just…they should be taken away because a mum or child wouldn't call 999 just to get a dad taken away for no reason. (Louis, Young People's Focus Group 5)

There was concern from some young people participating in the focus groups that temporary removal of the perpetrator from the scene might lead to further problems when they returned to the house. However, those who had experienced such interventions were more positive about removal. Young people wanted the police to use their powers to ensure that the perpetrator stayed away from the family home for some time:

> …lock him up and then like make, either charge him, do you know if he's broken something, or even disturbance of the peace or something like that, so that's on his record, he'll have to pay a fine, that'd even make him think and then like if, if it happens again…they should try and like get him with something bigger like, like harassment or something. (Rachel, Young People's Focus Group 3)

Removal of perpetrators is now a standard approach in the policing of domestic violence incidents. This approach may be difficult to implement immediately if the perpetrator is not present at the scene when the police arrive, as was the case for 63 incidents in the sample. However, the introduction of Domestic Violence Protection Orders as proposed by the former New Labour Government (HM Government 2009) and ACPO (2009) would consolidate this policy of removal, and these orders are discussed later in this chapter.

The most common outcome of the 251 incidents examined was that the perpetrator was arrested (44%) or left the location (27%) (sometimes before the police arrived). In the majority of the 110 incidents where an arrest was made and the time was recorded, it was made within 24 hours of the incident (86%); for the remaining 16 per cent of these incidents it took more than 24 hours for an arrest to be made. These families (n = 21) were likely to have experienced a considerable period of uncertainty and concern before the perpetrator was arrested.

In 29 incidents, police deemed that no offence had occurred. A further 11 incidents were either described as bordering on harassment or the paperwork included was not clear on what police action had been taken. Some of these incidents involved abusive text messages while others concerned non-crime incidents which had occurred in the past. While the majority of these were classified as having a low level of violence by the researchers, abusive text messages can be used as a long-term strategy to control and threaten victims, as evidenced by Barter and colleagues' study of abuse in teenagers' intimate relationships (Barter *et al.* 2009).

Police officers commented that separating adults at the scene was considered good practice and allowed them to investigate the incident and to encourage the victim to discuss it openly. Securing children's safety was a consideration in this approach:

> A lot of the time you might turn up and there's just two of you and one will obviously be dealing with the victim and one will be dealing with the suspect. The first thing you need to do is separate them and keep the children in the safest place which is normally with the victim, which is normally their mum. (Frontline Officer 5)

In line with ACPO positive action guidance, which notes that the function of an arrest is both to prevent further offences and to allow investigation to take place (ACPO 2008), officers interviewed stated that they would 'make efforts' to arrest perpetrators at the scene wherever possible:

> We've got a duty of care not only to the victim but to the children, to take the perpetrator out of that environment, so again regardless of what the victim says I would agree and stand by the policy of removing the perpetrator from the scene. (Domestic Violence Specialist 1)

Officers described difficulties in obtaining victims' statements due to the upsetting nature of the incident, fear of reprisals or a reluctance to engage with the court system as well as concerns about the impact a prosecution would have on family life. Some officers were sympathetic to the pressures that might lead to statements being retracted; however, in common with accounts provided by other studies (Hester 2005), some frontline officers appeared to find victims' retractions frustrating.

Specialist domestic violence officers were more likely to identify ways in which their role in supporting victims through the prosecution process could reduce the likelihood of retractions. One specialist officer described using his/her knowledge about the impact of violence on children as an argument for continuing with prosecutions:

> When they come back and say I don't want to make a complaint any more, we go through all the family history and we go through the family tree and we say, look you've got these children here in your house, they're six, they're four, they're two, how do you think they're going to be brought up looking at this all the time? (Domestic Violence Specialist 6)

Police communication with parents and children

Clarity of communication was also emphasised by all parents and young people interviewed who wanted explanations from the police about what would happen next. In particular, children and survivors wanted to know whether it was likely the perpetrator would or could return, and they also wanted information about relevant support services. Survivors were appreciative when the police provided them with clear information, such as feedback on the likely consequences of police intervention:

> ...they did ring me up and say 'all right, we're going to keep him over night and to court in the morning'. So I found it helpful that they'd actually got in contact with me and said what they were actually going to do with him. (Lisa, Survivor of Domestic Violence)

Perpetrators valued being spoken to in a direct manner by the police, even when this might prove personally challenging. This perpetrator stated how his encounters with police and social workers in respect of his abusive behaviour had functioned as a 'wake-up call':

> I needed somebody like the police and social services to lay it on the line and say well if this is the way it is, you know, it's not going to work the way you want to go. (Patrick, Domestic Violence Perpetrator)

This father also commented that police intervention had served to emphasise the impact his behaviour was having on his son. Acknowledgement of the effects of domestic violence on children has been identified as a key message motivating men to seek help to address abusive behaviour (Stanley *et al.* forthcoming 2012).

However, the young people participating in the focus groups were less likely to experience police communication as clear and helpful. For the most part, they described themselves as excluded from police communication which was focused on the adults at the scene of the incident:

> They listen to the adults more…they don't want to talk to you. (Nicola, Young People's Focus Group 1)

> …one of them [police] goes upstairs to talk to the kids and find out what they heard. They don't do that like but they should. (Tremayne, Young People's Focus Group 1)

This picture was confirmed by police officers interviewed. Nearly half the 33 officers interviewed expressed reservations about talking to children at the scene of an incident and four officers did not see talking to children as part of their role:

> …it's not something that's done as often as you would probably think. I think we go there and it's all happening and you are there, and I think we just take away the person that needs taking away and we probably don't really spend much time. There are some times when I've spoken to the children but you certainly don't say I'm taking your child into kitchen, I'm going to speak to them…it doesn't really work like that. (Frontline Officer 8)

Directing families to other agencies

All the 251 cases in the sample were selected on the basis that they had been notified to children's social services, although, in the event, the researchers were unable to locate 22 per cent of the original sample notifications in social services files. Many of these 'lost' notifications could be attributed to errors and omissions in the information conveyed by the police, although children's social services also failed to locate some files requested for the study. However, only a small proportion of cases (15%) notified in this way received either a family support or child protection service (see Stanley *et al.* 2011a). This response was in part constrained by resources, but omissions in police notifications may have resulted in some cases being allocated a lower priority than was warranted. The misspelling and omission of some parents' and children's names in notification forms made for difficulties in marrying notifications up with children's social services records and in contacting families. In 25 cases in the original sample, children were described as 'present' at the incident in police files, but this information was not included in the notification. In some notifications, the full extent of the violence was not conveyed to children's social services by the notification, and some notifications did not convey the extent to which children had been involved in incidents. For example, one notification described an 11-year-old girl as 'involved in the incident' but failed to communicate the information contained in police records which described her as 'dragged' downstairs during the incident. Social workers interviewed felt that the information conveyed in notification forms about children was often inadequate; they wanted more information about what was meant by police descriptions of children as 'present' at an incident, what children had seen or heard and whether there was evidence of distress.

Additional police activity in response to the 251 sample incidents and the timescales in which the response was delivered is shown in Table 16.1. While some interventions such as the provision of safety information, taking the victim to a place of safety (usually a refuge) and referral to the multi-agency domestic violence service were likely to happen within 24 hours of the incident, other interventions could take considerably longer. In six incidents in one site, the period spent investigating an incident took several weeks.

Most of the follow-up services provided by the police centred on the needs of the adult victim who was usually the mother. Just under half the victims were contacted by telephone (in some cases the calls were initiated by the victims); some follow-up contact with victims subsequent to an incident took the form of home visits and letters. These contacts were used for a variety of purposes including: to obtain information about the location of a perpetrator, to acquire statements or further information about the incident and to provide information about the progress of the case. However, they were also an opportunity to provide some services directly, such as safety planning, sanctuary schemes or the installation of panic alarms, and to signpost women to local support services. In some cases, joint visits were undertaken with children's services social workers. In one site, 'care packs' containing advice and information on local services such as housing, finances, counselling and local domestic violence support services were recorded as being issued in a third of all cases.

TABLE 16.1 Police interventions following incident

POLICE ACTIVITY	UNDERTAKEN WITHIN 24 HOURS	UNDERTAKEN AFTER 24 HOURS	UNDERTAKEN BOTH WITHIN 24 HOURS AND SUBSEQUENTLY	UNDERTAKEN BUT TIME NOT RECORDED	TOTAL
Safety information provided	31		3		34 (14%)
Referral to specialist domestic violence unit	6	12		45	63 (25%)
Victim taken/removed to place of safety	21	1			22 (9%)
Care pack provided (one site only)	10	30		3	43 (17%)
Referral to multi-agency domestic violence service (southern site only)	18	5	1	1	25 (10%)
Referral to place of safety (refuge)	5			1	6 (2%)
Referral to health visitor (one site only)	10	65			75 (30%)
Follow-up visit to victim	8	16	6	1	31 (12%)
Follow-up telephone call to victim	25	56	36	1	118 (47%)
Follow-up letter to victim	11	18		1	30 (12%)
Follow-up visit to perpetrator	2	3	1		6 (2%)
Follow-up telephone call to perpetrator	3	4	3		10 (4%)
Follow-up letter to perpetrator	2	3			5 (2%)

Only a small proportion of incidents involved removal of the victim to a place of safety or referral to a refuge; however, frontline officers interviewed appeared familiar with local refuge services and they emphasised the need for police officers to develop good working relationships with refuge staff. A number of specialist domestic violence officers were concerned about the lack of resources available to local refuges, and a specific lack of relevant services for victims of 'honour-based' violence – violence which the perpetrators consider to be a response to slights to their own or the family's honour – was noted. Officers also commented that asylum seeking or refugee victims who did not have 'recourse to public funds' were often unable to access refuge services (see Anitha 2010).

Referral to a one-stop Multi-Agency Domestic Violence Centre was standard practice for all domestic violence victims in one of the two sites. This agency brought independent advocates, victim support and domestic violence support staff, solicitors, housing officers and legal advisers, as well as police from the specialist domestic violence unit, together in one location. However, children's social workers were not included in this centre. Communication between centre staff and specialist domestic violence officers was described as good. However, frontline officers appeared less familiar with its work than specialist officers.

Seventy-five (30%) of incidents in one site involved a referral to health visiting services, and in this site an automatic referral was sent to health services in all cases where the victim was pregnant. However, such referrals were not integrated into procedure in the other site.

Independent Domestic Violence Advisers (IDVAs) were introduced in England and Wales during the period when the research was being undertaken (although they were not in post at the time the sample cases were collected) and they offer support, advocacy and co-ordination of services to high-risk victims. Specialist police officers interviewed described the IDVAs as of 'massive benefit' in relieving pressures on the police as well as offering an independent service that victims valued. However, the six IDVAs and advocates participating in the study were clear that they did not work directly with children and young people. An early evaluation (Howarth *et al.* 2009) of IDVA services noted that direct work with children was not part of the IDVA remit but emphasised the large numbers of children affected by high levels of domestic violence in the cases addressed by IDVAs. This evaluation suggested that IDVA responsibilities in relation to safeguarding children should be clarified.

Follow-up contact with perpetrators was confined to a small number of cases, as shown in Table 16.1. Contact with perpetrators tended to involve delivering 'warnings' in relation to their behaviour or providing information about legal sanctions (such as harassment orders). For perpetrators, there was little follow-up other than the steps towards criminal prosecution. Once embarked on this route, there appeared to be little consideration of alternative routes, although arrests were made in relation to less than half (44%) of the sample. Perpetrators interviewed for the study argued that earlier interventions were required for abusive men and saw the police as being in a position to play a role in this:

> Well I think it starts with the police being the ones because I mean every time that I was in the cells I had someone from the Drug Welfare come round and ask me if I wanted to chat about drugs and never anyone come and say, 'would you like to actually talk about what's gone wrong?'... For one of the officials that's already involved to actually point it out for you would be a lot easier than having to go and find it for yourself. (Craig, Domestic Violence Perpetrator)

Recent developments

The Coalition Government that came into power in England and Wales in 2010 initially cancelled plans for introducing domestic violence protection orders but subsequently announced that they would be piloted in three sites (HM Government 2010b). Domestic violence protection orders, or 'go orders' as they are known, are used in Austria, Germany, Switzerland and, more recently, Poland to exclude the perpetrator from the household for a short period. These are civil orders which become a criminal offence when breached, and an application to the court is required to extend or vary the order (Smartt and Kury 2007). An essential feature of the 'go order' is that the original short exclusion order is initiated by the police not the victim, although extensions or variations to the order can be initiated by the police alone, the victim or the police in collaboration with the victim (House of Commons Select Committee on Home Affairs 2008). They offer a form of immediate protection in situations where arrest and imprisonment are not possible and remove responsibility for short-term decision making from the victim. The police will need to monitor these orders and respond to any breaches, and this will place additional demands on their resources.

At present, it is currently unclear how such orders would take account of children's interests or contact arrangements. However, if fully implemented and monitored, such protection orders might go some way towards meeting survivors' and children's demands for perpetrators to be excluded from the home. Evidence from Austria suggests that while some women were initially opposed to the imposition of 'go orders' which they considered too draconian, they reported later that the order had been helpful in instigating changes in attitudes and behaviour (House of Commons Select Committee on Home Affairs 2008).

Currently, police communication at the scene of domestic violence incidents appears very focused on the adults present. This failure to engage with children is reflected in the quality of the information communicated to children's social services which social workers in our study found offered little detailed information about children. The police are increasingly incorporating information about children into the standardised risk assessments which previously were exclusively focused on risks to survivors (Humphreys 2007; Richards *et al.* 2008). These risk assessments can be communicated to children's social services as part of the notification. However, unless the police actually talk to children who are present at an incident, they are unlikely to have much detailed or relevant information about levels of harm that can be used to inform children's social services assessments and decisions about resource allocation.

Since the capacity of children's social services to intervene in families notified following a domestic violence incident is unlikely to increase dramatically, the availability of community-based services for children and families and the police's readiness to direct families to these services will continue to be crucial. While specialist domestic violence services increasingly offer support to children – for instance, many refuges now provide children's workers and services (Mullender *et al.* 1998; Poole, Beran and Thurston 2008) – at the time of writing such services are experiencing heavy cuts as a consequence of restrictions on public spending in England and Wales (Radford *et al.* 2011). It is also the case that most domestic violence services continue to maintain a focus on adult victims: for instance, as noted above, neither the IDVAs nor the multi-agency domestic violence centre included in this research provided services directly to children. However, there are some notable exceptions: integrated projects in the North of England (Donovan *et al.* 2010) provide support services for children in addition to IDVA services and perpetrator programs. Similarly, the Caledonian Service, which delivers perpetrator programs in Scotland, includes services for children in addition to support for perpetrators' partners (The Scottish Government 2010).

Conclusion

Currently, police intervention at incidents of domestic violence appears focused on the adults involved, and this positioning of children's and young people's needs on the periphery mirrors the approach of most community domestic violence services at present. Police reluctance to engage more fully with children at the scene of a domestic violence incident may be due in part to a lack of relevant services to which they can be referred. Without such services, engagement with children can feel like opening 'Pandora's Box' and letting loose uncontrollable and unmanageable needs which threaten to overwhelm the individual officer.

This study also found that police communication with other services may be undermined by gaps and errors which reflect the fact that much of the information is collected at a time of crisis when key participants are distressed and when police attention is directed onto other tasks such as the immediate protection of victims. Nevertheless, as the frontline service responding to domestic violence, police intervention in incidents of domestic violence embodies a 'window of opportunity' for children experiencing domestic violence to be connected to relevant services. Police capacity to identify those children most at risk and to direct them to appropriate services could be strengthened by multi-agency training and by the provision of relevant information on local services. Domestic violence protection orders may prove to be a means by which police intervention can become more responsive to the needs and interests of victims. It remains to be seen whether children's wishes and interests will be significant in the processes of introducing and operating such orders.

Acknowledgement

The research study described in this chapter was commissioned and funded by the NSPCC.

References

Anitha, S. (2010) 'No recourse, no support: State policy and practice towards South Asian women facing domestic violence in the UK.' *British Journal of Social Work 40*, 2, 462–479.

Applegate, R.J. (2006) 'Changing local policy and practice towards the policing of domestic violence in England and Wales.' *Policing: An International Journal of Police Strategies and Management 29*, 2, 368–383.

Association of Chief Police Officers (ACPO) (2004) *Guidance on Investigating Domestic Violence.* London: Association of Chief Police Officers/National Centre for Policing Excellence.

Association of Chief Police Officers (ACPO) (2008) *Guidance on Investigating Domestic Abuse*. London: National Policing Improvement Agency.
Association of Chief Police Officers (ACPO) (2009) *Tackling Perpetrators of Violence against Women and Girls: ACPO Review for the Home Secretary*. London: Association of Chief Police Officers.
Barter, C., McCarry, M., Berridge, D. and Evans, K. (2009) *Partner Exploitation and Violence in Teenage Intimate Relationships*. London: NSPCC/Bristol: University of Bristol School of Policy Studies.
Burton, M. (2000) 'Prosecution decisions in cases of domestic violence involving children.' *Journal of Social Welfare and Family Law 22*, 2, 175–191.
Cleaver, H., Nicholson, D., Tarr, S. and Cleaver, D. (2007) *Child Protection, Domestic Violence and Parental Substance Misuse: Family Experiences and Effective Practice*. London: Jessica Kingsley Publishers.
Donovan, C., Griffiths, S., Groves, N., Johnson, H. and Douglass, J. (2010) *Evaluation of Early Intervention Models for Change in Domestic Violence: Northern Rock Foundation Domestic Abuse Intervention Project, 2004–2009*. Newcastle upon Tyne: Northern Rock Foundation.
Edleson, J.L. (2004) 'Should Childhood Exposure to Adult Domestic Violence Be Defined as Child Maltreatment under the Law?' In P. Jaffe, L. Baker and A. Cunningham (eds) *Protecting Children from Domestic Violence: Strategies for Community Intervention*. New York: Guilford Press.
Hester, M. (2005) 'Making it through the Criminal Justice System: Attrition and domestic violence.' *Social Policy and Society 5*, 1, 79–90.
HM Government (2009) *Together We Can End Violence against Women and Girls: A Strategy*. London: Home Office.
HM Government (2010a) *Working Together to Safeguard Children: A Guide to Inter-Agency Working to Safeguard and Promote the Welfare of Children*. Nottingham: DCSF Publications.
HM Government (2010b) *Call to End Violence against Women and Girls*. London: Home Office.
House of Commons Select Committee on Home Affairs (2008) *Sixth Report*. London: House of Commons.
Howarth, E., Stimpson, L., Barran, D. and Robinson, A.L. (2009) *Safety in Numbers: A Multisite Evaluation of Independent Domestic Violence Advisor Services*. London: The Henry Smith Charity.
Humphreys, C. (2007) 'Domestic violence and child protection: Exploring the role of perpetrator risk assessments.' *Child and Family Social Work 12*, 360–369.
Humphreys, C. (2008) 'Problems in the system of mandatory reporting of children living with domestic violence.' *Journal of Family Studies 14*, 2, 228–239.
Jaffe, P.G., Crooks, C.V. and Wolfe, D.A. (2003) 'Legal and policy responses to children exposed to domestic violence: The need to evaluate intended and unintended consequences.' *Clinical Child and Family Psychology Review 6*, 3, 205–213.
Mullender, A., Debbonaire, T., Hague, G., Kelly, L. and Malos, E. (1998) 'Working with children in women's refuges.' *Child and Family Social Work 3*, 2, 87–98.
Mullender, A., Hague, G., Iman, U., Kelly, L., Malos, E. and Regan, L. (2002) *Children's Perspectives on Domestic Violence*. London: Sage.
Poole, A., Beran, T. and Thurston, W. (2008) 'Direct and indirect services for children in domestic violence shelters.' *Journal of Family Violence 23*, 8, 679–686.

Povey, D., Coleman, K., Kaiza, R. and Roe, S. (2009) *Homicides, Firearm Offences and Intimate Violence 2007/08*. Supplementary Volume to Crime in England and Wales 2007/08. London: Home Office.

Radford, L., Aitken, R., Miller, P., Ellis, J., Roberts, J. and Firkic, A. (2011) *Meeting the Needs of Children Living with Domestic Violence in London*. London: NSPCC.

Richards, L., Letchford, S. and Stratton, S. (2008) *Policing Domestic Violence*. Oxford: Oxford University Press.

Rivett, M. and Kelly, S. (2006) 'From awareness to practice: Children, domestic violence and child welfare.' *Child Abuse Review 15*, 4, 224–242.

Shields, J.P. (2008) 'An evaluation of police compliance with domestic violence documentation policy reform: Improving the identification of exposed children.' *Best Practices in Mental Health 4*, 1, 65–73.

Smartt, U. and Kury, H. (2007) 'Domestic violence: Comparative analysis of German and U.K. research findings.' *Social Science Quarterly 88*, 5, 1263–1280.

Stanley, N., Fell, B., Miller, P., Thomson, G. and Watson, J.P. (forthcoming 2012) 'Men's talk: Men's understandings of violence against women and motivations for change.' *Violence Against Women*.

Stanley, N., Miller, P., Richardson-Foster, H. and Thomson, G. (2011a) 'A stop–start response: Social services' interventions with children and families notified following domestic violence incidents.' *British Journal of Social Work 41*, 2, 296–313.

Stanley, N., Miller, P., Richardson-Foster, H. and Thomson, G. (2011b) 'Children's experiences of domestic violence: Developing an integrated response from police and child protection services.' *Journal of Interpersonal Violence 26*, 12, 2372–2391.

The Scottish Government (2010) *The Caledonian System*. Available at www.scotland.gov.uk/Topics/People/Equality/violence-women/CaledonianSystem, accessed on 10 October 2010.

Chapter 17

Relocation of Children in Family Law Disputes

Robert H. George

Introduction

A relocation dispute in the family court typically involves a proposal by one parent to move to a new geographic location with their child, where the other parent objects to that plan. When the parents are unable to agree, the courts are often asked to decide whether the relocation should be allowed or not. In making this assessment, most Western countries make the child's welfare or best interests the paramount consideration; in other words, the court should make the order which is best from the point of view of the child.

However, it is well known in general that there are significant disagreements about what is meant by 'best interests' and how to assess them in any particular case (Eekelaar 2002; Mnookin 1975). Those disagreements are particularly evident in relocation law, where different countries take markedly different approaches to the resolution of these increasingly frequent disputes (George 2009; Worwood 2005). Approaches range from those jurisdictions where relocation is normally allowed (*pro-relocation countries*) to those where obtaining permission is known to be difficult (*anti-relocation countries*), with many others falling in between (Foley 2006).

This chapter focuses on two common law countries which represent the two ends of that spectrum: England – thought to be pro-relocation; and New Zealand – thought to be anti-relocation. The chapter draws on qualitative interviews with family law practitioners in those two countries to illustrate just how differently relocation disputes are seen, despite both countries seeking the solution which best meets the child's welfare. After a brief overview of the legal provisions of England and New Zealand, the methodology of this research is summarised. From there, the chapter discusses three hypothetical relocation disputes which participants assessed, and concludes with some thoughts about what these findings might say about the welfare principle itself.

Legal provisions

English law divides relocation into a number of unofficial categories, though in all cases the welfare of the child concerned is paramount (*Children Act 1989*, s.1(1)). Where the proposed move is to another location within the United Kingdom, the courts currently say that orders restricting a parent's place of residence should be considered 'truly exceptional' (*Re B (Prohibited Steps Order)* [2008] 1 FLR 613, [7]). In practice, this means that few cases involving relocation within the UK are ever litigated because they are almost certain to be allowed, though the 'exceptionality' test has been criticised as representing an unjustified gloss on the welfare enquiry (*Re F (Internal Relocation)* [2011] 1 FLR 1382; for commentary, see George 2010, 2011a).

Where the proposed relocation is to an overseas destination, the leading case is *Payne v Payne* [2001] 1 FLR 1052. *Payne* is a subtle decision but, for present purposes, the 'discipline' proposed by Thorpe LJ in his judgment (as amended) will suffice:

> (a) Pose the question: is the mother's application genuine in the sense that it is not motivated by some selfish desire to exclude the father from the child's life? Then ask is the mother's application realistic, by which I mean founded on practical proposals both well researched and investigated? If the application fails either of these tests refusal will inevitably follow.
>
> (b) If however the application passes these tests then there must be a careful appraisal of the father's opposition: is it motivated by genuine concern for the future of the child's welfare or is it driven by some ulterior motive? What would be the extent of the detriment to him and his future relationship with the child were the application granted? To what extent would that be offset by extension of the child's relationships with the maternal family and homeland?
>
> (c) What would be the impact on the mother, either as the single parent or as a new wife, of a refusal of her realistic proposal? Where the mother cares for the child or proposes to care for

> the child within a new family, the impact of refusal on the new family and on the stepfather or prospective stepfather must also be carefully calculated.
>
> (d) The outcome of the second and third appraisals must then be brought into an overriding review of the child's welfare as the paramount consideration, directed by the statutory checklist insofar as appropriate.
>
> In suggesting such a discipline I would not wish to be thought to have diminished the importance that this court has consistently attached to the emotional and psychological well-being of the primary carer. In any evaluation of the welfare of the child as the paramount consideration great weight must be given to this factor. (*Payne v Payne* [2001] 1 FLR 1052, [40]–[41])

This approach applies unless the parents have an equal or near-equal shared care arrangement in place. In shared care cases, it is said that the Payne discipline should not be applied, and that the welfare checklist in s.1(3) of the *Children Act 1989* provides the best framework for decision-making (*K v K (Relocation: Shared Care Arrangement)* [2011] EWCA Civ 793; George forthcoming 2012). Consequently, judges assess shared care relocation applications without the framework of *Payne v Payne* or the 'exceptionality' test, using an unadulterated 'welfare' approach (though *Payne*'s 'discipline' is often seen as being a useful guide). There are few reported cases involving significantly shared care, and different judges seem to take different approaches.

In New Zealand, there is a single legal approach to relocation, regardless of whether the move is domestic or international, and regardless of the pre-existing care arrangements. Again, in all cases the welfare of the child concerned is paramount (*Care of Children Act 2004* ('COCA'), s.4). The English case of *Payne* was specifically rejected by the New Zealand Court of Appeal:

> presumptive or a priori weighing is inconsistent with the wider all-factor child-centred approach required under New Zealand law. Our law…requires the reasonableness of a parent's desire to relocate with the children to be assessed in relation to the disadvantages to the children of reduced contact with the other parent, along with all other factors. There will be no error of law if the decision as to residence is based on the welfare of the children looking at all relevant factors, including the need of the

> particular children for a continuing relationship with their father and with their mother… (*D v S* [2002] NZFLR 166, [47])

Section 5 of COCA super-imposes a series of 'principles relevant to child's welfare and best interests'. Amongst these principles, s.5(b) provides that 'there should be continuity in arrangements for the child's care, development and upbringing, and the child's relationships with his or her family…should be stable and ongoing (in particular, the child should have continuing relationships with both of his or her parents)'. This principle might reflect a general view that ongoing parental relationships are to be favoured, which can then militate against relocation (Boshier 2005), though no factor has pre-determined weight in the welfare analysis (*Kacem v Bashir* [2010] NZSC 112; George 2011b). In practice, New Zealand courts are willing to refuse permission to relocate even over very short distances (for example, *Brown v Argyll* [2006] NZFLR 705, refusing relocation to a town 30 minutes away), and it is thought to be difficult to obtain permission to relocate (George 2009; Mackenzie 2009).

As can be seen, there are obvious differences between the two countries about how to approach relocation disputes. The English law seeks to promote welfare by focusing on the wellbeing of a child's main carer (though the approach in cases of real shared care is less clear), while New Zealand law seeks to promote welfare by preserving and strengthening a child's relationships with both parents. The question being addressed in this chapter is how these differences manifest themselves in practice.

The views of family law practitioners in England and New Zealand

To address this question, family law practitioners in England and New Zealand were interviewed about their experiences of relocation disputes. Interviews took place between November 2008 and June 2009. There were 22 participants in each country, comprising trial judges, barristers, solicitors and court welfare advisors. After a general discussion of their experiences and analyses of their respective laws, these practitioners were asked to read and discuss three hypothetical relocation disputes, presented as 350-word vignettes (Finch 1987).

The practitioners in this study are referred to using 'tags' which indicate nationality and professional group. English participants start with an 'E', New Zealanders with an 'N'. Judges are marked with a 'J', barristers a 'B', solicitors an 'S', and court advisors a 'C' – so, NJ3 is a

New Zealand judge and ES5 is an English solicitor. Table 17.1a and b includes information about all the participants, showing nationality, professional group, sex, time in practice and the approximate number of relocation trials done each year. Two participants (EB2 and NB3) did not discuss the vignettes, and so their contributions to this part of the research are limited.

TABLE 17.1A List of participants by identifying tag, showing nationality, professional group, sex, time in practice, and approximate number of relocation trials per year

English participants

IDENTIFYING TAG	PROFESSIONAL GROUP	SEX	TIME IN PRACTICE (YEARS)	APPROXIMATE NUMBER OF RELOCATION TRIALS PER YEAR
EJ1	Judge	–	–	4
EJ2		–	–	2/3
EJ3		–	–	2
EJ4		–	–	3
EJ5		–	–	2/3
EJ6		–	–	3/4
EJ7		–	–	2/3
EB1	Barrister	M	7	1
[EB2]		[M]	[18]	[4/5]
EB3		M	19	2/3
EB4		F	8	1
EB5	Barrister, QC	M	30	2/3
EB6		F	24	5/6
EB7		F	24	1/2
ES1	Solicitor	M	28	1
ES2		F	9	1/2
ES3		M	15	2
ES4		F	18	1/2
ES5		M	12	6/8
EC1	Court Welfare Officer	F	20	1/2
EC2		M	25	3/4
EC3		F	33	1/2

TABLE 17.1B List of participants by identifying tag, showing nationality, professional group, sex, time in practice, and approximate number of relocation trials per year

New Zealand participants

IDENTIFYING TAG	PROFESSIONAL GROUP	SEX	TIME IN PRACTICE (YEARS)	APPROXIMATE NUMBER OF RELOCATION TRIALS PER YEAR
NJ1	Judge	–	–	9–14
NJ2		–	–	5/6
NJ3		–	–	3/4
NJ4		–	–	5/6
NJ5		–	–	5/6
NJ6		–	–	10/12
NB1	Barrister	F	23	2/3
NB2		M	25	1/2
[NB3]		[F]	15	[1/2]
NB4		M	40	3/4
NB5		F	35	3/4
NB6		F	21	3
NB7		M	25	1/2
NS1	Solicitor/barrister	M	23	2/3
NS2		F	30	1/2
NS3		F	22	3
NS4		F	18	2/3
NS5		F	19	2/3
NS6		F	31	1
NC1	Psychologist	M	25	7/8
NC2		F	25	12
NC3		M	13	6

To preserve anonymity, some information for judges is omitted. There were five men and two women amongst the English judges, and three men and three women amongst the New Zealand judges. Five of the English judges were Circuit Judges and two sat in the Family Division of the High Court; the average time sitting full time was 9.5 years. All six New Zealand judges sat in the Family Court, and the average time sitting full time was 8.5 years.

While much could be said about participants' discussions of these case studies (George 2011c), the focus here is on differences between the two national groups.

Case studies

Mark and Hannah's case

The first case was a proposed relocation within the country. The primary-carer father wants to move from a big city to a rural, coastal area; the contact mother objects to the move and seeks a court order requiring the father to remain with the children in the city (see Box 17.1).

Box 17.1 Mark and Hannah's case

Mark and Hannah, aged ten and seven, have been living near [London/Auckland] with their father for four years since their mother left the family to pursue a City career. The father has dedicated himself to being Mark and Hannah's primary carer, giving up his own career to care for them. The mother has maintained regular contact with the children, seeing them at least fortnightly and often more frequently. However, she finds her job very stressful, works long hours, and drinks heavily. At an earlier hearing, a judge suggested that the mother would be generally more suited to being the children's primary carer because of her warmer character, but concluded that her alcohol use and long hours precluded her from having the day-to-day care of Mark and Hannah. The father has announced his intention of moving from [London/Auckland] to [Cornwall/Whakatane]. The father has close friends in [Cornwall/Whakatane], and has visited many times. He says that the children would have a better quality of life and that living costs would be lower in that region. The mother opposes the move and seeks a court order imposing conditions on Mark and Hannah's place of residence. A report from a [welfare officer/psychologist] suggests that the father is 'strong minded, determined, and possibly obstinate in character', while the mother, although warm, shows no signs of being able to control her alcohol use. It is suggested that the absence of the children from the mother's normal routine may cause her to lose what control she has over her drinking, and put at risk her ability to support the children financially. The father has been offered part-time work by his friends if the move goes ahead, and he says that contact with the mother could be maintained on a reasonably regular basis. The [welfare officer/psychologist] is concerned that the children may react badly to losing regular contact with the mother, but makes no specific recommendation.

The general view in both countries was that the relocation would be permitted, though some participants disagreed. However, although there is some similarity in participants' views between the two countries, there were differences as well. In particular, the English were more firmly of the view that relocation would go ahead than were the New Zealanders. Figure 17.1 is a graphical representation of participants' views on the likely outcome of the case.

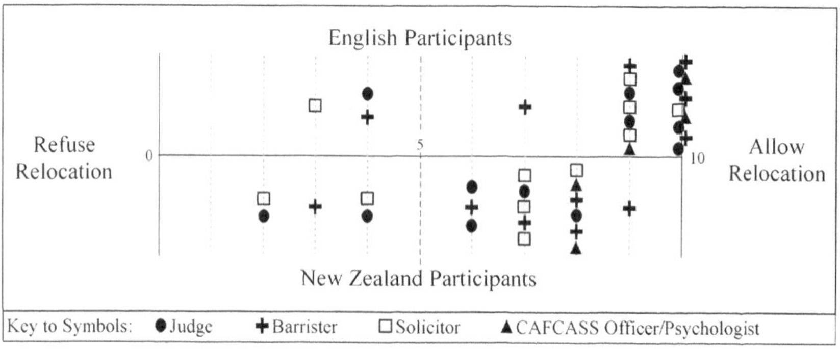

FIGURE 17.1 Illustration of participants' views on the likely outcome of Mark and Hannah's case on a scale of 0 to 10 where 10 is most likely to allow relocation, arranged by nationality and professional group

It was seen earlier that the English law makes restrictions on a parent's movement within the UK 'truly exceptional', which makes it unsurprising that most English participants thought the move likely to go ahead. Even though some English participants described themselves as 'lacking in sympathy for father', they thought that there was little chance of stopping the move because 'the law stands in the way of doing that' (EJ3). As an English barrister explained, the law required an 'exceptional' case before restrictions could be imposed, and 'there are plainly no exceptional features whatever in this case, and so the mother's claim...would be bound to fail' (EB5).

New Zealanders, on the other hand, not restricted by any test of 'exceptionality', tended to look at the case in more detail. They were often unimpressed by the father's reason for wanting to move, and said that they would like to know more about the children's own views. However, although there was some concern about the difficulty of maintaining contact with the mother if the children lived four to five hours' drive away, most thought that a reasonable contact plan could be devised, and therefore that the move would probably be allowed.

Overall, although the law on internal relocation is very different in the two countries, the end result seems relatively similar. What really differed between the countries was the way in which the case was analysed, though New Zealand participants were also more willing to think that the move should be stopped, and were less optimistic about the father's chances of being allowed to move.

Jane's case

The second case was a proposed international move where the parents had a near-equal shared care arrangement. The mother of 12-year-old Jane is unhappy living in her present location and wants to return to her home country, South Africa. Jane is a child with mixed cultural heritage, having South African and Welsh or Māori heritage, depending. She is torn between wanting to live with both her parents and wanting her parents to be happy (see Box 17.2).

As with Mark and Hannah's case, there was general similarity between the two national groups when assessing the likely outcome of this case, with most participants thinking that the relocation application would be refused. Participants were less sure about the outcome of this case, with a large proportion thinking it to be a borderline decision which could change depending on subtleties which they could not judge from the facts given. Looking at participants' predictions of the likely outcome (Figure 17.2), it can be seen that New Zealanders were marginally more certain in their predictions than were the English. Whereas ten New Zealanders put the mother's chances of success at between zero and two out of ten, only three English participants did so; by contrast, where 14 English put the mother's chances of success at three or four out of ten, only six New Zealanders did so.

Box 17.2 Jane's case

Jane is 12 years old. She is an only child with a [Welsh/Māori] father and a South African mother, currently living [in Pembrokeshire/near Taupo]. Before her parents separated three years ago, Jane's parents were both very involved in her day-to-day care. Although they have had some difficulties in their post-separation relationship, the parents have managed to co-operate well over issues to do with Jane. They live close to one another and, by flexible and informal agreement, Jane normally spends three nights a week with her father and the rest with her mother. The father views his cultural background as particularly important and, with the mother's support, has ensured that Jane is fully aware of her bi-cultural heritage. Both the father and Jane are fluent in [Welsh/Māori], and the mother has what she calls a workable use of the language. Jane's mother has begun to feel increasingly isolated in [Wales/New Zealand], and has several times mentioned that she would prefer to live in Cape Town with her family. The mother has kept close ties with her family, and South Africa generally, and she and Jane have returned many times for visits. The mother has now decided that she wants to return permanently to Cape Town, and take Jane with her. She says she would facilitate generous contact, both in [the UK/New Zealand] and South Africa, and continue to promote Jane's [Welsh/Māori] heritage. The mother has suggested that she might go even if leave to take Jane is refused because she feels so trapped and unhappy, but says that she would be torn and hopes not to have to make that choice. The father opposes the move because of the impact it would have on his relationship with Jane, and on her exposure to the [Welsh/Māori] culture and language. He says he is happy to have full-time care of Jane if the mother decides to move, and would facilitate generous contact both in [the UK/New Zealand] and South Africa. Jane says she wants the present arrangement of shared care to continue, but also that she wants her parents to be happy.

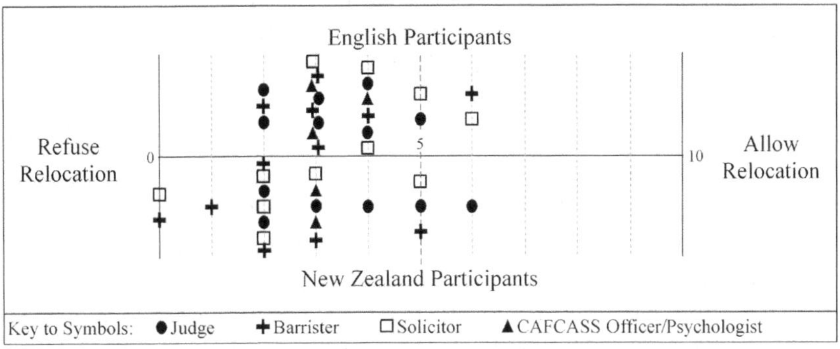

FIGURE 17.2 Illustration of participants' views on the likely outcome of Jane's case on a scale of 0 to 10 where 10 is most likely to allow relocation, arranged by nationality and professional group

There were a number of points of difference in participants' analyses of Jane's case. One was that many English participants thought the care arrangement itself to be 'most unusual' (EJ1), whereas New Zealanders thought that it fitted a fairly standard pattern of split care. The English also had to contend with moving outside the *Payne v Payne* framework and into the lesser-known shared care relocation cases. Despite these differences, participants were agreed about the general consequence of this kind of arrangement, namely that 'the closer to shared care you are, the harder it is to move, because the child is losing more' (NS4). In Jane's case, because 'both parents...are perfectly capable of looking after the child' (EB3), most participants in both countries agreed that, other things being equal, 'the balance would fall in favour of the child going to live with her father and her mother leaving the country, rather than going to live with her mother and leaving the country' (EB5).

The two national groups were also largely agreed about the relevance of Jane's views. Most participants took Jane's desire for continued shared care to be a more dominant factor than her wish for her parents to be happy. For those participants (mostly English) who thought that Jane's case overall was a difficult one to decide, Jane's views offered a way to determine the best outcome: as an English judge explained, 'if one were looking for a [deciding] factor – because this is a very nicely balanced case – ...her apparent wish might be it, against the application' (EJ6).

Jane's mother's suggestion that she might go to South Africa even if she could not take Jane was met with different reactions in the two countries. The English thought this a reasonable position to take and, indeed, the only position Jane's mother could take if she was to have any chance of success in her relocation application. New Zealanders, on the other hand, thought that it reflected badly on the mother, and described her as 'bloody-minded' (NC1) and as 'thinking more of herself than of the child' (NJ6).

Finally, there is the issue of Jane's mixed culture. There are different policy backgrounds in the English and New Zealand contexts here, which can be seen in the two countries' respective legislative focuses. While cultural considerations would be one of the factors addressed by an English court in its general assessment of welfare and best interests, there is no specific guidance on the issue. In New Zealand, by contrast, the *Care of Children Act 2004* makes particular reference, in s.5(f), to the importance of preserving and strengthening 'the child's identity (including, without limitation, his or her culture [and] language...)'.

Given this difference, it may be unsurprising that English participants had different views about the weight to give to Jane's mixed culture. While some thought Jane's Welsh culture to be an 'important heritage' (ES2) which would likely be lost if she moved to South Africa, others described it as 'something to weigh in the balance' but 'not a determinative factor' (EJ3). New Zealanders, by contrast, were clear that cultural issues were likely to be important in determining the case. They pointed to 'principles in the *Care of Children Act 2004* about children having access to their culture and having that preserved' (NS4 – see COCA, s.5(f)), and stressed the importance of the wider family (called *whānau*) in New Zealand, especially Māori, culture: 'being part of the whānau is very important... In Māori culture, the child is very much part of the wider family' (NJ6).

Overall, although participants in England and New Zealand discussed similar issues, they often evaluated their significance to the case differently. The English tended to see the case as quite borderline, and had to find individual issues (notably Jane's views) which pointed towards one outcome rather than the other. New Zealand practitioners, by contrast, were more inclined to see all the factors present in Jane's case as pointing against relocation. Consequently, although the outcome predicted by both national groups was the same, New Zealanders were more confident that the relocation would be refused than were the English.

Tom's case

Looking from an English perspective, Tom's case reflects the core facts of the vast majority of relocation cases. Tom is a young child with a clear primary-carer mother and frequent contact with his father. His mother has re-partnered, and the relocation application has come about because the mother's new partner wants to return to his home country (see Box 17.3).

Box 17.3 Tom's case

Tom's parents separated when he was two years old. Now aged six, Tom lives with his mother. He has always had good contact with his father, which has been increasing since the parents separated and now includes overnight stays once or twice a fortnight. Although the parents' relationship has been reasonably amicable, Tom's father thinks the mother is indifferent about contact, and she has sometimes resisted increases in the amount of contact between Tom and the father. About a year ago, the mother married an American and is four months pregnant with their first child. The mother's husband is very keen to return to California to be nearer his family, to make a home there, and because he thinks it will provide better opportunities for his growing family. Tom's mother lived in California for a year when she was a student and strongly supports her husband's desire to move home. The father opposes the move because of the great difficulties of contact and otherwise maintaining his relationship with Tom. He is unconvinced by the mother's plans for webcam chat, thinking it more likely he will be sidelined, given Tom's age and the mother's history of indifference to contact generally. The father points out that the mother and Tom are both happy living in [the United Kingdom/New Zealand], and all of the mother's wider family and support networks are here. He is also worried that the mother was unable to tell him what she would do if Tom did not settle well in the USA. The mother counters that her husband's family will all be nearby if they move, and is worried that her husband would be very resentful if he were stopped from returning home because Tom could not be taken too. She also stresses her role as primary carer and the fact that Tom's father works long hours and is not well placed to care for Tom if she went to America anyway.

Tom's case drew out remarkable differences between the two countries. This case falls squarely within *Payne v Payne* for English practitioners; we saw earlier that this approach was specifically rejected in the New Zealand courts, and therefore a difference in approach is not entirely surprising. Nonetheless, the sharp division of analysis and predicted outcome (Figure 17.3) suggests that there is a deep difference of opinion about how a case like Tom's would be seen in the two countries.

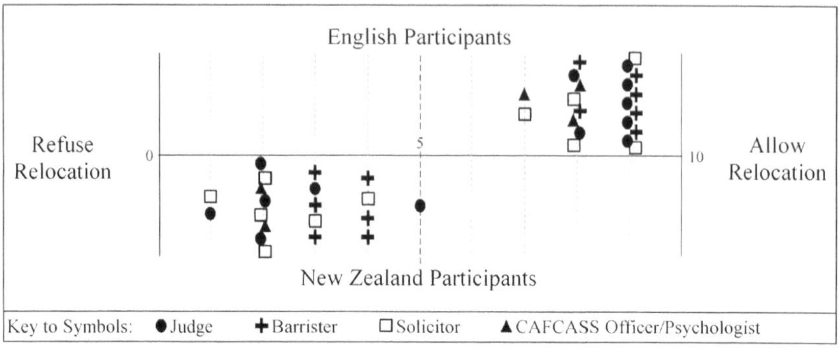

FIGURE 17.3 Illustration of participants' views on the likely outcome of Tom's case on a scale of 0 to 10 where 10 is most likely to allow relocation, arranged by nationality and professional group

English participants were unanimous in predicting that the relocation would be allowed; most participants gave the mother an eight- or nine-out-of-ten chance of success. By contrast, with the exception of one judge who thought that Tom's case 'could go either way' (NJ6), all New Zealanders thought that the relocation application would fail; most New Zealand practitioners gave the mother a two- or three-out-of-ten chance of success. So, not only were the two national groups not in agreement about the outcome, but most participants thought that the case was fairly clear-cut. As we turn to look at the factors which participants focused on in their discussions, it will become clear why there was such a difference in the predicted outcomes.

Starting with the English analysis, participants tended to think 'that the mother was wanting to relocate for sound reasons' (EJ3), and accepted that going to California would likely provide 'better opportunities', as suggested in the facts. There was concern that stopping the relocation would have a bad effect on the mother's relationship with her new partner, which in turn would be bad for Tom: as one judge explained, the relocation should be allowed 'because otherwise it looks as though it is going to have a very negative impact on [the mother's] new family unit' (EJ5).

Looking at Tom's existing relationship with his father, the English saw this as a good relationship, but also one that, 'in terms of days and nights spent between father and son, can almost be made up' with a carefully planned contact arrangement after relocation (EJ6). English participants tended to down-play the father's concerns about the mother's indifference to contact – 'a certain amount of indifference is to be expected in a situation like this' (EB3) – and in any case thought that it would be hard to prove that there was a problem.

Given their views on all these factors, it is perhaps unsurprising that English participants predicted so clearly that relocation would be allowed.

The contrast between this approach and that seen in New Zealand interviews is striking. Many New Zealanders questioned the mother's motivation for wanting to move, seeing it as 'not the best reason in the world to go' (NJ2). They were unconcerned about the effect of refusing relocation on the mother's new partner and on their relationship: as one judge explained, 'her husband may be unhappy, and that may spill over onto the mother, but when you keep your eye on Tom, on Tom's needs, I think that is not a good enough reason' (NJ2).

When it came to Tom's relationship with his father, New Zealanders were 'surprised that he only has overnight stays once or twice a fortnight' (NC2). They thought that, other things being equal, it would be in Tom's interests to have more contact, 'moving into a shared care type of arrangement' (NC3). As to the mother's alleged indifference to contact, New Zealand practitioners were very concerned, and thought this likely to be highly significant to the outcome of the case:

> The mother's history of indifference – well, she's sunk before she starts... Sorry mum, you can't head off and be indifferent – that's not what it's about. You have got to promote, improve, maintain, and indifference is not enough. (NS3)

Consequently, it is again unsurprising that most New Zealanders were clear that the relocation was not going to be allowed.

Discussion

As noted earlier, relocation cases in both England and New Zealand are subject to the overriding statutory obligation that decisions should be made which best promote the welfare of the children concerned. Despite this common starting point, relocation disputes in the two countries are seen differently by practitioners. In all three hypothetical cases discussed here, practitioners in the two countries focused on different aspects when assessing what they thought mattered. While the headline outcomes in two of the cases were the same – Mark and Hannah would relocate, Jane would not – English practitioners were consistently more inclined towards allowing the proposed moves than were their New Zealand counterparts. In Tom's case – which represents the majority of cases in many countries, including England – both the analyses and predicted outcomes of the two jurisdictions were markedly different: English practitioners were sure the relocation would be allowed, while New Zealanders were sure it would not.

One possible explanation for these findings is that English and New Zealand family lawyers have different ideas about what 'welfare' means in the relocation context. While there were individual practitioners in both countries who questioned whether their law's approach to relocation disputes truly did promote the best interests of the children involved, it was agreed that the different positions reached by England and New Zealand represented legitimate attempts to promote children's welfare in difficult cases. If that is true, it might cast doubt on any view that there is a single conception of what welfare means which can be applied in an international context.

Such a conclusion is not entirely surprising. With reference to Article 3(1) of the United Nations Convention on the Rights of the Child 1989, which also uses the language of best interests, Stephen Parker (1994, p.27) was keen to 'caution against the assumption that there is only one best interests standard in currency', since the interpretation of welfare would depend on local and national cultural views about children's upbringing. The question of what is in the best interests of a child is not only incapable of being answered in the abstract, rather than in reference to a particular child in his or her particular circumstances, but may also be incapable of being answered without reference to a particular society (Alston 1994; Eekelaar 2004; Parker 1994). Different societies reflect their values regarding children in different ways. One example was seen earlier regarding statutory provisions about children's cultural heritage. Another which is relevant to the issues raised by this chapter would be societal views on shared care in post-separation families. New Zealand has moved further and faster than England in embracing shared care as being in children's best interests (Harris-Short 2010; Henaghan 2007; Mackenzie 2009); while English courts often make orders for 'shared residence' (Gilmore 2006), these are often mere 'labels' which bear little resemblance to the child's day-to-day care in practice (Harris and George 2010).

This apparent variation in the interpretation given to children's best interests in different countries, caused in part at least by differing policy backgrounds, may indicate both a great strength and a great weakness of the welfare principle. On the one hand, it makes the principle flexible and usable in a wide variety of contexts, capable of being applied in different places as well as over time as societies develop. On the other hand, for those who hope to achieve greater international consistency to disputes over children's upbringing, including relocation cases, social variation in our understandings of welfare may mean that more substantive standards need to be negotiated. Any such standards would, almost inevitably, be contested and difficult to agree. One reason that the welfare principle is so universally accepted may be that it can mean anything to anyone.

Acknowledgement

The research reported in this chapter formed part of the author's doctoral thesis, which was funded by the UK Arts and Humanities Research Council (Grant Number 135597).

References

Alston, P. (1994) 'The best interests principle: Towards a reconciliation of culture and human rights.' *International Journal of Law and the Family 8*, 1–25.

Boshier, P. (2005) 'Relocation cases: An international view from the bench.' *New Zealand Family Law Journal 5*, 77–90.

Eekelaar, J. (2002) 'Beyond the welfare principle.' *Child and Family Law Quarterly 12*, 237–249.

Eekelaar, J. (2004) 'Children between cultures.' *International Journal of Law, Policy and the Family 18*, 178–194.

Finch, J. (1987) 'The vignette technique in survey research.' *Sociology 21*, 105.

Foley, T. (2006) *International Child Relocation: Varying Approaches Among Member States to the 1980 Hague Convention on Child Abduction*. Available at www.family-justice-council.org.uk/docs/International_Child_Relocation_research_paper.pdf, accessed on 20 April 2011.

George, R. (2009) 'The shifting law: Relocation disputes in New Zealand and England.' *Otago Law Review 12*, 107–130.

George, R. (2010) 'Re *L* (Internal Relocation: Shared Residence Order) [2009] EWCA Civ 20, [2009] 1 FLR 1157.' *Journal of Social Welfare and Family Law 32*, 71–80.

George, R. (2011a) 'Re *F* (Internal Relocation) [2010] EWCA Civ 1428, [2010] All ER (D) 263 (Oct).' *Journal of Social Welfare and Family Law 33*, 169.

George, R. (2011b) 'Principles relevant to child's welfare and best interests.' *New Zealand Family Law Journal 7*, 26–30.

George, R. (2011c) 'Practitioners' views on children's welfare in relocation disputes: Comparing approaches in England and New Zealand.' *Child and Family Law Quarterly 23*, 178.

George, R. (forthcoming 2012) 'Reviewing Relocation? Re W (Children) (*Relocation: Removal Outside Jurisdiction*) [2011] EWCA Civ 345 and K v K (*Relocation: Shared Care Arrangement*) [2011] EWCA Civ 793.' *Child and Family Law Quarterly 24*.

Gilmore, S. (2006) 'Court decision-making in shared residence order cases: A critical examination.' *Child and Family Law Quarterly 18*, 478–498.

Harris, P. and George, R. (2010) 'Parental responsibility and shared residence orders: Parliamentary intentions and judicial interpretations.' *Child and Family Law Quarterly 22*, 151–171.

Harris-Short, S. (2010) 'Resisting the march towards 50/50 shared residence: Rights, welfare and equality in post-separation families.' *Journal of Social Welfare and Family Law 32*, 257–274.

Henaghan, M. (2007) 'Legally Rearranging Families: Parents and Children after Break-up.' In M. Henaghan and W. Atkin (eds) *Family Law Policy in New Zealand* (3rd edition). Wellington: LexisNexis.

Mackenzie, F. (2009) *Uneasy Trends in Relocation Law*. Unpublished LLM thesis, Victoria University of Wellington.

Mnookin, R. (1975) 'Child-custody adjudication: Judicial functions in the face of indeterminacy.' *Law and Contemporary Problems 39*, 226–293.

Parker, S. (1994) 'The best interests of the child: Principles and problems.' *International Journal of Law and the Family 8*, 26–41.

Worwood, A. (2005) 'International relocation – the debate.' *Family Law 35*, 621-627.

Chapter 18

Working with Separated Families

Helen Rhoades

Introduction

Over the past decade, family law policies in several jurisdictions have increasingly emphasised the benefits of non-adversarial dispute resolution services for managing post-separation disputes over children. Whilst some countries, such as the UK, are presently considering 'mandatory mediation' reforms, Australia has already acquired some experience of this model. In 2006, the Australian government amended the *Family Law Act 1975* (Cth) to introduce legislative changes which require most parents to attempt to resolve their conflict through a family dispute resolution process before approaching the courts. Behind this shift was a desire to reduce the costs of the justice system, and to ensure that the involvement of lawyers in post-separation disputes becomes 'the exception rather than the rule' (Australian Government House of Representatives Standing Committee on Family and Community Affairs 2003, 4.47). However, recent evaluations of Australia's policy revealed that it has not reduced the need for legal services, and that parents who use family dispute resolution are highly likely to also engage a solicitor. Perhaps more significantly, the research revealed significant tensions between the legal and family dispute resolution professions which have operated to the detriment of clients, including suggestions that this problem has been exacerbated by the very reforms that were designed to benefit separated families.

This chapter engages with research data to examine the factors that enhance and inhibit effective collaboration between family lawyers and family dispute resolution practitioners and explores the potential for more recent government proposals to build integration across the service sector. Before turning to that analysis, the following section outlines the key legislative reforms that came into effect in July 2006.

Australia's 2006 family law reforms

Reflecting similar debates in other countries, the 2006 changes to Australia's family dispute resolution sector were part of a larger policy initiative focused on encouraging the use of shared care arrangements by separated parents. According to the government's press release at the time, the *Family Law Amendment (Shared Parental Responsibility) Act 2006* (Cth) ('the *Shared Parental Responsibility Act*') was designed 'to bring about a cultural shift in how family separation is managed: away from litigation and towards cooperative parenting' (Australian Government Attorney-General's Department 2005). As this suggests, the legislation had a mixed agenda. On the one hand, it aimed to reduce reliance on the legal profession and encourage separated parents to use alternative conflict resolution processes to settle their disputes. On the other, the government hoped the reforms would see a greater involvement by both parents in their children's lives, whenever this was safe (Chisholm 2007). Much like the Family Justice Review in England, which has recently released its Interim Report (Family Justice Review 2011), this design mix reflects the political background to the reforms, including agitation by fathers' rights groups for a joint custody law and a desire by government to reshape the justice system and provide disputants with an increased range of non-adversarial dispute resolution options.

The *Shared Parental Responsibility Act* was the end result of a parliamentary inquiry into the law governing children's post-separation care. Fathers' rights groups were 'the prime movers and shakers' behind this development (Rhoades 2006, p.125). Their demand for law reform was based on concerns that the legal profession was doing too little to facilitate men's involvement with their children after relationship breakdown, and that the courts were governed by traditional views about children's primary attachment to mothers. In their submissions to the parliamentary committee, these groups sought a joint custody presumption, in the hope that lawyers and judges would then be forced to make 'equal care time' orders. The committee also received numerous submissions from mediation practitioners, who argued that the inquiry's focus on law reform was misguided, and that the more pressing need was for increased conflict resolution services and a greater use of social science professionals who had 'an in-depth understanding of child development' (Rhoades and Boyd 2004, p.134).

The committee ultimately decided against an equal time presumption, noting there were 'dangers in a one size fits all approach' to children's living arrangements (Australian Government House of Representatives Standing Committee on Family and Community Affairs 2003, 2.39, 2.4). Nevertheless, it recommended that '50/50 shared residence' should become the new starting point for decision-making and negotiation, and expressed a hope that shared care arrangements would become the new post-separation norm (Australian Government House of Representatives Standing Committee on Family and Community Affairs 2003, 2.38, 2.43). The committee also suggested the need to create a new kind of family law system, where alternative dispute resolution services, rather than lawyers, would be the first port of call for parents in conflict. The government acted to implement both of these recommendations. As a result, the *Family Law Act* now contains provisions that require judges to consider making orders for the child to spend equal time, and failing that 'substantial and significant' time, with both parents, unless there is a history of violence of abuse (*Family Law Act 1975* (Cth), ss 61DA and 65DAA). Coupled with these amendments is a new legislative provision that requires parents to make a 'genuine effort' to resolve their conflict through a family dispute resolution process before they can apply for court orders (*Family Law Act 1975* (Cth), s 60I(1)).

Evaluations of the reforms

In February 2010 a different Australian government released a series of research reports on the reforms, including a comprehensive three-year evaluation conducted by the Australian Institute of Family Studies ('AIFS') (Kaspiew *et al.* 2009). At the same time as the AIFS evaluation was taking place, my colleagues and I were conducting a parallel investigation of interprofessional relationships in the Australian family law system (Rhoades *et al.* 2008). Together, these studies provide valuable insights into how the system is working, and how the reforms have affected services.

The AIFS evaluation suggested a picture of significant success. It revealed a marked decline in court applications since the introduction of the *Shared Parental Responsibility Act*, as well as a marked increase in shared care arrangements (Kaspiew *et al.* 2009). Its data also showed that family dispute resolution programs have achieved high satisfaction rates. While many surveyed parents had left services without reaching a formal agreement, the research suggested that the process of family dispute resolution had empowered them to 'take charge of their dispute', and had helped 'to sow the seeds for future reconciliation of differences' (Kaspiew *et al.* 2009, p.104, p.110). Moreover, the report indicated that family dispute resolution programs were producing high levels of durable agreements, with a majority of surveyed parents indicating that their care arrangements were working well for themselves and their children (Kaspiew *et al.* 2009).

On the other hand, the AIFS research disclosed some unintended consequences of the reforms, as well as some troubling implications for the service system. Contrary to the policymakers' hopes, the reforms had not reduced reliance on the legal profession. Instead, reflecting the experience of other jurisdictions (Collier 1999), the survey of family dispute resolution clients showed that most parents who used a family dispute resolution service also engaged a lawyer (Kaspiew *et al.* 2009). While this dynamic was not anticipated by the policymakers, it was greeted with relief by many in the system, particularly those who were aware of the benefits of legal representation for vulnerable clients (Hunter 2003). However, the AIFS evaluation, like our own research, pointed to a more worrying development.

As with the AIFS research, the passage of the 2006 reforms was the impetus for our study of interprofessional relationships. In light of the experience of other jurisdictions with well-developed mediation programs, we anticipated that, despite the emphasis on alternative dispute resolution processes, separating couples would continue to approach lawyers for advice and assistance about a wide range of legal issues (Douglas and Moorhead 2005). Given the dominance of the legal profession within the family law system, it was also clear that lawyers would play an important referral role for family dispute resolution services (Field 2004). Together, these factors suggested that the success of Australia's reforms was likely to be affected by the capacity of the two professional groups to work together effectively. Yet previous research had shown that interprofessional relationships within legal settings are often 'fraught with tension and misunderstanding' (Dickens 2004, p.17), particularly where practitioners have different perspectives on a client's needs. On the other hand, there was some anecdotal evidence at the time of the 2006 reforms that successful collaboration between lawyers and mediators was a feature of a number of agencies within the system.

The aim of our project was to gain an empirical understanding of how practitioners from these professions regard and manage their working relationships and the factors that enhance and inhibit collaborative practices (Rhoades *et al.* 2008). To this end, the research employed a sequential design of two studies. Study 1, which took place in 2006, involved the collection and analysis of qualitative data obtained from in-depth semi-structured interviews with dispute resolution practitioners from four well-known programs in the Australian family law system and with family lawyers who had an established and reputedly good working relationship with one or more of these services. In order to allow us to tease out the extent to which the program's nature and proximity to the formal justice system had an impact on relationships with the legal profession, the sample of services included a mix of community-based, court-based and legal aid dispute resolution services.[1]

The sample of participants in Study 1 comprised 59 practitioners: 30 family law solicitors and 29 family dispute resolution practitioners. Each of the dispute resolution practitioners was employed by or worked for one of the four dispute resolution services chosen for this study. The sample of family lawyers included solicitors who regularly referred clients to or worked with one or more of the four programs. The interviews explored the issues identified in earlier research on interprofessional relationships, with a focus on eliciting information about facilitators and inhibitors of successful collaboration between the two professions. The questions were designed to examine participants' knowledge, attitudes and beliefs about the role and function of their own profession and that of the 'other' profession, as well as aspects of their interprofessional relationships.

Study 2 involved an on-line questionnaire which drew on the qualitative information collected in the first study to survey a broader range of interprofessional relationships of varying quality and levels of establishment. Data collection for this stage took place in early 2007, six months after the introduction of the *Shared Parental Responsibility Act*. This largely quantitative study was designed to test the understanding of good collaborative relationships revealed in Study 1 and to gauge the extent to which such relationships were reflective of the wider family law community. A total of 456 practitioners completed the questionnaire, including 134 family dispute resolution practitioners and 322 family lawyers. The sample included dispute resolution practitioners from community-based organisations, legal aid services and Family Relationship Centres. Legal practitioners who completed the questionnaire comprised solicitors in private practice as well as legal aid and community-based family lawyers, and were drawn from a diverse range of locations, including capital cities and regional and rural areas. The questionnaire asked practitioners for information about their professional responsibilities and interprofessional practices and their understanding of the practices and responsibilities of the 'other' profession in relation to a range of practice issues. Respondents were also asked about their attitudes towards the other profession and their satisfaction with their interprofessional relationships.

The data collected from these studies indicated that many practitioners working in the sector enjoy good working relationships with members of the 'other' profession, but that there were also significant misunderstandings and tensions between the two groups. The findings also confirmed the influence of many of the disciplinary and cultural factors revealed in earlier studies of interprofessional relationships, including tensions created by their different roles and overlapping responsibilities. But they also suggested that the 2006 reforms had themselves had a negative impact on successful collaboration.

Impediments to interprofessional collaboration

Different roles

A key problem affecting the interprofessional relationships we surveyed was the different ways in which the two professions approached their work with separated parents. This tension centred on the distinction between the lawyer's advocacy role and the family dispute resolution practitioner's obligation of neutrality. For family lawyers, partisanship on the client's behalf is a core principle of legal professionalism (Mather, McEwen and Mainman 2001; Wright 2007). Lawyers have a single client whose interests they are required to 'advance and protect', and their professional ethics mean that they cannot represent both parties to the dispute (Law Council of Australia 2002, Rule 12.1). In contrast, the work of the family dispute resolution practitioner has a more holistic orientation, which encompasses the interests of all the disputants and imports a duty to act impartially (*Family Law Act 1975* (Cth), s 10F(b)).

For many family dispute resolution practitioners in our project, this distinction was cause for concern. These participants complained that the lawyer's advocacy role tended to exacerbate hostilities, impeding their collaboration-building work with separated parents. For their part, a number of lawyers expressed concerns about the dispute resolution practitioner's obligation of impartiality. While this concept has been used to denote a variety of meanings in the mediation literature (Furlong and Lipp 1994; Taylor 1997), it was the obligation to be 'disinterested' in the outcome of the dispute which proved to be contentious (see Walker 1988). Lawyers generally supported the dispute resolution profession's duty to be 'unaligned' with either disputant, but some were concerned that, without the intervention of the family dispute resolution practitioner, a vulnerable parent might feel pressured to agree to a care arrangement that did not support their safety needs. As one family lawyer in our study commented:

> I don't actually know what responsibility they assume for the content of the outcome. In other words, if they see something being agreed that alarms them, I don't know if they feel an obligation to intervene.

Different goals and responsibilities

A further source of conflict revolved around a perception that the two groups were working towards different goals. Whereas family lawyers were focused on achieving a workable parenting agreement, family dispute resolution practitioners tended to describe relationship-based aims, such as behavioural change and better parenting. This tension was summed up in the following comment by one dispute resolution practitioner:

> [W]e don't see people as parties to a disagreement, we see people as parents who need to work out how they are going to bring up their children, and we are focused on relationships, not agreements... We couldn't care less if people have an order or not. That's not necessarily going to help them be better parents. So in some ways our emphasis and our focus are on different things.

Even apparently shared responsibilities were the subject of conflict for some practitioners. In his 2003 study of social workers and lawyers working on child protection matters, Dickens concluded:

> Sometimes they might seem to have the same responsibility – for example, they both have a responsibility to the child – but those apparently identical responsibilities can still clash, because each profession understands them differently in the light of all the other responsibilities that they have. (Dickens 2004, p.29)

Our research suggested that this was also true for family lawyers and family dispute resolution practitioners who work with separated parents. Despite their duty of impartiality, the majority of family dispute resolution practitioners we surveyed identified their primary or overriding duty as being owed to the child. As many of these participants saw it, safeguarding the child's wellbeing was the foundation of good family dispute resolution practice. In contrast, family lawyers described a more complex array of multilayered obligations, including professional responsibilities as officers of the court and advocates for their client, and statutory responsibilities to advise parents about the 'best interests' principle (*Family Law Act 1975* (Cth), s 63DA(2)(c)). Unlike the dispute resolution profession, family lawyers have no direct responsibility to the child unless acting as an Independent Children's Lawyer. Rather, their primary duty is to 'advance and protect' the interests of their (adult) client. As suggested, this orientation was a matter of some concern for many family dispute resolution practitioners, who regarded lawyers as failing in their responsibility to children.

Different status

In addition to these practice-based differences, a further source of tension centred on the different cultural signifiers and relative status of the two professions within the family law system. Far from being regarded as a valued part of the family law community, a number of family dispute resolution practitioners in our sample felt that their skills and expertise were not valued by the legal profession, or suggested that lawyers had little respect for therapeutic processes. The data also revealed that some family dispute resolution practitioners believed that lawyers regarded their work as a secondary service or a 'support role' to that of the legal profession. As one such participant described it:

> It's like 20 years ago in the hospital framework, where the doctors thought that they were the top of the pecking order and that everybody underneath were assisting them.

Separate spheres and negative stereotypes

A more fundamental obstacle to effective collaboration was a lack of familiarity with one another's work practices (Kaspiew *et al.* 2009). To a large extent, the legal and family dispute resolution sectors operate in silos. One of the consequences of this phenomenon was a tendency to stereotype the 'other' profession. For example, some responses to our questionnaire survey contained descriptions of lawyers as 'hired guns', or references to dispute resolution practitioners being 'touchy feely'. Another consequence was that lawyers and family dispute resolution practitioners often had little accurate knowledge of how the other profession worked with family law clients. It was clear from our study that there is no standard family dispute resolution model operating in the Australian family law sector, and that different agencies have different methods of working with families.

A distinctive feature of the successful collaborative relationships in our study was that lawyers had a good understanding of these differences and made referrals accordingly. But many lawyers confessed to having little detailed knowledge about the nature of the services provided by dispute resolution agencies in their local area. As a practitioner from one of the Study 1 dispute resolution services noted:

> I guess if you speak to solicitors and you asked them, 'What do they think they're doing over there at [the dispute resolution service]?', they might go, 'Counselling?', or they don't know... I think they might not have actually a detailed clue about what happens.

The shared parenting reforms

Each of these cultural and disciplinary factors – issues of status, the differences in roles, goals and responsibilities to children – reflect the findings of earlier research on interprofessional relationships. However, our data also revealed the presence of some unique policy-based influences, which suggest that Australia's 2006 reforms have themselves played a significant role in shaping relationships between the two professions. At the heart of this dynamic are the different knowledge bases used by the two professions in working with separated parents – law *versus* child development.

A core part of the lawyer's professional role is a duty to give clients accurate advice about the law, and this obligation assumes particular prominence when reality testing a parent's proposals for their children's care. In accordance with this duty, legal practitioners in our study described measuring their clients' instructions against the relevant legal principles, and realigning their plans if the client's proposals were not consistent with these. As a result of the *Shared Parental Responsibility Act*, this process has seen lawyers obliged to advise clients about the legislation's shared parenting presumption, and that the courts must consider making orders for children to spend equal time with both parents unless there has been violence or abuse. Family dispute resolution practitioners, on the other hand, are able to draw on their knowledge of the child development research when working with separated parents.

Not surprisingly, the AIFS evaluation showed that the legal profession and the courts felt more significantly constrained by the legislative reforms than did their family dispute resolution colleagues. While there has been an overall rise in shared care arrangements since the 2006 reforms, this has been most pronounced in judicially determined outcomes. Ironically, this is the population of parents most likely to have complex support needs and high levels of conflict, making them poor candidates for a successful co-parenting project. Moreover, family lawyers reported that they had found it increasingly difficult since the reforms to achieve child-focused agreements, with many clients, particularly fathers, believing they were now entitled to 50–50 share time, and negotiating from a parental rights perspective, rather than a child-centred stance (Fehlberg, Millward and Campo 2009; Kaspiew *et al.* 2009). In contrast, the work of family dispute resolution practitioners, who are legally prohibited from giving legal advice to clients, has not suffered the same fate.

It is understandable then that the advisory practices of family lawyers were a source of concern for many family dispute resolution practitioners in our survey. However, few dispute resolution practitioners appeared to appreciate the role of the law in shaping the legal profession's work. Instead, many criticised lawyers for not challenging clients who sought a shared time arrangement that was not, in the opinion of the family dispute resolution practitioner, compatible with their child's wellbeing. As one participant commented:

> Look, the number of times that especially fathers come in going, 'I am going for [shared] residence', and it would be completely bonkers for their relationship with their children for that to actually happen, and there's someone behind the scenes saying, 'This is a good punt', I've got to be a bit worried about whether in fact some family lawyers do have the best interests of children at heart in that situation.

Enhancing interprofessional relationships

The present Australian government has identified the building of 'an integrated family law system' as a policy priority (Attorney-General for Australia 2009). Our study of interprofessional relationships provides a number of insights into how this might be achieved. Whilst the findings suggest that successful collaboration between lawyers and family dispute resolution practitioners is not widespread within the system, they also provided valuable information about the characteristics of effective working relationships and how these were formed and supported.

The central characteristic of positive relationships identified by our research was a 'complementary services' outlook, in which practitioners from each group saw themselves and the other profession as contributing different but equally valuable skills and expertise to the dispute resolution process. In contrast to the negative views reported in the previous section, practitioners who worked closely together exhibited a high level of understanding and respect for the different roles and responsibilities of the other profession, and regarded their input into family law disputes as adding value to their own work with separated parents. Lawyers, for example, valued the dispute resolution sector's communication-building skills and expert guidance to parents about children's needs, while family dispute resolution practitioners valued family lawyers for their expert legal advice and advocacy skills, particularly for vulnerable clients. For these practitioners, the 'other' profession's input added value to their own work with separated parents, rather than being a site of tension.

The key variable distinguishing these positive relationships from others in our sample was the amount of contact practitioners had with members of the other profession. The transformative potential of personal contact was captured well by one family dispute resolution practitioner who described this feature as having altered her previous negative perceptions of the family lawyer's advocacy role:

> And that's been refreshing to me because I think I've thought that the legal profession have a nicer job in that they can entirely – this was my belief – entirely support their client's view and their client's wishes and they only have to listen to one side of the situation. But as I talk to more legal professionals, I realise that they think more broadly than just their client's view and their client's wishes, so they do have a sense that there's another party here who may in fact have an entirely different view and so how do I work knowing that? So I think the legal profession, I'm finding that I have to give them more credit for that.

However, the data analysis suggested that contact *per se* is not sufficient of itself to counter the kind of stereotypes harboured by those who had little experience of working with the other profession, and may even reinforce negative perceptions. Instead, the research indicates that what is important is the *nature* of the contact between practitioners. Two forms of contact stood out as being influential in this regard. The first involved a teamwork approach, where practitioners from the two professions worked together as a multidisciplinary team on individual cases. This is the primary model used by Legal Aid Commissions in Australia. The success of this model in generating respectful working relationships was reflected in our survey where practitioners who identified themselves as working in partnership with members of the other profession were the most satisfied with their interprofessional relationships. As one Legal Aid Commission participant remarked:

> To me the best interaction is created by working together and actually doing the work together… I think that creates the best sort of rapport because you get hands-on understanding of each other's roles and each other's backgrounds and each other's approaches and stuff. So I think just the working together in the field I've found that to be the best bridge builder.

The second form of positive contact involved local cross-professional development activities with members of the other profession. This model was well illustrated by the monthly professional development meetings run by Relationships Australia Victoria for its dispute resolution personnel and members of the legal profession. The interviews with relevant participants indicated a number of ways in which these meetings had helped to foster collaboration between the professions. First, practitioners from both groups highlighted the information-sharing benefits, such as keeping mediators up to date with developments in the law, and demonstrating to lawyers how mediators approach their work with family law clients. Second, practitioners described the meetings as having helped to break down negative stereotypes, and allay fears about the other profession. For example, one family dispute resolution practitioner explained:

> [W]e get to hear what is going on for lawyers, so we get an understanding of what they're presented with, and they of us. So that's really good learning, and it removes that barrier of 'us and them'.

Third, practitioners provided examples of how the meetings had been used to address concerns about the practices of one or other profession. As an example, one family lawyer illustrated this point by describing how family dispute resolution practitioners had responded to family lawyers' concerns about the 'systems abuse' potential of the program's proposal to introduce child-inclusive mediation, and how the meeting had been used to reassure them that family dispute resolution practitioners were mindful of the issue. Finally, participants reported improved interprofessional communication. Having made contact at the professional development meetings, practitioners suggested they were more likely than before to phone members of the other profession to discuss concerns and provide feedback about mutual clients.

Conclusion: Towards an integrated service system

Since the publication of our report, the Australian government has acted on its findings to increase opportunities for cross-professional development and teamwork approaches to managing family disputes. In January 2009, the Federal Attorney-General launched the first of what has become an annual Family Law System Conference, which brings together practitioners from the various legal and family relationships communities to share and discuss professional practice concerns. In February 2009, a Family Law System Reference Group was assembled to advise the government on strategies for improving integration across the sector. In October 2009, the government introduced a Legal Assistance Partnership program to enhance collaboration between Family Relationships Centres and legal assistance services (Attorney-General's Department 2009). Subsequently, in March 2011, it introduced family violence legislation which aims to ensure protective outcomes for families whenever a shared care arrangement is not consistent with the child's safety needs (*Family Law Legislation Amendment (Family Violence and Other Measures) Bill 2011* (Cth)).

These are important initiatives that respond to the insights gleaned from the survey data collected for our project. Together they represent a significant step towards building a coherent service delivery system for family law clients. However, these measures do little to address one of the key problems identified by our study, namely the present disjunction between the law governing children's best interests and the child development evidence base. The new emphasis on family safety is a welcome development. But such tinkering with the present legal framework will not be sufficient to change the pattern of inappropriate shared care arrangements being made where parents are incapable of effective collaboration, or to overcome the professional tensions this has engendered. The interprofessional relationships study suggests that the government will need to go further than supplementing the law's shared care emphasis with principles about family violence if it wants to build a truly coordinated service system for separated families.

Endnote

1. The four dispute resolution programs were: Relationships Australia's Family Mediation Service in Victoria; Victoria Legal Aid's Roundtable Dispute Management Program; UnitingCare Unifam's Keeping Contact Parenting Order Program in Parramatta, New South Wales; and the Family Court of Australia's Mediation Section (as it was then known) in the Melbourne Registry.

References

Attorney-General for Australia (2009) *Opening Address: Inaugural Family Law System Conference.* Canberra: Commonwealth of Australia.

Attorney-General's Department (2009) 'Building better partnerships between family relationship centres and legal assistance services.' *Media Release*, 4 December 2009.

Australian Government Attorney-General's Department (2005) 'Bill marks "cultural shift" in dealing with family breakdown.' *Press Release*, 8 December 2005.

Australian Government House of Representatives Standing Committee on Family and Community Affairs (2003) *Every Picture Tells a Story: Report on the Inquiry into Child Custody Arrangements in the Event of Family Separation.* Canberra: Commonwealth of Australia.

Chisholm, R. (2007) 'Making it work: The Family Law Amendment (Shared Parental Responsibility) Act 2006.' *Australian Journal of Family Law 21*, 1, 143–172.

Collier, R. (1999) 'The dashing of a "Liberal dream"? The information meeting, the "new family" and the limits of law.' *Child and Family Law Quarterly 11*, 3, 257–270.

Dickens, J. (2004) 'Risks and responsibilities: The role of the local authority lawyer in child care cases.' *Child and Family Law Quarterly 16*, 1, 17–30.

Douglas, G. and Moorhead, R. (2005) 'Providing advice for lone parents: From parent to citizen.' *Child and Family Law Quarterly 17*, 1, 55–74.

Family Justice Review (2011) *Interim Report* (March). London: Ministry of Justice.

Fehlberg, B., Millward, C. and Campo, M. (2009) 'Shared post-separation in 2009: An empirical snapshot.' *Australian Journal of Family Law 23*, 3, 247–275.

Field, R. (2004) 'A feminist model of mediation that centralizes the role of lawyers as advocates for participants who are victims of domestic violence.' *Australian Feminist Law Journal 20*, 65–91.

Furlong, M. and Lipp, J. (1994) 'The multiple relationships between neutrality and therapeutic influence.' *Australia and New Zealand Journal of Family Therapy 16*, 113–122.

Hunter, R. (2003) 'Adversarial mythologies: Policy assumptions and research evidence in family law.' *Journal of Law and Society 30*, 1, 156–176.

Kaspiew, R., Gray, M., Weston, R., Moloney, L., Hand, K. and Qu, L. (2009) *Evaluation of the 2006 Family Law Reforms.* Melbourne: Australian Institute of Family Studies.

Law Council of Australia (2002) *Model Rules of Professional Conduct and Practice.* Canberra: Law Council of Australia.

Mather, L., McEwen, C.A. and Mainman, R.J. (2001) *Divorce Lawyers at Work: Varieties of Professionalism in Practice.* New York: Oxford University Press.

Rhoades, H. (2006) 'Yearning for Law: Fathers' Groups and Family Law Reform in Australia.' In S. Sheldon and R. Collier (eds) *Fathers' Rights Activism and Law Reform in Comparative Perspective.* Oxford: Hart Publishing.

Rhoades, H. and Boyd, S.B. (2004) 'Reforming custody laws: A comparative study.' *International Journal of Law, Policy and the Family 18*, 119–146.
Rhoades, H., Astor, H., Sanson, A. and O'Connor, M. (2008) *Enhancing Inter-Professional Relationships in a Changing Family Law System: Final Report.* The University of Melbourne, May 2008.
Taylor, A. (1997) 'Concepts of neutrality in family mediation: Contexts, ethics, influence and transformative process.' *Mediation Quarterly 14*, 3, 215–236.
Walker, G.B. (1988) 'Training mediators: Teaching about ethical concerns and obligations.' *Mediation Quarterly 19*, 33–42.
Wright, K. (2007) 'The role of solicitors in divorce: A note of caution.' *Child and Family Law Quarterly 19*, 4, 481–495.

Chapter 19

Deciding the Best Interests of the Child

Legal Responses to Child Protection Concerns

Rosemary Sheehan

Introduction

This chapter examines how the aims of child welfare legislation fail to address the practical concerns of child protection. Studies undertaken in the Children's Court, Victoria, Australia, together with other related studies, reveal that effective child protection is a shared enterprise across child and community welfare professions. The framing of child protection as a socio-legal enterprise limits this enterprise and distracts from a broader child welfare focus. The implications of this for children, and the legal context, are debated. So too are approaches that offer a more integrated response to child protection concerns, where legal process is part of a collaborative response.

Child protection: A socio-legal enterprise

The series of public inquiries into child deaths in the UK from those in the mid-1980s (Jasmine Beckford, Kimberley Carlisle and Tyra Henry) to the more recent deaths of Victoria Climbié (2003) and Baby P (2007) reveal how forcefully the law asserts itself in the child welfare jurisdiction (Braye and Preston-Shoot 2006). Child protection workers were criticised in each inquiry for failing to understand their legal obligations, and calls were made for the development of even more legal criteria to define risk and procedural standards for intervention to ensure children were adequately protected. The legal system exerts the same influence on the child protection system in Australia and specifically directs system and service responses. Court proceedings have become part of the core business of the child protection service, and great emphasis is given to using highly structured and standardised risk assessment measures to gather evidence that is acceptable to the Court (Allen Consulting Group 2003). The Office of the Victorian Ombudsman (2009) reported that 'approximately 50 per cent of child protection worker time is spent servicing Children's Court work and subsequent Protection Orders, even though only 7.3 per cent of the total number of reports made to the department result in legal intervention being initiated in the Children's Court' (p.12).

Child protection in Australia turns on argument about parental incapacity (Allen Consulting Group 2003); it is aligned with judicial and adversarial processes and separated from the broader child welfare and family support systems set up to respond to vulnerable families. The Victorian Ombudsman, in his 2009 review of the child protection program, noted that 'the current legal system perversely encourages disputation rather than cooperation in the protection of children' (Office of the Victorian Ombudsman 2009, p.57), when the remit of the child welfare jurisdiction is to respond 'to concerns about child abuse and neglect often in circumstances of acute family disadvantage or marginalisation' (VLRC 2010, p.312), and what is needed to decide these matters is expertise other than legal training. A further consequence of the law becoming the standard by which cases are judged, and maltreatment defined, is that this influences child protection practice about thresholds for intervention according to what might or might not be accepted by the court.

Although there is common acknowledgement that child protection legislation needs to move away from looking for episodes of abuse as isolated events, and attention is given in Victorian legislation to the effects of cumulative harm (*Children, Youth and Families Act 2005*, s.10), the legislative grounds for a child protection application are still constructed around an event-oriented approach (Glaser and Prior 1997). Child protection workers have to demonstrate to the Court incidents of abuse or evidence of behaviours that have caused harm or are likely to harm the child. The emphasis on discrete episodes of maltreatment excludes the majority of child protection cases which, in Victoria, are generally of a more chronic nature and about cumulative harm rather than 'specific dangerous parental behaviours' (Allen Consulting Group 2003, p.29).

Confining child protection intervention to restricted interventions is, Braye and Preston-Shoot (2006) argue, usually ineffective for the often long-term and complex problems of individuals and families. It also constrains the identification of 'at risk' or maltreating families in order to offer help and limits the independence of child protection services to decide the best responses to vulnerable children (Sheehan 2008).

The aims of child welfare legislation

The protection of the privacy of family life and parental autonomy is a long-held tradition in Australia, reflected not only in the framing of child welfare legislation but also in the choice of legal remedies to perceived problems in child-rearing. The United Nations Convention on the Rights of the Child (UNCROC) has also had a particular impact on frameworks that have been developed in Australia about standards for the care of children. Legislation such as Victoria's *Children, Youth and Families Act 2005* supplies the legal framework for child protection investigations and interventions. The Act provides for the protection of children where a child is believed to have suffered, or is likely to suffer, significant physical, sexual or emotional harm, or a parent fails to provide for a child's physical development, or is unavailable to care for the child. Child protection intervention is to be at the minimum necessary to secure the child's welfare and safety (s.10(2)(a)), a service of last resort, rather than as a gateway to child and family services. The legislation sets out a series of best interests principles (s.10) as the paramount concern of the court, as is the protection of the child from harm, protecting the child's rights and promoting the child's development taking into account their age and stage of development. How best interests are defined is not set out, nor is there any guidance about how they might be materially understood.

When determining the most appropriate outcome for a child, this principle must be balanced with other legislative principles (s.11) such as giving weight to the child's views, preserving family relationships, whether the child is in the care of parents or in alterative care, and to protect the distinctive cultural needs of Aboriginal children. This emphasis given to maintaining children with their parents and to developing case plans which support family reunification has led to criticism of the child protection service for persevering far too long with a small group of families that are unlikely ever to be able to provide adequate care for their children (Allen Consulting Group 2003).

Understanding risk and significant harm

There are no clear definitions in the *Children, Youth and Families Act 2005* about what is considered 'harm to a child'; how this is to be understood is left to the discretion of the individual legal decision-maker. Masson (2010) reminds us that the application of the test of significant harm is highly variable and contested and shaped by who is applying the lens for its definition. Whilst the Act states that harm 'may be constituted by a single act, omission or circumstance or accumulate through a series of continuing acts, omissions or circumstances' (s.162(2)) – what is commonly referred to as the 'cumulative harm' provision – none of the grounds of the Act explicitly accommodate concerns that are less about specific dangerous parental behaviours but rather about ongoing risk that comes from broad family circumstances and levels of functioning (Allen Consulting Group 2003).

The dominance of 'risk' as the benchmark for deciding harm or likelihood of harm to a child pervades these legal processes. There has been considerable attention given to developing risk assessment instruments as an important way of gathering the hard evidence favoured by the legal system to identify situations of child maltreatment and to justify decisions made by the child protection service. The problem is that no checklist or model can include every possible risk factor, and Tomison (2002a, p.49) argues that instruments alone cannot identify what combination of factors and their interactions might be important in a case.

Presenting best interests

The *Children, Youth and Families Act 2005* considers children's views and wishes as central to deciding their best interests (s.11). In Victoria, children aged seven and over instruct a solicitor appointed by Victorian Legal Aid, and the child's wishes are conveyed to the Court by adult legal practitioners. The legislation also provides in exceptional circumstances for best interests representation for children who are not mature enough to provide instruction. In these cases the legal representative must act according to what s/he believes are the best interests of the child and communicate these to the Court. Whilst giving voice to the child's wishes about matters that directly concern them is of fundamental importance, how this is done and whether or not it is the child's voice may be debatable. In Victoria, a legal representative appointed to act on a child's behalf is not required to have any particular training in working with children or knowledge of child welfare. Training in how, how often and where instructions are taken; about a child's understanding of what is being asked of them; and knowledge about the impact of court attendance on a child and being the subject of adult discussions about them is left to the individual legal practitioner to develop (Sheehan 2003).

Certainly, court outcomes are often perceived by the child protection service as a compromise, legally driven and based on an accommodation of parents' and children's instructions to their legal representatives, and on what they will agree to do rather than based on the child's developmental and welfare needs (Sheehan 2006a). Such outcomes are often difficult to implement, and viewed by families as too intrusive and by child protection workers as insufficient for the child's safety.

Child welfare legislation is challenged by the difficult and uncertain nature of the social and individual problems that child protection workers respond to on a daily basis (Braye and Preston-Shoot 2006). Moreover, child protection legislation in Victoria – and this is typical of Australian child protection legislation in general – sets out overlapping interests that are not easily reconciled: the family's interest to live as it chooses without external interference; the state's interest in the protection of vulnerable children; and the child's interest in exercising their own rights, which might differ from those of family and state especially when their wellbeing is being determined. How the child welfare, legal and adult service systems (mental health, substance abuse and family violence, for example) define child abuse and neglect may overlap, but will differ because they each serve a different purpose. In the absence of shared frameworks, legal and child protection systems find it almost impossible to develop agreed approaches about risks and consequences of maltreatment.

Court responses to children's matters

Child protection matters brought before the Court increasingly involve long-term factors impacting on the lives of the children and their families: low income, sole parenthood, parental mental illness, substance abuse and domestic violence (Allen Consulting Group 2003). They typically are more difficult to prove legally, there is little agreement between legal and welfare systems about definition and recognition of the impact of these factors on children, and the child protection service struggles to present the type of evidence of demonstrated behaviour and events that the Court seeks and fits readily into legislative parameters about proof of harm and the need for care and protection. Sheehan

(2006b) confirmed the difficulties in demonstrating significant harm for children affected, for example, by parental addiction or significant mental illness, when the child welfare concerns did not readily fit into legislative grounds for the making of a child protection order.

Dickens (2007) found that the key legal criterion of significant harm raised particular challenges in cases of child neglect. Although legislation in England and Wales does not require a 'decisive event' to satisfy the courts when making a child protection order, he found the focus of both social work and legal practice remains very much on incidents. He found the tensions about incidents and reasonable parenting epitomise the dilemmas of intervening in child neglect cases. They are cases, he notes, that are frequently characterised by parents 'facing great challenges of deprivation or vulnerability' (2007, p.79).

Although legal practitioners acknowledged there was legal provision for neglect, and that a child's best interests might be better served by child protection involvement, they still looked for a specific event or a change of circumstance that justified legal action. The study also exemplified how 'best interests' is determined not solely by child welfare concerns but by a 'trade-off' between how such concerns can be accommodated by legal frameworks.

The adversarial paradigm that operates in the Children's Court in Victoria creates considerable tension between the child protection and legal systems and distracts from concentrating on the nature and merit of child protection concerns and how a child's best interests are best determined. The Victorian Law Reform Commission, in their report on the child protection system (2010), described how the legal practitioners they interviewed used the language of criminal procedure when speaking about child protection processes at court, referring to the child protection service as 'the prosecution' and comparing interim orders to bail applications. Magistrates acknowledged the adversarial nature of court, saying it was their role to hear and determine issues raised by parties. It is the responsibility of the litigants to define what is in dispute; it is not for the Magistrate to decide what is to be discussed.

What emerges in these studies (Office of the Victorian Ombudsman 2009; VLRC 2010) is that the legislative requirements currently in place in Victoria do not reflect 'contemporary thinking regarding child protection' (PAEC 2001, p.65). Freiberg, Kirby and Ward (2004) proposed, in their report on directions for reforms in the child protection system, that attention needed to be turned away from the Court to allow the child protection service to work with families away from the legal system, recognising that a child's best interests are better understood when all facets of concerns are assessed rather than just those which meet legal criteria.

Addressing the practical concerns of child protection

The number of children on care and protection orders in Australia continues to rise despite significant attempts by many jurisdictions to divert children and families away from statutory intervention and increasing family supports to maintain children in their family's care. However, in Victoria, on 30 June 2009, five in 1000 Victorian children were the subject of a care and protection order, the largest proportion of whom were aged between birth and four years of age. The rates of Indigenous children on care and protection orders were more than seven times as high as for other children, and the rate of Indigenous children in out-of-home care was almost nine times the rate of other children (VLRC 2010). Bromfield and Arney (2008) suggest one explanatory factor for the overall increase in child protection concerns is the complex family situations of these children, previously noted: the strong connection between child abuse and neglect, domestic violence, parental substance abuse and parental mental health. Certainly there is a clear relationship between socio-economic disadvantage and contact with child protection services (VLRC 2010), characterised by housing instability, poverty, low education, social isolation and neighbourhood disadvantage (Bromfield and Arney 2008).

Parents with intellectual disability (known in the UK as 'learning disabilities'), whilst representing a small – but increasing – number of parents in Australia, are also over-represented in child protection matters. In 2007–2008, parental intellectual disability was a characteristic in 12.5 per cent of cases reviewed by the Victorian Child Death Review Committee (2008). Better opportunities for community living, the banning of involuntary sterilisation and repeal of anti-discrimination laws (McConnell and Llewellyn 2002) have given adults with intellectual disability the opportunity to be parents. However, they are vulnerable to problems and stressors associated with child abuse and neglect: social isolation, poverty, domestic violence and substance misuse (Stanley 2011), the latter two the most common reasons for referral to child protection services.

Families in which there is parental substance misuse have high rates of child maltreatment: 33 per cent of parents involved in substantiated cases of child abuse or neglect in Victoria in 2000–2001 experienced significant problems with substance abuse, 31 per cent with alcohol abuse, and 19 per cent with mental illness (Department of Human Services 2002), together with financial disadvantage and many other problems. Despite this, Dawe, Harnett and Frye (2008) found there was little focus on the needs of children and young people affected by parental substance misuse in national and state drug and alcohol policy. At the national level, the 2004–2009 National Drug Strategy, in particular, and the Aboriginal and Torres Strait Islander Peoples Complementary Action Plan, did not prioritise the needs of children who are negatively affected by parental substance misuse, despite the overwhelming connection between substance abuse and child maltreatment in Indigenous families.

Complex needs of child protection: The limits of legal enterprise

Sammut and O'Brien (2009) observe that child protection service systems across Australia are struggling to respond to the increasingly complex problems and multiple needs of vulnerable families. Whilst child protection authorities have broadened their mandate to protect children from a wider spectrum of acts and behaviours that damage child development, legislation and legal process fails to support this. There remains a heavy emphasis on 'child rescue' through the tertiary and out of home care systems (Bromfield *et al.* 2010), with a 115 per cent rise in the number of children in out of home care in the past ten years. The latest Australian data shows 31,166 children in out of home care (AIHW 2009).

In Victoria, most child protection notifications are about child neglect or emotional harm; the latter formed 44 per cent of the notifications made, in 2000–2001, to the Victorian child protection service, followed by physical abuse (38%) and child sexual abuse (6%) (Sheehan 2006b). Yet, child welfare legislation in Australia continues to maintain adversarial and highly legalised processes to deal with child abuse which diminish the significance and utility of welfare contributions. There is little accommodation of the kind of multi-disciplinary contributions that are necessary to both make sense of, and effectively respond to, these increasingly complex problems.

Competing needs: Child welfare and the legal context

It was believed that the introduction of mandatory reporting would bring to attention abused children who could then be supported by appropriate intervention (Lonne *et al.* 2009). What has happened, however, is that child protection systems have become overloaded, and although 'at risk' families may require assistance, they do not require child protection intervention (Jacob and Fanning 2006; Tomison 2002b). When all instances of concern are identified as cases of child abuse or neglect, this becomes the way in which child welfare concerns are understood, and the need for broader family services that are actually needed is given less priority. Humphreys *et al.* (2009) argue that the 'child rescue' model which embraces a 'one size fits all' approach pushes nearly all resources into the tertiary child protection and out of home care systems. It also sets up a fragmentation of services, what Bromfield *et al.* (2010) describe as service 'silos', funded by both government and non-government sectors to concentrate on individual parent and family problems. It is an approach that obliges families to attend numerous agencies – for substance abuse treatment, parenting courses and mental health supports, for example, creating difficulties with access, causing frustration and placing additional stress on vulnerable individuals.

Humphreys *et al.* (2009) observe that in Victoria, as in many other jurisdictions in Australia, there has been renewed investment in early intervention/prevention approaches, particularly those targeting the first three years of life, and the development of initiatives to enhance child and family health and wellbeing. However, the 'forensic lens' is still evident in policy and practice, given the interrelationship between legislation and intervention in child protection matters. This 'forensic lens' has led to a greater focus on addressing child, parent and family-related factors that are associated with a likelihood of child maltreatment, what Libesman (2004) describes as 'individualising' and 'pathologising a particular family – rather than looking also to the societal and community factors that cause harm to children'. This is especially evident for Indigenous Australians, who very often live in communities with inadequate and poorly maintained infrastructure, and are in poorer health. This socio-economic disadvantage is closely entwined with substance abuse and family violence, and O'Donoghue (2001) notes that many Indigenous children are growing up in communities where violence has become 'a normal and ordinary part of life'.

The impact of the Stolen Generation of children is felt strongly in Australia; the forced removal of Indigenous children fragmented both families and communities, many of whom are still struggling to function effectively. It is this legacy, combined with a strong human rights orientation, that places great emphasis on family preservation in child welfare policy (Lynch 2001). Holding fast to this principle is particularly problematic in the situation of Indigenous children, with the complexity associated with protecting Aboriginal children from abuse and allowing the Indigenous community cultural independence and self-determination (Lynch 2001).

Bromfield and Holzer (2008) document new child protection approaches emerging in Australia which recognise the key role played by the broader child and family welfare system in supporting families and reducing or preventing child abuse and neglect. Such approaches situate statutory child protection services as one facet in an overall welfare system for children and their families rather than the driver of the system. However, there is a disconnect between legislation and these approaches as there is no provision for child protection to work with families, where risks are low but services needed, without court orders, and all that the forensic approach brings with this.

Effective child protection: A shared enterprise

Humphreys *et al.* (2009) observe there is no argument that there is a need for a well-funded tertiary statutory child protection and out of home care system. However, the more it is constructed as the principal conduit for welfare concerns about children, the more closely aligned it is with legal obligation, and children's best interests are predominantly cast in terms of legislative parameters around risk and safety. They argue that a child protection system 'should be a lean and efficient system well connected to community based services' (Humphreys *et al.* 2009, p.7), offering a more targeted and effective response to a smaller group of vulnerable and abused children. The *National Framework for Protecting Australia's Children* (The Council of Australian Governments 2009) provides the impetus for this shift in approach.

The Victorian Ombudsman's investigation into the child protection system raised fundamental questions about the legal framework and its 'one size fits all' model of child protection (Scott 2009). He observed that the resources spent on 'responding to the forensic examination of activity...leads more families [to] becoming ensnared in resource intensive and often counter-productive contested processes' (2009, p.65). Given the overlap between the mental health, disability, drug and alcohol and domestic violence sectors, he noted – as have others – that the protection of children needs to reflect the shared responsibility that is evident in other jurisdictions. Certainly, the Victorian Law Reform Commission suggested a process be designed that reflects the unique role of the child welfare jurisdiction, which minimises disputation and works on agreement, as a better way to resolve the child's best interests – especially 'when parties will usually have important ongoing relationships' (VLRC 2010, p.209).

The VLRC proposed that a range of measures be introduced, such as family group conferences, that are agreement-focused and more child-centred in their approach (2010). They suggested also the development of legislative principles which encourage early resolution of child protection matters – with emphasis on agreement. The legal process should be problem-solving in its approach and accommodate the kind of inter-professional contributions decision-makers need to decide about a child's development and wellbeing. It was noted that the legal and statutory approach in England and Wales appears to better provide for this. The incorporation of child welfare guidance for the Court and child protection case conferences into statutory processes provides a way to assess the relevant information about a child and family and develop an agreed child protection plan to be put to the Court. What is not provided for in Victorian legislation, and yet is key to understanding care and protection matters, is that legal decision-makers have formal knowledge and education in child development, the effect of trauma on children, and the impact of parental mental illness and exposure to drugs and family violence on children (submission by the Director of Victorian Paediatric Forensic Medical Service to the VLRC, 2010).

Tertiary child protection services are designed to respond to abuse and neglect situations where children have been harmed or are in immediate danger; they have a limited capacity to prevent abuse and neglect (Bromfield *et al.* 2010). The need for service integration is a theme common to both Victorian reports and other commentators. It is generally acknowledged that families with multiple problems are the primary client group in child protection services, and their isolation and disadvantage places their children at great risk of abuse and neglect. A more holistic approach reduces situations where families are referred from one service to another, and when such services do not work collaboratively families struggle to gain assistance for the combination of problems they experience (Tomison 2002a).

Key to the success of such an approach is that adult-focused services (for example, drug and alcohol services or domestic violence programs) are child-sensitive, and identify when adult clients are parents in need of family as much as individual assistance (Scott 2009). An example of this 'whole of family' approach is the 'Think Family' program, developed in 2008, in the UK. Bromfield *et al.* (2010) observe that the principles on which it is based exemplify both the joined-up support families need and an understanding of how parental problems affect the whole family. Key principles, such as there is no 'wrong door', an individual's contact with any service offers entry to support services, that adult services will consider clients as parents, and that working with family strengths will better serve a child's best interests, offer interventions that are more tailored to child and family need – rather than a 'one size fits all' approach of the legal system (Scott 2009).

Families turn to governments and to a range of family support services to help them deal with social changes around them and the specific issues they may face. These approaches, however, need to be grounded in understanding how the wider social environment, in which poor housing, unemployment and social isolation are key factors, influences children's outcomes (Dawe *et al.* 2008). Tomison (2002b, p.68) reminds us that the importance of 'community' is increasingly recognised in policy and practice, mindful that improving the physical and social environment of communities improves the living circumstances of vulnerable children.

The Council of Australian Governments (2009) believes that applying a public health model, rather than focusing solely on legal and rights-based approaches to child protection, may help to reduce the burden on child protection services and deliver better outcomes for children and families. The significance of the public health model is that it offers a service continuum, ranging from primary services available to all families, such as health and education, to having secondary interventions available to families who are seen as at risk of child maltreatment, to tertiary child protection services which are a last resort for families when child abuse and neglect has occurred (Horsfall, Bromfield and McDonald 2010; Scott 2006). Moreover, it is an approach that reinforces community membership, significant for children and families whose vulnerability and poor functioning places them on the margins of social exclusion. It also brings a broader understanding to deciding a child's best interests and seeing these in terms of the loss of social capital these children experience, referring to the loss of family relationships, as well as the strain of economic deprivation, the loss of parental support and supervision, and the stigma and shame of societal labelling. Stone and Hughes (2001) remind us that good quality family relationships are important to a whole range of outcomes for family members, including the development of children and their capacity to engage with the broader community.

References

Allen Consulting Group (2003) *Protecting Children: The Child Protection Outcomes Project.* Melbourne: Victorian Department of Human Services.

Australian Institute of Health and Welfare (AIHW) (2009) *Child Protection Australia 2007–08.* Child Welfare Series No. 45. Canberra: AIHW. Available at www.aihw.gov.au/publications/index.cfm/title/10687 [purchase only].

Braye, S. and Preston-Shoot, M. (2006) *Teaching, Learning and Assessment of Law in Social Work Education.* Bristol: The Policy Press.

Bromfield, L. and Arney, F. (2008) *Developing a Road Map for Research: Identifying the Priorities for a National Child Protection Research Agenda* (Child Abuse Prevention Issues No. 28). Melbourne: Australian Institute of Family Studies, National Child Protection Clearinghouse.

Bromfield, L. and Holzer, P. (2008) *A National Approach for Child Protection: Project Report.* Melbourne: Australian Institute of Family Studies, National Child Protection Clearinghouse.

Bromfield, L., Lamont, A., Parker, R. and Horsfall, B. (2010) *Issues for the Safety and Wellbeing of Children in Families with Multiple and Complex Problems: The Co-occurrence of Domestic Violence, Parental Substance Misuse, and Mental Health Problems* (Child Abuse Prevention Issues No. 33). Melbourne: Australian Institute of Family Studies, National Child Protection Clearinghouse.

Dawe, S., Harnett, P. and Frye, S. (2008) *Improving Outcomes for Children Living in Families with Parental Substance Misuse: What Do We Know and What Should We Do?* (Child Abuse Prevention Issues No. 29). Melbourne: Australian Institute of Family Studies, National Child Protection Clearinghouse.

Department of Human Services (2002) *Annual Report 2002–03.* Victoria: Victorian Government Department of Human Services.

Dickens, J. (2007) 'When a child care case is taken to court in England and Wales, child neglect and the law: Catapults, thresholds and delay.' *Child Abuse Review 16*, 77–92.

Freiberg, A., Kirby, P. and Ward, L. (2004) *The Report of the Panel to Oversee the Consultation on Protecting Children: The Child Protection Outcomes Project.* Melbourne: Department of Human Services, Victoria.

Glaser, D. and Prior, V. (1997) 'Is the term child protection applicable to emotional abuse?' *Child Abuse Review 6*, 315–329.

Horsfall, B., Bromfield, L. and McDonald, M. (2010) *Are Social Marketing Campaigns Effective in Preventing Child Abuse and Neglect?* (Child Abuse Prevention Issues No. 32). Melbourne: Australian Institute of Family Studies, National Child Protection Clearinghouse.

Humphreys, C., Harries, M., Healy, K., Lonne, B. *et al.* (2009) 'Shifting the child protection juggernaut to earlier intervention.' *Children Australia 34*, 3, 5–8.

Jacob, A. and Fanning, D. (2006) *Report on Child Protection Services in Tasmania.* Hobart: Tasmania Department of Health and Human Services and Commissioner for Children.

Libesman, T. (2004) *Child Welfare Approaches for Indigenous Communities: International Perspectives* (Child Abuse Prevention Issues No. 20). Melbourne: Australian Institute of Family Studies, National Child Protection Clearinghouse. Available at www.aifs.gov.au/nch/pubs/issues/issues20/issues20.html, accessed on 3 February 2012.

Lonne, B., Parton, N., Thomson, J. and Harries, M. (2009) *Reforming Child Protection.* Hoboken, NJ: Routledge.

Lynch, P. (2001) 'Keeping them home: The best interests of indigenous children and communities in Canada and Australia.' *Sydney Law Review 23*, 4, 501–542.

Masson, J. (2010) '(Mis)understandings of significant harm.' *Child Abuse Review 19*, 291–298. Published online 21 June 2010 on Wiley InterScience (www.interscience.wiley.com), doi:10.1002/car.1129.

McConnell, D. and Llewellyn, G. (2002) 'Stereotypes, parents with intellectual disability and child protection.' *Journal of Social Welfare and Family Law 24*, 3, 297–317.

O'Donoghue, L. (2001) 'Indigenous violence: It's everyone's business.' *The Age*, 22 October, p.15.

Office of the Victorian Ombudsman (2009) *Own Motion Investigation into the Department of Human Services Child Protection Program.* Melbourne: Victorian Government Printer.

Public Accounts and Estimates Committee (PAEC) (2001) *Report on the Review of the Auditor-General's Special Report No. 43 – Protecting Victoria's Children: The Role of the Department of Human Services*, Report No. 44. Melbourne: Victorian Government Printer.

Sammut, J. and O'Brien, T. (2009) *Fatally Flawed: The Child Protection Crisis in Australia.* New South Wales: Centre for Independent Studies.

Scott, D. (2006) 'Towards a public health model of child protection in Australia.' *Communities, Children and Families Australia 1*, 9–16.

Scott, D. (2009) 'Think child, think family: How adult specialist services can support children at-risk of abuse and neglect.' *Family Matters 81*, 37–42.

Sheehan, R. (2003) 'The marginalisation of children by the legal process.' *Australian Social Work 56*, 1, 12–25.

Sheehan, R. (2006a) 'Alternative dispute resolution in child protection matters: The Victorian experience.' *Australian Social Work 59*, 2, 157–171.

Sheehan, R. (2006b) 'Emotional abuse and neglect: The legal response.' *Child Abuse Review 15*, 1, 38–54.

Sheehan, R. (2008) 'Social Work and the Law.' In M. Connolly and L. Harms (eds) *Social Work: Contexts and Practice* (2nd edition). Melbourne: Oxford University Press.

Stanley, N. (2011) *Children Experiencing Domestic Violence: A Research Review.* Research in Practice Series. Totnes: Dartington and the University of Sheffield.

Stone, W. and Hughes, J. (2001) 'Social capital: Linking family and community?' Australian Institute of Family Studies. Paper presented to *Family Strengths: Everybody's Business, Everybody's Gain.* Family Strengths Conference, 2–5 December 2001, Newcastle, NSW, Australia.

The Council of Australian Governments (2009) *Protecting Children is Everyone's Business: National Framework for Protecting Australia's Children 2009–2020* (the National Framework). Annual Report. Available at www.fahcsia.gov.au/sa/families/pubs/Pages/pac_report_to_COAG.aspx, accessed on 6 October 2011.

Tomison, A.M. (2002a) 'Child Protection and Child Abuse Prevention "Down Under": Key Trends in Policy and Practice.' In M. Hill, A. Stafford and P. Green Lister (eds) *International Perspectives on Child Protection: Report of a Seminar Held on 20 March 2002* (Scottish Executive Child Protection Review: Protecting Children Today and Tomorrow). Glasgow: Scottish Executive.

Tomison, A.M. (2002b) *Preventing Child Abuse: Changes to Family Support in the 21st Century* (Child Abuse Prevention Issues No. 17). Melbourne: Australian Institute of Family Studies, National Child Protection Clearinghouse.

Victorian Child Death Review Committee (2008) *Annual Report of the Victorian Child Death Review Committee.* Victoria: Office of the Child Safety Commission.

Victorian Law Reform Commission (VLRC) (2010) *Protection Applications in the Children's Court: Final Report.* Melbourne: Victorian Law Reform Commission.

Chapter 20

Conclusion

Rosemary Sheehan, Helen Rhoades and Nicky Stanley

The rapid growth of child protection concerns and the need for legal interventions challenges policy makers, professionals and governments internationally. As we noted in the Introduction, this book examines the diverse array of contemporary settings in which children's lives intersect with the law. In this concluding chapter, we identify a number of cross-cutting themes that reveal the historical legacy and emerging struggles facing vulnerable children and those who work with them, and the need for a range of practice and policy strategies to address them. Contributing authors have focused on both specific groups of children, such as asylum seekers and unaccompanied minors and children in the justice system, and on the pervasive impact of child abuse, evidenced in the extraordinary increase in the frequency with which family violence is identified and the fracturing of children's relationships and life contexts. The book provides a comprehensive analysis of issues of children and vulnerability and what approaches might more effectively protect their rights in the context of recent social challenges.

Children's rights

One of the key themes in the book concerns the struggle for access to fundamental human rights by children and young people, and their continuing exclusion from legal protections, despite the presence of domestic laws and international rights guarantees. Research conducted in several jurisdictions has shown that while disadvantaged groups, such as Indigenous families, are more likely than others in the community to come into contact with the legal system, they are less likely to seek the assistance of legal support services (Coumarelos, Wei and Zhou 2006;

Genn 1999). Among the factors that were found to impede access to the justice system for such groups were a lack of knowledge of the law, a lack of capacity and disempowerment. More recent studies suggest that these factors may be amplified for refugee and new-arrival communities by a series of additional difficulties, including language and literacy issues, housing and economic barriers, racism and a fear of government authorities (The Australian Muslim Women's Centre for Human Rights 2011). The contributions in this book illustrate powerfully that childhood is also a central part of this picture, and that many of the legal frameworks that are meant to protect vulnerable children are failing to do so.

Deena Haydon (Chapter 1) used an empirical study of disadvantaged young people in conflict with the law to highlight the failure of the British legal system to respond to their needs or protect their rights. Drawing on their stories, Haydon exposed the gaps between the rhetoric and reality of children's rights in Northern Ireland where young people who enter the care system are frequently denied the right to participate in decision-making processes that affect their lives, and where little effort is made to ensure that children from disadvantaged backgrounds are provided with adequate educational and health services. Haydon found that this occurs notwithstanding the UK's implementation of UNCRC which provides children with a right 'to be heard' and express their views (Article 12), a right to enjoy 'the highest attainable standard of health' (Article 24) and a right to education 'on the basis of equal opportunity' (Article 28). Haydon's study recommended the introduction of international 'minimum standards' which can be used to measure state compliance with human rights obligations.

Other chapters identified myriad contraventions and denials of children's citizenship rights, including the frequent failure to accord children access to information (UNCRC Article 17). Nicky Stanley and her colleagues (Chapter 16) examined police practices at the scene of domestic violence incidents and the failure of the police to engage with and provide information and referrals to children and young people who are present. The authors' research revealed that most police time and referrals centred on the needs of the adults, and that children remained very much on the periphery of, if not entirely excluded from, police attention at domestic violence incidents, despite the clear desire of children for information, including information about the legal process, support services and the return rights of the perpetrator.

In a different geographical and legal context, Gladis Molina (Chapter 5) discussed the processing of unaccompanied children who arrive in the United States, one of only two countries in the world that have not ratified the UNCRC. Molina documented the traumatic legal process that unaccompanied children who arrive in the US must negotiate, which include detention and intimidating interrogation techniques, noting the lack of legal representation and information about the process accorded to children which are guaranteed by the Convention.

Although Australia has enacted domestic legislation giving effect to international human rights charters, including the International Convention on the Elimination of All Forms of Racial Discrimination, Suzanne Oliver's critique of the Australian Government's 'Emergency Response' legislation (Chapter 7), which was designed to protect Aboriginal children from abuse, illustrated the vulnerability of such guarantees to local political agendas. As Terri Libesman noted in Chapter 10, despite the existence of the *Racial Discrimination Act 1975*, Aboriginal families in Australia continue to have significantly higher levels of contact with child welfare systems than non-Aboriginal families do, and Indigenous children continue to be placed in out of home care at a higher rate than non-Indigenous children. This chapter proposed recognition of 'cultural safety', such as the Aboriginal and Torres Strait Islander Child Placement Principle (Australian Law Reform Commission 1986, Chapter 16), as an antidote to paternalistic government responses to child abuse in Indigenous communities like the Northern Territory Emergency Response discussed by Oliver in Chapter 7. An international human rights framework, especially the right to self-determination, could offer a means of achieving recognition of Indigenous cultural rights, including the right of Indigenous people to participate in decisions that impact on their children. As Libesman argues, such a framework might offer the potential to transform mainstream understandings of Aboriginal children's welfare.

Professional responsibilities, skills and training

A second thematic thread in the book highlights the needs and training requirements of professionals working with vulnerable children in a wide range of settings. Patrick O'Leary and Jason Squire (Chapter 2) explored professional responses to child protection in the context of humanitarian emergencies, when children are at heightened risk of exposure to exploitation and violence due to the increased fragility of natural protection systems within families and communities. While the aim of emergency aid programs is to harness and support family resilience with the goal of a return to normalcy as quickly as possible, the authors highlighted the complex intersections in these circumstances. These include pre-existing child protection problems which combine with the effects of humanitarian emergencies, the need to balance the needs of children with responses to the immediate crisis and the importance of supporting community self-determination. They argued that given the grave nature of the risks – from child trafficking to opportunistic sexual assault and forced recruitment into the armed forces – aid workers need to be given a clear child protection mandate that prioritises children's safety.

Other contributions raised more pragmatic concerns, such as shortcomings in professional training programs for staff working with vulnerable children. Una Convery and Linda Moore (Chapter 6) noted the limited training in work with children available for staff who process unaccompanied children in custody – and proposed specialist training for care staff in remand centres to help them deal with the complex range of mental health issues affecting detained children. They argued that training of this nature could be built into international standards for staff working with children in custody. Likewise, Gladis Molina (Chapter 5) emphasised the importance for border control personnel to understand the trauma of pre-arrival experiences of children who come to developed countries seeking refuge from conflict and civil war.

Goos Cardol (Chapter 8) made a similar case for improved training for childcare workers in the Youth Care Office in the Netherlands, arguing that they lack an adequate legal understanding of the rights of refugee children and have little information about the educational and psychological health services that can be accessed for children in this circumstance. Cardol advocated legal literacy education for childcare workers who work with refugee children, including education about the international rights of children who arrive without documentation.

Other authors focused on the need for careful recruitment and training of practitioners to ensure cultural competence across the full range of professional groups. Rawiri Taonui (Chapter 9) called for an across-the-board presence of Maori professionals in child welfare services for Maori children, not just as social workers and in support services, but as lawyers and administrators also. James Reid (Chapter 13) considered the 'Assessment Framework' used in England for evaluating child protection needs and its purported holistic approach across three domains (children's developmental needs, parenting capacity and family and environmental factors). He critiqued the absence of anything directing the social work practitioner to consider their own 'lens' through which they view the child and argued that social workers should be required to incorporate reflection of their own personal, professional and cultural mores, values and experiences into their assessments.

Political influences and media stereotypes

A number of chapters in this book highlighted the roles of politics and the media in lawmaking, and explored the current constructions and popular images of children and young people involved with welfare services in particular jurisdictions and how these have shaped policy responses.

Robert George's comparative examination of the professional practices of family lawyers in New Zealand and England (Chapter 17) illustrated the impact of differing political constructions of children's post-divorce welfare on legal advice given to parents who wish to relocate to a new country with their children following separation. Lisa Young (Chapter 15) revealed how, even while Australian family law governing post-separation parenting expressly addresses safety concerns, its protections are routinely 'trumped' in litigated cases by an overriding policy message embedded in the law which encourages shared parenting arrangements. Young's chapter illustrates how the tensions created by these divergent messages about safety and shared parenting have impeded the delivery of intended protective measures for children.

In the child protection context, Cathy Humphreys and Meredith Kiraly (Chapter 11) described an empirical research project that exposed a similar problem in the Victorian jurisdiction, where a policy of high frequency contact between infants and birth parents designed to improve the chances of family reunification is seen to impede the healthy brain development of young children in care.

Other chapters focused on the role of the media in shaping community expectations and legal responses to children and young people. Una Convery and Linda Moore (Chapter 6) explored the role of the British media in generating community fears about young people and their impact on the law. Rawiri Taonui's discussion of Maori child abuse cases in New Zealand (Chapter 9), where Maori children are overrepresented in child protection statistics, also highlighted the media's repeated representations of Maori as violent. Goos Cardol (Chapter 8) engaged in a similar exploration of the Netherlands policy response to 'minor aliens', which aims to discourage the arrival of refugees and minimise government expenditure on illegal immigrants. Cardol showed how, in this context, child protection services to non-resident children are framed by policy concerns to allay community fears and discourage a higher influx of refugees.

Professional collaboration, communication and consultation

Contributors to this book have also highlighted the need for greater cooperation between the full range of professionals working with vulnerable families. Cathy Humphreys and Meredith Kiraly (Chapter 11) drew on their research data to argue that all professionals in the child protection system, including judicial officers and lawyers who act for parents, need to have an understanding of infant development and its connection to secure attachment relationships for children, as well as the importance of quality rather than frequency of contact. They advocated for enhanced professional collaboration between different professional communities in the child protection system, and a shift away from adversarial contests towards a case planning approach.

Nicky Stanley and her colleagues (Chapter 16) emphasised the need for improved communication between police who attend domestic violence incidents and children's social services, while Helen Rhoades (Chapter 18) called for greater harmonisation of the law governing post-separation parenting with the child development evidence base and increased cross-professional development opportunities for lawyers and mediators who work with separated families. Rosemary Sheehan (Chapter 19) argued that the law with its emphasis on child protection and maltreatment has too dominant a role in child welfare and that the promotion of children's safety and wellbeing should be a shared enterprise across child and community welfare professions. Sheehan concludes that its statutory framing as a socio-legal enterprise limits this enterprise and distracts from a broader child welfare focus.

Other contributors raised concerns about the lack of government consultation with communities targeted by recent child protection policies, particularly in relation to Indigenous children in Australia. Suzanne Oliver (Chapter 7) critiqued the Australian government's unilateral response to evidence of abuse of Aboriginal children, despite recommendations to develop a collaborative response with Aboriginal communities. The failure of the government's intervention, which involved the imposition of income and alcohol management regimes on Aboriginal families, to address systemic problems of isolation, illiteracy and intergenerational violence, is evident in the continuing prevalence of abuse and violence in Indigenous communities. Terri Libesman (Chapter 10) called for a greater use of Cultural Consultants in Aboriginal child protection cases to provide an Indigenous perspective on risk and safety assessments. As Libesman sees it, Cultural Consultants would have the capacity to work as partners with the child protection department, involving family and community in case management of Indigenous children who come into contact with the child protection system.

The value of the contributions to this book is that, whilst they address child vulnerability in a range of domestic contexts, they also highlight the globalised nature of these concerns and the need to adopt an international perspective on the questions they raise for policy makers and practitioners. The research-based critiques described here demonstrate the critical importance of agreed international minimum standards which can be used to measure state compliance with international human rights obligations, and the need for international human rights treaties to be enacted into domestic law. This then would provide for a set of international standards for those working with vulnerable children – most particularly those in custody – with particular attention to training requirements around knowledge of mental health issues. The chapters in the book present a range of national responses to managing children's rights and best interests within a context of contemporary – and often unexpected – social conditions that challenge national systems designed to respond to children at risk of harm. Children's rights as citizens must be protected, and as the contributions in this book demonstrate, this demands that the best interests of all children remain a high priority on public and policy agendas.

References

Australian Law Reform Commission (1986) *Recognition of Aboriginal Customary Laws: Report 31*. Canberra: Australian Law Reform Commission.

Coumarelos, C., Wei, Z. and Zhou, A.Z. (2006) *Justice Made to Measure: NSW Legal Needs Survey in Disadvantaged Areas*. Sydney: Law and Justice Foundation of New South Wales.

Genn, H. (1999) *Paths to Justice: What People Do and Think About Going to Law*. Oxford: Hart Publishing.

The Australian Muslim Women's Centre for Human Rights (2011) *Muslim Women, Islam and Family Violence*. Northcote: The Australian Muslim Women's Centre for Human Rights.

List of Contributors

Christine Beddoe is Director of ECPAT UK (End Child Prostitution, Pornography and Trafficking of Children for Sexual Purposes), based in London, England. Her work has led to significant campaigns against child trafficking that have resulted in legal reform and increased protection for sexually exploited children.

Goos Cardol is a lecturer at Zuyd University of Applied Sciences, Heerlen, in the Netherlands. He is also a legal adviser with the Child Protection Board in Utrecht. His research and publications have examined policy and welfare responses to unaccompanied children arriving in the Netherlands, child protection and children's rights.

Una Convery is Lecturer in Criminology at the University of Ulster in Northern Ireland. Her research has looked at the use of custody for children and the rights of children with a parent in prison. She has worked as a researcher for the Northern Ireland Human Rights Commission.

Chaitali Das is Lecturer in Social Work in the School of Sociology, Social Policy and Social Work, Queens University Belfast, Northern Ireland. Her research draws on her work in India with vulnerable children, including child labourers, street children and children in prostitution.

Robert H. George, previously Senior Law Tutor at Jesus College, Oxford University, England, is now undertaking postdoctoral work at University College Oxford. He is a member of the Oxford Centre for Family Law and Policy. His research is in child and family law, especially private law parenting disputes, and he has published widely in this field.

Deena Haydon is a postgraduate researcher within the Childhood, Transition and Social Justice Initiative at Queens University Belfast, Northern Ireland. She has published widely on the issue of socially excluded young people and children's rights.

Cathy Humphreys is Professor and Alfred Felton Chair of Child and Family Welfare in the Department of Social Work, School of Health Sciences, University of Melbourne, Australia. Her work has specialised in the area of domestic violence and children and young people in care.

Greg Kelly has recently retired as Senior Lecturer in Social Work in the School of Sociology, Social Policy and Social Work, Queens University Belfast, Northern Ireland.

He has actively researched and contributed to the development of childcare policy and practice in Northern Ireland.

Meredith Kiraly is Honorary Research Fellow, the Alfred Felton Research Program, the Department of Social Work, School of Health Sciences, University of Melbourne, Australia, with research interests in children in out of home care and child and family services.

Terri Libesman is a senior lecturer in the Law Faculty at the University of Technology, Sydney, Australia. Her research focuses on international and comparative human rights frameworks for Indigenous children's wellbeing and national, state and territory reviews into Australian child welfare legislation.

Pam Miller is a Research Officer at the National Society for the Prevention of Cruelty to Children (NSPCC), England. She was a Research Fellow at the University of Central Lancashire and was a primary researcher in the UK study of police and children's social services responses to children and families experiencing domestic violence.

Gladis E. Molina is an attorney at law with Kids in Need of Defense, Inc. (KIND), based in Los Angeles, California, the United States, representing unaccompanied immigrant children who have entered the United States without legal status.

Linda Moore is Lecturer in Criminology at the University of Ulster in Northern Ireland. From 2000 to 2007 she was investigations worker at the Northern Ireland Human Rights Commission, investigating the rights of children in custody and of women in prison.

Patrick O'Leary is Professor and Head of the School of Human Services and Social Work at Griffiths University, Queensland, Australia. Patrick also holds a professorship at the University Southampton, United Kingdom. His research addresses the long-term effects of child sexual abuse as well as gendered violence and child protection in humanitarian emergencies and social development.

Suzanne Oliver is a Magistrate in the Northern Territory, Australia. She conducts hearings in regional and remote Aboriginal communities, balancing justice matters with the needs and beliefs of Indigenous peoples.

James Reid is Senior Lecturer in Childhood Studies at the University of Huddersfield, England. His research interests are in work with fathers, and he has worked with UNICEF.

Helen Rhoades is an associate professor in the Melbourne Law School at the University of Melbourne, Australia. She is Chair of the Family Law Council which provides policy advice to the Australian Government on family law matters, with particular attention to contact arrangements between children and their parents.

Helen Richardson-Foster was a Research Fellow at the University of Central Lancashire, England, on the UK study of police and children's social services responses to children and families experiencing domestic violence between 2007 and 2009.

Rosemary Sheehan is an associate professor in the Department of Social Work, Monash University, Victoria, Australia; she holds a Governor-in-Council appointment to the Children's Court of Victoria to conduct alternative dispute resolution conferences and is a member of the Victorian Child Death Review Committee.

Jason Squire is the current Country Representative of Foundation Terre des hommes Lausanne in Lebanon. He has worked in emergency settings such as Sri Lanka, Sudan and Lebanon and provided child protection consultation in countries such as Albania, Greece and China.

Nicky Stanley is Professor of Social Work at the University of Central Lancashire, England. She researches in the fields of domestic violence, parental mental health and child welfare, young people's mental health and interagency work and publications, including research commissioned by the UK and local government, and a national study (2007–2009) of police and children's social services responses to children and families experiencing domestic violence.

Rawiri Taonui was most recently Associate Professor and Head of Aotahi – School of Maori and Indigenous Studies at the University of Canterbury, New Zealand. His research areas include Indigenous peoples, oral traditions, Maori and indigenous development (entrepreneurial, government, tribal and international), and human rights.

Gill Thomson is a Research Fellow in the School of Nursing at the University of Central Lancashire, England. She was a Research Fellow on the UK study of police and children's social services responses to children and families experiencing domestic violence from 2008 to 2009.

Jackie Turton is Senior Lecturer in the Department of Sociology at Essex University, England. Her research projects for the Home Office, Department of Health and the Royal College of Paediatrics and Child Health in the UK and for the Irish Government have examined the social and health needs of marginalised groups, refugees and asylum seekers, child protection, and women as offenders.

Shelly L. Whitman is Deputy Director of the Centre for Foreign Policy Studies, Dalhousie University, Halifax, Nova Scotia, Canada. Her current research concentrates on child soldiers and women in peacebuilding, with previous published research attending to small arms proliferation, the international criminal court, and human rights violations.

Lisa Young is Associate Professor in the School of Law at Murdoch University, Western Australia. She teaches and researches in the area of family law and works as a decision-maker for the Australian Government's Child Support Agency.

Subject Index

Author Index